D1451383

A Bibliography of Business Ethics, 1981-1985

Center for the Study of Applied Ethics
at the University of Virginia

A Bibliography of Business Ethics 1981-1985

edited by
Donald G. Jones
Patricia Bennett

Center for the Study of Applied Ethics
at the University of Virginia

The Edwin Mellen Press
Lewiston/Queenston

Library of Congress Cataloging-in-Publication Data

Jones, Donald G.
A bibliography of business ethics, 1981-1985.

(Mellen studies in business ; vol. 2)
Produced by the Center for Study of Applied Ethics at University of Virginia.
Includes index.
1. Business ethics--Bibliography. 2. Industry--Social Aspects--Bibliography. I. Bennett, Patricia. II. Colgate Darden Graduate School of Business Administration. Center for the Study of Applied Ethics. III. Title. IV. Series.
Z7164.C81J595 1986 (HF5387) 016.174'4 86-23545
ISBN 0-88946-154-6

This is volume 2 in the continuing series
Mellen Studies in Business
Volume 2 ISBN 0-88946-154-6
MSB Series ISBN 0-88946-152-X

The Edwin Mellen Press
Box 450
Lewiston, New York
USA 14092

The Edwin Mellen Press
Box 67
Queenston, Ontario
CANADA L0S 1L0

Printed in the United States of America

Contents

Foreword

Every business organization has an ethic. The question of relevance is, what does the ethic look like? What effect does the ethic have on the organization? Some organizations have an ethic (ethical system) we would applaud, find praiseworthy. Other organizations have an ethic (ethical system) we would fault, find blameworthy.

Whether it be praise or blame, never before in our industrial history have the issues of business ethics been as widely discussed. It is certainly not overstating the case to suggest that the success or failure of many of today's corporations will be decided by how well or poorly their corporate ethic will help them deal with the very difficult decisions they face.

This bibliography reflects the importance of the business ethics field. It is intended to assist students, researchers, teachers, and practitioners in their search for ways to do things in "a better way."

The Center for the Study of Applied Ethics is dedicated to helping academics and business people deal with ethical issues. This bibliography reflects this dedication and our commitment to the field.

Alexander B. Horniman
Director, Center for the Study of
Applied Ethics
Colgate Darden Graduate School
of Business Administration
University of Virginia

Acknowledgments

While this bibliography represents the efforts of several people, a few individuals have made exceptional contributions. To Henry Wingate go our thanks for his unstinting administrative and material support. Libby Eschbach kept the information retrieval process alive during the interval between volumes, and became our computer literature searcher. Karen Dickinson devoted many hours to assisting in the manuscript preparation. John Feldmann, a recent Ph.D. in Religious Studies and a former CSAE research assistant, helped a new entrant into the field of business ethics develop an awareness of the philosophical concepts embedded in ethics issues. April Downer and Chris May provided the computer and the necessary training and support for the development of a business ethics database.

Several other persons have assisted us in various ways, especially the staff at the University of Virginia libraries. Their contributions have helped make the preparation of this volume a rewarding experience.

Patricia I. Bennett
Donald G. Jones

Charlottesville, Virginia
Summer 1986

Introduction

Background and Scope

This is the fourth *Bibliography of Business Ethics* produced by the Center for the Study of Applied Ethics at the Colgate Darden Graduate School of Business Administration, at the University of Virginia. The last three volumes covered the years, 1950-1970, 1971-1975, and 1976-1980. This volume covers the five years between 1981-1985. Like the previous volume, this one provides coverage of English language materials published primarily in North America.

Virtually any ethical issue arising in the private sector work place and marketplace, as well as those issues emerging from business and social relations has been considered. The items selected were those which reflected ongoing ethical concerns which appear in a variety of new situations, as well as those situations which have appeared many times before. Materials excluded from this volume were most government documents, conference reports and proceedings, audiovisual materials, unpublished papers from professional meetings, and newspapers (*The Wall Street Journal* being the only exception).

This volume presents a number of issues such as computer security and privacy, genetic screening and drug testing of present and potential employees, terrorism directed at consumers and corporations through product tampering, corporate mergers and takeovers, golden parachutes, toxic waste disposal, nuclear power plant accidents, and the politicizing of corporate boardrooms by shareholders and social activists.

Methodology

The methodology used to retrieve articles and books included direct review of books and articles, perusal of footnotes and bibliographies in books and journals covering business ethics, and a review of the standard journal indexes. The main resources consulted were Business Periodicals Index, Social Sciences Index, Humanities Index, Public Affairs Information Service, Religion Index, Philosopher's Index, and The Wall Street Journal Index. Computer literature searching was done on ABI/Inform. Citations for books were verified on the OCLC bibliographic data base and Books in Print. Whenever possible, journal articles were verified directly at the University of Virginia libraries. Any articles not verified were included when their source was considered reliable and the information appeared complete.

Organization

The main body of this bibliography is structured according to issues arising out of business practices within the firm, in the marketplace, and in society. A fourth category, "Theoretical and Applied Ethics," was designed to capture such materials as cases and texts, issues of economic justice, religious perspectives on business, and teaching and training in ethics.

This volume is our first to have a subject index to books and articles, providing a much-needed source of access. Our intention is to encourage perusal of the categories in the Contents as the initial approach to the citations. The subject index provides further access to citations covering more than a single topic named in the categories. For example, articles or books on women in banking could be found in either the categories, "Women in Organizations" or "Banking and Finance," depending upon the perceived emphasis. The subject index should be used as an adjunct, rather than a substitute, to consulting the categories in the Contents.

An Emerging Discipline

The virtual explosion of interest in business ethics in the past 15 years can be linked, in part to such matters as Watergate, bribery, financial scandals, environmental horror stories, and product safety issues. The continued interest in the subject is linked to more recent scandals: corporate overcharges to the Defense Department, the Bhopal disaster, major banks neglecting to report billions of dollars in currency transfers, unfriendly takeovers, and personal injury lawsuits, among others.

There is no question that a powerful stimulus for much of the writing on business ethics has to do with the current exposure of business misdeeds. However, the explosion of interest is not simply a response to these scandals. In fact, many of the items in this book reflect serious and positive efforts to undergird business ethics as a solid discipline.

A study commissioned by the Ford Foundation and Carnegie Corporation 20 years ago resulted in a book comprising a series of reports, *The Education of American Businessmen.* A central recommendation of this study was that adequate education for business managers in the 60's, 70's and 80's would have to include close attention to "the problems of business ethics and social responsibility." Since that time there have been numerous studies and reports—some within the past five years—pointing to large scale implementation of the Ford and Carnegie study recommendations.

What are some indicators that business ethics is more than a surface phenomenon? Nearly 400 schools of higher education are offering courses in business ethics. Within the past decade major corporations have instituted training programs in ethics. There are now over three dozen centers and institutes in the U.S. involved in advancing business ethics. Finally, one of the clearest signs that business ethics is becoming a bona fide discipline is the explosion of books and articles written on the subject. More than 4,000 entries in this volume bear witness to the fact that the study of business ethics is alive and well.

Patricia I. Bennett
Donald G. Jones

Professional Ethics Centers

Analysis of Values Program
St. John's University
Collegeville, Minnesota 56321

Business Ethics
P.O. Box 672
Batesville, South Carolina 29006

Business, Government, Society Research Institute
Mr. Barry Metnick
University of Pittsburgh

Center for Business Ethics
Mr. W. Michael Hoffman, Director
Bentley College
Beaver and Forest Streets
Waltham, Massachusetts 02154

Center for Ethics and Religious Values in Business
Mr. John Houck, Co-Director
Notre Dame University
South Bend, Indiana 46556

Center for Ethics and Social Policy
Graduate Theological Union
2465 LeConte Avenue
Berkeley, California 94709

Center for Philosophy and Public Policy
Dr. Douglas MacLean, Director
University of Maryland
College Park, Maryland 20742

Center for Private and Public Sector Ethics
Dr. Mark Pastin, Director
Arizona State University
Tempe, Arizona 95281

Center for Professional Ethics
Mr. Robert Clark
Case Western Reserve University
11300 Juniper Road
Cleveland, Ohio 44106

Center for the Study of Business in Society
School for Business and Economics
5151 State University Drive
Los Angeles, California 90032

Center for the Study of Ethics in the Professions
Illinois Institute of Technology
Dr. Mark S. Frankel
3300 South Federal Street
Chicago, Illinois 60616

Center for the Study of Values
Mr. Norman Bowie
University of Delaware
Newark, Delaware 19711

Center for Values in Business
Father Thomas F. McMahon
10 East Pearson Street
Chicago, Illinois 60611

Ethics and Public Policy Center
Ernest Lefevre, President
1030 15th Street, N.W.
Washington, D.C. 20005

Ethics Resource Center
Mr. Gary Edwards, Director
1025 Connecticut Avenue, N.S.
Suite 1003
Washington, D.C. 20036

The Forum for Corporate Responsibility, Inc.
593 Park Avenue
New York, New York 10021

The Hastings Center
Dr. Daniel J. Callahan, Director
360 Broadway
Hastings-on-Hudson, New York 10706

Henry Salvatori Center
Dr. George Benson
Pitzer Hall
Claremont University
Claremont, California 91711

Institute for Business Ethics
Dr. Robert Cooke, Director
DePaul University
25 East Jackson Boulevard
Chicago, Illinois 60604

Institute for Humane Studies
Leonard Liggio, President
George Mason University
Fairfax, Virginia 22030

Institute on Ethics in Management
Mr. Charles W. Powers
215 First Street
Cambridge, Massachusetts 02142

Interfaith Center on Corporate Responsibility
475 Riverside Drive
Room 566
New York, New York 10027

Investor Responsibility Research Center
1755 Massachusetts Avenue, N.W.
Washington, D.C. 20036

Kennedy Institute of Ethics
Georgetown University
Washington, D.C. 20057

Society for Business Ethics
Father Manuel Vilasquez
311 Bannan Hall
University of Santa Clara
Santa Clara, California 95053

Society for the Study of Professional Ethics
University of Rhode Island
Kingston, Rhode Island 02881

Trinity Center for Ethics and Corporate Policy
74 Trinity Place
New York, New York 10006

Lester G. Wendt Center for the Advancement of Ethics
University of Dubuque
Dubuque, Iowa 52001

Westminster Institute for Ethics and Human Values
Mr. Benjamin Freedman
Westminster College
London, Ontario N6G 2M2
Canada

Journals Featuring Business Ethics Articles

Academy of Management Journal
Academy of Management Review
Across the Board
American Business Law Journal
Business
Business (UK)
Business and Economic Review
Business and Professional Ethics Journal
Business and Society Review
Business Horizons
Business Lawyer
Business Quarterly
Business Week
California Management Review
Dun's Business Month
Employee Relations Law Journal
Employment Relations Today
Harvard Business Review
Journal of Business Ethics
Personnel
Personnel Journal
Sloan Management Review

A Bibliography of Business Ethics, 1981-1985

Center for the Study of Applied Ethics
at the University of Virginia

Business Ethics: General Works

Business Ethics: General Works

Books

Arthur, Henry B. *Making Business Ethics Useful.* Boston: Harvard University, 1983.

Baier, Kurt, et al. *Just Business: New Introductory Essays in Business Ethics.* Philadelphia: Temple Univ. Press, 1983.

Bayles, Michael D. *Professional Ethics.* Belmont, Calif.: Wadsworth Pub. Co., 1981.

Behrman, Jack N. *Discourses on Ethics and Business.* Cambridge, Mass.: Oelgeschlager, Gunn & Hain, 1981.

Benson, George C. S. *Business Ethics in America.* Lexington, Mass.: Lexington Books, 1982.

Berleant, Arnold, ed. *The Ethical Factor in Business Decisions: Essays Toward Criteria.* Greenvale, N.Y.: C.W. Post Center, 1982.

Bond, Kenneth M., and Robert B. Daugherty, eds. *Bibliography of Business Ethics and Business Moral Values.* 3d ed. Omaha, Neb.: Creighton University, 1985.

Bowie, Norman. *Business Ethics.* Englewood Cliffs, N.J.: Prentice-Hall, 1982.

Bowman, James S. *Essentials of Management: Ethical Values, Attitudes, and Actions.* Port Washington, N.Y.: Associated Faculty Press, 1983.

Bowyer, J. B. *Cheating.* New York; St. Martin Press, 1982.

Braybrooke, David. *Ethics in the World of Business.* Totowa, N.J.: Rowman & Allanheld, 1983.

Caplan, Arthur L., and Daniel Callahan, eds. *Ethics in Hard Times.* New York: Plenum Press, 1981.

Cavanagh, Gerald F. *American Business Values.* 2d ed. Englewood Cliffs, N.J.: Prentice-Hall, 1984.

Chewning, Richard C. *Business Ethics in a Changing Culture.* Reston, Va.: Reston Pub. Co., 1984.

Cunningham, Robert M., Jr. *The Healing Mission and the Business Ethic.* Chicago: Pluribus Press, 1982.

Des Jardins, Joseph R., and John J. McCall. *Contemporary Issues in Business Ethics.* Belmont, Calif.: Wadsworth Pub. Co., 1985.

Grundstein, Nathan. *The Managerial Kant.* Cleveland: Case Western Reserve U., 1981.

Heyne, Paul T. *Private Keepers of the Public Interest.* New York: McGraw-Hill, 1983.

Hoffman, W. M., and Thomas J. Wyly. *The Work Ethic in Business.* Cambridge, Mass.: Oelgeschlager, Gunn & Hain, 1981.

Jones, Donald G., ed. *A Bibliography of Business Ethics, 1976-1980.* Charlottesville, Va.: University Press of Va., 1982.

Natale, Samuel M. *Ethics and Morals in Business.* Birmingham, Ala.: REP, 1983.

Robison, Wade L., Michael S. Pritchard, and Joseph Ellin. *Profits and Professions: Essays in Business and Professional Ethics.* Clifton, N.J.: Humana Press, 1983.

Snoeyenbos, Milton, Robert Almeder, and James Humber. *Business Ethics: Corporate Values and Society.* Buffalo: Prometheus Books, 1983.

Solomon, Robert C., and Kristine R. Hanson. *Above the Bottom Line: an Introduction to Business Ethics.* New York: Harcourt, Brace, Jovanovich, 1983.

Solomon, Robert C., and Kristine R. Hanson. *It's Good Business.* New York: Atheneum Pubs., 1985.

Stevens, Edward. *Making Moral Decisions.* New York: Paulist Press, 1981.

Articles

Arthur, H. B. "Making Business Ethics Useful." *Strategic Management Journal* 4 (October-December 1984), 319-333.

Bahm, Archie J. "The Foundations of Business Ethics." *Journal of Business Ethics* 2 (May 1983), 107-110.

Barach, Jeffrey A. "The Ethics of Hardball." *California Management Review* 27 (Winter 1985), 132-139.

Barnett, John H. "A Business Model of Enlightenment." *Journal of Business Ethics* 4 (February 1985), 57-63.

Bell, K. D. "Accountability in the Private Sector." *Practising Manager* 5 (October 1984), 12-16.

Bowie, Norman E. "Are Business Ethics and Engineering Ethics Members of the Same Family?" *Journal of Business Ethics* 4 (February 1985), 43-52.

Brennan, Joseph G. "Thomas Mann and the Business Ethic." *Journal of Business Ethics* 4 (October 1985), 401-407.

Brown, Daniel J. "Business Ethics: Is Small Better?" *Policy Studies Journal* 13 (June 1985), 766-775.

Brummer, James J. "Business Ethics: Micro and Macro." *Journal of Business Ethics* 4 (Spring 1985), 81-91.

Burger, Chester. "Ethics and the Real World." *Public Relations Journal* 38 (December 1982), 13, 16-17.

"Business Credibility and Ethics." *Public Relations Review* 11 (Winter 1985), 67-71.

Camenisch, Paul F. "Business Ethics: On Getting to the Heart of the Matter." *Business and Professional Ethics Journal* 1 (Fall 1981), 59-69. Commentary: by Robert N. Wilson, 71.

Cunningham, Mary E. "Productivity: Does Business Need Values?" *Across the Board* 18 (December 1981), 7-11.

De George, Richard T. "Can Corporations Have Moral Responsibility?" *University of Dayton Review* 15 (Winter 1981-82), 3-15.

De George, Richard T. "What Is the American Business Value System?" *Journal of Business Ethics* 1 (November 1982), 267-275.

Delattre, Edwin J. "Ethics in the Information Age." *Public Relations Journal* 40 (June 1984), 12-15.

Drucker, Peter F. "Ethical Chic." *Forbes* 128 (September 4, 1981), 160-162+.

Drucker, Peter F. "What Is 'Business Ethics'?" *Public Interest* 63 (Spring 1981), 18-36.

Drucker, Peter F. "Doing Good Makes Cents." *Reason* 17 (November 1985), 39-43.

Elliston, Frederick A. "The Philosopher in the Workplace." *Journal of Business Ethics* 4 (August 1985), 331-339.

Free, William T. "Strictly Speaking." *Journal of the American Society of CLU* 38 (January 1984), 19-20.

French, Peter A. "What Is Hamlet to McDonnell-Douglas or McDonnell-Douglas to Hamlet: DC-10." *Business and Professional Ethics Journal* 1 (Winter 1982), 1-14. Commentary: by Homer Sewell, 15.

Friedman, Hershey H., and Linda W. Friedman. "Ethics: Everybody's Business." *Collegiate News and Views* 2 (Winter 1981-1982), 11-13.

Gatewood, Emmette T., Jr. "Ethics: The Starting Point of Success." *Real Estate Today* 18 (February 1985), 46-48.

Goodpaster, Kenneth E. "Business Ethics, Ideology, and the Naturalistic Fallacy." *Journal of Business Ethics* 4 (August 1985), 227-232.

Goodpaster, Kenneth E. "Business Ethics: Tilling a New Field." *Ethics* 91 (1981), 525-530.

Griffith, William B. "Ethics and the Academic Professional: Some Open Problems and a New Approach." *Business and Professional*

Ethics Journal 1 (Spring 1982), 75-96. Commentary: by Willard F. Enteman, 97.

Hall, Robert T. "Emile Durkheim on Business and Professional Ethics." *Business and Professional Ethics Journal* 2 (Fall 1982), 51-60.

Hanson, Kristine, and Robert Solomon. "The Real Business Ethics." *Business and Society Review* 41 (Spring 1982), 58-59.

Hanson, Kirk O. "Ethics and Business: A Progress Report." *Stanford Graduate School of Business* 51 (Spring 1983), 10+.

Hayes, Thomas J. "Ethics in Business: Problem Identification and Potential Solutions." *Hospital Material Management Quarterly* 4 (May 1983), 35-42.

Henderson, Verne E. "The Ethical Side of Enterprise." *Sloan Management Review* 23 (Spring 1982), 37-47.

Henderson, Verne E. "The Spectrum of Ethicality." *Journal of Business Ethics* 3 (May 1984), 163-171.

Hennessey, John W., Jr. and Bernard Gert. "Moral Rules and Moral Ideals: A Useful Distinction in Business and Professional Practice." *Journal of Business Ethics* 4 (April 1985), 105-115.

Hill, Ivan. "A Turning Point for Individuals and Societies—Common Sense and Everyday Ethics Continued." *Security Management* 25 (August 1981), 116-123.

Hoffman, W. M. and Jennifer M. Moore. "What Is Business Ethics? A Reply to Peter Drucker." *Journal of Business Ethics* 1 (November 1982), 293-300.

James, Gene C. "The Crisis of American Business." *Journal of Business Ethics* 1 (November 1982), 285-291.

Jones, Donald G. "Business Ethics: An Emerging Discipline." *Darden Report (University of Virginia)* 8 (Winter 1982), 13-16.

Kahn, Robert. "The Practical Philosophy of Ethics." *Management Consulting* 1 (Fall 1984), 9-13.

Kavka, Gregory S. "When Two 'Wrongs' Make a Right: An Essay on Business Ethics." *Journal of Business Ethics* 2 (February 1983), 61-66.

Klein, Sherwin. "Two Views of Business Ethics: A Popular Philosophical and a Value Based Interdisciplinary One." *Journal of Business Ethics* 4 (February 1985), 71-79.

Lewis, Philip V. "Defining 'Business Ethics': Like Nailing Jello to a Wall." *Journal of Business Ethics* 4 (October 1985), 377-383.

Linden, Eugene. "Beating the System." *Output* 2 (July 1981), 199-731.

Massey, Stephen J. "Marxism and Business Ethics." *Journal of Business Ethics* 1 (November 1982), 301-312.

McCoy, Bowen H. "Applying the Art of Action Oriented Decision Making to the Knotty Issues of Everyday Business Life." *Management Review* 72 (July 1983), 20-24.

Miller, William H. "Business' New Link: Ethics and the Bottom Line." *Industry Week* 223 (October 29, 1984), 49+.

Mintz, Jim. "Moral, Ethical, and Practical Questions." *Venture* 6 (February 1984), 54-59.

Mitias, Michael H. "Introduction: On Raising Value Questions in Business." *Journal of Business Ethics* 1 (November 1982), 255-258.

Moskowitz, Milton, "Trumpeting the New Values." *Communication World* 1 (November 1983), 39-41.

Natale, Samuel M. "Ethics and Enterprise." *Journal of Business Ethics* 2 (February 1983), 43-49.

Nersoyan, H. J. "An Analysis of Collectivity." *University of Dayton Review* 15 (Winter 1981-82), 82-96.

Norris, George A. "The Ethical Struggle." *Life Association News* 79 (May 1984), 62-64.

Opitz, Edmund A. "Business and Ethics." *Freeman* 33 (December 1983), 735-740.

Pastin, Mark. "Why?" *Business Horizons* 26 (January-February 1983), 2-6.

Pattan, John E. "The Business of Ethics and the Ethics of Business." *Journal of Business Ethics* 3 (February 1984), 1-20.

Rickover, Hyman G. "The Moral Responsibility of Business." *Technology Review* 85 (May-June 1982), 12-14.

Roterbury, Harry C. "Erosion of Ethics." *Management World* 10 (March 1981), 44+.

Schorr, Philip. "Learning Ethics: The Search for an Ideal Model." *Public Administration* 7 (Fall 1983), 323-345.

Seligman, D. "Up From Aristotle." *Fortune* 112 (October 14, 1985), 197-198.

Senia, Al M. "Can Business Ethics Turn on U.S. Industry?" *Iron Age* 225 (November 10, 1982), 217+.

Sherwin, Douglas S. "The Ethical Roots of the Business System." *Harvard Business Review* 61 (November-December 1983), 183-192.

Solomon, Robert C., et al. "The Case Against Corporate Virtue." *Business and Society Review* 48 (Winter 1984), 4-12.

Stearns, Mary. "What Are Business Ethics?" *Data Management* 19 (May 1981), 26-27+.

Talbott, Frederick. "Business Ethics: Do They Exist?" *Tidewater Virginian* 7 (February 1984), 36-39.

Verity, C. W., Jr. "Verity's Truth Center for Enlightened Business." *Business and Society Review* 48 (Winter 1984), 60-62.

Wakin, Edward. "Business Ethics and the Bottom Line." *Today's Office* 19 (February 1985), 22-30.

Wilkins, Bryan. "Ethics of Big Eight Involvement in DP Services Debated." *Computerworld* 18 (May 28, 1984), 19.

Wright, Donald K. "Philosophy of Ethics." *Public Relations Journal* 38 (December 1982), 12, 14-16.

The Firm

The Firm

Acquisitions and Divestitures

Books

Fernandez, Ronald. *Excess Profits: The Rise of United Technologies.* Reading, Mass.: Addison-Wesley, 1983.

Gargiulo, Albert F. *Leveraged Buyout.* New York: American Management Assn., 1982.

Kudla, Ronald J. and Thomas H. McInish. *Corporate Spin-offs: Strategy for the 1980's.* Westport, Conn.: Greenwood Press, 1984.

Shooshan Harry M., III. *Disconnecting Bell: The Impact of the AT&T Divestiture.* New York: Pergamon, 1984.

Articles

Carey, Susan. "Bell Breakup Places Stress on Employees." *Wall Street Journal* (December 30, 1983), 11.

Cavanagh, John. "The Conglomerate Universe." *Engage/Social Action* 12 (November 1984), 10-14.

Chernoff, J., and C. Paustian. "Attempt to Pre-empt Divestiture Laws Dies." *Pensions Investment Age* 13 (July 22, 1985), 8.

Cook, D. "Thinking of Using an ESOP to Buy Your Company? Think Again." *Business Week* (August 26, 1985), 34.

Crandon, David, and Kevin Schultz. "Approving Acquisitions: A New Board Danger Zone." *Directors & Boards* 5 (Winter 1981), 17-21.

Ferenbach, Carl. "In Praise of the Leveraged Buyout." *Wall Street Journal* (May 30, 1984), 30.

"GTE and ITT Object Again to ATT's Plan to Keep 'Bell' Name." *Wall Street Journal* (April 14, 1983), 21.

Greenberger, Robert S. "AT&T Sees New Pact with Major Union Before Deadline Tomorrow Despite Snags." *Wall Street Journal* (August 5, 1983), 10.

Greenwald, John. "Let's Make a Deal." *Time* 126 (December 23, 1985), 42-47.

Hennessey, Edward L., Jr. "Mergers: Good and Bad." *Vital Speeches of the Day* 51 (June 15, 1985), 535-538.

Kreisman, R. "Selling Your Company: The Ties that Bind." *Inc.* 7 (July 1985), 102.

Langley, Monica. "AT&T Breakup Brings Calls for Staff Cuts as Thousands Are Asked to Retire Early." *Wall Street Journal* (November 3, 1983), 4.

Loewenstein, Louis. "Management Buyouts." *Columbia Law Review* 85 (May 1985), 730-784.

Ogle, George. "Concentration of Power in the Hands of a Few: Ethical Characteristics of Conglomerates." *Engage/Social Action* 12 (November 1984), 15-18.

Ring, T. "$738 Million Is Divested by 51 Tax-Exempt Funds." *Pensions Investment Age* 13 (August 5, 1985), 1+.

Rock, Milton L. "Greenmail: The Destabilizer of the American Corporation." *Directors & Boards* 8 (Summer 1984), 3.

Schulman, Stephen H., and Alan Schenk. "Shareholders' Voting and Appraisal Rights in Corporate Acquisition Transactions." *Business Lawyer* 38 (August 1983), 1529-1555.

Smith, Mark W., and Mark S. Pulliam. "Congress Wrote Continental's Ticket." *Wall Street Journal* (October 11, 1983), 30.

Twomey, Harry F. "The Human Resources Element in Buyouts and Acquisitions." *Journal of Buyouts & Acquisitions* 2 (June-July 1984), 3-7.

Werner, Jesse. "Divestiture Can Be Humane and Effective." *Industry Week* 215 (November 15, 1982), 13.

"What to Do about a Pension Plan in a Merger or Acquisition." *Practical Accountant* 14 (June 1981), 43-45.

White, James A. "AT&T Bows to Judge, Gives Up Most Use of Bell Name to Proceed with Divestiture." *Wall Street Journal* (August 4, 1983), 4.

Codes of Conduct and Self Regulation

Books

Corporate Governance and Codes of Ethics: A Guide for Bankers. Park Ridge, Ill.: Bank Administration Inst., 1980.

Cressey, Donald R., and Charles A. Moore. *Corporation Codes of Ethical Conduct: Final Report to the Peat, Marwick, Mitchell Foundation*. Santa Barbara, Calif.: Dept. Sociology Univ. Cal., 1980.

Hammaker, Paul M., Alexander B. Horniman, and Louis T. Rader. *Standards of Conduct in Business*. Charlottesville, Va.: The Darden School, Univ. Va., 1981.

Hoffman, W. M., Jennifer M. Moore, and David A. Fedo. *Corporate Governance and Institutional Ethics.* Lexington, Mass.: Lexington Books, 1984.

Implementation and Enforcement of Codes of Ethics in Corporations and Associations. Princeton, N.J.: The Corporation, 1980.

Tulloch, Henry, and W. S. Bauman. *The Management of Business Conduct.* Charlottesville, Va.: The Darden School, Univ. Va., 1981.

Articles

Abraham, Kenneth S. "Efficiency and Fairness in Insurance Risk Classification." *Virginia Law Review* 71 (April 1985), 403-451.

Achenbaum, Alvin A. "Can We Tolerate a Double Standard in Marketing Research?" *Journal of Advertising Research* 25 (June-July 1985), RC3-RC7.

Adams, John R., et al. "Bankers' Code of Conduct: Stumbling Blocks or Stepping Stones?" *ABA Bank Compliance* 6 (Winter 1985), 37-40, 47.

Ambrose, James. "The Credit Executive's Credo." *Credit World* 72 (November-December 1983), 26-29.

Bacon, Ernest. "Ethical Conduct in the Measure of Excellence: How to Survive in the Eighties." *Hospital & Health Services Administration* 28 (March-April 1983), 15-23.

Berkeley, Edmund C. "Editorial: The Computer Cottage." *Computers and People* 32 (September-October 1983), 6.

Bowman, James S. "The Management of Ethics: Codes of Conduct in Organizations." *Public Personnel Management* 10, no.1 (1981), 59-66.

Burgess, Carole, et al. "Self-Regulation Vs. Public Regulation." *Woman CPA* 47 (April 1985), 6-8.

"A Code of Ethics: Patterning Your Collection Policies After the Fair Debt Collection Practices Act." *Credit Union Magazine* 5 (July 1985), 50-52.

Conway, Jeremiah, and John Houlihan. "The Real Estate Code of Ethics: Viable or Vaporous?" *Journal of Business Ethics* 1 (August 1982), 201-210.

Cressey, Donald R., and Charles A. Moore. "Managerial Values and Corporate Codes of Ethics." *California Management Review* 25 (Summer 1983), 53-77.

Darr, Kurt. "Administrative Ethics and the Health Services Manager." *Hospital & Health Services Administration* 29 (March-April 1984), 120-136.

"Do Organizational Codes of Conduct Really Affect Employees' Behavior?" *Management Review* 71 (June 1982), 53.

Dubinsky, Alan J. "Ethics in Industrial Selling: How Product and Service Salespeople Compare." *Journal of the Academy of Marketing Science* 13 (Winter-Spring 1985), 160-170.

"Ethics, 1982: The St. Paul Companies Revises Its Code." *Directors & Boards* 7 (Fall 1982), 48-52.

Fenwick, P. R. "DPMA Code of Ethics and Standards of Conduct." *Data Management* 19 (May 1981), 9.

Free, William T. "Society's Code of Ethics." *Journal of the American Society of CLU* 38 (July 1984), 29-30.

Garvin, David A. "Can Industry Self-Regulation Work?" *California Management Review* 25 (Summer 1983), 37-52.

Gregory, Charles L. "Ethics: A Management Tool? A Profile of the Values of Hospital Administrators." *Hospital & Health Services Administration* 29 (March-April 1984), 102-119.

Heerema, Douglas. "The Cathedral and the Parish—Tenets of the Market System vs. Ethics as a Guide to Business Behavior." *Business Horizons* 27 (May-June 1984), 2-6.

Jackson, Brooks. "Some Corporate Political Funds Consider Code of Ethics Dealing with Legislators." *Wall Street Journal* (February 9, 1984), 29.

Kelly, Lincoln G. "THe Value to the Individual Professional Man of Strict Adherence to His Code of Ethics." *Journal of Accountancy* 156 (November 1983), 140-144.

Kokus, John, Jr. "Ethics for the Real Estate Appraiser." *Appraisal Journal* 51 (October 1983), 540-545.

Kolton, Paul. "A Question of Ethics." *FE: The Magazine for Financial Executives* 1 (June 1985), 12-22.

Leary, Thomas B., Martin Michaelson, and Timothy J. Dowling. "ASAE Government Affairs Position—10." *Association Management* 36 (March 1984), 39-43.

Luegenbiehl, Heinz C. "Codes of Ethics and Moral Education of Engineers." *Business and Professional Ethics Journal* 2 (Summer 1983), 41-61. Commentary: by Bill Puka, 63.

Maitland, Ian. "The Limits of Business Self-Regulation." *California Management Review* 27 (Spring 1985), 132-147.

McGraw, Harold W., Jr. "The Information Industry: The Principles that Endure." *Computers and People* 32 (May-June 1983), 7-10.

McIntyre, Kathryn J. "Do Risk Managers Need an Ethics Code?" *Business Insurance* 16 (May 3, 1982), 13, 18.

Reinfeld, George. "Adhering to a Sales Code of Ethics Benefits Both the Customer and the Sales Person." *American Printer and Lithographer* 187 (May 1981), 76.

Relman, Arnold S. "Private Hospitals: Ethics and Profits." *Business and Society Review* 47 (Fall 1983), 28-30.

Rickner, Gale, Jr. "Are Ethics Rules for Replacement in Your Future?" *National Underwriter (Life/Health)* 88 (November 5, 1984), 26, 40-41.

Sanderson, Glen R., et al. "What's Wrong with Corporate Codes of Conduct?" *Management Accounting* 66 (July 1984), 28-31, 35.

Schultz, Brad. "Expert Warns DP Standards Could Endanger Legal Cases." *Computerworld* 15 (November 16, 1981), 31.

Smith, Peter. "Questions of Conduct." *IPRA Review* 9 (February 1985), 8-12.

Snapper, John W. "Whether Professional Associations May Enforce Professional Codes." *Business and Professional Ethics Journal* 3 (Winter 1984), 43-54. Commentaries: by John Ladd, 55; Milton F. Lunch, 61; Donald E. Wilson, 65.

Spiro, Bruce E., et al. "DPMA Code of Ethics and Standards of Conduct for Information Processing Professionals: Viewing the Need, Development." *Data Management* 19 (May 1981), 26A-26D.

Spiro, Bruce E. "Ethics—the Next Step Is Crucial." *Data Management* 21 (November 1983), 32-33.

Stein, M. L. "Ethics and Small Newspapers." *Editor and Publisher* 117 (December 22, 1984), 10-11.

Stevens, Mark. "Who Will Audit the Auditors?" *Across the Board* 22 (September 1985), 57-61.

Stevenson, J. T. "Regulation, Deregulation, Self-Regulation: The Case of Engineers in Ontario." *Journal of Business Ethics* 4 (August 1985), 253-267.

Turner, J. C., Jr. "Why Standards?" *Data Management* 19 (May 1981), 43.

Wozniak, Kenneth. "Rethinking Ethics for DP Professionals." *Computerworld* 16 (September 13, 1982), 61+.

Wright, Donald K. "Can Age Predict the Moral Values of Public Relations Practitioners?" *Public Relations Review* 11 (Spring 1985), 51-60.

Computers and Automation

Books

Baetz, Mary L. *The Human Imperative: Planning for People in the Electronic Office*. Homewood, Ill.: Dow Jones-Irwin, 1985.

Bequai, August. *How to Prevent Computer Crime: A Guide for Managers*. New York: Wiley, 1983.

Ferguson, Anne E. *Legal and Ethical Dilemmas of Computer Software: An Exploratory Study*. Logan, Utah: Utah State University, 1983.

Fitch, Philip. *Computer Ethics: A Philosophical Problem Book*. New York: Trillium Press, 1983.

Hoffman, W. M., and Jennifer M. Moore, eds. *Ethics and the Management of Computer Technology*. Cambridge, Mass.: Oelgeschlager, Gunn, & Hain, 1982.

Hulteng, John L. *Playing It Straight*. Chester, Conn.: The Globe Pequot Press, 1981.

Hunt, H. A., and Timothy L. Hunt. *Human Resource Implications of Robotics*. Kalamazoo, Mich.: W.E. Upjohn Institute, 1983.

Johnson, Deborah G. *Computer Ethics*. Englewood Cliffs, N.J.: Prentice-Hall, 1985.

Johnson, Deborah G., and John W. Snapper. *Ethical Issues in the Use of Computers*. Belmont, Calif.: Wadsworth Pub. Co., 1985.

Parker, Donn B. *Fighting Computer Crime*. New York: Scribner, 1983.

Scott, Peter B. *The Robotics Revolution*. Oxford, U.K.: Basil Blackwell, 1984.

Van Duyn, Julia A. *The Human Factor in Computer Crime*. Princeton, N.J.: Petrocelli Books, 1985.

Werneke, Diane. *Microelectronics and Office Jobs: The Impact of the Chip on Women's Employment*. Geneva: International Labour Office, 1983.

Articles

Albus, James S. "Robots in the Workplace: The Key to a Prosperous Future." *Futurist* 17 (February 1983), 22-27.

Allen, Brandt. "Threat Teams: A Technique for the Detection and Prevention of Fraud in Automated and Manual Systems." *Computer Security Journal* 1 (Spring 1981), 1-13.

Argote, Linda, Paul S. Goodman, and David Schkade. "The Human Side of Robotics: How Workers React to a Robot." *Sloan Management Review* 24 (Spring 1983), 31-41.

Arthur, Alcott. "Robots, RIFs, and Rights." *Journal of Business Ethics* 4 (June 1985), 197-203.

Atkins, William. "Jesse James at the Terminal." *Harvard Business Review* 63 (July-August 1985), 82-87.

Baab, John G., Stephen M. Paroly, and William H. Marquand. "A Three-Dimensional Look at Computer Fraud." *Financial Executive* 52 (October 1984), 21-28.

Bailey, Douglas M. "White Collar Software Piracy/Inside the Pirate's Cove." *New England Business* 6 (September 17, 1984), 18-22.

Bequai, August. "Computers Plus Business Equal Liabilities." *Personnel Administrator* 29 (September 1984), 35-52.

Bequai, August. "Identify and Avoid Computer-Related Liability—Part 2." *Security Management* 29 (May 1985), 69-76.

Bequai, August. "Lack of Ethics as a Cause of Computer Crime." *Computers and People* 33 (May-June 1984), 7-14.

Bequai, August. "What Can Be Done to Stem Rising Electronic Crime?" *Office* 98 (November 1983), 47-48+.

Betts, Mitch. "U.S. Attorneys Push to Clarify Vague '84 DP Crime Law." *Computerworld* 19 (July 1, 1985), 22.

Bezdek, Jiri, and Sanford Sheriden. "Across-the-Board Training Protects Data/Computer Crime, Requires Preventive Action by Execs." *Computerworld* 18 (October 29, 1984), 10-11.

Blackey, Robert. "Will Robots Carry Union Cards?" *Business and Society Review* 53 (Spring 1985), 33-35.

Block, Fred L., and John B. Judis. "Computerization Changes the Rules." *Commonweal* 111 (November 2-16, 1984), 592-595.

Bologna, Jack. "Internal Security: Issues and Answers." *Office Administration & Automation* 46 (July 1985), 33-37.

Brightman, Harvey J., Lawrence L. Schkade, and Dick Schoech. "Managing the Decision Science Technology: A Case for Ethical Analysis?" *Decision Sciences* 12 (October 1981), 690-701.

Britton, Herchell. "Computer Crime: The Continuing Problem." *Security World* 18 (August 1981), 71+.

Brod, Craig. "Managing Technostress: Optimizing the Use of Computer Technology." *Personnel Journal* 61 (October 1982), 753-757.

Buss, Martin D. J., and Lynn M. Salerno. "Common Sense and Computer Security." *Harvard Business Review* 62 (March-April 1984), 112-121.

Byron, Christopher, and Paul A. Witteman. "Dropping by to Keep His Hand In." *Time* 117 (March 9, 1981), 64.

Campbell, Robert P. "Locking up the Mainframe (Part 2)." *Computerworld* 17 (October 17, 1983), 1-13.

Carroll, John M. "The Control of Computer-Based Fraud." *Computers & Security* 1 (June 1982), 123-138.

Cirillo, David J. "Office Ergonomics: Coping With Causes of Stress in the Automated Work Place." *Management Review* 72 (December 1983), 25.

Clevenger, M. "The Ergonomics Ball Is Rolling." *Office Administration and Automation* 46 (July 1985), 90.

Coates, Joseph, F. "Computers and Business: A Case of Ethical Overload." *Journal of Business Ethics* 1 (August 1982), 239-248.

Colvard, Robert G., et al. "Computer Fraud in the Banking Industry." *Tennessee's Business* 9 (November 1982), 10-19.

"Computer Security: What Can Be Done." *Business Week* (September 26, 1983), 126-127+.

Conrath, David W. "White Collar Productivity: The Search for the Holy Grail." *Journal of Business Ethics* 3 (February 1984), 29-33.

Cooper, Frederick L., III, and Cynthia B. Somervill. "Software Piracy: Is Your Company Liable?" *Business* 35 (Oct.-Nov.-Dec. 1985), 34-38.

Courtney, Robert H., Jr. "Part II. Computer Security Goals of the DoD —Another Opinion." *Computer Security Journal* 3 (Summer 1984), 61-63.

Desmond, John. "Clear and Present Danger." *Computerworld* 18 (January 7, 1985), 15-19.

Egger, Steven A. "The New Predators: Crime Enters the Future." *Futurist* 19 (April 1985), 15-18.

"Ergonomics: The Cure for Computer Blues." *Savings Institutions* 105 (January 1984), 97-99.

Faurer, Lincoln D. "Part I. Computer Security Goals of the Department of Defense." *Computer Security Journal* 3 (Summer 1984), 55-60.

Foegen, J. H. "Telecommuting: New Sweatshops at Home Computer Terminals?" *Business and Society Review* 51 (Fall 1984), 52-55.

Gassaway, Paul. "Keep Computers Safe from Unauthorized Use." *Security Management* 29 (September 1985), 113.

Geiser, Ken. "The Chips Are Falling: Health Hazards in the Microelectronics Industry." *Science for the People* 17 (July-August 1985), 8-11+.

Gengler, Michael J., and Richard J. Tersine. "ROBOTS: Coming to Work in America." *Business and Economic Review* 30 (July 1984), 26-32.

Henriques, Vico, and Charlotte LeGates. "A Look at VDTs and Their Impact on the Workplace and an Overview of a New Science Called Ergonomics." *Personnel Administrator* 29 (September 1984), 64-68.

Hoffman, Lance J., and Alan F. Westin. "A Survey: Office Automation Security and Privacy Practices." *Computer Security Journal* 3 (Winter 1985), 69-76.

"Information Technology-Bugbusters." *Canadian Business* 58 (September 1985), 131-135.

Johnson, Bob. "DP 'Hacking' Seen as Addiction to be Squelched." *Computerworld* 17 (April 18, 1983), 32.

Johnson, Bob. "Stop Thief!" *Computerworld* 15 (December 28, 1981-January 4, 1982), 72-76.

Johnson, Deborah G. "Privacy, Power, and Property: Ethical Dilemmas for Computer Professionals." *Small Systems World* 11 (June 1983), 17-22.

Ketchum, Sally E. "Technology with a Human Touch." *Computer Decisions* 15 (September 15, 1983), 162-172.

Kirchner, Jake. "August Bequai, Fighter for Ethics." *Computerworld* 18 (May 21, 1984), 1-14.

Kizilos, Tolly. "Kratylus Automates His Urnworks." *Harvard Business Review* 62 (May-June 1984), 136-144.

Kneale, Dennis. "Special Report: Technology in the Workplace: The Unfinished Revolution." *Wall Street Journal* (September 16, 1985), 1C-100C.

Laberis, Bill. "CPU Programmed to Hide Theft." *Computerworld* 15 (June 8, 1981), 2.

Large, Peter. "Coping With Computer Crime." *World Press Review* 28 (July 1981), 57.

Lasden, Martin, "Computer Crime." *Computer Decisions* 13 (June 1981), 104-124.

Lewis, Mike. "Computer Crime: Theft in Bits and Bytes." *Nation's Business* 73 (February 1985), 57-58.

Lydecker, Toni H. "Computer Crime." *Association Management* 36 (November 1984), 62-66.

Main, Jeremy. "Work Won't Be the Same Again." *Fortune* 105 (June 28, 1982), 58-65.

Martin, Alexia. "Facing Up to Reality: Dilemma of the Dislocated Office Worker." *Office Administration and Automation* 45 (September 1984), 27-28+.

McArthur, Donald W. "What Good Is Technology if You Are Faced With Disenchanted Employees?" *Office* 101 (January 1985), 128.

McKibbin, Wendy L. "Who Gets the Blame for Computer Crime?" *Infosystems* 30 (July 1983), 34-36.

McLellan, Vin. "Of Trojan Horses, Data Diddling, and Logic Bombs: How Computer Thieves Are Exploiting Companies' Hidden Vulnerabilities." *Inc.* 6 (June 1984), 104+.

McNitt, Jim. "Making Computers and People Compatible." *Nation's Business* 72 (March 1984), 50, 52.

Meldman, Jeffrey A. "Educating Toward Ethical Responsibility in MIS." *Sloan Management Review* 23 (Winter 1982), 73-75.

Meldman, Jeffrey A. "Privacy Expectations in an Information Age." *Computer Security Journal* 1 (Winter 1982), 81-89.

Middaugh, J. K., II. "Data Transmission: Guarding the System." *Business* 35 (Jan.-Feb.-Mar. 1985), 3-15.

Miller, Marc. "The 'Wild Card' of Business: How to Manage the Work Ethic in the Automated Workplace." *Management Review* 72 (September 1983), 8-12.

Mitsch, Robert J. "Ensuring Privacy and Accuracy of Computerized Employee Record Systems." *Personnel Administration* 28 (September 1983), 37-41.

Nussbaum, Karen. "The Hazards of Office Automation." *Business and Society Review* 40 (Winter 1981-82), 45-48.

Page, John, and Paul Hooper. "Internal Control in Computer Systems." *Financial Executive* 50 (June 1982), 14-20.

Paris, Michael. "CIM and the Art of Management." *Vital Speeches of the Day* 51 (February 15, 1985), 264-267.

Parker, Donn B. "A Strategy for Preventing Program Theft and System Hacking." *Computer Security Journal* 3 (Summer 1984), 21-32.

Piel, Gerard. "Reentering Paradise: The Mechanization of Work." *McKinsey Quarterly* (Summer 1984), 35-44.

Polis, Richard I. "Information Security: Reality and Fiction." *Computers and Security* 3 (August 1984), 225-228.

Rothman, Steven. "Computer Crime: The Menace Grows." *D & B Reports* 29 (July-August 1981), 6-12.

Saddler, Jeanne. "Home Work: Personal Computers Increase Independence of Handicapped Users." *Wall Street Journal* (February 7, 1984), 1+.

Schnabolk, Charles. "Protecting Against the Electronic Thief." *Security Management* 28 (August 1984), 41-47.

Schultz, Brad. "Computer Found Cutting Worker's Tie to Job." *Computerworld* 15 (July 27, 1981), 5.

"Sour Notes Still Soil a Sweet Idea." *Modern Office Procedures* 28 (April 1983), 46-52.

"Spreading Danger of Computer Crime." *Business Week* (April 20, 1981), 86-92.

Stark, Craig. "Are They Clean?" *PC Magazine* 4 (January 22, 1985), 79+.

Steinbrecher, D. "As Computer Systems Transform the Way Business Is Done, Users Must Address Ethical and Moral Issues." *Office Administration and Automation* 46 (May 1985), 10.

Taylor, Ron. "The Dark Age of Office Ergonomics Isn't Over Yet." *Computing Canada* (Fall 1984), 15-16.

Thackeray, Gail. "Planning a Corporate Defense Against Communications Crime." *Information Strategy* 1 (Summer 1985), 15-19.

Thackeray, Gail. "Why Are We Reluctant to Prosecute Computer Crime?" *Office* 100 (August 1984), 81-82.

Wasch, Kenneth A. "Software Thievery Is a Crime." *Security Management* 29 (February 1985), 50-56.

Webb, Dan K. "Recent Developments in White Collar Crime: Electronic Eavesdropping." *Vital Speeches of the Day* 51 (January 1, 1985), 175-178.

Weiss, W. H. "Ergonomics—Making Work Fit for Humans." *Supervision* 46 (November 1984), 14-17.

Williams, Bob, et al. "Office of the Future: Implications of High Technology." *Accountancy* 94 (September 1983), 84-90.

Wood, Charles C. "Countering Unauthorized Systems Accesses." *Journal of Systems Management* 35 (April 1984), 26-28.

Employee Rights and Personnel Management

Books

Abolishing Mandatory Retirement. Washington, D.C.: Government Printing Off., 1981.

Burud, Sandra L., Pamela R. Aschbacher, and Jacquelyn McCroskey. *Employer-Supported Child Care: Investing in Human Resources.* Dover, Mass.: Auburn House, 1984.

Dilts, David A., Clarence R. Deitsch, and Robert J. Paul. *Getting Absent Workers Back on the Job.* Westport, Conn.: Quorum Books, 1985.

Eglit, Howard C. *Age Discrimination.* New York: McGraw-Hill, 1982.

Employer's Manual of Affirmative Action in Employment. Indianapolis: Indiana Civil Rights Commission, 1981.

Ewing, David W. *Do It My Way or You're Fired: Employee Rights and the Changing Role of Management Prerogative.* New York: Wiley, 1983.

International Labour Conference. *Equal Opportunities and Equal Treatment for Men and Women in Employment.* Geneva: International Labour Organisation, 1985.

Larson, Lex K. *Unjust Dismissal.* New York: Matthew Bender, 1985.

Luce, Sally R. *Retrenchment and Beyond: The Acid Test of Human Resource Management.* Ottawa: Conference Board of Canada, 1983.

McCullough, Kenneth J. *Selecting Employees Safely Under the Law.* Englewood Cliffs, N.J.: Prentice-Hall, 1981.

Morin, William J. *Outplacement Techniques.* New York: American Management Association, 1982.

Pati, Gopal C., and John I. Adkins. *Managing and Employing the Handicapped: The Untapped Potential.* Lake Forest, Ill.: Brace-Park, 1981.

Pohier, Jacques, and Dietmar Mieth, eds. *Unemployment and the Right to Work.* New York: Seabury Press, 1982.

Saunders, Christopher T., and David Marsden. *Pay Inequalities in the European Community.* London, U.K.: Butterworth, 1981.

Shawe, Stephen D., and Bruce S. Harrison. *Avoiding Employment Discrimination Charges.* New York: Matthew Bender, 1984.

Smith, Robert E. *Workrights.* New York: Dutton, 1983.

Snell, M., W. P. Glucklich, and M. Povall. *Equal Pay and Opportunities.* London, U.K.: Dept. of Employment, 1981.

Werhane, Patricia, and H. Persons. *Rights and Corporations.* Englewood Cliffs, N.J.: Prentice-Hall, 1985.

Willman, Paul. *Fairness, Collective Bargaining, and Incomes Policy.* Oxford, U.K.: Clarendon Press, 1982.

Wolff, Richard H. *Fire Me and I'll Sue: A Manager's Survival Guide to Employee Rights.* New York: Alexander Hamilton Inst., 1984.

Articles

Acton, Norman. "Employment of Disabled Persons: Where Are We Going?" *International Labour Review* 120 (January-February 1981), 1-14.

Adams, Jane M. "The Problem Employee." *New England Business* 4 (April 19, 1982), 62-63, 65.

Adamson, Barry, et al. "Managing Large-Scale Staff Reductions." *Business Quarterly (Canada)* 48 (Summer 1983), 40-52.

Adler, Philip, Jr., Charles K. Parsons, and Scott B. Zolke. "Employee Privacy: Legal and Research Developments and Implications for Personnel Administration." *Sloan Management Review* 26 (Winter 1985), 13-22.

Agarwal, Naresh C. "Pay Discrimination: A Comparative Analysis of Research Evidence and Public Policy in Canada, the United States and Britain." *Columbia Journal of World Business* 18 (Summer 1983), 28-38.

"Age Discrimination: Terminated Employees Sue Roche." *Chemical Engineering News* 63 (May 13, 1985), 4-5.

"The Age-Old Problems of Discrimination." *Personnel Journal* 64 (April 1985), 11.

Aikin, Olga. "Mitigation of Loss After Dismissal." *Personnel Management* 15 (March 1983), 44.

America, Richard F. "Rethinking Affirmative Action in Banks." Banker's Magazine 167 (January-February 1984), 80-83.

Angarola, Robert T. "Drug Testing in the Workplace: Is it Legal?" *Personnel Administrator* 30 (September 1985), 79-89.

Antonucci, Joseph T. "Proprietary Information: Employee Loyalty Makes the Difference." *Security Management* 29 (September-October 1985), 42-45.

Applebaum, Steven H. "A Human Resource Counseling Model: The Drug-Abused Employee." *Colorado Business Review* 54 (January 1981), 2-4.

"Are the Parachutes Working? a CEO Debate." *Directors & Boards* 6 (Summer 1982), 26-28.

"Associations Rely on Polygraphs." *Savings and Loan News* 104 (April 1983), 90-92.

Austin, Glenn. "Consistent, Preventive Care Lead to Payoff." *Business and Health* 2 (September 1985), 10-13.

Axmith, Murray. "The Art of Firing: A Constructive Approach." *Business Quarterly* (Canada) 46 (Spring 1981), 36-45.

Bakaly, Charles G., Jr., and Joel M. Grossman. "How to Avoid Wrongful Discharge Suits." *Management Review* 73 (August 1984), 41-46.

Baker, George H. "The Unwritten Contract: Job Perceptions." *Personnel Journal* 64 (July 1985), 36-41.

Baldwin, James J. "The Employer and Employee Laws: The Continued Adherences to the Terminable-at-will Rule in South Carolina." *Business and Economic Review* 27 (April-May 1981), 15-17.

Baldwin, James J. "The Employer and Employment Laws; Comparable Worth Theory Survives Round One as Supreme Court Decides Gunther Case." *Business and Economic Review* 28 (October 1981), 16-18.

Bates, Jeffrey W. "Smokers vs. Nonsmokers: The Common Law Right to a Smoke-Free Environment." *Missouri Law Review* 48 (Summer 1983), 783-800.

Batt, William L. "Canada's Good Example With Displaced Workers." *Harvard Business Review* 61 (July-August 1983), 6+.

Becker, Peter. "Being Fired Is No Big Thing." *Association Management* 35 (April 1, 1983), 86-88.

Belt, John A. "The Polygraph: A Questionable Personnel Tool." *Personnel Administrator* 28 (August 1983), 69, 91.

Benfield, C. J. "Problem Performers: The Third-Party Solution." *Personnel Journal* 64 (August 1985), 96-101.

Benjamin, Gerald A. "Shift Workers." *Personnel Journal* 63 (June 1984), 72-76.

Bierman, Leonard, Joseph C. Ullman, and Stuart A. Youngblood. "Making Disputes Over Dismissals 'Win-Win' Situations." *Business and Economic Review* 31 (July 1985), 26-28.

Bilyea, Cliff. "Managing the Marginal Performer." *Management World* 10 (April 1981), 39-40.

Bishop, D. W. "Affirmative Action Cases: Bakke, Weber, and Fullilove." *Journal of Negro History* 67 (Fall 1982), 229-244.

Bistline, Susan M. "How to Buy . . . The Services of an Outplacement Consultant." *Association Management* 36 (March 1984), 181-189.

Black, Sheila. "Facing the Future: Career Counselling." *Director (UK)* 38 (October 1984), 38-40.

Bloch, Howard R., and Robert L. Pennington. "An Econometric Analysis of Affirmative Action." *Review of Black Political Economy* 11 (Winter 1981), 267-276.

Blomquist, Ceil. "Study Shows Relocation Resistance Reversing." *Personnel Administrator* 27 (December 1982), 55-56.

Bluestone, Miriam. "Right-to-Know: An Ongoing Battle Grows Hotter." *Chemical Week* 136 (January 16, 1985), 8-10.

Blum, David J. "Donors' Backlash: Many Workers Oppose Employers' Pressures to Give to Charities." *Wall Street Journal* (January 12, 1982), 1, 12.

Bookser Feister, John. "The Struggle for Workplace Justice." *Other Side* 21 (April-May 1985), 46-49.

Brenkert, George G. "Privacy, Polygraphs and Work." *Business and Professional Ethics Journal* 1 (Fall 1981), 19-36. Commentary: by David Linowes, 37.

Bright, Thomas L. and Charles J. Hollon. "EEO: Where We Stand Now." *Management World* 12 (February-March 1983), 14-16.

Bright, Thomas L. and Charles H. Hollon. "State Regulation of Polygraph Tests at the Workplace." *Personnel* 62 (February 1985), 50-55.

Brown, Howard B. "Time Is Running Out on Right-to-Know Compliance." *Risk Management* 31 (December 1984), 60-62.

Bryant, James A., et al. "Employment at Will: Where Is It Going and What Can Be Done?" *Advanced Management Journal* 49 (Autumn 1984), 12-21.

Buckley, Joseph P. "The 9 Steps of Interrogation." *Security Management* 27 (May 1983), 45-47.

Bullard, Perry. "The Right to Fire: Under Fire." *Corporate Board* (May-June 1984), 6-11.

Bullock, Kathy. "Downsizing: Opportunities and Dilemmas." *Cost & Management* 59 (July-August 1985), 60-63.

Burchett, S. R. "Performance Appraisal and the Law." *Personnel* 62 (July 1985), 29-37.

Bushardt, Stephen C., and Aubrey R. Fowler. "Compensation and Benefits: Today's Dilemma in Motivation." *Personnel Administrator* 27 (April 1982), 23-26.

Buss, Dale D. "Auto Firms' Blue-Collar Transfers Result in Troubles at Work, Home." *Wall Street Journal* (May 15, 1984), 31.

Byrne, John A. "Undoctoring the Resume." *Forbes* 134 (July 16, 1984), 144-145.

Calonius, L. E., and Erik Larson. "Long Road Home: Georgia-Pacific's Trek From West to South Rattles Many Workers." *Wall Street Journal* (September 30, 1982), 1+.

Camden, Carl, and Bill Wallace. "Job Application Forms: A Hazardous Employment Practice." *Personnel Administrator* 28 (March 1983), 31+.

Camden, Thomas M. "Outplacement." *Magazine of Bank Administration* 58 (May 1982), 53-56.

Camden, Thomas M. "The Role of Outplacement Counseling in a Changing Economy." *Management World* 10 (March 1981), 1, 7.

Cann, Arnie, William D. Siegfried, and Lorena Pearce. "Forced Attention to Specific Applicant Qualifications: Impact of Physical Attractiveness and Sex of Applicant Biases." *Personnel Psychology* 34 (Spring 1981), 65-75.

Carey, Justin P. "Business Ethics, Employee Privacy and the Management of Insurance Information." *Review of Business* 3 (Fall-Winter 1981), 21-24.

Carmean, Gene. "Preplacement Medical Screenings." *Personnel Journal* 64 (June 1985), 124-131.

Carson, John J. "Is There Any Merit in the Merit System Today?" *Optimum* 12 (1981), 73-76.

Cawsey, Thomas F., et al. "Human Needs and Job Satisfaction: A Multidimensional Approach." *Human Relations* 35 (September 1982), 703-715.

Chafee, John H. "Ensuring the Health of Children." *Business and Health* 2 (September 1985), 5-8.

Challenger, J.E. "The Threat of Age Discrimination Has Increased in Recent Years." *Office Administration and Automation* 46 (March 1985), 92.

"Child Care Benefits: A Plus for Management and Employees." *Effective Manager* 4 (June 1981), 3-5.

Christiansen, Hanne D. "Equality and Equilibrium: Weaknesses of the Overlap Argument for Unisex Pension Plans." *Journal of Risk & Insurance* 50 (December 1983), 670-680.

Christie, Claudia M. "Who's Watching the Children?" *New England Business* 3 (October 1981), 21-23.

Cleveland, Harlan. "How Much Sunshine Is Too Much?" *Across the Board* 22 (July-August 1985), 15-21.

Collins, Denis. "Ex-cultists Need Not Apply." *Across the Board* 21 (December 1984), 59-64.

"Comparable Worth: Employers Can No Longer Pass the Buck." *Personnel Journal* 64 (November 1985), 110-111.

Condon, Thomas J. and Richard H. Wolff. "Procedures That Safeguard Your Right to Fire." *Harvard Business Review* 63 (November-December 1985), 16-18.

Conner, Caryl. "Beyond the Fringes." *Across the Board* 22 (April 1985), 8-12.

Couger, J. D. "Providing Norms on Ethics to Entering Employees." *Journal of Systems Management* 35 (February 1984), 40-41.

Coulson, Robert. "How Fair Are Your Grievance Procedures?" *Association Management* 37 (February 1985), 17-120.

Coulson, Robert, "Rules of the Game—How to Fire." *Across the Board* 19 (February 1982), 30-48.

Crapnell, Stephen G. "Worker Notification: The New Right-to-Know Battleground." *Occupational Hazards* 43 (December 1981), 59-62.

"Creative Fiction." *Time* 117 (May 11, 1981), 64.

Criscuoli, E. J., Jr. "What Personnel Administrators Should Know About Computer Crime." *Personnel Administrator* 26 (September 1981), 53-56.

"Curtailing the Freedom to Fire." *Business Week* (March 19, 1984), 29+.

Dahl, Robert A. "Democracy in the Workplace: Is It a Right or a Privilege?" *Dissent* 31 (Winter 1984), 54-60.

Daspin, Eileen. "Outplacement for Hourly Workers." *Management Review* 74 (March 1985), 57-60.

Davis, George and Glegg Watson. "Backlash." *Across the Board* 19 (December 1982), 47-54.

De Long, David. "The Employee Who's No Longer Useful." *Inc.* 4 (January 1982), 86.

Deitsch, Clarence R., et al. "Getting Absent Workers Back on the Job: The Case of General Motors." *Business Horizons* 24 (September-October 1981), 52-58.

Delaney, W. A. "The Misuse of Bonuses." *Supervisory Management* 29 (January 1984), 28-31.

Denis, Martin K. "The Roots of Age Discrimination Claims." *Employment Relations Today* 12 (Autumn 1985), 257-263.

Des Jardins, Joseph R., and John J. McCall. "A Defense of Employee Rights." *Journal of Business Ethics* 4 (October 1985), 367-376.

Dickens, Linda. "Unfair Dismissal Law: A Decade of Disillusion?" *Personnel Management* 14 (February 1982), 24-27.

Dilks, Carol. "Employers Who Help with the Kids." *Nation's Business* 72 (February 1984), 59-60.

Dipboye, Robert L. "Some Neglected Variables in Research on Discrimination in Appraisals." *Academy of Management Review* 10 (January 1985), 116-127.

Dube, L. E., Jr. "OSHA's Hazard Communication Standard: Right to Know Comes to the Workplace." *Labor Law Journal* 36 (September 1985), 696-701.

Dubin, R. A. "Guess Who Wants Your Frequent-Flier Coupons?" *Business Week* (August 5, 1985), 37.

Duff, Karl J., and Eric T. Johnson. "A Renewed Employee Right to Privacy." *Labor Law Journal* 34 (December 1983), 747-762.

Duffy, D. J. "Conducting Work-Place Investigations: Potential Liabilities for Employers." *Employment Relations Today* 12 (Spring 1985), 63-72.

Duffy, D. J. "Defamation." *Employment Relations Today* 10 (Autumn 1983), 267-280.

Duffy, D. J. "Defamation and Employer Privilege." *Employee Relations Law Journal* 9 (Winter 1983-84), 444-454.

Duffy, D. J. "Privacy in the Work Place: Constitutional Restrictions on Employers." *Employment Relations Today* 11 (Autumn 1984), 305-310.

Duffy, D. J. "Privacy in the Workplace: Statutory Restrictions on the Employer." *Employment Relations Today* 11 (Spring 1984), 57-65.

Duffy, D. J. "Privacy vs. Disclosure: Balancing Employee and Employer Rights." *Employee Relations Law Journal* 7 (Spring 1982), 594-609.

Duffy, D. J. "Tortious Invasion of Privacy." *Employment Relations Today* 10 (Winter 1983-84), 381-390.

Dunn, D. H. "When a Lie Detector Is Part of the Job Interview." *Business Week* (July 27, 1981), 85-86.

Durling, Bette B. "Retaliation: A Misunderstood Form of Employment Discrimination." *Personnel Journal* 60 (July 1981), 555-558.

Edwards, Mark R., and J. R. Sproull. "Safeguarding Your Employee Rating System." *Business* 35 (Apr.-May-June 1985), 17-27.

"Employee Benefit Program Based on Moral Commitment." *Business Insurance* 17 (April 17, 1983), 123-124.

"Employer-Provided Day Care." *Supervision* 47 (July 1985), 10-11.

"Employers Respond to Two-Career Families/Corporate Child Care: Making an Impact on Productivity." *Chain Store Age Executive* 61 (July 1985), 11-13.

Engel, Paul G. "No Smoking: More Companies Are Imposing Bans." *Industry Week* 227 (November 11, 1985), 20-21.

Engel, Paul G. "Preserving the Right to Fire." *Industry Week* 224 (March 18, 1985), 39-40.

Englade, Kenneth F. "The Business of the Polygraph." *Across the Board* 19 (October 1982), 20-27.

English, Carey W. "Getting Tests for Jobs Stir Hopes and Fears." *U.S. News and World Report* 94 (April 11, 1983), 72+.

"The ESOP Fable: Employee Stock Ownership Plan Fall Short." *Dollars and Sense* (July-August 1983), 12-14.

"ESOP Used to Avoid Takeover, Raise Productivity." *Employee Benefit Plan Review* 36 (August 1983), 67-68.

Estreicher, Samuel. "At-Will Employment and the Problem of Unjust Dismissal: The Appropriate Judicial Response." *New York State Bar Journal* 54 (April 1982), 146-149+.

Ewing, David W. "A Bill of Rights for Employees: Constitutionalizing the Corporation." *Across the Board* 18 (March 1981), 42-49.

Ewing, David W. "Case of the Disputed Dismissal." *Harvard Business Review* 31 (September-October 1983), 38+.

Ewing, David W. "Due Process: Will Business Default?" *Harvard Business Review* 60 (November-December 1982), 114-122.

Ewing, David W. "Your Right to Fire." *Harvard Business Review* 61 (March-April 1983), 32-42.

Faley, Robert H., Lawrence S. Kleiman, and Mark L. Lengnick-Hall. "Age Discrimination and Personnel Psychology: A Review and Synthesis of the Legal Literature with Implications . . ." *Personnel Psychology* 37 (Summer 1984), 327-350.

Fenn, Donna. "The Kids Are All Right." *Inc.* 7 (January 1985), 48-54.

Fenton, James W., Jr., and Sherman A. Timmins. "The At-Will-Employment Doctrine: Implications and Recommendations for the Small Business Firm." *Journal of Small Business Management* 20 (January 1982), 32-37.

"The Fiery Debate Over Smoking at Work." *Business and Society Review* 51 (Fall 1984), 4-12.

Filer, Randall K. "Male-Female Wage Differences: The Importance of Compensating Differentials." *Industrial and Labor Relations Review* 38 (April 1985), 426-437.

Fisher, Anne B. "Businessmen Like to Hire by the Numbers." *Fortune* 112 (September 16, 1985), 26-30.

Flynn, W. R., et al. "Managing Problem Employees." *Human Resource Management* 20 (Summer 1981), 28-32.

Foegen, J. H. "The New Cottage Industries Create New Issues in Benefits." *Personnel Journal* 64 (February 1985), 28-30.

Foegen, J. H. "Pink Slips for Troublemakers: Employes Fight the Firing Squad." *Business and Society Review* 48 (Winter 1984), 19-22.

Foegen, J. H. "Job Loyalty Works Both Ways." *Enterprise* 2 (Summer 1983), 25-27.

Foegen, J. H. "Sick Leave Is No Vacation." *Business Horizons* 26 (March-April 1983), 52-54.

Francesco, A. M., and M. D. Hakel. "Gender and Sex Ad Determinants of Hireability of Applicants for Gender-Typed Jobs." *Psychology of Women Quarterly* 5 (1981), 747-757.

Fulk, J., et al. "Trust-in-Supervisor and Perceived Fairness and Accuracy of Performance Evaluations." *Journal of Business Research* 13 (August 1985), 301-313.

Fulmer, William E., and Caroline Fryman. "A Managerial Guide to Outplacement Services." *Advanced Management Journal* 50 (Summer 1985), 10-13.

Gaden, Herman. "Termination-at-Will: A Test of Morality in Organizations." *International Journal of Applied Philosophy* 2 (Spring 1984), 23-24.

Gallagher, James J. "How to Fire an Executive." *Today's Office* 17 (March 1983), 55-59.

Gandz, Jeffrey, and James C. Rush. "Human Rights and the Right Way to Hire." *Business Quarterly (Canada)* 48 (April 1983), 70-77.

Garfinkel, Perry. "Smoker Seg: A New Kind of Regulation Is Compelling Many Businesses to Put Smokers in Their Place." *Across the Board* 21 (July-August 1984), 28-36.

Gerson, Herbert E., and Louis P. Britt, III. "The Expanding Rights of Unrepresented Employees." *Personnel Journal* 62 (May 1983), 350-356.

Gersuny, Carl. "Employment Seniority: Cases from Iago to Weber." *Journal of Labor Research* 3 (Winter 1982), 111-119.

Gest, Ted. "Using Drugs? You May Not Get Hired." *U.S. News and World Report* 99 (December 23, 1985), 38.

Gibson, G. B. "Worker Right-to-Know Laws Suggest New Safety Role for Risk Managers." *National Underwriter* (Property/Casualty) 89 (August 2, 1985), 6+.

Giglioni, Giovanni B., Joyce B. Giglioni, and James A. Bryant. "Performance Appraisal: Here Comes the Judge." *California Management Review* 24 (Winter 1981), 14-23.

Gillespie, R. J. "Suit Seeks to Halt A&P Asset Distribution." *Pensions Investment Age* 13 (May 27, 1985), 63.

Gillo, Martin. "Comparable Worth vs. Equal Pay—The U.S. Controversy and Some Candid Questions." *Benefits International (UK)* 14 (January 1985), vi-xii.

Goldberg, Matthew S. "Discrimination, Nepotism, and Long-Run Wage Differentials." *Quarterly Journal of Economics* 97 (May 1982), 307-319.

Golen, Steven, et al. "The Personal Touch." *Management World* 12 (September 1983), 40-41.

Grafton, Kermit S. "The Laws That Apply to Honesty Testing." *Security Management* 29 (August 1985), 33-36.

Graser, Rick. "Employer-Sponsored Child Care on the Rise." *Appalachia* 17 (November-December 1983), 15-21.

Greenberg, Karen, et al. "How Companies Feel About Outplacement Services." *Personnel* 60 (January-February 1983), 55-57.

Greene, Richard. "Don't Panic." *Business Week* (August 29, 1983), 122.

Greenlaw, Paul S., and John P. Kohl. "Sexual Harassment: Homosexuality, Bisexuality and Blackmail." *Personnel Administrator* 26 (June 1981), 59-62.

Greenwood, Daphne. "The Institutional Inadequacy of the Market in Determining Comparable Worth." *Journal of Economic Issues* 18 (June 1984), 57-464.

Guiley, Rosemary. "When Your Employees Work from Home." *Working Woman* 10 (March 1985), 27-30.

Guynes, Carl S., and Michael T. Vanecek. "Computer Security: The Human Element." *Personnel Administrator* 26 (April 1981), 71-75.

Haight, Gretchen G. "But What Happens to the Kids While We Work?" *Across the Board* 19 (October 1982), 28-35.

Hambley, Thomas J., et al. "Employment Termination: What Do You Do If It Affects You, Personally?" *Canadian Insurance* 87 (September 1982), 28, 30.

Harrison, Edward L. "Legal Restrictions on the Employer's Authority to Discipline." *Personnel Journal* 61 (February 1982), 136-141.

Hartmann, Heidi I., and Donald J. Treiman. "Notes on the NAS Study of Equal Pay for Jobs of Equal Value." *Public Personnel Management* 12 (Winter 1983), 404-417.

Hatano, Daryl G. "Employee Rights and Corporate Restrictions: A Balance of Liberties." *California Management Review* 24 (Winter 1981), 5-13.

Hayden, Trudy. "Employers Who Use Lie Detector Tests." *Business and Society Review* 41 (Spring 1982), 16-21.

Hayes, James L. "Loyalty and Today's Manager." *Security Management* 25 (February 1981), 102.

Hayes, Mary. "OSHA Final Rule Gives Employees the Right to See Their Exposure and Medical Records." *Personnel Administrator* 27 (March 1982), 71-75.

Heiland, Constance R., John P. Daniels, and Jerry L. Wall. "The Ethical Imperative: Myth or Reality?" *Journal of Business Ethics* 3 (May 1984), 119-125.

Helburn, I.B., and John R. Hill. "The Arbitration of Religious Practice Grievances." *Arbitration Journal* 39 (June 1984), 3-13.

"Helping Laid-Off Workers Find New Employment." *Chemical Week* 129 (November 4, 1981), 55-56.

Hendriksen, Dane. "Outplacement: Program Guidelines that Ensure Success." *Personnel Journal* 61 (August 1982), 583-589.

Hergenrather, E. R. "Mature and Motivated: The Strength of the Gray Boomers." *Management World* 14 (May 1985), 1+.

Heshizer, Brian. "The Implied Contract Exception to At-Will-Employment." *Labor Law Journal* 35 (March 1984), 131-141.

Hiatt, Arnold. "Child Care: A Business Responsibility." *Industry Week* 215 (November 29, 1982), 13.

Hilaski, Harvey J., and Chao Ling Wang. "How Valid Are Estimates of Occupational Illness?" *Monthly Labor Review* 105 (August 1982), 27-35.

Hiley, David R. "Employee Rights and the Doctrine of At Will Employment." *Business and Professional Ethics Journal* 4 (Fall 1985), 1-10. Commentary: by Robert Sass, 11.

Hill, Marvin F., Jr., and Terry Bishop. "Aging and Employment: The BFOQ Under the ADEA." *Labor Law Journal* 34 (December 1983), 763-775.

Hill, M., Jr., and D. Dawson. "Discharge for Off-Duty Misconduct in the Private and Public Sectors." *Arbitration Journal* 40 (June 1985), 24-37.

Hollon, Charles J., and Thomas L. Bright. "Avoiding Religious Discrimination in the Workplace." *Personnel Journal* 61 (August 1982), 590-594.

Horton, Norman R. "Dear New Hire: We Reserve the Right to Fire You." *Management Review* 73 (August 1984), 3.

Horton, Thomas R. "Employment at Will: Two Approaches in Dealing with Employees." *Vital Speeches of the Day* 52 (December 15, 1985), 150-153.

"How Banks Are Grappling with Smokers' Rights." *ABA Banking Journal* 77 (March 1985), 19-20.

"How to Fire—and Not Get into Trouble: The Laws Are Changing." *Business Owner* 7 (June 1983), 17-18.

Howard, John. "Good News, Bad News—What to Tell the Workers?" *Chief Executive (UK),* (May 1981), 12-14.

Hughes, Hunter R., III, and Carl C. Hoffman. "Employee Surveys in Employment Discrimination Litigation." *Employee Relations Law Journal* 9 (Summer 1983), 42-69.

Hurd, Sandra N. "Use of the Polygraph in Screening Job Applicants." *American Business Law Journal* 22 (Winter 1985), 529-549.

"Individual Rights in the Workplace: The Employment-at-Will Issue." *Univ. Mich. Journal Law Reform* 16 (Winter 1983), 199-305.

"It's Getting Harder to Make a Firing Stick." *Business Week* (June 27, 1983), 104-105.

Jablin, Fredric M. "Use of Discriminatory Questions in Screening Interviews." *Personnel Administrator* 27 (March 1982), 41-44.

Jablin, Fredric M., and Craig D. Tengler. "Facing Discrimination in On-Campus Interviews." *Journal of College Placement* 42 (Winter 1982), 57-61.

Jacobs, Bruce A., "Are CEOs Worth $1 Million?" *Industry Week* 221 May 14, 1984), 43-46.

Jaegerman, Megan. "Who'd Hurt a Flower?" *Security Management* 25 (May 1981), 89-91.

Jain, Harish C. "Management of Human Resources and Productivity." *Journal of Business Ethics* 2 (November 1983), 273-289.

James, Jennifer. "Sex Harassment/Detecting and Preventing Harassment." *Communicator's Journal* 1 (July-August 1983), 52-57.

Jamir, Vinson. "The European Economic Community: Paying Men and Women Equally." *World Order* 15 (Fall-Winter 1980-81), 48-68.

Janner, Greville. "Implied Terms: The Unwritten Law of the Employment Contract." *Personnel Management (UK),* (September 1985), 44-45.

Johnson, Greg. "Shrinking the White-Collar Ranks." *Industry Week* 215 (October 4, 1982), 54-59.

Johnson, Robert J., et al. "The Use of Polygraphs to Screen Potential Employees." *Texas Business Review* 55 (March-April 1981), 90-92.

Jones, Paul D., and Edward C. Brewer, III. "Smokers and Nonsmokers in the Work Place." *Employment Relations Today* 11 (Summer 1984), 188-204.

Kalt, Sandra W. "Value the Human—Confront the Behavior." *Small Systems World* 10 (March 1982), 24-26.

Kamalich, Richard F., and Solomon W. Polachek. "Discrimination: Fact or Fiction? An Examination Using an Alternative Approach." *Southern Economic Journal* 49 (October 1982), 450-461.

Kanner, Rikke, et al. "Relocation Overview." *Personnel Journal* 63 (November 1984), 28-50.

Kastiel, Diane. "Work-and-Family Seminars Help Parents Cope." *Business Insurance* 18 (May 28, 1984), 26-28.

Katz, David M. "Baby Fae and the Ethics of Benefits." *National Underwriter (Life/Health)* 88 (November 24, 1984), 2, 12-13.

Kaufman, Roger T. "Nepotism and the Minimum Wage." *Journal of Labor Research* 4 (Winter 1983), 81-89.

Keenan, Tony. "Where Application Forms Mislead." *Personnel Management* 15 (February 1983), 40-43.

Kelly, Laurence. "A Weekend's Work, A Week's Pay." *Worklife (Canada)* 4 (1984), 4-5.

Kemmer, Rick. "Honest Tests: Applicant Exams that Help Stop Stealing." *Magazine of Bank Administration* 58 (March 1982), 36-42.

Kennedy, R.D., and J.A. Roberts. "Insurance Coverage for Wrongful Termination Claims." *Employee Relations Law Journal* 10 (Spring 1985), 654-668.

Kennish, John W. "Employee Theft: A System Approach." *Internal Auditor* 42 (August 1985), 26-29.

Kent, Donald C., et al. "Smoking in the Workplace; A Review of Human and Operating Costs." *Personnel Administrator* 27 (August 1982), 29-33, 83.

Ketchum, Robert H. "Retrenchment: The Uses and Misuses of LIFO in Downsizing an Organization." *Personnel* 59 (November-December 1982), 25-30).

Kingstrom, Paul O., and Larry E. Mainstone. "An Investigation of the Rater-Ratee Acquaintance and Rater Bias." *Academy of Management Journal* 28 (September 1985), 641-653.

Kirby, Donald. "Situating the Employee Rights Debate." *Journal of Business Ethics* 4 (August 1985), 269-276.

Kleiman, Lawrence S., and Richard L. Durham. "Performance Appraisal, Promotion and the Courts: A Critical Review." *Personnel Psychology* 34 (Spring 1981), 103-121.

Kleinmutz, Benjamin. "Lie Detectors Fail the Truth Test." *Harvard Business Review* 63 (July-August 1985), 35-42.

Klotchman, Janisse, and Linda L. Neider. "EEO Alert: Watch Out for Discrimination in Discharge Decisions." *Personnel* 60 (January-February 1983), 60-66.

Koral, Alan M. "Section 4(f)(2) of ADEA—A Vanishing Haven for Employers." *Employment Relations Today* 11 (Summer 1984), 130-136.

Kovach, Kenneth. "Subconscious Stereotyping in Personnel Decisions." *Business Horizons* 25 (September-October 1982), 60-66.

Koziara, Karen S. "Comparable Worth: Organizational Dilemmas." *Monthly Labor Review* 108 (December 1985), 13-16.

Kronenberger, George K., and David L. Bourke. "Effective Training and the Elimination of Sexual Harassment." *Personnel Journal* 60 (November 1981), 879-883.

Kruchko, John G., and Lawrence E. Dube. "A New Right for Non-Union Workers." *Personnel* 60 (November-December 1983), 59-64.

LaMarre, Sandra E., and Kate Thompson. "Industry-Sponsored Daycare: An Outlook for the '80's." *Personnel Administration* 29 (February 1984), 53-55+.

Lansing, Paul, and Richard Pegnetter. "Fair Dismissal Procedures for Non-Union Employees." *American Business Law Journal* 20 (Spring 1982), 45-91.

Lapp, John S. "Mandatory Retirement as a Clause in an Employment Insurance Contract." *Economic Inquiry* 23 (January 1985), 69-92.

Lasden, Martin. "The End of Firing at Will." *Computer Decisions* 16 (October 1984), 132-140.

Lasden, Martin. "Moonlighting: A Double Standard?" *Computer Decisions* 15 (March 1983), 82-92.

Lasden, Martin. "Unacceptable Behavior: How Much Should You Take?" *Computer Decisions* 15 (February 1983), 78-85.

Lawler, Edward E. "Merit Pay: Fact or Fiction?" *Management Review* 70 (April 1981), 50-53.

LeRoux, Margaret. "No Smoking." *Madison Avenue* 26 (August 1984), 92-97.

LeRoux, Margaret. "Where There's Smoke . . ." *Madison Avenue* 26 (March-April 1984), 98-99.

Leach, Daniel E., and Elizabeth L. Werley. "Comparable Worth, Job Evaluation and Wage Discrimination: The Employer Approaches Wage Gap Issues of the 1980s." *Public Personnel Management* 12 (Winter 1983), 345-357.

Lehr, Richard I. "Work Force Reductions: Facing Up to the Issue." *Telephony* 207 (August 6, 1984), 64-70.

Leonard, Maria. "Challenges to the Termination-at-Will Doctrine." *Personnel Administrator* 28 (February 1983), 49-56.

Levin, Michael. "Do Workers 'Own' Their Jobs?" *Fortune* 107 (February 7, 1983), 109-111.

Levin, Michael E. "Equality of Opportunity." *Philosophy Quarterly* 31 (April 1981), 110-125.

Levine, Hermine Z. "Child-Care Policies." *Personnel* 61 (March-April 1984), 4-10.

Levine, Hermine Z. "Employee Assistance Programs." *Personnel* 62 (April 1985), 14-19.

Linenberger, Patricia, and Timothy J. Keaveny. "Performance Appraisal Standards Used by the Courts." *Personnel Administrator* 26 (May 1981), 89-94.

Linnen, Beth M. "Employee Reviews Should be Tailored to the Institution." *Savings Institutions* 106 (June 1985), 114-115.

Linsen, Mary Ann. "An Employee Benefit That's Not Just Child's Play." *Progressive Grocer* 64 (January 1985), 50-52.

Lissy, William E. "Circumstantial Evidence and Refusal to Talk." *Supervision* 45 (April 1983), 18-20.

Locher, Alan H. "Short-Time Compensation: A Viable Alternative to Layoffs." *Personnel Journal* 60 (March 1981), 213-216.

Lopatka, Kenneth T. "The Emerging Law of Wrongful Discharge—A Quadrennial Assessment of the Labor Law Issue of the 80's." *Business Lawyer* 40 (November 1984), 1-31.

Lorber, Lawrence Z., and J. R. Kirk. "A Status Report on the Theory of Comparable Worth: Recent Developments in the Law of Wage Discrimination." *Public Personnel Management* 12 (Winter 1983), 332-344.

Lublin, Joann S. "Resisting Advances: Employers Act to Curb Sex Harassing on Job: Lawsuits, Fines Feared." *Wall Street Journal* (April 24, 1981), 1.

Lumpkin, Julie. "Corporate Child Care." *Business and Economic Review* 30 (April 1984), 10-14.

Lyons, Terry. "The Right Approach to Redundancy." *Director (UK)* 37 (March 1984), 48-49.

Macleod, Jennifer S. "Integrating Handicapped People into the Work Force." *Employment Relations Today* 11 (Autumn 1984), 261-265.

Macleod, Jennifer S. "The Real Nature of the 'Handicap' Problem and What Can Be Done About It." *Employment Relations Today* 11 (Summer 1984), 163-168.

Madison, James R. "The Employee's Emerging Right to Sue for Arbitrary or Unfair Discharge." *Employee Relations Law Journal* 6 (Winter 1980-81), 422-436.

Mager, Robert F., et al. "The Regulators Are Coming!" *Training* 22 (September 1985), 40-45.

Magid, Renee Y. "Parents and Employers: New Partners in Child Care." *Management Review* 71 (March 1982), 38-44.

Majerus, Raymond E. "Workers Have a Right to a Share of Profits." *Harvard Business Review* 62 (September-October 1984), 42-50.

Malone, P., and M. Reid. "Industrial Social Work: Is There a Case for the Development of an In-House Social Work Service?" *Human Resource Management (Australia)* 20 (November 1982), 11+.

Martin, Edward. "Is There a Right to Work?" *Quarterly Review (National Westminster Bank)*, (November 1982), 66-74.

Matejka, J. K., and D. N. Ashworth. "The Employee's Hierarchy of Greeds." *Association Management* 46 (October 1985), 24-25.

Matusewitch, Eric P. "Fear of Lying: Polygraphs in Employment." *Technology Review* 33 (January 1981), 10-11.

Mauro, Tony. "Age Bias Charges: Increasing Problem." *Nation's Business* 71 (April 1983), 44-46.

McLenahan, John S. "The Privacy Invasion: In a Job Setting, How Personal Is 'Too Personal'?" *Industry Week* 227 (November 11, 1985), 50-53.

Megranahan, Mike. "Manpower Matters: Changing Attitudes to Redundancy." *Journal of General Management (UK)* 9 (Winter 1983/1984), 98-103.

Metzger, Michael B. "Job Security in the 1980s." *Indiana Business Review* 56 (August 1981), 3-6.

Miles, J. B. "How to Help Troubled Workers." *Computer Decisions* 17 (February 12, 1985), 66-76.

Miles, Mary. "Fighting That Losing Feeling." *Computer Decisions* 17 (June 4, 1985), 64, 111.

Milite, George A. "A Catalyst for Change." *Management Review* 74 (January 1985), 34-36.

Miller, M. A. "Age-Related Reductions in Workers' Life Insurance." *Monthly Labor Review* 108 (September 1985), 29-34.

Mills, D. Q. "Seniority Versus Ability in Promotion Decisions." *Industrial and Labor Relations Review* 38 (April 1985), 421-425.

Morgan, Philip I., et al. "The Complaint Interview." *Supervisory Management* 29 (June 1984), 25-30.

Muir, John, "Incompetence at Work." *Management Services (UK)* 28 (October 1984), 14-16.

Mulvihill, K. "Another Step Forward for Right to Know." *Chemical Week* 137 (July 17, 1985), 12.

Murphy, B. S., et al. "No Private Waiver of ADEA Rights." *Chemical Engineering News* 63 (July 8, 1985), 7.

Murphy, B. S., et al. "Weingarten Rights in State of Flux." *Personnel Journal* 64 (August 1985), 19-20+.

Murray, Thomas H. "Genetic Testing at Work: How Should It Be Used?" *Technology Review* 88 (May-June 1985), 50-59.

"Narrowing Right to Fire: How Chemical Companies Are Coping." *Chemical Week* 132 (June 22, 1983), 46-50.

Nelson, Bruce A., Edward M. Opton, Jr., and Thomas E. Wilson. "Wage Discrimination and Title VII in the 1980's: The Case Against 'Comparable Worth.' " *Employee Relations Law Journal* 6 (Winter 1980-81), 380-405.

Newby, A. C. "Ethical Issues for Training Practitioners." *Journal of European Industrial Training* 6 (1982), 10-14.

Nicholson, N. and G. Johns. "The Absence Culture and the Psychological Contract—Who's in Control of Absence?" *Academy of Management Review* 10 (July 1985), 397-407.

Noel, Al. "Privacy: A Sign of Our Times." *Personnel Administrator* 26 (March 1981), 59-62.

Novit, Mitchell S. "Defamation: Management's New Predicament." *Business* 32 (April-June 1982), 2-7.

Novit, Mitchell S. "Employees, Too, Have Legal Obligations." *Advanced Management Journal* 48 (Summer 1983), 12-18.

Novit, Mitchell S. "Genetic Screening: New Challenge for Human Resource Management." *Human Resource Management* 20 (Summer 1981), 2-9.

Nye, David L. "Fire at Will—Careful, Now, Careful." *Across the Board* 19 (November 1982), 37-40.

Nye, David L. "Fire At Will: New Rules for Managers." *Business (Atlanta)* 32 (April-June 1982), 8-11.

O'Boyle Thomas F. "More Firms Require Employee Drug Testing: Legal Questions Surround Spread of Mandatory Screening." *Wall Street Journal* (August 8, 1985), 6.

Olian, Judy D., and Tom C. Snyder. "The Implications of Genetic Testing." *Personnel Administrator* 29 (January 1984), 19-27.

Oliver, Adela. "Outplacement Plans Cut Costs." *National Underwriter (Life/Health)* 89 (June 15, 1985), 13, 24.

Oliver, Anthony T., Jr. "The Disappearing Right to Terminate Employees at Will." *Personnel Journal* 61 (December 1982), 910-917.

Orlov, Darlene. "Truth in Hiring." *Executive Female* 8 (March-April 1985), 18-20.

Ostroff, J. M. "Health Care Costs and Your Retirees." *Personnel Administrator* 30 (August 1985), 64+.

Patten, Thomas H., Jr. "Pay Cuts: Will Employees Accept Them?" *National Productivity Review* 1 (Winter 1981-1982), 110-118.

Paul, Karen, and George Sullivan. "Equal Employment Opportunity vs. Seniority Rights: The Emergence of a Social Policy." *Business and Society* 23 (April 1984), 8-14.

Paustian, C. "Claim United Violated Law: Pilots Fight Termination." *Pensions Investment Age* 13 (August 19, 1985), 1+.

"Pay Incentives Motivate Some, Disturb Others." *Savings Institutions* 104 (July 1983), 125.

"Paying Workers What They're Worth." *Christianity & Crisis* 45 (June 24, 1985), 243-244.

Pelfrey, William V. "Keeping Honest Employees Honest." *Security Management* 28 (June 1984), 22-24.

Pendleton, Clarence M. Jr. "Comparable Worth Is Not Pay Equity." *Vital Speeches of the Day* 51 (April 1, 1985), 382-384.

Pepe, Stephen P., and Michael A. Curley. "Fire at Will?" Not Necessarily." *ABA Banking Journal* 76 (July 1984), 24+.

Perham, John. "Big Surge in Age Bias Suits." *Dun's Business Month* 120 (September 1982), 56-62.

Perry, Lee T. "Cutbacks, Layoffs, and Other Obscenities: Making Human Resource Decisions." *Business Horizons* 28 (July-August 1985), 68-75.

Perry, Lee T., and Jay B. Barney. "Performance Lies Are Hazardous to Organizational Health." *Organizational Dynamics* 9 (Winter 1981), 68-80.

Pesci, Michael L. "Morale Management." *Personnel Administrator* 28 (May 1983), 14.

Peters, Laurence H., et al. "Sex Bias and Managerial Evaluations: A Replication and Extension." *Journal of Applied Psychology* 69 (May 1984), 349-352.

Peters, Robert B. "In Hiring, When Is a Risk a Risk?" *Security Management* 29 (August 1985), 51-53.

Pilla, Lou. "Unjust Discharge Arises." *Management World* 14 (March 1985), 14-16.

Pingpank, Jeffrey C., and Thomas B. Mooney. "Wrongful Discharge: A New Danger for Employers." *Personnel Administrator* 26 (March 1981), 31-35.

Pluhar, Evelyn B. "Preferential Hiring and Unjust Sacrifice." *Philosophical Forum* 12 (Spring 1981), 214-224.

Powell, Jon T. "Listening to Help the Hostile Employee." *Supervisory Management* 26 (November 1981), 2-5.

Pritchard, Robert D., Scott E. Maxwell, and W. C. Jordan. "Interpreting Relationships Between Age and Promotion in Age-Discrimination Cases." *Journal of Applied Psychology* 69 (May 1984), 199-206.

Profusek, Robert A. "Golden Parachutes and the Law." *Directors & Boards* 8 (Winter 1984), 31-33.

Rankin, K. "Polygraph Test Problem Refuses to Go Away." *Chain Store Age Executive* 61 (August 1985), 7.

Rich, Laurie A., James Schwartz, and Vicky Cahan. "UAW's Right-to-Know Breakthrough." *Chemical Week* 136 (January 23, 1985), 19-20.

Rones, Philip L. "Response to Recession: Reduce Hours or Jobs?" *Monthly Labor Review* 104 (October 1981), 3-11.

Rosenblum, Marc, and George Biles. "The Aging of Age Discrimination—Evolving ADEA Interpretations and Employee Relations Policies." *Employee Relations Law Journal* 8 (Summer 1982), 22-36.

Rothwell, Sheila. "Manpower Matters: New Equal Pay Legislation." *Journal of General Management* 10 (Autumn 1984), 83-88.

Rowe, Mary P. "Ideas for Action: Dealing with Sexual Harassment." *Harvard Business Review* 59 (May-June 1981), 42+.

Rowe, Mary P., and Michael Baker. "Are You Hearing Enough Employee Concerns?" *Harvard Business Review* 62 (May-June 1984), 127-135.

Sackett, Paul R. "Honesty Testing for Personnel Selection." *Personnel Administrator* 30 (September 1985), 67-76+.

Sackett, Paul R., and Michael M. Harris. "Honesty Testing for Personnel Selection: A Review and Critique." *Personnel Psychology* 37 (Summer 1984), 221-245.

Sape, George P. "Coping With Comparable Worth." *Harvard Business Review* 63 (May-June 1985), 145-152.

Saunders, Basil. "Helping Unwanted Staff Start Again." *Chief Executive (UK),* (July-August 1983), 20-21.

Schacter, Victor, and JoAnne Dellaverson. "Cleaning Out the Deadwood." *Across the Board* 22 (January 1985), 51-55.

Schmidt, Frank L. and John E. Hunter. "The Money Test." *Across the Board* 19 (July-August 1982), 35-37.

Schmidt, Robert H. "Efficient Detectors Improve Morale." *Security Management* 26 (November 1982), 38-42.

Schonberger, Richard J., and Harry W. Hennessey, Jr. "Is Equal Pay for Comparable Work Fair?" *Personnel Journal* 60 (December 1981), 964-968.

Schreiber, Glenn P. "Relocation: The Human Element." *Mortgage Banking* 44 (June 1984), 78-80.

Schroeder, Harold H. "Discharge: Is It Industrial Capital Punishment?" *Arbitration Journal* 37 (December 1982), 65.

Schuster, Michael H., and Christopher S. Miller. "Evaluating the Older Worker: Use of Employer Appraisal Systems in Age Discrimination Litigation." *Aging and Work* 4 (Fall 1981), 229-243.

Schwab, Donald P., and Dean W. Wichern. "Systematic Bias in Job Evaluation and Market Wages: Implications for the Comparable Worth Debate." *Journal of Applied Psychology* 68 (February 1983), 60-69.

Schwab, Donald P., and Robert Grams. "Sex-Related Errors in Job Evaluation: A 'Real World' Test." *Journal of Applied Psychology* 70 (August 1985), 533-539.

Schweitzer, Nancy J., and John Deely. "Interviewing the Disabled Job Applicant." *Personnel Journal* 61 (March 1982), 205-209.

Sculnick, Michael W. "Discipline for Off-Site Conduct." *Employment Relations Today* 12 (Summer 1985), 95-100.

Sculnick, Michael W. "Front Pay: The Remedy Whose Time Has Come." *Employment Relations Today* 11 (Winter 1984-85), 347-350.

Sculnick, Michael W. "Plant Relocations—Between a Rock and a Hard Place." *Employment Relations Today* 10 (Autumn 1983), 213-219.

Sculnick, Michael W. "Update on Pregnancy Leave." *Employment Relations Today* 11 (Winter 1984-85), 351-353.

Sculnick, Michael W., and Alan M. Koral. "New York Joins the States Overturning the Employment-at-Will Doctrine: Employee Handbooks Are the Key." *Employment Relations Today* 10 (Spring 1983), 3-13.

Sethi, S. P., and Carl Swanson. "How Japanese Multinationals Skirt Our Civil Rights Laws." *Business and Society Review* 44 (Winter 1983), 46-51.

Sewell, Carole. "Preventing Pilferage: Screening Potential Employees Thwarts Theft." *Business Insurance* 15 (May 11, 1981), 41.

Shahzad, Nadeem. "Outplacement Services Generate Good Will." *Healthcare Financial Management* 39 (August 1985), 71-72.

Sheridan, Peter J. "Congress to Probe Polygraph Testing." *Occupational Hazards* 45 (June 1983), 40-44.

Shub, Allen N., and William J. Connelly. "In Search of an Honest Employee." *Security Management* 29 (August 1985), 24-30.

Sicilian, John J. "Job Security: Employee Concerns and Management's Response." *Employment Relations Today* 12 (Autumn 1985), 241-247.

Siegel, Jay S. "Treating Staff Fairly During Force Reductions." *New England Business* 4 (July 5, 1982), 69-70.

Silverman, Leonard. "Corporate Childcare: Playpen in the Boardroom or Productivity Investment?" *Vital Speeches of the Day* 51 (June 1, 1985), 503-506.

Slowik, Stanley M. "Why Applicants Lie and What to Do About It." *Security Management* 29 (August 1985), 41-43.

Smith, Larry. "Corporate-Funded Day Care." *Employment Relations Today* 12 (Autumn 1985), 267-271.

Smith, M. E. "Shrinking Organizations: A Management Strategy for Downsizing." *Business Quarterly* 47 (Winter 1982), 30-33.

Smith, Pamela K. "Wrongful Termination of Employees at Will: The California Trend." *Northwestern U. Law Review* 78 (March 1983), 259-285.

Sosnowski, Daniel E. "Curbing Employee Theft—How Firms Do It." *Security Management* 29 (September 1985), 109-112.

Spang, Steve, "Business Besieged by Bogus Resumes." *Business and Society Review* 48 (Winter 1984), 39-40.

Staff, Marcia J., and Charles Foster. "Current Issues Affecting the Private Employee's Right to Freedom of Expression." *American Business Law Journal* 23 (Summer 1985), 257-280.

Stein, Jane. "Industry's New Bottom Line on Health Care Costs: Is Less Better?" *Hastings Center Report* 15 (August 1985), 14-18.

Stevens, George E. "Freedom of Speech in Private Employment: Overcoming the 'State Action' Problem." *American Business Law Journal* 20 (1982-83), 102-109.

Stickler, K. B. "Limitations on an Employer's Right to Discipline and Discharge." *Employee Relations Law Journal* 9 (Summer 1983), 70-80.

Stiff, Cyndy R. "Bringing Up Baby Is a Corporate Conundrum." *Florida Trends* 25 (February 1983), 71-74.

Stressin, Lawrence. "Moonlighting: The Employer's Dilemma." *Personnel* 58 (January-February 1981), 32-36.

Stybel, Laurence J., Robin Cooper, and Maryanne Peabody. "Planning Executive Dismissals: How to Fire a Friend." *California Management Review* 24 (Spring 1982), 73-80.

Sullenberger, Tom E. "Is the Polygraph Suited to Preemployment Screening?" *Security Management* 29 (August 1985), 44-48.

Superson, Anita M. "The Employer-Employee Relationship and the Right to Know." *Business and Professional Ethics Journal* 3 (Fall 1983), 45-58.

Sweeney, Terrance, and Randall S. Echlin. "Recent Developments in the Law of Wrongful Dismissal." *Business Quarterly* 46 (Spring 1981), 18-22.

Tarrant, John. "Can Loyalty Be Locked Up?" *Across the Board* 22 (May 1985), 51-55.

Tiffany, Susan. "Firing—What You Should, Shouldn't Do." *Credit Union Executive* 22 (Winter 1982), 12-14.

Toiv, H. "What Is Merit?" *GAO Review* 16 (Spring 1981), 68-70.

Trott, Betty. "Ethics and the Executive: What Works Is Not Always Enough." *Executive* 25 (April 1983), 60-64.

Tucker, Irvin B., and Louis Amato. "Equal Pay." *Business and Economic Review* 31 (October 1984), 11-13.

Tyska, Louis A. "Taking Positive Action on Employee Crime." *Office* 93 (January 1981), 146.

"Unwitting Accomplices." *Training and Development Journal* 39 (November 1985), 12+.

"Use Exit Interviews to Assess the Employee Climate." *Effective Manager* 4 (January 1981), 4-5.

Van Buren, D. M. "The Seduction of the Honest Employee." *Security Management* 29 (November 1985), 53.

Vella, Carolyn M. "Employment at Will: A Dying Concept." *Supervision* 44 (August 1982), 3-4, 15.

Wall, Jerry L., and H. M. Shatshat. "Controversy Over Mandatory Retirement Age." *Personnel Administrator* 26 (October 1981), 25+.

Wallace, Fran A. "Walking a Tightrope: Ethical Issues Facing HR Professionals." *Personnel* 62 (June 1985), 32-36.

Walls, Jim. "One of Your Employees Is Stealing." *Supervision* 47 (February 1985), 14-16, 23.

Waterman, Robert H. "The Human Element of Enterprise." *Perkins Journal* 38 (Fall 1984), 32-42.

Weis, William L. "Can You Afford to Hire Smokers?" *Personnel Administrator* 26 (May 1981), 71-78.

Weis, William L. "Profits Up in Smoke." *Personnel Journal* 60 (March 1981), 162-165.

Weiss, William L., et al. "Smoking: Burning a Hole in the Balance Sheet." *Personnel Management (UK)* 13 (May 1981), 24-29.

Wendell, Herbert. "Pooling for Jobs." *Management World* 12 (August 1983), 36-37.

Werhane, Patricia H. "Accountability and Employee Rights." *International Journal of Applied Philosophy* 1 (Spring 1983), 15-26.

Wertheimer, Alan. "Jobs, Qualifications, and Performances." *Ethics* 94 (October 1983), 99-112.

Westin, Alan F. "New Issue of Employee Privacy: Apply Basic Principles to the Workplace." *New Jersey Bell Journal* 6 (Spring 1983), 22-33.

Wheelock, Keith. " 'No Fault' Corporate Divorce." *Personnel Administrator* 30 (March 1985), 112-116.

Williams, Thomas H. "Fire at Will." *Personnel Journal* 64 (June 1985), 72-77.

Wise. L. "Trial by Machine." *Human Rights* 12 (Fall 1984), 30-34.

Wood, Robert C. "Life Without Layoffs." *Inc.* 4 (September 1982), 115-118.

Wooten, Bob E., and Lynn Godkin. "The Specter of Malpractice: Are Personnel Managers Liable for Job-Related Actions?" *Personnel* 60 (November-December 1983), 53-58.

"Worker Drug Tests Spread Despite Deep Controversy." *Money* 14 (October 1985), 13.

Wrich, James T. "EAPs: Ethical Considerations." *Personnel Administrator* 30 (August 1985), 12, 14.

Wright, Philip C. "How Managers Should Approach Alcoholism and Drug Abuse in the Work Place." *Business Quarterly* 48 (Winter 1983), 53-56.

Wright, Philip C. "Should Your Company Stop Smoking?" *Canadian Manager* 7 (March-April 1982), 16-18.

Young, Terry H. " 'Finding' Lost Days: A Little Incentive Can Go Far to Reduce Absenteeism, Improve Morale." *Business Insurance* 16 (September 27, 1982), 35.

Youngblood, Stuart A., and Gary L. Tidwell. "Termination at Will—Some Changes in the Wind." *Personnel* 58 (May-June 1981), 22-23.

Zemke, Ron. "Sexual Harassment: Is Training the Key?" *Training* 18 (February 1981), 22+.

Zimmerman, David. "Coercive Wage Offers." *Philosophy and Public Affairs* 10 (Spring 1981), 121-145.

Zippo, Mary. "Consensus: Equal Pay for Comparable Work." *Personnel* 58 (November-December 1983), 4-10.

Zippo, Mary. "Smoking in the Workplace: The Controversy Intensifies." *Personnel* 60 (November-December 1983), 50-52.

Zippo, Mary, et al. " 'Insearch': Salvaging the Morale of Internal 'Also Rans.' " *Personnel* 59 (November-December 1982), 51.

Health and Safety

Books

Denenberg, Tia S., and R. V. Denenberg. *Alcohol and Drugs: Issues in the Workplace*. Washington, D.C.: BNA, Inc., 1984.

Freedman, Audrey. *Industry Response to Health Risk*. New York: Conference Board, 1981.

Gersuny, Carl. *Work Hazards and Industrial Conflict*. Hanover, N.H.: U. Press of New England, 1981.

Gibson, Mary. *Workers' Rights*. Totowa, N.J.: Rowman and Allanheld, 1983.

Glen, Douglas S. *Business and Stress Management* (M.B.A. Thesis). Austin, Tex.: University of Texas, 1982.

Green, Mark, and Norman Waitzman. *Business War on the Law: An Analysis of the Benefits of Federal Health/Safety Enforcement*. Washington, D.C.: Corporate Accountability Research Group, 1981.

Lee, Jeffrey S., and William N. Rom, eds. *Legal and Ethical Dilemmas in Occupational Health*. Ann Arbor, Mich.: Ann Arbor Science Pub., 1982.

MacCarthy, Mark. *Beyond OSHA: Improving Workplace Safety and Health*. College Park, Md.: Ctr. Philosophy & Public Policy, 1983.

Nelkin, Dorothy, and Michael S. Brown. *Workers at Risk: Voices from the Workplace*. Chicago: Univ. Chicago Press, 1984.

Pelletier, Kenneth R. *Healthy People in Unhealthy Places: Stress and Fitness at Work*. New York: Delacorte, 1984.

Reasons, Charles E., et al. *Assault on the Worker: Occupational Health and Safety in Canada*. Toronto: Butterworth, 1981.

Viscusi, W. K. *Risk by Choice*. Cambridge, Mass.: Harvard University Press, 1983.

White, Lawrence. *Human Debris: The Injured Worker in America*. New York: Seaview/Putnam, 1983.

Articles

Abrams, Lori. "The Human Tragedy of Uranium Mining." *Business and Society Review* 51 (Fall 1984), 21-25.

Adams, John D. "Health, Stress, and the Manager's Life Style." *Group & Organization Studies* 6 (September 1981), 291-301.

Adams, Michael. "Warning: Smoking May Be Harmful to Your Meeting." *Successful Meetings* 33 (January 1984), 10-14.

"AIDS Costs—Employers and Insurers Have Reason to Fear." *Wall Street Journal* (October 18, 1985), 1.

Allen, Frank. "Battle Building Over 'Right to Know' Laws Regarding Toxic Items Used by Workers." *Wall Street Journal* (January 4, 1983), 31.

Allen, Robert E., and Patricia Linenberger. "The Employee's Right to Refuse Hazardous Work." *Employee Relations Law Journal* 9 (Autumn 1983), 251-275.

Allen, Steven G. "Compensation, Safety, and Absenteeism: Evidence from the Paper Industry." *Industrial & Labor Relations Review* 34 (January 1981), 207-218.

Andrade, Vibiana M. "The Toxic Workplace: Title VII Protection for the Potentially Pregnant Person." *Harvard Women's Law Journal* 4 (1981), 71-103.

"Asbestos Lawsuits." *Economist* 284 (September 18-24, 1982), 18.

Avetisov, E. S. "Eyesight and Modern Industry." *Impact of Science on Society* 31 (April-June 1981), 165-171.

Barefoot, J. K. "Fact or Fraud: Is Your Employee's Injury the Real Thing?" *Security Management* 29 (October 1985), 65-68.

Bayer, Ronald. "Women, Work, and Reproductive Hazards." *Hastings Center Report* 12 (August 1982), 14-19.

Beeman, Don R. "Is the Social Drinker Killing Your Company?" *Business Horizons* 22 (January-February 1985), 54-58.

Belohlav, James A., and Paul O. Popp. "Employee Substance Abuse: Epidemic of the Eighties." *Business Horizons* 26 (July-August 1983), 29-34.

Bollier, David."The Emasculation of OSHA." *Business and Society Review* 51 (Fall 1984), 37-41.

Boyd, D. P. "Managerial Stress: Causes and Cures." *Thought* 58 (September 1983), 319-328.

Brooks, Lovic A., Jr. "An Analysis of Employee's Right to Refuse to Work Based on Perceived Unsafe or Unhealthy Working Conditions." *Business and Economic Review* 28 (April 1982), 13-16.

"Burn-Out: Sign of Management Failure." *ZIP/Target Marketing* 8 (March 1985), 37, 40.

Buzzeo, Ronald W. "Drug Abuse in Industry: Is It America's Number One Health Problem?" *Security Management* 29 (October 1985), 49-50.

Cain, C. "Execs Convicted of Murder in Worker's Death." *Business Insurance* 19 (June 24, 1985), 1+.

Collingwood, Thomas R. "Office Fitness: Fledgling Programs Prove Good Business." *Business Insurance* 15 (February 2, 1981), 21.

Collins, James W., Lee M. Sanderson, and James D. McGlothlin. "Death by Robot: Safety Issues in Automated Plants." *Business and Society Review* 54 (Summer 1985), 56-59.

Conte, Christopher. "How Railroads Avoided Laws on Alcohol." *Wall Street Journal* (June 11, 1984), 27.

Cooper, J. C., et al. "Employee Stress: The Great Leveller." *CA Magazine (Canada)* 115 (May 1982), 64-65, 67.

Crapnell, Stephen G. "Mystery Lingers: What's Causing Brain Cancer Among Chemical Workers?" *Occupational Hazards* 44 (February 1982), 67-70.

Crapnell, Stephen G. "Special Report on OSHA's New Hearing Conservation." *Occupational Hazards* 45 (May 1983), 65-68.

Crawford, James. "The Deregulation of Worker Health." *Business and Society Review* 40 (Winter 1981-1982), 9-14.

Cutler, J. "Cover-Up on Asbestos Victims." *New Statesman* 104 (October 15, 1982), 4.

D'Ambrosio, Dominick. "Workers and the Environment: The OSHA/Environmental Network." *Health and Medicine* 2 (Winter 1983-84), 3-7.

Dixon, Norman. "Some Thoughts on the Nature and Causes of Industrial Incompetence." *Personnel Management* 14 (December 1982), 26-30.

"Do Puffing Employees Send Profits Up in Smoke?" *Business and Society Review* 49 (Spring 1984), 4-9.

Fidell, Eugene R., and William C. Marcout. "The Nuclear Industry Employee Protection Provisions of Federal Law." *Public Utilities Fortnightly* 110 (November 11, 1982), 15-19.

Fishman, A. E. "Establish Company Policies for Alcohol and Drug Abuse." *Merchandising* 10 (August 1985), 73-74.

Freedman, Martin, and A. J. Stagliano. "Industry Rekindles the Cotton Dust Storm." *Business and Society Review* 44 (Winter 1983), 62-64.

Freifeld, K. "In the Lion's Case." *Forbes* 136 (October 7, 1985), 142+.

Frese, M. "Stress at Work and Psychosomatic Complaints: A Causal Interpretation." *Journal of Applied Psychology* 70 (May 1985), 314-328.

Gampel, Joanne C., and Kevin B. Zeese. "Are Employers Overdosing on Drug Testing?" *Business and Society Review* 55 (Fall 1985), 34-38.

Gellhorn, Ernest. "Arguments Heat Up Over Burn Hazard Protection." *Occupational Hazards* 44 (January 1982), 22-23.

Gildea, Joyce A. "Safety and Privacy: Are They Compatible?" *Personnel Administrator* 27 (February 1982), 80-83.

Goldstein, Mitchell H. "The Facts of Ergonomics: Part I." *National Productivity Review* 4 (Fall 1984), 449+.

Graebner, William. "Doing the World's Unhealthy Work: The Fiction of Free Choice." *Hastings Center Report* 14 (August 1984), 38-45.

Greenberger, Robert S. "Sobering Method: Firms Are Confronting Alcoholic Executives with Threat of Firing." *Wall Street Journal* (January 13, 1983), 1.

Greenfield, Paul E., et al. "High Price of Stress Taking Its Toll on Your DP Staff?—Part 1." *Computerworld* 18 (June 18, 1984), 20.

Greenfield, Paul E., et al. "Watch for Signs of Stress That Threaten Your DP Site—Part 2." *Computerworld* 18 (June 18, 1984), 20.

Gruning, Carl F. "VDTs and Vision—New Problems for the 80's." *Office* 101 (February 1985), 19-22, 34.

Guest, R. G. "Employee Health and Safety: Can You Afford to Ignore It?" *Canadian Manager* 7 (December 1982), 18-19.

Hall, Robert H. "The Truth About Brown Lung." *Business and Society Review* 40 (Winter 1981-1982), 15-20.

Handman, Edward. "OSHA's Being Destroyed from Within." *Management Review* 74 (July 1985), 52-53.

"Hazards on the Line." *Progressive* 49 (October 1985), 21.

Hembree, Diana. "Dead End in Silicon Valley: The High-Tech Future Doesn't Work." *Progressive* 49 (October 1985), 18-20+.

Herzberg, Frederick. "Down the Staircase to Depression." *Industry Week* 216 (January 24, 1983), 34-38.

Herzberg, Frederick. "Remedies for Depression and Burnout." *Industry Week* 216 (February 7, 1983), 38-39.

Hetzler, A. "Work and Sickness—Ideology and Law." *Acta Sociologica* 24 (1981), 75-92.

Hosty, Robert E., and Francis J. Elliott. "Drug Abuse in Industry: What Does It Cost and What Can Be Done?" *Security Management* 29 (October 1985), 53-58.

Hymowitz, Carol. "Managers' Malaise: Fear of Unemployment Takes Emotional Toll at White Collar Levels." *Wall Street Journal* (July 19, 1982), 1+.

"Industry Changes Pose Environmental Problems." *Chemical Engineering News* 63 (June 7, 1985), 7.

"Industry's Large Stake in Curbing Alcoholism." *Occupational Hazards* 45 (October 1983), 97-101.

Ivancevich, John M., and Michael Matteson. "See You In Court: Employee Claims for Damages Add to the High Cost of Job Stress." *Management Review* 72 (November 1983), 9+.

Jackson, S. E., and C. Maslack. "After-Effects of Job-Related Stress: Families as Victims." *Journal of Occupational Behavior* 3 (January 1982), 63-78.

Jacobs, Sanford L. "Small Business: Industrial Hygienists Increase Firms' Output and Efficiency." *Wall Street Journal* (March 5, 1984), 33.

Jamal, M. "Relationship of Job Stress to Job Performance: A Study of Managers and Blue-Collar Workers." *Human Relations* 38 (May 1985), 409-424.

"Job Safety and Health: A Canadian Perspective." *Occupational Hazards* 44 (March 1982), 51-54.

Kahn, Steven C. "Drugs and Alcohol in the Work Place." *Employment Relations Today* 12 (Summer 1985), 127-136.

Kast, S. V., et al. "Impact of the Accident at the Three Mile Island on the Behavior and Well-Being of Nuclear Workers." *American Journal of Public Health* 71 (May 1981), 484-495.

Katz, David M. "Divided Loyalties and Health Risks." *National Underwriter (Life/Health)* 88 (August 11, 1984), 4, 6.

Kauffman, C. W. "Grain Dust Elevators: Workplaces of Doom." *Business and Society Review* 52(Winter 1985), 26-30.

"Keep Deaf Workers Safe." *Personnel Journal* 63 (August 1984), 49-51.

Kemery, Edward R., et al. "Outcomes of Role Stress: A Multisample Constructive Replication." *Academy of Management Journal* 28 (June 1985), 363-375.

Kimmerling, George F. "Warning: Workers at Risk, Train Effectively." *Training and Development Journal* 39 (April 1985), 50-55.

King, Resa W., and Irene Pave. "Stress Claims Are Making Business Jumpy." *Business Week* (October 14, 1985), 152+.

Klokis, Holly. "Asbestos: Wreaking Havoc on Remodeling." *Chain Store Age Executive* 60 (October 1984), 17-19.

Kuntz, Mary. "Everybody Out of the Pool." *Forbes* 136 (December 16, 1985), 83+.

Kuntz, M. "Open Wide and Say Ahhh—Or You're Fired." *Working Woman* 10 (October 1985), 30-31.

Lancianese, Frank W. "Criminal Penalties Coming for Concealing Hazards?" *Occupational Hazards* 43 (December 1981), 45-47.

Lappe, Marc. "Ethical Issues in Testing for Differential Sensitivity to Occupational Hazards." *Journal of Occupational Medicine* 25 (November 1983), 797-808.

Lappe, Marc. "The Predictive Power of the New Genetics." *Hastings Center Report* 14 (October 1984), 18-21.

Leigh, J. P. "Compensating Wages for Occupational Injuries and Diseases." *Social Science Quarterly* 62 (December 1981), 772-778.

Levine, Carol. "A Cotton Dust Study Unmasked." *Hastings Center Report* 14 (August 1984), 17-22.

Logan, Shelley R. "Adapting Fetal Vulnerability Programs to Title VII: Wright v. Olin." *Employee Relations Law Journal* 9 (Spring 1984), 605-628.

Lublin, Joann S. "Workplace Perils: Occupational Diseases Receive More Scrutiny Since the Manville Case." *Wall Street Journal* (December 20, 1982), 1+.

Marmo, Michael. "Arbitrators View Alcoholic Employees: Discipline or Rehabilitation?" *Arbitration Journal* 37 (March 1982), 17-27.

Martins, J. K. "A Year-Long, Hour by Hour Accident Occurrence Study." *Industrial Management* 24 (January-February 1982), 5-8.

Masi, Dale A., and Maura A. O'Brien. "Drug Abuse in the Work Place." *Business and Health* 3 (December 1985), 29-32.

Massen, Sharon, "Safety: Thwarting Workplace Dangers." *Management World* 11 (February 1982), 9+.

McClure, Walter. "Buying Right: The Consequences of Glut." *Business and Health* 2 (September 1985), 43-46.

McLennan, Barbara N. "Product Liability in the Workplace: Product Liability Legislation and Worker Compensation Laws." *Labor Law Journal* 34 (March 1983), 160-171.

Meer, J. "Blue-Collar Stress Worse for Boys." *Psychology Today* 19 (June 1985), 15.

Milbourn, Gene, Jr. "Alcoholism, Drug Abuse, Job Stress: What Small Business Can Do." *American Journal of Small Business* 8 (April-June 1984), 36-48.

Miljus, Robert C., et al. "The Work Environment: How Safe Are Video Display Terminals?" *Personnel Journal* 64 (March 1985), 36-37.

Miller, Matt. "Words Still Speak Louder Than Deeds: India Hasn't Come to Grips with Plant Safety." *Wall Street Journal* (November 26, 1985), 24.

Murray, Thomas H. "The Lethal Paradox in Occupational Health Research." *Business and Society Review* 53 (Spring 1985), 20-24.

Murray, Thomas H. "The Social Context of Workplace Screening." *Hastings Center Report* 14 (October 1984), 21-23.

Murray, Thomas H. "Warning: Screening Workers for Genetic Risk." *Hastings Center Report* 13 (February 1983), 5-8.

Nelkin, Dorothy. "Observations on Workers' Perceptions of Risk in the Dangerous Trades." *Science, Technology and Human Values* 9 (Spring 1984), 3+.

"Nobody Is Fire-Proof in the Realm of Asbestos." *Economist* 284 (September 4-10, 1982), 79-80.

"Noise or Bacteria—Which Was Greater Health Threat?" *Occupational Hazards* 44 (January 1982), 42-44.

Novit, Mitchell S. "Mental Distress: Possible Implications for the Future." *Personnel Administrator* 27 (August 1982), 47-53.

"Occupational Health Risks and the Workers' Right to Know." *Yale Law Journal* 90 (July 1981), 1792-1810.

Pace, Nicholas A. "Sobering Advice on Office Alcoholics." *Wall Street Journal* (November 19, 1984), 32.

Pati, Gopal C., et al. "The Employer's Role in Alcoholism Assistance." *Personnel Journal* 62 (July 1983), 568-572.

Pave, Irene. "Fear and Loathing in the Workplace: What Managers Can Do About AIDS." *Business Week* (November 25, 1985), 126.

Puleo, Matthew J., et al. "Communicating About Substance Abuse." *Communication World* 1 (May 1984), 19-22.

Rea, Samuel A., Jr. "Workmen's Compensation and Occupational Safety Under Imperfect Information." *American Economic Review* 71 (March 1981), 80-93.

Reber, Robert A., and Jerry Wallin. "The Effects of Training, Goal Setting, and Knowledge of Results on Safe Behavior: A Component Analysis." *Academy of Management Journal* 27 (September 1984), 544-560.

Rice, Berkeley, "Can Companies Kill?" *Psychology Today* 15 (June 1981), 78-85.

Schaeffer, Dorothy. "Burnout—The Headache of the 1980s." *Supervision* 44 (February 1982), 11-12, 23.

Sculnick, Michael W. "Hazardous Substances: The Debate Revives." *Employment Relations Today* 10 (Spring 1983), 17-27.

Sheridan, Peter J. "Drug Abuse Demands Action from Industry." *Occupational Hazards* 43 (March 1981), 62-65.

Sheridan, Peter J. "Genetic Screening: Its Promise and Peril." *Occupational Hazards* 45 (April 1983), 75-79.

Sheridan, Peter J. "NIOSH Puts Job Stress Under the Microscope." *Occupational Hazards* 43 (April 1981), 70-73.

Sheridan, Peter J. "Reproductive Hazards: Probing the Ethical Issues." *Occupational Hazards* 45 (May 1983), 72-75.

Shipley, L. B. "Hearing Loss Comp Becoming Today's Major Industry Issue." *National Safety Health News* 132 (July 1985), 35-38.

Simison, Robert L. "Living in Fear." *Wall Street Journal* (January 3, 1983), 1+.

Smith, D. M., and N. P. Gillies. "Health and Safety Training Is Key to Implementing Right to Know Rule." *Pulp & Paper* 59 (June 1985), 134-137.

Smith, Michael J. "Health and Safety Consequences of Shift Work in the Food Processing Industry." *Ergonomics* 25 (February 1982), 133-144.

Squires, Stephen F. "Ergonomics Can Prevent Many Work Injuries." *Business Insurance* 18 (September 24, 1984), 40.

Starr, B. "Drug Abuse at Nuclear Plants: The Alarms Are Ringing." *Business Week* (October 28, 1985), 27-28.

Stoner, Charles R., et al. "Developing a Corporate Policy for Managing Stress." *Personnel* 60 (May-June 1983), 66-76.

Stow, Derek. "Are Managers Safe Enough?" *Personnel Management* 15 (April 1983), 36-39.

"Study Tracking Stress Responses." *Training* 18 (June 1981), 21, 87.

Tersine, Richard J., and James Hazeldine. "Alcoholism: A Productivity Hangover." *Business Horizons* 25 (November-December 1982), 68-72.

"VDU-Related Health Risks: Facts and Fallacies." *International Management* 38 (December 1983), 75-76.

Vanderwaerdt, Lois. "Resolving the Conflict Between Hazardous Substances in the Workplace and Equal Employment Opportunity." *American Business Law Journal* 21 (Summer 1983), 157-184.

Viscusi, W. K. "Cotton Dust Regulation: An OSHA Success Story?" *Journal Policy Analysis and Management* 4 (Spring 1985), 325-343.

Viscusi, W. K. "Health and Safety." *Regulation* 6 (January-February 1982), 34-36.

Von Magnus, Eric. "Rights and Risks." *Journal of Business Ethics* 2 (February 1983), 23-26.

"Warning: Asbestos May Cost You More Than Money." *Economist* 280 (July 11-17, 1981), 83-89.

"What's in a Name? Workers See Truth about Workplace Chemicals." *Dollars and Sense* (April 1983), 6-7+.

Wines, Michael. "They're Still Telling OSHA Horror Stories, But the Victims Are New." *National Journal* 13 (November 7, 1981), 1985-1989.

"Workers and AIDS—Uncle Sam Speaks." *U.S. News and World Report* 99 (November 25, 1985), 14.

Labor Unions

Books

Babson, Steve. *Working Detroit: The Making of a Union Town.* New York: Adama Books, 1984.

Beer, Chris, et al. *Gay Workers: Trade Unions and the Law*. New York: State Mutual Book, 1981.

Bowling, W. K., and Waldon Loving. *Management Fumbles and Union Recoveries*. Dubuque, Iowa: Kendall-Hunt, 1982.

Campbell, Alan, and John Bowyer. *Trade Unions and the Individual*. New York: State Mutual Book, 1981.

Clark, Paul F. *The Miners' Fight for Democracy: Arnold Miller and the Reform of the United Mine Workers*. Ithaca, N.Y.: ILR Press, 1981.

Foner, Philip S. *Fellow Workers and Friends: IWW Free Speech Fights as Told by Participants*. Westport, Conn.: Greenwood, 1981.

Sexual Harassment and Labor Relations. Washington D.C.: Bureau of National Affairs, 1981.

Articles

Beattie, Margaret. "Women, Unions, and Social Policy." *Journal of Business Ethics* 2 (August 1983), 227-231.

Bensman, David. "Greedy Steelworkers?" *Commonweal* 109 (December 17, 1982), 677-678.

Bensman, David, and Jack Metzgar. "Steel-ing for Battle." *Commonweal* 109 (October 8, 1982), 526-528.

"Big Labor Grooms Strategy for the Twenty-first Century." *Business and Society Review* 53 (Spring 1985), 62-67.

Bowers, David G. "What Would Make 11,500 People Quit Their Jobs?" *Organizational Dynamics* 11 (Winter 1983), 5-19.

Bowie, Norman E., et al. "Should Collective Bargaining and Labor Relations Be Less Adversarial?/Commentary." *Journal of Business Ethics* 4 (August 1985), 283-295.

Brown, Linda. "Ethics in Negotiation." *Executive Female* 7 (January-February 1984), 34-37.

Burrough, Bryan. "Continental Air's Bankruptcy-Law Filing Is Challenged as Attempt to Break Unions." *Wall Street Journal* (December 12, 1983), 43.

Burtless, Gary. "Are Targeted Wage Subsidies Harmful? Evidence from a Wage Voucher Experiment." *Industrial and Labor Relations Review* 39 (October 1985), 105-114.

Carling, F. "What Happened to the Threat of White-Collar Unionization?" *Management Review* 75 (March 1985), 52-54.

Carson, Thomas L., et al., "Bluffing in Labor Negotiations: Legal and Ethical Issues." *Journal of Business Ethics* 1 (February 1982), 13-22.

Cort, John C. "Labor on the March: A Hungry Giant." *Commonweal* 108 (October 9, 1981), 450-451.

Engel, Paul G. "Union Busters or Morale Builders?" *Industry Week* 221 (April 2, 1984), 56-58.

English, Carey W. "Women Flex Muscles in Union Movement." *U.S. News and World Report* 97 (October 29, 1984), 76-77.

Farkas, D. L. "White Collars With Union Labels." *Modern Office Technology* 30 (May 1985), 118+.

Greer, C. R., and J. C. Shearer. "Do Foreign-Owned U.S. Firms Practice Unconventional Labor Relations?" *Monthly Labor Review* 104 (January 1981), 44-48.

Hughes, M. J. "White-Collar Organizing: We're Not Giving Up Yet." *Management Review* 75 (March 1985), 54-56.

Jacobs, Louis A., et al. "Fair Coverage in Internal Union Periodicals." *Industrial Relations Law Journal* 4 (1981), 204-257.

Kaplan, Elizabeth. "Labor Borrows the Tools of Capital from Wall Street." *Dun's Business Month* 126 (November 1985), 60-62.

Kovach, Kenneth A., and Peter E. Millspaugh. "The Plant Closing Issue Arrives at the Bargaining Table." *Journal of Labor Research* 4 (Fall 1983), 367-374.

Levitan, Sar A., and Clifford M. Johnson. "Thinking Ahead: Labor and Management: The Illusion of Cooperation." *Harvard Business Review* 61 (September-October 1983), 8-16.

Levitan, Sar A. and Diane Werneke. "Worker Participation and Productivity Change." *Monthly Labor Review* 107 (September 1984), 28-33.

Lublin, Joann S. "Unions Try New Kinds of Resistance as Anger Over Plant Closings Grow." *Wall Street Journal* (January 27, 1982), 29.

Lublin, Joann S. "Most Workers End Walkout Against AT&T." *Wall Street Journal* (August 29, 1983), 3.

McKenzie, Richard B., and Bruce Yandle. "State Plant Closing Laws: Their Union Support." *Journal of Labor Research* 3 (Winter 1982), 101-110.

McLennan, Barbara N. "Sex Discrimination in Employment and Possible Liabilities of Labor Unions." *Labor Law Journal* 33 (January 1982), 26-35.

Newman, Winn, and Carole W. Wilson. "The Union Role in Affirmative Action." *Labor Law Journal* 32 (June 1981), 323-342.

O'Reilly, James T. "Driving a Soft Bargain: Unions, Toxic Materials, and Right to Know Legislation." *Harvard Environmental Law Review* 9 (1985), 307-329.

Rabby, Rami. "Employment of the Disabled in Large Corporations." *International Labour Review* 122 (January-February 1983), 23-26.

Rubin, Mori. "To Cross or Not to Cross: Picket Lines and Employee Rights." *Industrial Relations Law Journal* 4 (Summer 1981), 419-447.

Sabban, Yitzchak, and Philip Harris. "Safety and Health Grievances in Labor Arbitration: Pre and Post OSHA." *Akron Business and Economic Review* 13 (Spring 1982), 15-19.

Smith, Randall. "Constructive Plan?: Use of Pension Funds to Create Union Jobs Raises Issue of Legality." *Wall Street Journal* (January 17, 1984), 1.

Solomon, Norman A., and Rebecca A. Grant. "Canadian Trade Unionism and Wage Parity for Women: Putting the Principle into Practice." *Journal of Business Ethics* 2 (August 1983), 213-219.

Terry, Jim. "Campbell Soup in Hot Water With Organized Labor." *Business and Society Review* 46 (Summer 1983), 37-41.

Wines, William A. "Seniority, Recession, and Affirmative Action: The Challenge for Collective Bargaining." *American Business Law Journal* 20 (Spring 1982), 37-58.

Wisniewski, Stanley C. "Achieving Equal Pay for Comparable Worth Through Arbitration." *Employee Relations Law Journal* 8 (Autumn 1982), 236-255.

Worrall, John D., and Richard J. Butler. "Health Conditions and Job Hazards: Union and Non-Union Jobs." *Journal of Labor Research* 4 (Fall 1983), 339-347.

Wurf, Jerry. "Labor's View of Quality of Working Life Programs." *Journal of Business Ethics* 1 (May 1982), 131-137.

Minorities in Organizations

Books

Block, Walter, and M. A. Walker. *Discrimination, Affirmative Action, and Equal Opportunity: An Economic and Social Perspective.* Vancouver, B.C.: Fraser Institute, 1982.

Davis, George, and Glegg Watson. *Black Life in Corporate America: Swimming in the Mainstream.* New York: Doubleday, 1982.

Fernandez, John P. *Racism and Sexism in Corporate Life: Changing Values in American Business.* Lexington, Mass.: Lexington Books, 1981.

Fujita, Kuniko. *Black Workers' Struggles in Detroit's Auto Industry, 1935-1975*. Ann Arbor, Mich.: UMI Press, 1981.

Jain, Harish C., and Peter J. Sloane. *Equal Employment Issues: Race and Sex Discrimination in the United States, Canada and Britain*. New York: Praeger, 1981.

Lewis, Ronald L. *The Black Worker from the Founding of the CIO to the AFL-CIO Merger, 1936-1955*. Philadelphia: Temple Univ. Press, 1983.

Nixon, Regina. *Climbing the Corporate Ladder*. Washington, D.C.: National Urban League, 1985.

Parcel, Toby L., and Charles W. Mueller. *Ascription and Labor Markets: Race and Sex Differences in Earnings*. New York; Academic Press, 1983.

Smith, Robert C. *Equal Employment Opportunity: A Comparative Micro-Analysis of Boston and Houston*. Totowa, N.J.: Allanheld, Osmun, 1982.

Stasz, Clarice. *The American Nightmare: Why Inequality Persists*. New York: Schocken, 1981.

Articles

"Ability Tests: A Shift in Policy from Equal Treatment to Equal Outcome." *Across the Board* 19 (July-August 1982), 25-26.

America, Richard F. "Public Relations and Affirmative Action." *Public Relations Quarterly* 28 (Summer 1983), 24-28.

Aptheker, Herbert. "Affirmative Action: A Response to Critics." *Political Studies* 60 (June 1981), 23-27.

"Are Blacks, Women, and Hispanics Getting 'More Than Their Fair Share'?" *Employment Relations Today* 10 (Spring 1983), 93-96.

Baldwin, James J. "Avoiding Discrimination Against the Handicapped in the Employment Setting." *Business and Economic Review* 29 (June 1983), 11-13.

Bolton, Brian, et al. "After the Interview: How Employers Rate Handicapped Employees." *Personnel* 62 (July 1985), 38-44.

Bowe, Frank. "Intercompany Action to Adapt Jobs for the Handicapped." *Harvard Business Review* 63 (January-February 1985), 166-168.

Bubb, Debra. "How Banks Provide Real Opportunities for the Disabled." *ABA Banking Journal* 73 (August 1981), 50-52.

Buckwalter, Nancy. "Women and Minorities in Banking: Are the Employment Gains Real or Token?" *U.S. Banker* 93 (April 1982), 44-45.

Carr, C. R. "Unfair Sacrifice—Reply to Pluhar's 'Preferential Hiring and Unjust Sacrifice.' " *Philosophical Forum* 14 (Fall 1982), 94-97.

Chegwidden, Paula, and Wendy R. Katz. "American and Canadian Perspectives on Affirmative Action: A Response to the Fraser Institute." *Journal of Business Ethics* 2 (August 1983), 191-202.

Coil, James H., III. "Action Needed on Affirmative Action." *Employment Relations Today* 10 (Winter 1983-1984), 351-357.

Cole, Craig W. "Affirmative Action: Change It or Lose It?" *EEO Today* 8 (Autumn 1981), 262-271.

Crocker, Jennifer. "After Affirmative Action: Barriers to Occupational Advancement for Women and Minorities." *American Behavioral Scientist* 27 (January-February 1984), 287-407.

Davis, Michael. "Race as Merit." *Mind* 92 (July 1983), 347-367.

Davis, Michael. "Racial Quotas, Weights and Real Possibilities: A Moral for Moral Theory." *Social Theory and Practice* 7 (Spring 1981), 49-84.

De Lone, Richard H. "Creating Incentives for Change." *Christian Century* 41 (March 30, 1981), 92-94.

DeForest, Mariah E. "Spanish-Speaking Employees in American Industry." *Business Horizons* 27 (January-February 1984), 14-17.

Denis, Martin K. "Race Harassment Discrimination: A Problem That Won't Go Away." *Employee Relations Law Journal* 10 (Winter 1984-1985), 415-436.

Eames, Elizabeth R. "Quotas, Goals, and Ideal for Equality." *Journal of Social Philosophy* 13 (January 1982), 10-15.

Elgart, Lloyd D., and Lillian Schanfield. "More Blacks on Boards of Fortune 500 Companies; A Dream Deferred." *Business and Professional Ethics Journal* 2 (Spring 1983), 41-50. Commentary: by Richard E. Hart, vol.2, no.4, 94.

Emer, William H., and Catherine B. Frink. "Hiring the Handicapped—What Every Employer Should Know." *Employment Relations Today* 11 (Spring 1984), 69-85.

Fant, Ora D. "Racial Diversity in Organizations and Its Implications for Management." *Personnel* 59 (September-October 1982), 60-68.

Grant, Charles T. "Blacks Hit Racial Roadblocks Climbing up the Corporate Ladder." *Business and Society Review* 52 (Winter 1985), 56-59.

Green, Philip. "The New Individualism: Guarding the Ramparts of Privilege." *Christianity and Crisis* 41 (March 30, 1981), 74-80.

Greenberger, Robert S. "Job Bias Alert: Firms Prod Managers to Keep

Eye on Goal of Equal Employment." *Wall Street Journal* (May 17, 1982), 1+.

Greenberger, Robert S. "Up the Ladder: Many Black Managers Hope to Enter Ranks of Top Management." *Wall Street Journal* (June 15, 1981), 1.

Guzda, M. K. "At the Jobs Fair." *Editor & Publisher* 118 (August 31, 1985), 12-13.

Guzda, M. K. "No Room at the Top." *Editor & Publisher* 118 (August 17, 1985), 18-19.

"Hiring Quotas May Creep North." *Business Week* (June 21, 1982), 137.

Hollon, Charles J., and Thomas L. Bright. "National Origin Harassment in the Work Place: Recent Guideline Developments from the EEOC." *Employee Relations Law Journal* 8 (Autumn 1982), 282-293.

Hook, S. "Rationalization for Reverse Discrimination." *New Perspective* 17 (Winter 1985), 9-11.

Jennings, Kenneth, Steven Williamson, and Carl Stotts. "The Man Behind the Stotts Case." *Personnel Journal* 64 (July 1985), 74-77.

Johnson, William G., and James Lambrinos. "Wage Discrimination Against Handicapped Men and Women." *Journal of Human Resources* 20 (Spring 1985), 264-277.

Jones, James E. " 'Reverse Discrimination' in Employment; Judicial Treatment of Affirmative Action Programmes in the United States." *International Labour Review* 120 (July-August 1981), 453-472.

Jones, Nathaniel, and Jerry C. Wofford. "Nineteen Hundred Ninety-Nine, the Year of the Black CEO." *Business Horizons* 26 (May-June 1983), 51-57.

Kaufman, R. L., and T. N. Daymont. "Racial Discrimination and the Social Organization of Industries." *Social Science Research* 10 (September 1981), 225-255.

Kilberg, William J., and Stephen E. Tallent. "From Bakke to Fullilove: The Use of Racial and Ethnic Preferences in Employment." *Employee Relations Law Journal* 6 (Winter 1980-81), 364-379.

Kramnick, Isaac. "Equal Opportunity and 'The Race for Life.' " *Dissent* 28 (April 1981), 178-187.

Lawrence, Daniel G., et al. "Design and Use of Weighted Application Blanks." *Personnel Administrator* 27 (March 1982), 47-53.

Leap, Terry L., and Larry R. Smeltzer. "Racial Remarks in the Workplace: Humor or Harassment?" *Harvard Business Review* 62 (November-December 1984), 74-78.

Lebacqz, Karen. "Professional Treatment—Women and Minority Groups: Recent Studies." *Religious Studies Review* 7 (April 1981), 97+.

Lebed, Hartzel Z. "Employing the Disabled Is Good Business." *Industry Week* 227 (October 28, 1985), 49-52.

Leigh, J. P. "Racial Differences in Compensating for Wages for Job Risks." *Industrial Relations* 20 (Fall 1981), 318-321.

Lempert, Rich. "The Force of Irony: On the Morality of Affirmative Action and United Steelworkers versus Weber." *Ethics* 95 (October 1984), 86-89.

Leonard, Jonathan S. "Antidiscrimination or Reverse Discrimination." *Journal of Human Resources* 19 (Spring 1984), 145-174.

Leonard, Jonathan S. "The Effect of Unions on the Employment of Blacks, Hispanics and Women." *Industrial and Labor Relations Review* 39 (October 1985), 115-132.

Leonard, Jonathan S. "Employment and Occupational Advance Under Affirmative Action." *Review of Economics and Statistics* 66 (August 1984), 377-385.

Leonard, Jonathan S. "What Promises Are Worth: The Impact of Affirmative Action Goals." *Journal of Human Resources* 22 (Winter 1985), 1-20.

Loury, Glenn C. "Economics of Affirmative Action: Is Equal Opportunity Enough?" *American Economic Review* 71 (May 1981), 122-126.

Massey, Stephen J. "Rethinking Affirmative Action." *Social Theory and Practice* 7 (Spring 1981), 21-47.

Massing, M. "Blackout in Television." *Columbia Journalism Review* 21 (November-December 1982), 38-39+.

Matusewitch, Eric P. "Employment Discrimination Against the Overweight." *Personnel Journal* 62 (June 1983), 446-450.

Morishima, James. "The Special Employment Issues for Asian Americans." *Public Personnel Management* 10 (Winter 1981), 384-392.

Mosk, Stanley. "Affirmative Action, Si—Quotas, No." *Employee Relations Law Journal* 9 (Summer 1983), 126-135.

Moskowitz, Milton R. "The 1982 Black Corporate Directors Lineup." *Business and Society Review* 43 (Fall 1982), 51-54.

Murphy, Thomas S. "Making Sure Minority Recruitment Is Not Just for Show." *Wall Street Journal* (November 18, 1985), 30.

Nelson, F. H. "Black Computer Workers: Closing the Gap in High

Technology Employment." *Journal of Negro Education* 54 (Fall 1985), 548-557.

Nelson, William. "Equal Opportunity." *Social Theory and Practice* 10 (Summer 1984), 157-184.

"The New Bias on Hiring Rules: Cuts in Affirmative Action Could Bring Big Business the Fights it Prefers to Avoid." *Business Week* (May 25, 1981), 123+.

Peden, Creighton. "Rise of Numerical Equality: Fullilove v. Klutznick." *Journal of Social Philosophy* 13 (January 1982), 1-9.

Prashar, Usha. "Evening Up the Odds for Black Workers." *Personnel Management* 15 (June 1983), 34-37.

Rabkin, Jeremy. "The Stroke of a Pen." *Regulation* 5 (May-June 1981), 15-18.

Reed, Leonard. "What's Wrong With Affirmative Case." *Washington Monthly* 12 (January 1981), 24-26.

Rosen, Benson, Thomas H. Jerdee, and John Huonker. "Are Older Workers Hurt by Affirmative Action?" *Business Horizons* 25 (September-October 1982), 67-70.

"A Ruling That Could Roll Back Affirmative Action." *Business Week* (July 2, 1984), 31.

Russell, James S. "A Review of Fair Employment Cases in the Field of Training." *Personnel Psychology* 37 (Summer 1984), 261-276.

Schapire, Julie A., and Florence Berger. "Responsibilities and Benefits in Hiring the Handicapped." *Cornell Hotel and Restaurant Management Quarterly* 24 (February 1984), 58-67.

Sculnick, Michael W., and Michael R. Zeller. "Handicap Discrimination Cases." *Employment Relations Today* 10 (Winter 1983-84), 343-347.

Sculnick, Michael W., and Michael R. Zeller. "Update on Age Discrimination." *Employment Relations Today* 10 (Winter 1983-84), 335-342.

Seligman, Daniel. "Affirmative Action Is Here to Stay." *Fortune* 105 (April 19, 1982), 143-144+.

Sheahan, Robert H. "Responding to Employment Discrimination Charges." *Personnel Journal* 60 (March 1981), 217-220.

Siegler, Mark. "Another Form of Age Discrimination." *Across the Board* 22 (February 1985), 7-10.

"The Son of an Affluent Mathematics Professor Scores 700. A Working Class Woman Scores 650." *Across the Board* 19 (July-August 1982), 32-35.

Sowell, Thomas. "A Dissenting Opinion About Affirmative Action." *Across the Board* 18 (January 1981), 64-72.

Szafran, Robert F. "Female and Minority Employment Patterns in Banks." *Work and Occupations* 11 (February 1984), 55-76.

"They Can Provide Useful Information about the Probability of an Applicant's Performing Successfully on the Job." *Across the Board* 19 (July-August 1982), 27-32.

Thomas, Laurence. "Sexism, Racism, and the Business World." *Business Horizons* 24 (July-August 1981), 62-68.

Tinsley, Dillard B., and Jose A. Rodriguez. "Mexican-American Employees—Stereotypes or Individuals?" *Business and Society* 21 (Spring 1982), 40-45.

Vaughn, Dennis H. "Employment Quotas—Discrimination or Affirmative Action?" *Employee Relations Law Journal* 7 (Spring 1982), 552-566.

Vile, J. R., and K. R. McCoy. "The Memphis Case: Another Precedent?" *Personnel* 62 (July 1985), 72-76.

Waltz, Anne. "Integrating Disabled Workers into Your Workforce." *Public Personnel Management* 10 (Winter 1981), 412-417.

Welch, Finis. "Affirmative Action and Its Enforcement." *American Economic Review* 71 (May 1981), 127-131.

"Women and Minorities: Their Proportions Grow in the Professional Work Force." *Monthly Labor Review* 108 (February 1985), 49-50.

Organizational Behavior, Corporate Culture, and Managerial Style

Books

Bensman, Joseph. *Dollars and Sense: Ideology, Ethics, and the Meaning of Work in Profit and Non-Profit Organizations.* New York: Schocken Books, 1983.

Birdzell, L. E., Jr. *Ethical Problems of Inside Counsel.* New York: Matthew Bender, 1984.

Callan, Hilary, and Shirley Ardener, eds. *Incorporated Wife.* London, U.K.: Croom Helm, 1984.

Cangemi, Joseph P., Casimir J. Kowalski, and Jeffrey C. Claypool. *Participative Management: Employee-Management Participation.* New York: Philosophical Library, 1985.

Chamberlain, Neil W. *Social Strategy and Corporate Structure.* New York: Macmillan, 1982.

Chapman, Elwood N. *Scrambling: Zig-Zagging Your Way to the Top.* Los Angeles: Tarcher, 1981.

Clark, John P., and Richard C. Hollinger. *Theft by Employees in Work Organizations.* Washington, D.C.: Nat'l. Inst. of Justice, 1982.

Clinard, Marshall B. *Corporate Ethics and Crime: The Role of Middle Management.* Beverly Hills, Calif.: Sage Pubs., 1983.

Clutterbuck, David. *How to Be a Good Corporate Citizen: A Manager's Guide to Making Social Responsibility Work—and Pay.* New York: McGraw-Hill, 1981.

Collins, Eliza G. C., ed. *The Executive Dilemma: Handling People Problems at Work.* New York: Wiley, 1985.

Cooper, Terry L. *The Responsible Administrator: An Approach to Ethics for the Administrative Role.* Port Washington, N.Y.: Associated Faculty Press, 1982.

Cox, Allan. *The Cox Report on the American Corporation.* New York: Delacorte Press, 1982.

Cushing, Harry A. *Voting Trusts: A Chapter in Modern Corporate History.* Buffalo: W.S. Hein, 1983.

Davis, Stanley M. *Guiding Beliefs: Managing Corporate Culture.* Cambridge, Mass.: Ballanger, 1984.

Deal, Terrence E., and Allan A. Kennedy. *Corporate Cultures: The Rites and Rituals of Corporate Life.* Reading, Mass.: Addison-Wesley, 1982.

Donaldson, Thomas. *Corporations and Morality.* Englewood Cliffs, N.J.: Prentice-Hall, 1982.

Elkins, Arthur, and Dennis Callaghan. *A Managerial Odyssey: Problems in Business and Its Environment.* 3d ed. Reading, Mass.: Addison-Wesley, 1981.

Ermann, M. D., and Richard J. Lundman, eds. *Corporate and Governmental Deviance: Problems of Organizational Behavior in Contemporary Society.* 2d ed. New York: Oxford Univ. Press, 1981.

Ermann, M. D., and Richard J. Lundman. *Corporate Deviance.* New York: Holt, Rinehart & Winston, 1982.

Evans, William A. *Management Ethics: An Intercultural Perspective.* Boston: M. Nijhoff Pub., 1981.

Finn, David. *The Corporate Oligarch.* Lanham, Md.: Univ. Press of America, 1983.

Freeman, R. E. *Strategic Management: A Stakeholder Approach.* Marshfield, Mass.: Pitman, 1983.

Ginzberg, Eli, and George Voijta. *Beyond Human Scale: The Large Corporation at Risk.* New York: Basic Books, 1985.

Glenn, James R. *Ethics in Decision Making.* New York: Wiley, 1985.

Golchin, Mostafa. *Values in Management: A Cross-Cultural Study.* Ann Arbor, Mich.: UMI Press, 1982.

Goodpaster, Kenneth E. *Adding Value to Value Added: The Moral Agenda of Corporate Leadership.* Boston: Harvard Business School, 1985.

Goodpaster, Kenneth E., comp. *Ethics in Management.* Boston: Harvard Business School, 1984.

Greanias, George C., and Duane Windsor, eds. *The Changing Boardroom: Making Policy and Profits in an Age of Corporate Citizenship.* Houston, Tex.: Gulf Pub., 1982.

Hamilton, Peter. *The Administration of Corporate Security.* Dover, N.H.: Woodhead-Faulkner, 1985.

Handy, Charles. *The Future of Work.* Oxford, U.K.: Basil Blackwell, 1984.

Harrison, Bruce S., and Eric Hemmendinger. *Responding to Employment Discrimination Charges.* New York: Marcel Bender, 1985.

Horn, Patrice C., and Jack D. Horn. *Sex in the Office: Power and Passion in the Workplace.* Reading, Mass.: Addison-Wesley, 1982.

Jackall, Robert, and Henry M. Levin. *Worker Cooperatives in America.* Berkeley, Calif: Univ. of California Press, 1984.

Kakabadse, Andrew, and Christopher Parker. *Power, Politics, and Organizations.* Chichester, U.K.: John Wiley, 1984.

Kidder, Tracy. *The Soul of a New Machine.* New York: Little, Brown and Company, 1981.

Kochan, Thomas A., et al. *Worker Participation and American Unions: Threat or Opportunity?* Kalamazoo, Mich.: W.E. Upjohn Institute, 1984.

Laureau, William. *Conduct Expected: The Unwritten Rules for a Successful Career.* Piscataway, N.J.: New Century Publications, 1985.

Maccoby, Michael. *The Leader.* New York: Simon & Schuster, 1981.

Manning, Frank V. *Managerial Dilemmas and Executive Growth.* Reston, Va.: Reston Publishing Co., 1981.

McCoy, Charles S. *Management of Values: The Ethical Difference in*

Corporate Policy and Performance. Mansfield, Mass.: Pitman, 1985.

McKersie, Robert B., and Werner Sengenberger, eds. *Job Losses in Major Industries: Manpower Strategy Responses*. Paris: OECD, 1983.

Megill, Robert E. *Life in the Corporate Orbit*. Tulsa, Okla.: PennWell Pub., 1981.

Miller, Gifford W. *The Ethical Conduct and Behavior of Public Executives as Compared to That of Corporate Exectives*. Claremont, Calif.: Claremont Graduate School, 1981.

Millstein, Ira M., and S. M. Katsh. *The Limits of Corporate Power: Existing Constraints on the Exercise of Corporate Discretion*. New York: Macmillan, 1981.

Mindell, Mark G., and William J. Gordon. *Employee Values in a Changing Society*. New York: American Management Association, 1981.

Missirian, Agnes K. *The Corporate Connection: Why Executive Women Need Mentors to Reach to the Top*. Englewood Cliffs, N.J.: Prentice-Hall, 1982.

Mitroff, Ian I. *Corporate Tragedies: Product Tampering, Sabotage, and Other Catastrophes*. New York: Praeger, 1984.

Peacock, William E. *Corporate Combat*. New York: Facts on File Pubs., 1984.

Peters, Thomas J., and Robert H. Waterman, Jr. *In Search of Excellence: Lessons from America's Best-Run Companies*. New York: Harper & Row, 1982.

Pfeffer, Jeffrey. *Power in Organizations*. Marshfield, Mass.: Pitman, 1981.

Reskin, Barbara, ed. *Sex Segregation in the Workplace: Trends, Explanations, Remedies*. Washington, D.C.: National Academic Press, 1984.

Sathe, Vijay. *Culture and Related Corporate Realities*. Homewood, Ill.: Richard D. Irwin, 1985.

Schein, Edgar H. *Organizational Culture and Leadership*. San Francisco: Jossey-Bass Pubs., 1985.

Seibert, Donald, and William Proctor. *The Ethical Executive: A Top CEO's Program for Success with Integrity in the Corporate World*. New York: Cornerstone, 1984.

Sengoku, Tamotsu. *Willing Workers: The Work Ethic in Japan, England and the United States*. Westport, Conn.: Quorum Books, 1985.

Sethi, S. P. *Crime in the Executive Suites: Executive Criminal Liability for Corporate Law Violation*. Cambridge, Mass.: Oelgeschlager, Gunn & Hain, 1982.

Simon, David R., and D. S. Eitzen. *Elite Deviance*. Newton, Mass.: Allyn & Bacon, 1982.

Slavin, Stephen L., and Mary H. Pradt. *The Einstein Syndrome: Corporate Anti-Semitism in America Today*. Lanham, Md.: Univ. Press of America, 1982.

Spitzer, Carlton E. *Raising the Bottom Line: Business Leadership in a Changing Society*. New York: Longman, 1982.

Vaughan, Diane. *Controlling Unlawful Organizational Behavior: Social Structure and Corporate Misconduct*. Chicago: Univ. of Chicago Press, 1983.

Waldo, Charles N. *Boards of Directors: Their Changing Roles, Structure, and Information Needs*. Westport, Conn.: Quorum Books, 1985.

Whisler, Thomas L. *Rules of the Games: Inside the Corporate Boardroom*. Homewood, Ill.: Dow Jones-Irwin, 1984.

Yates, Douglas, Jr. *The Politics of Management*. San Francisco: Jossey-Bass, 1985.

Articles

Adams, Michael. "A Matter of Morality?" *Successful Meetings* 32 (December 1983), 38-39, 42.

Aldag, Ramon J., and Donald W. Jackson, Jr. "Measurement and Correlates of Social Attitudes." *Journal of Business Ethics* 3 (May 1984), 143-151.

"Alienation among Industrial Entrepreneurs and Industrial Workers." *Psychological Reports* 55 (December 1984), 774.

Allen, P. T. "Size of Workforce, Morale and Absenteeism: A Re-Examination." *British Journal of Industrial Relations* 20 (March 1982), 83-100.

America, Richard F. "The Social Debt and Personnel Policy." *Personnel Administrator* 29 (May 1984), 84+.

Andrews, Kenneth R. "Difficulties in Overseeing Ethical Policy." *California Management Review* 26 (Summer 1984), 133-137.

Anker, R., and C. Hein. "Why Third World Urban Employers Usually Prefer Men." *International Labour Review* 124 (January-February 1985), 73-90.

"Anti-Takeover Expenses Are Deductible, Says IRS." *Journal of Taxation* 63 (July 1985), 16-17.

"Are You an Ethical Manager?" *Working Woman* 6 (October 1981), 102-103.

Arlow, Peter, and Martin J. Gannon. "Social Responsiveness, Corporate Structure and Economic Performance." *Academy of Management Review* 7 (April 1982), 235-241.

Armstrong, J. S., Martin K. Starr, and Michael J. Mahoney. "The Ombudsman: Cheating in Management Science/Comments." *Interfaces* 13 (August 1983), 20-29.

Auerbach, Joseph. "Can Inside Counsel Wear Two Hats?" *Harvard Business Review* 62 (September-October 1984), 80-86.

Axel, Helen. "Working Families—Do(n't) Employers Care?" *Training and Development Journal* 39 (October 1985), 8-12.

Bailey, Douglas M. "It's Wonderful, But Can I Keep It? The Ethics of Corporate Gifts." *New England Business* 5 (December 5, 1983), 22-26.

Banner, David K., and Robert A. Cooke. "Ethical Dilemmas in Performance Appraisal." *Journal of Business Ethics* 3 (November 1984), 327-333.

Baron, Alma, S., et al. "Assertiveness Can Make Office Life Easier/Positive Criticism Sessions." *Modern Office Procedures* 27 (September 1982), 56-57.

Beach, John. "Bluffing: Its Demise as a Subject Unto Itself." *Journal of Business Ethics* 4 (June 1985), 191-196.

Benson, Bob. "A Question of Give and Take." *Financial Post Magazine* (April 1982), 15+.

Berkhout, Jan. "The Causes and Consequences of High Morale." *Personnel Journal* 61 (March 1982), 194-197.

Bernard, Thomas J. "The Historical Development of Corporate Criminal Liability." *Criminology* 22 (February 1984), 3-17.

Berry, W. "The Human Side of Control." *Supervisory Management* 30 (June 1985), 34-39.

Bhasin, Roberta. "It's on the House (Accepting Gifts)." *Pulp Paper* 58 (February 1984), 145.

Biesinger, Gerald G. "Corporate Power and Employee Relations." *Journal of Business Ethics* 3 (May 1984), 139-142.

Bigoness, William J., and Philip B. DuBose. "Effects of Gender on Arbitrators' Decisions." *Academy of Management Journal* 28 (June 1985), 485-491.

Biles, George E. "A Program Guide for Preventing Sexual Harassment in the Workplace." *Personnel Administrator* 26 (June 1981), 49+.

Bing, S. "The Finer Points of Firing." *Esquire* 104 (November 1985), 64.

"Blame the Tax System for the Debts of Corporate America." *Economist* 296 (July 20, 1985), 65-66.

Blasi, Joseph R., and William F. Whyte. "Worker Ownership and Public Policy." *Policy Studies Journal* 10 (December 1981), 320-337.

Boulanger, Robert, and Donald Wayland. "Ethical Management: A Growing Corporate Responsibility—Part I." *CA Magazine* 118 (March 1985), 54-57.

Boulanger, Robert, and Donald Wayland. "Ethical Management: A Growing Corporate Responsibility—Part II." *CA Magazine* 118 (April 1985), 50-53.

Box-Grainger, Jill. "Employers' Attitudes to Ex-Offenders." *Personnel Management* 15 (November 1983), 32+.

Brady, F. M. "A Defense of Utilitarian Policy Processes in Corporate and Public Management." *Journal of Business Ethics* 4 (February 1985), 23-30.

Brass, Daniel J. "Men's and Women's Networks: A Study of Interaction Patterns and Influences in an Organization." *Academy of Management Journal* 28 (June 1985), 327-343.

Braybrooke, David. "Work: A Cultural Ideal Ever More in Jeopardy." *Midwest Studies of Philosophy* 7 (1982), 321-341.

Brenner, O. C. "Playing Fair." *Supervisory Management* 27 (July 1982), 33-35.

Brown, David S. "The Case for a New Managerial Ethic." *Management Quarterly* 26 (Spring 1985), 6-14.

Brown, David S. "The Managerial Ethic and Productivity Improvement." *Public Productivity Review* 7 (September 1983), 223-250.

Brown, Mark. "How To Manage Minds." *Management Today (UK)* (December 1984), 56-57+.

Brown, Martha A. "Ethics and Management Style." *Journal of Business Ethics* 3 (August 1984), 207-214.

Brunson, Richard W. "A Top Management Personal Values Typology: Inverted Factor Analysis Approach to a Conglomerate." *Group & Organization Studies* 10 (June 1985), 118-124.

Burke, Jim. "Expense Account Umpires: What Do You Call Fair? Foul?" *Association Management* 36 (May 1984), 79-87.

Campbell, David N., R. L. Fleming, and Richard C. Grote. "Discipline Without Punishment—at Last." *Harvard Business Review* 63 (July-August 1985), 162-178.

"Can Workplace Democracy Boost Productivity?" *Business and Society Review* 43 (Fall 1982), 10-15.

Carter, R. "A Security Role in Corporate Morality." *Security Management* 29 (June 1985), 57-60.

Cassell, Frank H. "Reflections on Management Style and Corporate Social Policy." *Journal of Business Ethics* 2 (May 1983), 123-126.

Caudle, S. "The Bedrock Capping Uppity Women." *Bureaucrat* 14 (Summer 1985), 27-30.

Cavanagh, Gerald F., Dennis J. Moberg, and Manuel Velasquez. "The Ethics of Organizational Politics." *Academy of Management Review* 6 (July 1981), 363-374.

Chace, Susan, and James A. White. "Mum's the Word: Among the Ways IBM Leads Computer Rivals Is in Keeping Secrets." *Wall Street Journal* (July 2, 1982), 1+.

Cherrington, David J., and J. O. Cherrington. "Creating a Climate of Honesty." *BYU Today* (November 1981), 9-11.

Cherrington, David J., W.S. Albrecht, and Marshall B. Romney. "The Role of Management in Reducing Fraud." *Financial Executive* 49 (March 1981), 28-32.

Christie, Claudia M. "Employee Benefits: The End of the Free Lunch: More and More Companies Are Switching from Defined to Contributory Plans." *New England Business* 7 (March 4, 1985), 18-22.

Christie, Claudia M. "When Employees 'Fire' the Boss." *New England Business* 6 (October 15, 1984), 12-17.

Christon, Richard. "Can Companies Control Confidential Information?" *Personnel Management* 17 (March 1985), 26-29.

Clawson, James G., and Kathy E. Kram. "Managing Cross-Gender Mentoring." *Business Horizons* 27 (May-June 1984), 22-32.

Cloninger, Dale O. "The Moral Constraint to Managerial Behavior." *Collegiate Forum* (Fall 1983), 16.

Cochran, Philip L., and Steven Wartick. "Golden Parachutes: A Closer Look." *California Management Review* 26 (Summer 1984), 111-125.

Cochran, Philip L., Robert A. Wood, and Thomas B. Jones. "The Composition of Boards of Directors and Incidence of Golden Parachutes." *Academy of Management Journal* 28 (September 1985), 664-671.

Cohen, Cynthia F., and Joyce P. Vinceletti. "Notice, Remedy and Employer Liability for Sexual Harassment." *Labor Law Journal* 35 (May 1984), 301-307.

Cohen, G. A. "Are Workers Forced to Sell Their Labor Power?" *Philosophy and Public Affairs* 14 (Winter 1985), 99-105.

Collins, Eliza G. "Managers and Lovers." *Harvard Business Review* 61 (September-October 1983), 142-153.

Collins, Eliza G., and Timothy B. Blodgett. "Sexual Harassment: Some See It . . . Some Won't." *Harvard Business Review* 59 (March-April 1981), 76-94.

Copp, David, and Edwin Levy. "Value Neutrality in the Techniques of Policy Analysis: Risk and Uncertainty." *Journal of Business Administration* 13 (1982), 161-190.

Cort, John C. "Is Mondragon the Way?" *New Catholic World* 226 (July-August 1983), 152-154.

Creedon, John J. "Lawyer and Executive—The Role of the General Counsel." *Business Lawyer* 39 (November 1983), 25-31.

Cunningham, Mary E. "Corporate Culture Determines Productivity." *Industry Week* 209 (May 4, 1981), 82-84.

Cunningham, Mary E. "Planning for Humanism." *Journal of Business Strategy* 3 (Spring 1983), 87-90.

Cunningham, Mary. "Productivity and the Corporate Culture." *Vital Speeches of the Day* 47 (April 1, 1981), 363-367.

"Deductibility of Greenmail Payments." *Journal of Taxation* 63 (July 1985), 63-64.

"Devise Strategy for Fight Against Employee Theft." *Occupational Hazards* 44 (January 1982), 53-54.

Dickson, John W. "Beliefs About Work and Rationales for Participation." *Human Relations* 36 (October 1983), 911-932.

Dickson, John W. "Organizational Type, Formality of Participation, Beliefs about Work, and Rationales for Participation." *International Studies of Management & Organization* 13 (Fall 1983), 43-61.

Diffie-Couch, Priscilla. "Building a Feeling of Trust in the Company." *Supervisory Management* 29 (April 1984), 31-36.

"Do Employees Snipe, Snarl and Struggle? Consider Counseling." *New England Business* 4 (June 7, 1982), 27-29.

"Do You Trust the Home Office?" *Economist* 279 (June 13-19, 1981), 60.

Doan, Michael, Jeannye Thornton, and Ronald A. Taylor. "Executives Who Look Beyond the Bottom Line." *U.S. News and World Report* 97 (October 22, 1984), 61-62.

Dobel, J. P. "Doing Good by Staying In?" *Public Personnel Management* 11 (Summer 1982), 126-139.

Dolecheck, Maynard M., and Clayton C. Dolecheck. "How Do Male and Female Employees with Business Degrees Perceive Discrimination on the Job?" *Akron Business and Economic Review* 14 (Summer 1983), 12-15.

Donlan, Thomas G. "Hands in the Cookie Jar: Why Companies Are Tapping Their Pension Funds." *Barron's* 64 (May 21, 1984), 8-9.

Drapkin, Dennis B., and Robert A. Profusek. "Unfurling the New Golden Parachute Laws." *Directors and Boards* 9 (Fall 1984), 27-32.

Dreyfack, Madeleine. "Sexual Harassment: Can You Afford Not to Clamp Down?" *Supervision* 44 (April 1982), 8-10.

Driscoll, Jeanne B. "Sexual Attraction and Harassment: Management's New Problems." *Personnel Journal* 60 (January 1981), 33+.

Drucker, Peter F. "Executives Are 'Aging' at 42." *Wall Street Journal* (March 7, 1984), 30.

Dubinsky, Alan J., and Thomas N. Ingram. "Correlates of Salespeople's Ethical Conflict: An Exploratory Investigation." *Journal of Business Ethics* 3 (November 1984), 343-353.

Dubno, Peter. "Attitudes Toward Women Executives: A Longitudinal Approach." *Academy of Management Journal* 28 (March 1985), 235-239.

Dubno, Peter. "Is Corporate Sexism Passe?" *Business and Society Review* 53 (Spring 1985), 59-61.

Dunbar, Roger L., et al. "Crossing Mother: Ideological Constraints on Organizational Improvements." *Journal of Management Studies* 19 (January 1982), 91-108.

Dunfee, Thomas W., and Diana C. Robertson. "Work-Related Ethical Attitudes: Impact on Business Profitability." *Business and Professional Ethics Journal* 3 (Winter 1984), 25-40. Commentaries: by David Braybrooke, 41; Charles T. Hutchinson, vol.4, no.1, 74.

Dwight, Lee. "Patience Is a Market Virtue." *Reason* 16 (January 1985), 42-46.

Dyer, William G., and Jeffrey H. Dyer. "The M*A*S*H Generation: Implications for Future Organizational Values." *Organizational Dynamics* 13 (Summer 1984), 66-79.

Eckner, Jack O. "Integrity Awareness Training for Managers." *Training and Development Journal* 37 (July 1983), 46-49.

Elfin, Rodman M. "An Evaluation of a New Trend in Corporate Law: Dismissal of Derivative Suits by Minority Board Committees." *American Business Law Journal* 20 (Summer 1982), 179-202.

Engel, Paul G. "Bankruptcy: A Refuge for All Reasons?" *Industry Week* 220 (March 5, 1984), 63-68.

Ewing, David W. "How to Negotiate With Employee Objectors." *Harvard Business Review* 61 (January-February 1983), 103-110.

"Executive Ethics." *Forbes* 136 (November 4, 1985), 12.

Exton, William, Jr. "Ethical and Moral Considerations and the Principal of Excellence in Management Consulting." *Journal of Business Ethics* 1 (August 1982), 211-218.

Fasching, Darrell J. "A Case for Corporate and Management Ethics." *California Management Review* 23 (Summer 1981), 62-76.

Faux, Jeff. "Does Worker Ownership Work?" *Mother Jones* 10 (July 1985), 18-19.

Feinberg, Mortimer R., and Aaron Levenstein. "The Danger in Manipulating Employees." *Wall Street Journal* (March 3, 1985), 26.

Ferris, G. R., and V. L. Yates. "The Influence of Subordinate Age on Performance Ratings and Causal Attributions." *Personnel Psychology* 38 (Autumn 1985), 545-547.

Ferris, Kenneth R., et al. "A Comparison of Two Organizational Commitment Scales." *Personnel Psychology* 36 (Spring 1983), 87-98.

Feuer, Dale. "A World Without Layoffs: Wouldn't it Be Lovely?" *Training* 22 (August 1985), 23-25+.

Fleming, John E. "A Suggested Approach to Linking Decision Styles with Business Ethics." *Journal of Business Ethics* 4 (Spring 1985), 137-144.

Foegen, J. H. "Rethinking Retirement: Corporate Life after 65." *Business and Society Review* 45 (Spring 1983), 14-17.

Fombrun, Charles J. "Corporate Culture, Environment, and Strategy." *Human Resource Management* 22 (Spring 1983), 139-154.

Ford, Robert, and Frank McLaughlin. "Nepotism." *Personnel Journal* 64 (September 1985), 57-60.

Fores, Michael, et al. "The Decline of the Management Ethic." *Journal of General Management (UK)* 6 (Spring 1981), 36-50.

Frederick, William C. "Managing on the Ethics Frontier." *Managing* 1 (1982), 35-37.

French, Peter A. "The Principle of Responsible Adjustment in Corporate Moral Responsibility: The Crash on Mount Erebus." *Journal of Business Ethics* 3 (May 1984), 101-111.

Fritzsche, David J., and Helmut Becker. "Linking Management Behavior to Ethical Philosophy—An Empirical Investigation." *Academy of Management Journal* 27 (March 1984), 166-175.

Frost, Taggart F. "The Sick Organization, Part 1: Neurotic, Psychotic, Sociopathic." *Personnel* 62 (May 1985), 40-44.

Fuller, Stephen H. "Becoming the Organization of the Future." *Journal of Business Ethics* 1 (May 1982), 115-118.

Gallagher, Kathleen G. "Legal and Professional Responsibility of Corporate Counsel to Employees During an Internal Investigation." *Corporation Law Review* 6 (Winter 1983), 3-28.

Gardner, Meryl P. "Creating a Corporate Culture for the Eighties." *Business Horizons* 28 (January-February 1985), 59-63.

Gibson, W. D. "Lore and Order: The Traditional Annual Meeting Is Undergoing Radical Change." *Barron's* 64 (April 2, 1984), 45.

Ginsburg, Sigmund G. "Diagnosing and Treating Managerial Malaise." *Personnel* 61 (July-August 1984), 34-41.

Glinow, Mary Ann, and Luke Novelli, Jr. "Ethical Standards Within Organizational Behavior." *Academy of Management Journal* 25 (June 1982), 417-436.

Goddard, Robert W. "Management Malpractice: How to Avoid Employee Complaints that Could Lead to Litigation." *Management Review* 73 (February 1984), 58-61.

Goddard, Robert W. "Sign Up for High Performance." *Manage* 36 (July 1984), 27-28.

Goldburg, Leonard D., and Kenneth D. Walters. "No-Fault Criminal Liability for Executives." *California Management Review* 24 (Summer 1982), 25-32.

Goldwater, Leslie R. "Some Big Companies Manage Quite Well Without a Union." *Iron Age* 225 (August 20, 1982), 71, 74-76.

Golembiewski, Robert T., Robert Munzenrider, and Diane Carter. "Phases of Progresive Burnout and Their Work Site Covariants: Critical Issues in OD Research and Praxis." *Journal of Applied Behavioral Science* 19 (1983), 461-481.

Gooding, Judson. "Firing at the Top." *Across the Board* 18 (October 1981), 17-21.

Goodpaster, Kenneth E. "Testing Morality in Organizations." *International Journal of Applied Philosophy* 2 (Spring 1984), 35-38.

Goodpaster, Kenneth E., and John B. Matthews, Jr. "Can a Corporation Have a Conscience?" *Harvard Business Review* 60 (January-February 1982), 132-141.

Goodstein, Leonard D. "Managers, Values, and Organization Development." *Group and Organization Studies* 8 (June 1983), 203-220.

Gray, Bonnie J., and Robert K. Landrum. "Difficulties With Being Ethical." *Business* 33 (July-September 1983), 28-3.

Greenblat, Arleigh. "Salve for Burnouts." *Successful Meetings* 32 (June 1983), 16.

Greene, Richard. "Peeking Beneath the Corporate Veil." *Forbes* 134 (August 13, 1984), 58.

Greller, M. "Moral and Immoral Companies—A Review of Corporate Ethics and Crime: The Role of Middle Management." *Across the Board* 20 (December 1983), 59-61.

Gruner, Richard. "Employment Discrimination in Management by Objectives Systems." *Labor Law Journal* 34 (June 1983), 364-370.

Gulick, Walter B. "Is It Ever Morally Justifiable for Corporate Officials to Break the Law?" *Business and Professional Ethics Journal* 1 (Spring 1982), 25-47. Commentary: by Charles T. Hutchinson, 49.

Hacker, Robert C., et al. "Representing the Corporate Client and the Proposed Rules of Professional Conduct." *Corporation Law Review* 6 (Summer 1983), 269-273.

Hameed, Abdul. "Diagnosing Sickness in the Corporate Sector." *Pakistan Management Review* 23 (Fall 1982), 50-56.

Harmon, Frederick G., and Garry Jacobs. "Company Personality: The Heart of the Matter." *Management Review* 74 (October 1985), 36-40.

Harrison, Robert E. "Ethics in Employee Relations." *Northeast Louisiana Business Review* (Fall-Winter 1982), 16-20.

Hayes, James L. "Managing Conflict in the Organization." *Credit & Financial Management* 84 (February 1982), 31-32.

Hecker, Richard E. "The Human Side of Managing Complexity." *Vital Speeches of the Day* 48 (May 1, 1982), 428-434.

Heilman, M. E., and M. H. Stopeck. "Attractiveness and Corporate Success: Different Causal Attributions for Males and Females." *Journal of Applied Psychology* 70 (May 1985), 379-388.

Heims, Peter A. "Unethical, but Legal." *Security Management* 25 (November 1981), 10-11, 13+.

Henle, Robert J., S.J. "An Essay Toward a Philosophy of the Corporation." *Loyola Management Review* 1 (Spring 1981), 35-42.

Herrick, Neal Q. "The Means and End of Work." *Human Relations* 34 (July 1981), 611-632.

Hershman, Arlene. "The Spreading Wave of Stock Buybacks." *Dun's Business Month* 124 (August 1984), 40-46.

Hochner, Arthur, and Cherlyn Granrose. "Sources of Motivation to Choose Employee Ownership as an Alternative to Job Loss." *Academy of Management Journal* 28 (December 1985), 860-875.

Hofstede, G. G. "Culture and Organizations." *Intern. Studies of Management and Organization* 10 (Winter 1980-81), 15-41.

Horovitz, Bruce. "When Should an Executive Lie?" *Industry Week* 211 (November 16, 1981), 80-87.

Horton, Thomas R. "Shaping Business Values." *Management Review* 73 (April 1984), 2-3.

Hubben, Herbert. "Merit and Machiavelli." *Across the Board* 22 (March 1985), 3.

Izraeli, Dafna N., and Dove Izraeli. "Sex Effects in Evaluating Leaders: A Replication Study." *Journal of Applied Psychology* 70 (August 1985), 540-546.

Jackall, Robert. "Moral Mazes: Bureaucracy and Managerial Work." *Harvard Business Review* 61 (September-October 1983), 118-130.

Jacobs, Bruce A. "Sex in the Office." *Industry Week* 208 (February 9, 1981), 32-38.

Jacobson, C. K. "Resistance to Affirmative Action: Self-Interest or Racism." *Journal of Conflict Resolution* 29 (June 1985), 306-329.

Jamieson, David W. "Organizational Culture Is Our Business." *Training and Development Journal* 39 (October 1985), 22.

Jamison, Kaleel. "Managing Sexual Attraction in the Workplace." *Personnel Administrator* 28 (August 1983), 45-51.

Jennings, Eugene. "Are Corporations Stingy on Directors' Pay?" *Business and Society Review* 51 (Fall 1984), 35-36.

Johnson, Harold L. "Ethics and the Executive." *Business Horizons* 24 (May-June 1981), 53-59.

Jones, Peter T. "Sanctions, Incentives and Corporate Behavior." *California Management Review* 27 (Spring 1985), 119-131.

Josefowitz, Natasha. "Sexual Relationships at Work: Attraction, Transference, Coercion or Strategy." *Personnel Administrator* 27 (March 1982), 91-96.

Kangas, J. E. "Compatible Human Communities: The Role of Ethics in Modern Enterprise." *Journal of Business Ethics* 2 (May 1983), 127-133.

Kavanagh, John P. "Ethical Issues in Plant Relocation." *Business and*

Professional Ethics Journal 1 (Winter 1982), 21-33. Commentary: by Elmer W. Johnson, 35.

Kavanagh, John P. "The Sinking of Sun Ship: A Case Study in Managerial Ethics." *Business and Professional Ethics Journal* 1 (Summer 1982), 1-13. Commentaries: by George G. Brenkert, vol.2, no.3, 63; Joseph A. Pichler, 67.

Keeley, Michael. "Ethical Aspects of Organizational Governance: A Contractual View." *Review of Social Economy* 40 (December 1982), 375-392.

Keeley, Michael. "Values in Organizational Theory and Management Education." *Academy of Management Review* 8 (July 1983), 376-386.

Keim, Gerald D., Barry D. Baysinger, and Roger E. Meiners. "The Corporate Democracy Act: Would the Majority Rule?" *Business Horizons* 24 (March-April 1981), 30-35.

Kelso, Louis, and Patricia Hetter. "Could an ESOP Save General Motors?" *Business and Society Review* 40 (Winter 1981-82), 53-55.

Kennish, John W. "Prevention Starts From the Top." *Security Management* 29 (October 1985), 60-63.

Kessler, Felix. "Mergers Without a Company." *Fortune* 112 (October 28, 1985), 51-56.

Kets DeVries, Manfred F. R., and Danny Miller. "Unstable at the Top." *Psychology Today* 18 (October 1984), 26-28+.

Kilmann, R. H. "Corporate Culture." *Psychology Today* 19 (April 1985), 62-68.

Konrad, Armin R. "Business Managers and Moral Sanctuaries." *Journal of Business Ethics* 1 (August 1982), 195-200.

Koral, A. "Ethics in the Office: How Far Can—or Should—You Go to Protect Your Boss?" *Glamour* 79 (January 1981), 138-139.

Krugman, Dean O., and O. C. Ferrell. "Organizational Ethics of Advertising: Corporate and Agency Views." *Journal of Advertising* 10 (1981), 21-30+.

Kur, C. E. "OD: Perspectives, Processes and Prospects." *Training and Development Journal* 35 (April 1981), 28-30.

Labich, Kenneth. "Showdown Over Insuring Corporate Officers." *Fortune* 112 (December 9, 1985), 70.

"Labor's Voice on Corporate Boards: Good or Bad?" *Business Week* (May 7, 1984), 151-153.

Laczniak, Gene R. "Business Ethics: A Manager's Primer." *Business* 33 (January-March 1983), 23-29.

Ladd, John. "Corporate Mythology and Individual Responsibility." *International Journal of Applied Philosophy* 2 (Spring 1984), 1-21.

Lambert, Richard A., and David F. Larcker. "Golden Parachutes, Executive Decision-Making, and Shareholder Wealth." *Journal of Accounting and Economics* (April 1985), 179-203.

Larwood, Laurie, Barbara Gutek, and Urs E. Gattiker. "Perspectives on Institutional Discrimination and Resistance to Change." *Group and Organizational Studies* 9 (September 1984), 333-352.

Lasden, Martin. "Surviving Corporate Crises." *Computer Decisions* 15 (January 1983), 84-96.

Law, W. A. "Management Versus the Wild Bunch." *Across the Board* 22 (June 1985), 7-9.

Leary, Thomas B. "Is There a Conflict in Representing a Corporation and Its Individual Employees?" *Business Lawyer* 36 (March 1981), 591-595.

Lederer, Philip C. "Management's Right to Loyalty of Supervisors." *Labor Law Journal* 32 (February 1981), 83-104.

Lees-Haley, Paul R., et al. "Attitude Survey Norms: A Dangerous Ally." *Personnel Administrator* 27 (October 1982), 51-53, 89.

Leibig, Michael T., and Randy S. Rabinowitz. "Social Investment and the Regulation of Pension Investment: An Outline of Basic Materials." *Journal of Pension Planning & Compliance* 9 (June 1983), 173-214.

Leighton, Tony. "When Love Walks In . . ." *Canadian Business* 57 (May 1984), 78-83.

Levinson, Marc. "On the White-Collar Assembly Line." *Commonweal* 111 (June 1, 1984), 334-335.

Levy, Leslie. "Reforming Board Reform." *Harvard Business Review* 59 (January-February 1981), 166-172.

Lewicki, Roy J. "Organizational Seduction: Building Commitment to Organizations." *Organizational Dynamics* 10 (Autumn 1981), 5-21.

Lincoln, Douglas J., Milton M. Pressley, and Taylor Little. "Ethical Beliefs and Personal Values of Top Level Executives." *Journal of Business Research* 10 (December 1982), 475-487.

Linder, Jane. "Harnessing Corporate Culture." *Computerworld* 19 (September 23, 1985), 1-10.

Lippitt, Gordon L. "Managing Conflict in Today's Organizations." *Training & Development Journal* 36 (July 1982), 66-72, 74.

Longenecker, Justin G. "Management Priorities and Management Ethics." *Journal of Business Ethics* 4 (February 1985), 65-70.

Lorne, Simon M. "Why Outside Counsel Should Stay Outside." *Directors and Boards* 6 (Fall 1981), 26-28.

Louis, J. C. "Employee Ownership: The Rising Tide." *Management Review* 74 (March 1985), 40-43.

Maccoby, Michael. "Management, Leadership and the Work Ethic." *Modern Office Procedures* 28 (May 1983), 14+.

Maclagan, Patrick W. "The Concept of Responsibility: Some Implications for Organizational Behavior and Development." *Journal of Management Studies* 20 (October 1983), 411-423.

Majerus, Raymond. "Nowhere to Go but Up: Corporation Ethics in the U.S. Economy." *Review of Social Economics* 40 (December 1982), 407-416.

Marcus, Philip M., and Catherine B. Smith. "Absenteeism in an Organizational Context." *Work and Occupations* 12 (August 1985), 251-268.

Martel, Gilles. "Absenteeism Is Everybody's Business." *Canadian Business Review* 8 (Spring 1981), 53-55.

Masuch, A. "Vicious Circles in the Organization." *Administrative Science Quarterly* 30 (March 1985), 14-33.

Mawhinney, T. C. "Philosophical and Ethical Aspects of Organizational Behavior Management: Some Evaluative Feedback." *Journal of Organizational Behavior Management* 6 (Spring 1984), 5-31.

McConkie, Mark L., and R. W. Boss. "Lessons From Antiquity: The Wisdom of Solomon." *Leadership & Organization Development Journal* 4 (1983), 17-19.

McCoy, Bowen H. "The Parable of the Sadhu." *Harvard Business Review* 61 (September-October 1983), 103-108.

McCroskey, Jacquelyn. "Work and Families: What Is the Employer's Responsibility?" *Personnel Journal* 61 (January 1982), 30-38.

McCullough, Rose V. "Hostility—Its Causes and Cures." *Rough Notes* 127 (September 1984), 68-70.

McDonald, J. J. "Bankruptcy Reorganization: Labor Considerations for the Debtor-Employer." *Employee Relations Law Journal* 11 (Summer 1985), 7-31.

McIntyre, Kathryn J. "Hall Executive Defends Retroactive Cover." *Business Insurance* 17 (November 14, 1983), 75.

McIntyre, Shelby H., et al. "On Conducting Socially Responsible Organizational Research/Counterpoints." *Journal of Enterprise Management* 3 (1981), 103-113.

McKenna, Jack, and Paul L. Oritt. "Job Dissatisfaction: A Social Disease." *Business and Society* 21 (Spring 1982), 32-39.

McLaughlin, David J. "On Golden Parachutes: Following the Leader and Other Falacies." *Directors and Boards* 6 (Summer 1982), 22-25.

Miceli, Marcia P., and Janet P. Near. "The Relationships Among Beliefs, Organizational Position, and Whistle-Blowing Status: A Discriminant Analysis." *Academy of Management Journal* 27 (December 1984), 687-705.

Mikalachki, Alexander. "Does Anyone Listen to the Boss?" *Business Horizons* 26 (January-February 1983), 18-24.

Miller, Marc. "Workers' Owned." *Radical Religion* 5 (1981), 48-58.

Miller, Samuel R., and Irwin H. Warren. "Conflicts of Interest and Ethical Issues for the Inside and Outside Counsel." *Business Lawyer* 40 (February 1985), 631-668.

Mintzberg, Henry. "Why America Needs, But Cannot Have, Corporate Democracy." *Organizational Dynamics* 11 (Spring 1983), 5-20.

Moch, Michael, and Anne S. Huff. "Life on the Line." *Wharton Magazine* 6 (Summer 1982), 53-58.

Moore, John M. "The Role Relocation Plays in Management Planning." *Personnel Administrator* 27 (December 1982), 31-34.

Moritz, Milton E. "Straight Talk on How Management Can Help Keep Employees Honest." *Telephony* 203 (September 13, 1982), 67-68.

Morse, Mary. "The Day Care Dividend: Companies Find That It Pays to Offer Employees Child-Care Assistance." *Corporate Report* 16 (January 1985), 66-69.

Moskal, Brian S. "Corporate Responsibility: Putting Your Act Together." *Industry Week* 214 (July 26, 1982), 50-53+.

Moskowitz, Milton R. "Social Proxy Fights Spice Up Annual Meetings." *Business and Society Review* 45 (Spring 1983), 23-24.

Mumford, Enid. "Participation—What Does It Mean and How Can It Be Achieved?" *Manchester Business School Review (UK)* 5 (Summer 1981), 7-11.

Murphy, John W. "Organizational Issues in Worker Ownership." *American Journal of Economics and Society* 43 (July 1984), 287-299.

Myers, Donald W., and Neil J. Humphrey. "The Caveats in Mentorship." *Business Horizons* 28 (July-August 1985), 9-14.

Nader, Ralph. "Reforming Corporate Governance." *California Management Review* 26 (Summer 1984), 126-132.

Nadler, Paul S. "Nepotism in Banking?" *Banker's Monthly* 10 (October 15, 1983), 5-6, 22.

Nairn, Allan. "Mondragon: Where Workers Call the Shots: An Alternative to Multinationals." *Multinational Monitor* 5 (July 1984), 9-13.

Naisbitt, John. "Re-inventing the Corporation." *FE* 1 (March 1985), 38-43.

Neumann, Frederick L. "Corporate Audit Committees and the Foreign Corrupt Practices Act." *Journal of Accountancy* 151 (March 1981), 78-80.

Nielsen, John. "Management Layoffs Won't Quit." *Fortune* 112 (October 28, 1985), 46-49.

Nielsen, Richard P. "Alternative Managerial Responses to Ethical Dilemmas." *Planning Review* 13 (November 1985), 24-29+.

Nielsen, Richard P. "Pluralism in the Mass Media: Can Management Participation Help?" *Journal of Business Ethics* 3 (November 1984), 335-341.

Nystrom, Paul C., and William H. Starbuck. "Managing Beliefs in Organizations." *Journal of Applied Behavioral Science* 20 (August 1984), 277-287.

O'Donnell, John R. "Ethical Behavior in the Corporate Environment." *Review of Social Economy* 40 (December 1982), 371-374.

Oliver, Carl R. "A Psychological Approach to Preventing Computer Abuse—A Case History." *Computer Security Journal* 3 (Winter 1985), 51-56.

O'Toole, James. "Corporate Raiders May Destroy in a Week What It Took a Lifetime to Create." *New Management* 2 (Spring 1985), 4-5.

Ozar, David T. "Do Corporations Have Moral Rights?" *Journal of Business Ethics* 4 (August 1985), 277-280.

Packard, M. "Company Policies and Attitudes Toward Older Workers." *Social Security Bulletin* 48 (May 1985), 45-46.

Pascarella, Perry. "The Corporation Steps in Where Family, Church, and Schools Have Failed." *Industry Week* 220 (June 25, 1984), 34-35.

Pascarella, Perry. "Malcontent Managers: Will They Retard the Recovery?" *Industry Week* 220 (January 23, 1984), 32-38.

Pastin, Mark. "Ethics as an Integrating Force in Management." *Journal of Business Ethics* 3 (November 1984), 293-304.

Patton, William, and Randall Bartlett. "Corporate 'Persons' and

Freedom of Speech: The Political Impact of Legal Mythology." *Wisconsin Law Review* 3 (1981), 494-512.

Peach, L. "Managing Corporate Citizenship." *Personnel Management* 17 (July 1985), 32-35.

Pichler, Joseph A. "The Liberty Principle: A Basis for Management Ethics." *Business and Professional Ethics Journal* 2 (Winter 1983), 19-29. Commentaries: by Elliot Lehman, 31; Eric Mack, 35.

Posner, Barry Z., James M. Kouzes, and Warren H. Schmidt. "Shared Values Make a Difference: An Empirical Test of Corporate Culture." *Human Resource Management* 24 (Fall 1985), 293-309.

Posner, Barry Z., and J. M. Munson. "Gender Differences in Managerial Values." *Psychological Reports* 49 (December 1981), 867-881.

Posner, Barry Z., and Warren H. Schmidt. "Values and the American Manager: An Update." *California Management Review* 26 (Spring 1984), 202-216.

Potter, Earl H., III, and Fred E. Fiedler. "The Utilization of Staff Member Intelligence and Experience Under High and Low Stress." *Academy of Management Journal* 24 (June 1981), 361-376.

Powell, Brian, and Jerry A. Jacobs. "The Prestige Gap: Differential Evaluations of Male and Female Workers." *Work and Occupations* 11 (August 1984), 283-308.

Powell, Gary N., et al. "Sex Effects on Managerial Value Systems." *Human Relations* 37 (November 1984), 909-921.

Pringle, Charles D., and Justin G. Longenecker. "The Ethics of MBO." *Academy of Management Review* 7 (April 1982), 305-312.

Pritchett, M. J., III. "Corporate Ethics and Corporate Governance: A Critique of the ALI Statement on Corporate Governance Section 2.01(b)." *California Law Review* 71 (May 1983), 994-1011.

Purcell, Theodore V. "The Ethics of Corporate Governance." *Review of Social Economy* 40 (December 1982), 360-370.

"A Question of Leadership." *Datamation* 29 (February 1983), 119-128.

Raines, John C. "Capital, Community, and the Meaning of Work." *Christian Century* 43 (October 17, 1983), 375-379.

Rainey, Hal G. "Reward Preferences Among Public and Private Managers: In Search of the Service Ethic." *American Review of Public Administration* 16 (Winter 1982), 288-302.

Raudsepp, Eugene. "The Politics of Promotion." *Office Administration & Automation* 44 (April 1983), 28-31.

Redding, D. G., et al. "The Role of 'Face' in the Organizational Perceptions of Chinese Managers." *International Studies of Management & Organization* 13 (Fall 1983), 92-123.

Renfro, William L. "Managing the Issues of the 1980s." *Futurist* 16 (August 1982), 61-66.

Rhodes, S. R., and R. M. Steers. "Conventional vs. Worker-Owned Organizations." *Human Relations* 34 (December 1981), 1013-1035.

Rizzo, Ann-Marie, and Thomas J. Patka. "Organizational Imperative and Supervisory Control—Their Effects on Managerial Ethics." *Public Personnel Management* 10 (1982), 103-109.

Roberts, John. "The Moral Character of Management Practice." *Journal of Management Studies* 21 (July 1984), 286-302.

Robison, Wade L. "Management and Ethical Decision-Making." *Journal of Business Ethics* 3 (November 1984), 287-291.

Rohrlich, Jay. "Business Success and Personal Trauma." *Business and Society Review* 41 (Spring 1982), 36-40.

Romei, Lura. "Management by Harassment: Everyone Loses." *Modern Office Procedures* 26 (February 1981), 76, 78, 80.

Rosen, Corey. "Employee Stock Ownership Plans: A New Way to Work." *Business Horizons* 26 (September-October 1983), 48-54.

Rosen, Corey. "Next Step; Worker Ownership?" *Commonweal* 111 (August 10, 1984), 434-438.

Rosenbaum, W. C., Jr. "The Pension Swindle." *Association Management* 37 (October 1985), 107-108.

Rosenthal, Mark M., and Robert A. Miller. "Tactics to Employ When a Lawsuit Looms." *Harvard Business Review* 62 (July-August 1984), 42-44.

Roush, John A. "Loyalty in the Inner Circle." *Business Horizons* 26 (September-October 1983), 55-56.

Rowan, Roy. "Rekindling Corporate Loyalty." *Fortune* 103 (February 9, 1981), 54-59.

Rutherford, Denny G. "Managing Guest Intoxication: A Policy to Limit Third-Party Liability." *Cornell Hotel and Restaurant Administration Quarterly* 26 (November 1985), 64-69.

Ryan, Michael, and David L. Martinson. "The PR Officer as Corporate Conscience." *Public Relations Quarterly* 28 (Summer 1983), 20-23.

Safer, David A. "Institutional Body Language." *Public Relations Journal* 41 (March 1985), 26-28+.

Samiee, Saeed. "How Auto Workers Look at Productivity Measures: Lessons From Overseas." *Business Horizons* 25 (May-June 1982), 85-91.

Santilli, Paul C. "Moral Fictions and Scientific Management." *Journal of Business Ethics* 3 (November 1984), 279-285.

Sashkin, Marshall. "Participative Management Is an Ethical Imperative." *Organizational Dynamics* 12 (Spring 1984), 5-22.

Scheibla, S. H. "The Liability Syndrome: Why So Many Corporate Directors Suffer From It." *Barron's* 65 (November 4, 1985), 28+.

Schein, Edgar H. "Coming to a New Awareness of Organizational Culture." *Sloan Management Review* 25 (Winter 1984), 3-16.

Schrank, Robert. "The New Romanovs." *New Management* 2 (1984), 14-21.

Schwartz, Howard S. "A Theory of Deontic Work Motivation." *Journal of Applied Behavioral Science* 19 (May 1983), 204-214.

Schwartz, Howard S. "The Usefulness of Myth and the Myth of Usefulness: A Dilemma for the Applied Organizational Scientist." *Journal of Management* 11 (Spring 1985), 31-42.

Schwartz, Kenneth R., and Krishnagopal Menon. "Executive Succession in Failing Firms." *Academy of Management Journal* 28 (September 1985), 680-686.

Scotese, Peter G. "Fold Up Those Golden Parachutes." *Harvard Business Review* 63 (March-April 1985), 168-172.

Serpa, Roy. "Creating a Candid Corporate Culture." *Journal of Business Ethics* 4 (October 1985), 425-430.

Shapiro, Kenneth P. "Improvements in Attitudes of Employees Not Spreading to Middle Managers." *Business Insurance* 15 (December 7, 1981), 26.

Sherman, Stanley R. " 'Did Somebody Forget to Tell You? You're Fired.' " *Advanced Management Journal* 47 (Spring 1982), 29-30.

Shuter, Robert. "Assignment America: Foreign Managers Beware!" *International Management (UK)* 40 (September 1985), 93-96.

Siegel, Jay S. "Shielding the Worker From Crisis at the Top." *New England Business* 5 (September 19, 1983), 78, 80.

Sigelman, Lee, et al. "Organizational Responses to Affirmative Action: 'Elephant Burial Grounds' Revisited." *Administration and Society* 16 (May 1984), 27-40.

Sinetar, Marsha. "Entrepreneurs, Chaos, and Creativity—Can Creative People Really Survive Large Company Structure?" *Sloan Management Review* 26 (Winter 1985), 57-62.

Sjoberg, Gideon, Ted R. Vaughan, and Norma Williams. "Bureaucracy as a Moral Issue." *Journal of Applied Behavioral Science* 20 (1984), 441-454.

Slowik, Stanley M. "The Manager as Moralist." *Management World* 10 (October 1981), 25-28.

Smith, H. R., and Archie B. Carroll. "Organizational Ethics: A Stacked Deck." *Journal of Business Ethics* 3 (May 1984), 95-100.

Sockell, Diana. "Attitudes, Behavior, and Employee Ownership." *Industrial Relations (Berkeley)* 24 (Winter 1985), 130-138.

Solberg, S. L. "Changing Culture Through Ceremony: An Example From GM." *Human Resource Management* 24 (Fall 1985), 329-340.

Soothill, Keith. "The Extent of Risk in Employing Ex-Prisoners." *Personnel Management* 13 (April 1981), 35-37.

Sorensen, Allan C. "Controlling Our Needs in a Changing Work Force." *Office* 95 (January 1982), 123-124.

"Speakers Blast Corporate Misuse of Pension Plans." *Employee Benefit Plan Review* 38 (November 1983), 60-62.

Spooner, Peter. "The Two Faces of Business Morality." *Chief Executive (UK)* (March 1981), 15-17.

Spruell, Geraldine R. "Daytime Drama: Love in the Office." *Training and Development Journal* 39 (February 1985), 21-26.

Steele, Paul D., and Robert L. Hubbard. "Management Styles, Perceptions of Substance Abuse, and Employee Assistance Programs in Organizations." *Journal of Applied Behavioral Science* 21 (1985), 271-286.

Sturdivant, Frederick D., James L. Ginter, and Alan G. Sawyer. "Managers' Conservatism and Corporate Performance." *Strategic Management Journal* 6 (January-March 1985), 17-38.

Sullivan, Roger J. "A Response to 'Is Business Bluffing Ethical?' " *Business and Professional Ethics Journal* 3 (Winter 1984), 1-18). Commentaries: by Van C. Langley, 19; Donald C. Powell, 23.

Sussman, Lyle, Penny Ricchio, and James Belohlav. "Corporate Speeches as a Source of Corporate Values: An Analysis Across Years, Themes and Industries." *Strategic Management Journal* 4 (April-June 1983), 187-196.

Sutton, Robert I. "Managing Organizational Death." *Human Resource Management* 22 (Winter 1983), 391-412.

Szwajkowski, Eugene. "Organizational Illegality: Theoretical Integration and Illustrative Application." *Academy of Management Review* 10 (July 1985), 558-567.

Terry, P. "Organization and the Search for Community." *Leadership and Organizational Development Journal* 2 (1981), 13-16.

Thackray, John. "America's Management Mischief." *Management Today* 14 (February 1985), 80-84+.

Thackray, John. "The New Organization Man." *Management Today* 11 (September 1981), 74-77.

Thomas, Michael. "In Search of Culture: Holy Grail or Gravy Train?" *Personnel Management (UK),* (September 1985), 24-27.

Tinsley, Dillard B., and Michael F. d'Amico. "Cutting Management's Kudzu Vines." *Akron Business & Economic Review* 12 (Summer 1981), 35-39.

Turk, Harry N., and Robert K. Strauss. "Can Companies Regulate Marriage and Work? A Look at Antinepotism Policies in Corporate America." *Employment Relations Today* 11 (Winter 1984-85), 371-376.

Useem, Michael. "Classwide Rationality in the Politics of Managers and Directors of Large Corporations." *Administrative Science Quarterly* 27 (June 1982), 199-226.

Uttal, Bro. "The Corporate Culture Vultures." *Fortune* 108 (October 17, 1983), 66-72.

Vagts, Detlev F. "CEOs and Their Lawyers: Tension Strains the Link." *Harvard Business Review* 59 (March-April 1981), 6-8.

Vaughan, Diane. "Transaction Systems and Unlawful Organizational Behavior." *Social Problems* 29 (April 1982), 373-379.

Velasquez, Manuel G., S.J., Dennis J. Moberg, and Gerald F. Cavanagh. "Organizational Statesmanship and Dirty Politics: Ethical Guidelines for the Organizational Politician." *Organizational Dynamics* 12 (Autumn 1983), 65-80.

Veysey, Victor V. "Comparable Worth: What Is Management Doing?" *Advanced Management Journal* 50 (Summer 1985), 38-41.

Wagoner, S. S. "Pension Accounting: The Liability Controversy." *Management Accounting* 67 (July 1985), 54-57.

Wallace, Douglas. "John Le Carre: The Dark Side of Organizations." *Harvard Business Review* 63 (January-February 1985), 6-7+.

Walter, Gordon A. "Organizational Development and Individual Rights." *Journal of Applied Behavioral Science* 20 (November 1984), 423-439.

Waters, James A., and Peter D. Chant. "Internal Control of Managerial Integrity: Beyond Accounting Systems." *California Management Review* 24 (Spring 1982), 60-66.

Weber, James. "Institutionalizing Ethics into the Corporation." *MSU Business Topics* 29 (Spring 1981), 47-52.

Weiss, W. H. "Supervising Employees with Personality Problems." *Supervisory Management* 28 (February 1983), 8-13.

Weitzul, James B. "Fostering Employee Loyalty." *Best's Review* 82 (September 1981), 104.

Wente, M. A. "Golden Bullets." *Canadian Business* 55 (August 1982), 49-52.

Werhane, Patricia H. "Formal Organizations, Economic Freedom, and Moral Agency." *University of Dayton Review* 15 (Winter 1981-82), 33-39.

Werner, Gerald C. "O.D. Also Stands for Organizational Deception." *Manage* 33 (April 1981), 2-5.

Whieldon, David. "Ethics: MIS/DP's New Challenge." *Computer Decisions* 16 (October 1984), 92-110.

White, Louis P., and Kevin C. Wooten. "Ethical Dilemmas in Various Stages of Organizational Development." *Academy of Management Review* 8 (October 1983), 690-697.

White, Peter. "The Psychology of Pay—The Relationship Between Management Cultures and Remuneration Systems." *Benefits & Compensation International* 15 (September 1985), 23-27.

Wiener, Yoash. "Commitment in Organizations: A Normative View." *Academy of Management Review* 7 (July 1982), 418-428.

Williams, John D. "Buyouts Made with ESOPs Are Criticized." *Wall Street Journal* (February 21, 1984), 35.

Willimon, William H. "A Labor Day Reflection on the Work Ethic." *Christian Century* 100 (August 31, 1983), 776-778.

Willmer, Michael, and Jack Keiser. "The Ethics of Deviousness." *Manchester Business School Review* 6 (Summer-Autumn 1982), 11-15.

Wilson, Glenn T. "Ethics: Your Company or Your Conscience?" *Working Woman* 9 (June 1984), 62+.

Wilson, Glenn T. "Solving Ethical Problems and Saving Your Career." *Business Horizons* 26 (November-December 1983), 16-20.

Wintour, P. "Management by Stick and Carrot." *New Statesman* 102 (October 30, 1981), 102-104+.

Wise, Deborah, C., and Geoffrey C. Lewis. "A Split That's Sapping Morale at Apple." *Business Week (Ind./Tech. Ed.)* (March 11, 1985), 106, 108.

Woodworth, W. "Promethean Relations; Labor, ESOPs and the Boardroom." *Labor Law Journal* 36 (August 1985), 618-624.

Wooten, Kevin C., and Louis P. White. "Ethical Problems in the Practice of Organization Development." *Training and Development Journal* 37 (April 1983), 16-23.

Work, Clemens P., et al. "The New Star System: Executive Pay Goes Sky-High." *U.S. News and World Report* 98 (April 29, 1985), 60-65.

Wright, Donald K. "Men, Women and Social Responsibility." *Public Relations Journal* 39 (August 1983), 27-29.

Yankelovich, Daniel, and John Immerwahr. "The Changing American Workplace—Putting the Work Ethic to Work." *Technology Review* 86 (November-December 1983), 13, 16-17.

Yankelovich, Daniel, and John Immerwahr. "Management and the Work Ethic." *Directors & Boards* 8 (Fall 1983), 41-45.

Yao, Margaret. "Manager's Miseries: Middle-Aged Officials Find New Group Hit by Slump." *Wall Street Journal* (September 1, 1982), 1.

Yorks, Lyle, and David A. Whitsett. "Hawthorne, Topeka, and the Issue of Science Versus Advocacy in Organizational Behavior." *Academy of Management Review* 10 (January 1985), 21-30.

Zahra, Shaker A. "Background and Work Experience Correlates of the Ethics and Effect of Organizational Politics." *Journal of Business Ethics* 4 (October 1985), 419-423.

Zahra, Shaker A. "Managerial Views of Organizational Politics." *Management Quarterly* 25 (Spring 1984), 31-37.

Zemke, R. "Stalking the Elusive Corporate Credo." *Training* 22 (June 1985), 44-51.

Zey-Ferrell, Mary, and O. C. Ferrell. "Role-Set Configuration and Opportunity as Predictors of Unethical Behavior in Organizations." *Human Relations* 35 (July 1982), 587-604.

Zimmerman, Joel S. "The Human Side of Computer Security." *Computer Security Journal* 3 (Summer 1984), 7-19.

Zollers, Frances E. "Criminal Liability of Officers and Directors." *Indiana Business Review* 56 (August 1981), 29-33.

Zubrzycki, J. "Challenges of Change." *Practising Manager* 4 (October 1983), 9-19.

Plant Closings and Business Failure

Books

Davis, Lawrence J. *Bad Money*. New York: St. Martin's Press, 1982.

Hamer, John G. *Troubled Debt Restructuring: An Alternative to Bankruptcy*. Ann Arbor, Mich.: UMI Research Press, 1985.

Plant Closings: What Can Be Learned from Best Practice. Washington, D.C.: U.S. Dept. of Labor, 1982.

Platt, Harlan. *Why Companies Fail: Strategies for Detecting, Avoiding and Profiting from Bankruptcy*. Lexington, Mass.: Lexington Books, 1985.

Singer, Mark. *Funny Money*. New York: Knopf, 1985.

Wintner, Linda. *Employee Buyouts: An Alternative to Plant Closings*. New York: Conference Board, 1983.

Articles

Bailey, Jeff. "Continental Illinois Blames 3 Ex-Officers in Report on Penn Square Loan Purchases." *Wall Street Journal* (July 23, 1984), 3.

Bleiberg, Robert M. "Life After Lilco?" *Barron's* 64 (July 2, 1984), 9.

Blustein, Paul. "Ambrosiano's Fallout on International Banking." *Wall Street Journal* (September 1, 1982), 14.

Carrington, Tim. "Continental Scare Prompts Search for New Ways to Avert Bank Crisis." *Wall Street Journal* (June 11, 1984), 27.

Cifelli, Anna. "Management by Bankruptcy." *Fortune* 108 (October 31, 1983), 69-72.

"Closing Notice." *Wall Street Journal* (August 31, 1982), 1.

"Closing Shop: A Kentucky Plant Becomes a Model for 'Good' Plant Closings." *Wall Street Journal* (April 12, 1983), 1.

Colvin, Geoffrey. "How Sick Companies Are Endangering the Pension System." *Fortune* 106 (October 4, 1982), 72-74+.

Compa, Lance. "Fighting Back: Workers Challenge Plant Shutdowns." *Progressive* 49 (October 1985), 32-34.

Corrigan, Richard. "Workers and Weirton Steel See Only One Way to Save Their Failing Plant: Buy It." *National Journal* 15 (August 13, 1983), 1672-1679.

Eves, James H., Jr. "When a Plant Shuts Down: Easing the Pain." *Personnel* 62 (February 1985), 16-23.

Forbes, Daniel. "The No-Layoff Payoff." *Dun's Business Month* 126 (July 1985), 64-66.

Fulmer, William E. "Plant Closing: The Need for Compassionate Strategic Decisions." *Advanced Management Journal* 50 (Winter 1985), 20-25.

Gini, A. R. "Manville: The Ethics of Economic Efficiency?" *Journal of Business Ethics* 3 (February 1984), 63-70.

Gupta, U. "Standing on Shaky Ground." *Venture* 7 (April 1985), 66+.

Hill, G. C. "Penn Square Insiders Express Surprise at Failure, but Auditors Warned in May." *Wall Street Journal* (August 17, 1982), 6.

Janzen, L. T. "Company Rescue—An Example." *Long Range Planning* 16 (December 1983), 88-93.

Johnston, Philip D. "Personnel Planning for a Plant Shutdown." *Personnel Administrator* 26 (August 1981), 53-57.

Konrad, W. "Battered But Not Broken." *Working Woman* 10 (October 1985), 66+.

"Major Losses from a Plant Shutdown Are Turned into Gains." *World of Work Report* 7 (October 1982), 75-76.

McKenzie, Richard B. "Case for Plant Closures." *Policy Review* 15 (Winter 1981), 119-133.

McMahon, Philip. "Employee Response to Receivership." *Management Accounting (UK)* 59 (November 1981), 30-31.

Murphy, B. S. "Plant Closings: Cases," *Personnel Journal* 64 (November 1985), 22+.

Murphy, Thomas P. "When the Game Is Over." *Forbes* 130 (December 20, 1982), 180.

Nag, Amal. "Creditors Say DeLorean Data to Assist Claims." *Wall Street Journal* (December 29, 1983), 4.

Paltrow, Scot J. "DeLorean Is Acquitted on All Counts in Cocaine-Smuggling Conspiracy Case." *Wall Street Journal* (August 17, 1984), 3.

Paltrow, Scot J. "DeLorean's Chances of Being Acquitted Hinge on Credibility of Witness for U.S." *Wall Street Journal* (April 16, 1984), 12.

Rawlings, Charles W. "U.S. Steel vs. the People: Buying and Selling in Pittsburgh." *Christianity and Crisis* 42 (March 29, 1982), 75-80.

Rhine, Barbara. "Business Closings and Their Effects on Employees—The Need for New Remedies." *Labor Law Journal* 35 (May 1984), 268-280.

Rotbart, Dean. "Braniff Proposes Settlement Plan Under Chapter 11." *Wall Street Journal* (January 5, 1983), 2.

Rotbart, Dean. "Conflicting Claims: Manville Corporation Faces Increasing Opposition to Bankruptcy Failing." *Wall Street Journal* (January 31, 1984), 1+.

Sculnick, Michael W. "Resolving the Conflict Between the Bankruptcy and Labor Laws." *Employment Relations Today* 11 (Spring 1984), 3-12.

Sease, Douglas R. "ESOPs Weren't Meant to Be Bailouts." *Wall Street Journal* (December 12, 1985), 20.

Symonds, W. C. "A Steelmaker Tests the Bankrupcy Weapon." *Business Week* (July 1, 1985), 28-29.

Teague, Carroll H. "Easing the Pain of Plant Closure: The Brown and Williamson Experience." *Management Review* 70 (April 1981), 23-27.

Van Dam, Laura. "128's Layoff Season Threatens the Morale of Remaining Workers." *New England Business* 7 (July 1, 1985), 33-35.

Verespej, Michael A. "May a Profitable Firm Duck Its Liabilities?" *Industry Week* 214 (September 20, 1982), 17-18.

"What's a Continental Worth?" *Wall Street Journal* (July 26, 1984), 26.

"Why Edward Lloyd Is Turning in His Grave." *Economist* 285 (December 11, 1982), 93-94.

Wintour, P. "Law May Stop Workers' Sit-In." *New Statesman* 101 (May 8, 1981), 4.

Professional Responsibility

Books

Baumrin, Bernard H., and Benjamin Freedman. *Moral Responsibility and the Professions*. New York: Haven, 1983.

Bowman, James S., et al. *Professional Ethics: Dissent in Organizations, an Annotated Bibliography and Resource Guide*. New York: Garland Pub. Inc., 1984.

Camenisch, Paul F. *Grounding Professional Ethics in a Pluralistic Society*. New York: Haven Publishing Co., 1983.

Elliston, Frederick A. *Professional Dissent: An Annotated Bibliography and Resource Guide*. New York: Garland Pub. Inc., 1985.

Labacqz, Karen. *Professional Ethics: Power and Paradox*. Nashville: Abingdon, 1985.

Martin, Mike W., and Roland Schinzinger. *Ethics in Engineering*. New York: McGraw-Hill, 1983.

Merton, Robert. *Social Research and the Practicing Professions*. Cambridge, Mass.: Abt Books, 1982.

Phillips, Michael, and Salli Rasberry. *Honest Business: A Superior*

Strategy for Starting and Managing Your Own Business. San Francisco: Clear Glass Pub. Co., 1981.

Schaub, James H., Karl Pavlovic, and Michael D. Morris. *Engineering Professionalism and Ethics.* New York: Wiley, 1983.

Articles

Alpern, Kenneth D. "Moral Responsibility for Engineers." *Business and Professional Ethics Journal* 2 (Winter 1983), 39-48). Commentaries: by Andrew Oldenquist, 49; Samuel C. Florman, 53.

Alt, Susan J. "Ethical Questions: Risk Managers Must Learn to Walk a Fine Line." *Business Insurance* 16 (March 29, 1982), 17-18.

Bernzweig, Eli P. "A Client's Rights, a Planner's Duties." *Financial Planning* 13 (June 1985), 153-156.

Boland, Richard J., Jr. "Organizational Control, Organizational Power and Professional Responsibility." *Business and Professional Ethics Journal* 2 (Fall 1982), 15-25. Commentaries: by Charles T. Hutchinson, 27; John Ladd, 31.

Broadway, D. L. "Ethics Committee Develops Guidelines for the Professional Risk Manager." *Risk Management* 32 (October 1985), 81-82.

Burke, Maureen H. "The Duty of Confidentiality and Disclosing Corporate Misconduct." *Business Lawyer* 36 (January 1981), 239-295.

"Capital Offense: How *Washington Post* and the Pulitzer Board Were Duped by Writer." *Wall Street Journal* (April 17, 1981), 1.

Crisafulli, Nino D. "Discordant Notes." *Best's Review (Property/Casualty)* 85 (June 1984), 40, 42.

Crosby, Phillip B. "Confessions of a Sinner: I Waived Material." *Purchasing* 99 (September 12, 1985), 106A41.

Danco, Jeffrey C. "The Ethics of Fee Practices: An Analysis of Presuppositions and Accountability." *Journal of Psychology and Theology* 10 (Spring 1982), 13-21.

Davis, Michael. "Conflict of Interest." *Business and Professional Ethics Journal* 1 (Summer 1982), 17-27. Commentary: by William Snead, 29.

Dixon, J. D., and B.G.S. James. "The Honesty of the Technical Salesman." *Management Decision* 22 (1984), 47-52.

Dowst, Somerby. "Are Your Standards Changing With the Times?" *Purchasing* 91 (September 24, 1981), 84A9.

Ellin, Joseph S. "Special Professional Morality and the Duty of Veracity." *Business and Professional Ethics Journal* 1 (Winter 1982), 75-90. Commentary: by Milton Lunch, 91.

English, William. "The Moral Component of Our Professional Challenge." *Professional Safety* 30 (March 1985), 15-19.

Fallows, James. "The Case Against Credentialism." *Atlantic Monthly* 256 (December 1985), 49-67.

Flores, Albert, and Deborah G. Johnson. "Collective Responsibility and Professional Roles." *Ethics* 93 (April 1983), 537-545.

Free, W. T. "Ethics: American Society of CLU Style." *National Underwriter (Life/Health)* 89 (October 21, 1985), 537-545.

Freedman, David H. "Ethics: Who Decides Right from Wrong?" *Infosystems* 30 (August 1983), 34-36.

Friedman, Herbert V. "Ethics and the Life Underwriter." *National Underwriter (Life/Health)* 87 (October 17, 1983), 26, 48-49.

Fuke, John M. "Can Tax Advisers Successfully Serve Two Masters?" *CA Magazine (Canada)* 118 (March 1985), 32-37.

Gahala, Charles L. "Do You Measure Up? The Credit Exec as a Professional." *Credit & Financial Management* 87 (April 1985), 13-14.

Gantser, D. C. "Professional Ethic and Performance: A Re-Examination." *Psychological Reports* 48 (February 1981), 335-338.

Garcia, Arthur. "Journalism Contests: Ethical or Corrupt?" *Communication World* 1 (June 1984), 22-24.

Gert, Bernard. "Licensing Professions: Preliminary Considerations." *Business and Professional Ethics Journal* 1 (Summer 1982), 51-60. Commentary: by Donald Weinert, 61.

Gibbins, Michael. "Easing the Tension Between Professional Judgment and Standards." *CA Magazine (Canada)* 116 (May 1983), 38-43.

Graham, Fred. "Keeping Professional Ethics Professional." *Nebraska Humanist* 7 (Fall 1984), 14-19.

Gross, Laurence H. "Refining the Financial Planner." *Financial Planner* 12 (November 1983), 28-33.

Hall, Ridgway M., Jr. "Recent Developments in Professional Liability Affecting Corporate Environmental Lawyers." *Business Lawyer* 36 (January 1981), 461-483.

Head, George. "On Risk Management: Professional Questions." *National Underwriter (Property/Casualty)* 87 (April 22, 1983), 41, 46-47.

Heide, Dorothy, and James K. Hightower. "Organizations, Ethics and the Computing Professional." *Journal of Systems Management* 34 (November 1983), 38-42.

Hollander, Rachelle. "Conference Report: Engineering Ethics." *Science, Technology and Human Values* 8 (Winter 1983), 25-29.

Kipnis, Kenneth. "Professional Responsibility and the Responsibility of Professions." *University of Dayton Review* 15 (Winter 1981-82), 69-78.

Kultgen, John. "The Ideological Use of Professional Codes." *Business and Professional Ethics Journal* 1 (Spring 1982), 53-59. Commentary: by Robin Alexander-Smith, 71.

Laney, James T. "Moralizing the Professions: Commitment to the Public Interest." *Vital Speeches of the Day* 51 (June 1, 1985), 501-503.

Laurendeau, Normand M. "Engineering Professionalism: The Case for Corporate Ombudsmen." *Business and Professional Ethics Journal* 2 (Fall 1982) 35-42. Commentaries: by Michael R. Rion, 47; Albert J. Fritsch, 49.

Layton, Edwin T., Jr. "Engineering Needs a Loyal Opposition: An Essay Review." *Business and Professional Ethics Journal* 2 (Spring 1982), 51-60. Commentary: by Robert M. Anderson, et al., 61.

Levy, Michael, and Alan J. Dubinsky. "Identifying and Addressing Retail Salespersons' Ethical Problems: A Method of Application." *Journal of Retailing* 59 (Spring 1983), 46-66.

Lichter, Barry D., and Michael P. Hodges. "Perceptions of the Engineers' 'Professionalism' in the Chemical Industry." *Business and Professional Ethics Journal* 1 (Winter 1983), 1-8. Commentaries: by John D. Leckie, 9; Milton S. Gross, 11; Alan C. Nixon, 15.

Long, Thomas A. "Informed Consent and Engineering: An Essay Review." *Business and Professional Ethics Journal* 3 (Fall 1983), 59-66. Commentary: by Roland Schinzinger and Mike W. Martin, 67.

MacKenzie, Ian. "Deception Deserves No Role in Life Sales." *National Underwriter (Life/Health)* 87 (November 26, 1983), 2-33.

Maupin, Michael W. "Environmental Law, the Corporate Lawyer and the Model Rules of Professional Conduct." *Business Lawyer* 36 (January 1981), 431-460.

May, Cathy. "Moonlighting—It's a Question of DP Ethics." *Data Management* 23 (March 1985), 10.

May, Larry. "Professional Action and the Liabilities of Professional Associations: A.S.M.E. v. Hydrolevel Corp." *Business and Professional Ethics Journal* 2 (Fall 1982), 1-14.

McCammond, Donald B. "The Growth of Ethical Awareness." *Public Relations Journal* 41 (February 1985), 8-9.

McDermott, Jack C. "Professional?—'We Must Earn the Title.' " *Journal of Information and Image Management* 18 (May 1985), 20-22.

Merz, C. M., and David F. Groebner. "Ethics and the CPA in Industry." *Management Accounting* 64 (September 1982), 44-48.

Namorato, Cono R., and Scott D. Michel. "Criminal Exposure of the Tax Practitioner—An Increasing Risk." *Practical Accountant* 18 (February 1985), 41-50.

Newton, Lisa H. "Lawgiving for Professional Life: Reflections on the Place of the Professional Code." *Business and Professional Ethics Journal* 1 (Fall 1981), 41-51. Commentary: by Donald E. Wilson, 55.

Newton, Lisa H. "The Origin of Professionalism: Sociological Conclusions and Ethical Implications." *Business and Professional Ethics Journal* 1 (Summer 1982), 33-43. Commentary: by Bernadine Z. Paulshock, 45.

Porter, Margo V. "The Ethical Dilemma: What's Right? What's Wrong?" *Association Management* 33 (October 1981), 77-80.

Potter, Nelson. "Professional Ethics." *Nebraska Humanist* 7 (Fall 1984), 3-13.

Razza, Joseph C., Jr. "Ethics." *Life Association News* 79 (May 1984), 88-94.

Razza, Joseph C., Jr. "Here's What NALU Members Say About Ethics." *Life Association News* 79 (May 1984), 88-98.

Rich, Anne J. "The Controller Who Said No." *Management Accounting* 66 (February 1985), 34-36.

Rohr, John A. "The Problem of Professional Ethics." *Bureaucrat* 11 (Summer 1982), 47-50.

Salvona, W. J. "Limiting Conditions, or, Don't Compromise Your Reputation by Being Mr. Nice Guy." *Appraisal Institute Magazine* 25 (May 1981), 6-7.

Schaefer, Thomas E. "Professionalism: Foundation for Business Ethics." *Journal of Business Ethics* 3 (November 1984), 269-277.

Schilit, Howard M. "Deviant Behavior and Misconduct of Professionals." *Woman CPA* 46 (April 1984), 20-24.

Schneider, Karen, and Marc Gunther. "Those Newsroom Ethics Codes." *Columbia Journalism Review* 24 (July-August 1985), 55-57.

Schultz, Brad. "Would Certification Ensure 'Moral' DP Staff?" *Computerworld* 15 (September 21, 1981), 11.

Seavey, John. "Ok, God, I Guess You Want Me to Change . . ." *Across the Board* 21 (March 1984), 9.

Seigel, Michael. "Use of Privileged Information for Attorney Self-Interest: A Moral Dilemma." *Business and Professional Ethics Journal* 3 (Fall 1983), 1-11.

Shrader-Frechette, Kristin. "Engineering Ethics." *IEEE Spectrum* 21 (June 1984), 10.

Slattery, T. J. "Time to Reinvent the Insurance Business?" *National Underwriter (Property/Casualty)* 89 (November 22, 1985), 64-65.

Stanger, Abraham M. "The Arthur Young Decision—The Auditor's Dilemma." *Corporation Law Review* 7 (Fall 1984), 374-378.

Stewart, W. T., and Dennis J. Paustenbach. "Analysis Techniques Help IEs Evaluate Ethical Dimensions of On-the-Job Decisions." *Industrial Distribution* 71 (March 1981), 71.

"Study Suggests Ethical Awareness Is Greater Among Marketers Than Financial, Production Vice President." *Marketing News* 17 (June 10, 1983), 11.

Stybel, Laurence J. "Some Job Counselors Leave Clients in the Lurch." *New England Business* 7 (September 2, 1985), 83, 85.

Summers, James W. "Doing Good and Doing Well: Ethics, Professionalism, and Success." *Hospital & Health Services Administration* 29 (March-April 1984), 84-100.

Thomas, Julia. "Ethics and Professionalism: The Integrated Way." *Vital Speeches of the Day* 49 (July 1, 1983), 558-562.

Von Glinow, Mary Ann, and Luke Novelli, Jr. "Ethical Standards Within Organizational Behavior." *Academy of Management Journal* 25 (June 1982), 417-436.

Waldo, Charles. "In Selling—It's the Little Things That Count." *Industrial Distribution* 7 (March 1981), 71.

Walters, James J. "Foundations of the Professions and of Professional Ethics: A Critical and Constructive Study." *Horizons* 12 (Spring 1985), 91-115.

Walters, Jonathan. "Can an Association Uphold a Code of Ethics in the Eighties?" *Association Management* 35 (October 1983), 62-67.

Weber, Austin. "Ethics, Conduct Standards Brand Real Professionals." *Data Management* 23 (May 1985), 12-13.

Wermiel, Stephen. "ABA Rejects Proposed Ethics Guideline Designed to Encourage Whistleblowing." *Wall Street Journal* (February 8, 1983), 6.

Whinney, John. "PSC—The Gentle Disciplinarian." *Accountancy* 94 (December 1983), 104-106.

Williams, Kathy. "George E. Smith: Let Ethics Guide Your Decisions." *Management Accounting* 66 (February 1985), 18-22.

Wilson, William T. "Business Conduct, Public Responsibility and Regulation." *Life Association News* 79 (May 1984), 65-70.

Quality of Worklife

Books

Gustavsen, Bjorn, and Gerry Hunnius. *New Patterns of Work Reform.* New York: Columbia Univ. Press, 1981.

Hochschild, Arlie R. *The Managed Heart.* Berkeley, Calif.: Univ. California Press, 1983.

Howard, Robert. *Brave New Workplace.* New York: Viking, 1985.

Levering, Robert, Milton Moskowitz, and Michael Katz. *The Best 100 Companies to Work for in America.* Reading, Mass.: Addison-Wesley, 1984.

Lloyd, Tom. *Dinosaur & Co.* London, U.K.: Routledge & Kegan Paul, 1984.

Masi, Dale A. *Human Services in Industry.* Lexington, Mass.: Lexington Books, 1982.

Meltzer, H., and Walter R. Nord. *Making Organizations Humane and Productive: A Handbook for Practitioners.* New York: Wiley, 1981.

Skrovan, Daniel J., ed. *Quality of Work Life: Perspectives for Business and the Public Sector.* Reading, Mass.: Addison-Wesley, 1983.

Stoddart, L., ed. *Conditions of Work and Quality of Working Life: A Directory of Institutions.* Washington, D.C.: International Labour Office, 1981.

Articles

Bowman, James S. "Altering the Fabric of Work: Beyond the Behavioral Sciences." *Business Horizons* 27 (September-October 1984), 42-48.

Braun, Jerome. "Industrial Justice in a Practical Sense." *Review of Social Economy* 42 (December 1984), 318-327.

Colwill, Nina L., and Marilyn Erhart. "Have Women Changed in the Workplace?" *Business Quarterly* 50 (Spring 1985), 27-31.

"Computers and Motivation in the Workplace." *Management Services (UK)* 29 (March 1985), 34-35.

Danner, Peter L. "The Moral Foundations of Community." *Review of Social Economy* 42 (December 1984), 231-251.

D'Arcy, Carl, et al. "Perceived Job Attributes, Job Satisfaction, and Psychological Distress: A Comparison of Working Men and Women." *Human Relations* 37 (August 1984), 603-611.

"Discussion of Fuller and Jonsson Paper [on Quality of Work Life]." *Journal of Business Ethics* 1 (May 1982), 127-130.

Douglas, Martin. "Reflections From the Assembly Line." *Business and Society Review* 42 (Summer 1982), 44-47.

"Employee Alienation or Alignment?" *Infosystems* 30 (August 1983), 42-43.

Felts, Charlie. "Ethical Considerations in Employee Participation Groups." *Quality Circle Digest* (April 1985), 22-24.

Finn, Peter. "The Effects of Shift Work on the Lives of Employees." *Monthly Labor Review* 104 (October 1981), 31-35.

Foegen, J. H. "Job Socializing: 'Endangered Species'?" *Industrial Management* 26 (July-August 1984), 10-12.

"Frustration in the Workplace: Its Effects on Productivity." *Journal of Micrographics* 15 (March 1982), 16-21.

Graber, Jim M. "Let's Get a Handle on Quality of Work Life." *Supervisory Management* 28 (June 1983), 25-34.

Henson, Ronald C. "Coping with Fluctuating Work-Force Requirements." *Employment Relations Today* 12 (Summer 1985), 149-156.

Hitt, Michael A., Orley M. Amos, Jr., and Larkin Warner. "Social Factors and Company Location Decisions: Technology, Quality of Life and Quality of Worklife Concerns." *Journal of Business Ethics* 2 (May 1983), 89-98.

Hoyt, Kenneth B. "Getting to Work." *Training and Development Journal* 38 (September 1984), 71-80.

Jonsson, Berth. "The Quality of Work Life—The Volvo Experience." *Journal of Business Ethics* 1 (May 1982), 119-126.

Kamata, Satoshi, "Employee Welfare Takes a Back Seat at Toyota." *Business and Society Review* 46 (Summer 1983), 26-31.

Laberis, Bill. "Job Frustration Seen Incubator for DP Crime." *Computerworld* 15 (October 12, 1981), 25.

Lindo, David K. "Are You Polluting Your Work Environment?" *Managing* 3 (1982), 4, 37.

Macleod, Jennifer S. "Some Thoughts on Power, Powerlessness, and

Productivity." *Employment Relations Today* 10 (Winter 1983-1984), 373-377.

Macleod, Jennifer S. "The Work Place as Prison." *Employment Relations Today* 12 (Autumn 1985), 215-218.

Mankin, Don, Tora K. Bikson, and Barbara Gutek. "Office of the Future: Prison or Paradise?" *Futurist* 16 (June 1982), 33-36.

Miles, Mary. "Disgruntled Employees." *Computer Decisions* 15 (October 1983), 210-214.

Motowidlo, Stephan J. "Does Job Satisfaction Lead to Consideration and Personal Sensitivity?" *Academy of Management Journal* 27 (December 1984), 910-915.

Natale, Samuel M. "Endless Corridors: The Stress of Organizational and Industrial Life." *Thought* 58 (September 1983), 263-273.

Neffa, Julio C. "Improvement of Working Conditions and Environment." *International Labour Review* 120 (July-August 1981), 473-490.

Oates, David. "Forecasters Focus on the People Factor." *International Management* 36 (April 1981), 10-14.

"The Quality of Work Life." *National Forum* 62 (Spring 1982), 2-28.

Renfro, William L. "Second Thoughts on Moving the Office Home." *Futurist* 16 (June 1982), 43-45.

Rice, Robert W., et al. "Organizational Work and the Perceived Quality of Life: Toward a Conceptual Model." *Academy of Management Review* 10 (April 1985), 296-310.

Robinson, Donald A. "IEs Must Consider Ergonomic, Work Area Issues to Overcome Problems with VDTs." *Industrial Engineering* 16 (December 1984), 58-61.

Rosow, Jerome M. "Quality of Work Life Issues for the 1980s." *Training and Development Journal* 35 (March 1981), 33-52.

Shamir, B., and I. Salomon. "Work-at-Home and the Quality of Working Life." *Academy of Management Review* 10 (July 1985), 455-464.

Singer, G. "Quality of Life in Shift Work." *Human Resource Management (Australia)* 20 (November 1982), 29-32.

Thompson, Walt. "Is the Organization Ready for Quality Circles?" *Training and Development Journal* 36 (December 1982), 115+.

"Tough Economy Forcing Americans Back to 'Old Morality.' " *Marketing News* 15 (May 28, 1982), 6, 9.

Wakin, Edward. "Quality of Work Life: Labor's Love Found." *Today's Office* 18 (July 1983), 34-40.

Research and Development

Books

Abbey, Augustus. *Technological Innovation: The R & D Work Environment.* Ann Arbor, Mich.: UMI Research Press, 1982.

Sahal, Devendra, ed. *Research, Development, and Technological Innovation: Recent Perspectives on Management.* Lexington, Mass.: Lexington Books, 1980.

Spanner, Robert A. *Who Owns Innovation: The Rights and Obligations of Employers and Employees.* Homewood, Ill.: Dow Jones-Irwin, 1984.

Articles

"Animals in Testing: How the CPI Is Handling a Hot Issue." *Chemical Week* 135 (December 5, 1984), 36-40.

Ashford, Nicholas. "A Framework for Examining the Effects of Industrial Funding on Academic Freedom and the Integrity of the University." *Science, Technology, and Human Values* 8 (Spring 1983), 16-23.

Bach, M. L., and R. Thornton. "Academic-Industrial Partnerships in Biomedical Research: Inevitability and Desirability." *Educational Record* 64 (Spring 1983), 26-32.

Bozeman, Barry, and Albert Link. "Public Support for Private R & D: The Case of the Research Tax Credit." *Journal of Policy Analysis and Management* 4 (Spring 1985), 370-382.

"Business and Universities: A New Partnership." *Business Week* (December 20, 1982), 58-62.

Caldart, Charles C. "Industry Investment in University Research." *Science, Technology and Human Values* 8 (Spring 1983), 24-32.

"Conflict of Interest on the American Campus." *Economist* 283 (May 22, 1982), 107-108.

"Corporations Bet on Campus R & D." *Business Week* (December 20, 1982), 61-62.

Dagani, Ron. "In-Vitro Methods May Offer Alternatives to Animal Testing." *Chemical and Engineering News* 62 (November 12, 1984), 25-28.

David, Edward E., Jr. "The University-Academic Connection in Research: Corporate Purposes and Social Responsibility." *Social Research Administration Journal* 14 (Fall 1982), 5-12.

"Defense Marketers Get a Jump on New Business with I R & D." *Business Marketing* 70 (July 1985), 42+.

Ellifritt, Duane S. "Research Amid Vested Interests: Whose Truth Is Truest?" *Engineering Education* 74 (January 1984), 235-237.

Fingeret, A. "Who's in Control? A Case Study of University-Industry Collaboration." *New Directions in Cont. Education* 33 (1984), 39-63.

Foote, Edward T., II, and Jack R. Borsting. "Will Corporate Research Strangle University Independence?" *Business and Society Review* 53 (Spring 1985), 15-19.

Gibson, G. T. "Research for Sale." *Venture* 6 (March 1984), 78-86.

Hill, Judith M. "The University and Industrial Research: Selling Out?" *Business and Professional Ethics Journal* 2 (Summer 1983), 27-35. Commentary: by L. Leon Campbell, 37.

Horwitz, Bertrand, and Richard Kolodney. "Financial Reporting Regulation and Small Research-Intensive Firms." *Journal of Small Business Management* 20 (January 1982), 44-49.

Jacobson, R. L. "Industry's Emphasis on Profits Cited as Bar to Business-University Ties." *Chronicle of Higher Education* 24 (July 21, 1982), 3.

Krebs, Robert E. "A Dilemma: Scholarship vs. Entrepreneurship." *Social Research Administration* 15 (Spring 1984), 19-28.

Krimsky, Sheldon. "The Corporate Capture of Genetic Technologies." *Science for the People* 17 (May-June 1985), 32-37.

Large, Arlen J. "Of Mice and Men." *Wall Street Journal* (June 21, 1983), 60.

McDonald, Kim. "Commercialization of University Science Is Decried." *Chronicle of Higher Education* 23 (January 13, 1982), 9.

McDonald, Kim. "Company May Not Force Researchers to Reveal Results, Court Rules." *Chronicle of Higher Education* 24 (March 24, 1982), 3.

McDonald, Kim. "Plan for Private Research Institute Near MIT Draws Complaints." *Chronicle of Higher Education* 23 (October 14, 1981), 6.

McDonald, Kim. "Universities Urged to Bar Secrecy in Pacts With Private Industry." *Chronicle of Higher Education* 24 (April 7, 1982), 1+.

Norman, Colin. "Basic Research Questions at MIT: Should It Accept an Industrialist's Offer of a $120-Million Research Institute?" *Across the Board* 18 (December 1981), 71-73.

"Research Partnership: Hastening the Process of Discovery." *Enterprise* 7 (August 1983), 4-17.

Richards, Robin. "Animal Test Alternatives: A Progress Report." *Drug and Cosmetic Industry* 134 (April 1984), 24+.

Simpson, James R., and Bernard E. Rollin. "Economic Consequences of Animal Rights Programs." *Journal of Business Ethics* 3 (August 1984), 215-225.

Singer, Eleanor. "Public Reactions to Some Ethical Issues of Social Research: Attitudes and Behavior." *Journal of Consumer Research* 11 (June 1984), 501-509.

Sjoberg, Gideon, Ted R. Vaughan, and Andree F. Sjoberg. "Morals and Applied Behavioral Research: A Prefatory Essay." *Applied Behavioral Science* 20 (1984), 311-322.

Stevens, Christine. "Animal Torture in Corporate Dungeons." *Business and Society Review* 49 (Spring 1984), 39-43.

Therrien, Lois, et al. "Cruelty in the Lab: The Growing Outcry Against Animal Research." *Business Week* (December 10, 1984), 146D-146G.

Whistleblowing

Books

Beyond Whistleblowing: Defining Engineers' Responsibility. Chicago: Ill. Inst. of Tech., 1983.

Box, Steven, *Power, Crime and Mystification*. London, U.K.: Tavistock, 1983.

Elliston, Frederick, et al. *Whistleblowing: Managing Dissent in the Workplace*. New York: Praeger, 1985.

Mitchell, Greg. *Truth—and Consequences: Seven Who Would Not Be Silenced*. New York: Dembner Books, 1981.

Rashke, Richard L. *The Killing of Karen Silkwood: The Story Behind the Kerr-McGee Plutonium Case*. Boston: Houghton Mifflin, 1981.

Westin, Alan F., ed. *Whistle Blowing! Loyalty and Dissent in the Corporation*. New York; McGraw-Hill, 1981.

Articles

Amara, Roy, and Gregory Schmid. "Case of a Suspicious Scientist." *Harvard Business Review* 60 (September-October 1982), 6-14.

"Armor for Whistle-Blowers." *Business Week* (July 6, 1981), 97-98.

Bamford, J. "When Do You Blow the Whistle?" *Forbes* 136 (October 21, 1985), 166+.

Becker, G. S. "Tailoring Punishment to White-Collar Crime." *Business Week* (October 28, 1985), 20.

Bowman, James S., ed. "Whistle Blowing: Literature and Resource Materials." *Public Administration Review* 43 (May-June 1983), 271-276.

Cook, Daniel D. "Whistle-Blowers—Friend or Foe?" *Industry Week* 211 (October 5, 1981), 50-54, 56.

Deevy, William J. "Loyalty and Whistleblowing." *Nebraska Humanist* 7 (Fall 1984), 36-49.

Elliston, Frederick A. "Anonymity and Whistleblowing." *Journal of Business Ethics* 1 (August 1982), 167-177.

Elliston, Frederick A. "Anonymous Whistleblowing: An Ethical Analysis." *Business and Professional Ethics Journal* 1 (Winter 1982), 39-58. Commentary: by Robert Coulson, 59.

Elliston, Frederick. "Civil Disobedience and Whistleblowing: A Comparative Appraisal of Two Forms of Dissent." *Journal of Business Ethics* 1 (February 1982), 23-28.

Feretic, James J. "Blowing the Whistle on White Collar Crime." *Today's Office* 16 (February 1982), 52-55.

Glazer, Myron. "Ten Whistleblowers and How They Fared." *Hastings Center Report* 13 (December 1983), 33-41.

Hanrahan, John. "Whistleblower!" *Common Cause Magazine* 9 (March-April 1983), 16-23.

Jacobson, Michael, et al. "Is Whistle-Blowing the Same as Informing?" *Business and Society Review* 39 (Fall 1981), 4-17.

Johnson, Douglas A., et al. "Exposed or Cover-Up: Will an Employee Blow the Whistle?" *Management Accounting* 63 (July 1981), 32-36.

Karlen, N. "Nuclear-Powered Murder?" *Newsweek* 106 (November 4, 1985), 29.

Malin, Martin H. "Protecting the Whistleblower From Retaliatory Discharge." *University of Michigan Journal of Law Reform* 16 (Winter 1983), 1-47.

McGowan, William. "The Whistleblowers' Hall of Fame." *Business and Society Review* 52 (Winter 1985), 31-36.

Near, Janet P., and T. C. Jensen. "The Whistleblowing Process: Retaliation and Perceived Effectiveness." *Work and Occupations* 10 (February 1983), 3-28.

Near, Janet P., and Marcia P. Miceli. "Organizational Dissidence: The Case of Whistle-Blowing." *Journal of Business Ethics* 4 (February 1985), 1-16.

Parmerlee, Marcia A., Janet P. Near, and Tamila C. Jensen. "Correlates of Whistle-Blowers' Perceptions of Organizational Retaliation." *Administrative Science Quarterly* 27 (March 1982), 17-34.

Perry, Tekla S. "Knowing How to Blow the Whistle." *IEEE Spectrum* 18 (September 1981), 56-61.

Rosenstein, Jay. "An Insider's Guide to Whistleblowing." *NABW Journal* 61 (January-February 1985), 12-14.

Seligman, Daniel. "Rat Protection." *Fortune* 103 (May 18, 1981), 36.

Sheler, Jeffrey L. "When Employees Squeal on Fellow Workers." *U.S. News and World Report* 91 (November 16, 1981), 81-82.

"Whistle-Blowers: Heroes or Heels?" *Office* 102 (August 1985), 55.

White Collar Crime

Books

Albanese, Jay S. *Organizational Offenders: Why Solutions Fail to Political, Corporate, and Organized Crime.* Niagara Falls, N.Y.: Apocalypse Pub. Co., 1982.

Albrecht, W. S., et al. *How to Detect and Prevent Business Fraud.* Englewood Cliffs, N.J.: Prentice-Hall, 1982.

Bologna, Jack. *Corporate Fraud: The Basics of Prevention and Detection.* Boston: Butterworth, 1984.

Braithwaite, John. *Corporate Crime in the Pharmaceutical Industry.* London, U.K.: Routledge and Kegan Paul, 1984.

Carroll, John M. *Controlling White Collar Crime: Design and Audit for Systems Security.* London, U.K.: Butterworth Pub., 1982.

Clark, Douglas L. *Preventing Crime in Small Business.* Sunnyvale, Calif.: PSI Research, 1984.

Edelhertz, Herbert, and Thomas D. Overcast, eds. *White-Collar Crime: An Agenda for Research.* Lexington, Mass.: Lexington Books, 1982.

Fisse, Brent. *The Impact of Publicity on Corporate Offenders.* Albany: S.U.N.Y. Press, 1983.

Geis, Gilbert. *On White Collar Crime.* Lexington, Mass.: Lexington Books, 1982.

Glekel, Jeffrey. *Business Crimes: A Guide for Corporate and Defense Counsel.* New York: Practicing Law Inst., 1982.

Hollinger, Richard C., and John P. Clark. *Theft by Employees.* Lexington, Mass.: Lexington Books, 1983.

Leigh, L. H. *The Control of Commercial Fraud.* London, U.K.: Heinneman, 1982.

Levi, Michael. *The Phantom Capitalists: Control of Long-Firm Fraud.* London, U.K.: Heinneman, 1982.

Mars, Gerald. *Cheats at Work: An Anthropology of Workplace Crime.* London, U.K.: Allen & Unwin, 1983.

McCullough, William W. *Sticky Fingers: A Close Look at America's Fastest-Growing Crime.* New York: AMACOM, 1981.

Sutherland, Edwin A. *White Collar Crime: The Uncut Version.* New Haven: Yale University Press, 1983.

Wickman, Peter, and Timothy Dailey, eds. *White-Collar and Economic Crime: Multidisciplinary and Cross-National Perspectives.* Lexington, Mass.: Lexington Books, 1982.

Articles

Abend, Jules. "Why, What, and How Some Steal." *Stores* 64 (January 1982), 71-74.

Adkins, Lynn. "The High Cost of Employee Theft." *Dun's Business Month* 120 (October 1982), 66-76.

Albanese, Jay S. "When the Company Is the Culprit: Accepted Corporate Behavior May Bend the Law." *Security Management* 28 (September 1984), 121-126.

Alexander, Charles P. "Crime in the Suites." *Time* 125 (June 10, 1985), 56-57.

Alsop, Ronald. "Gambling Fever: Embezzlement Surge Follows an Increase in Employee Wagering." *Wall Street Journal* (November 23, 1983), 1.

Anderson, G. "White-Collar Crime." *America* 144 (May 1981), 445-448.

Andresky, Jill. "Crime and Punishment." *Forbes* 134 (September 10, 1984), 114+.

Arkin, Joseph. "Employee Theft and Fidelity Insurance." *Journal of Property Management* 49 (September-October 1984), 64-65.

Babb, Dan K. "Recent Developments in White-Collar Crime—An Electronic Eavesdropping." *Vital Speeches of the Day* 51 (January 1, 1985), 175-178.

Bailey, Douglas M. "Is Business Fighting Crime?" *New England Business* 4 (March 1982), 35-37.

Barefoot, J. K. "Curtailing Fraud Through Worker's Comp Investigation." *Risk Management* 32 (February 1985), 38-42.

Barnett, Harold C. "Corporate Capitalism, Corporate Crime." *Crime and Delinquency* 27 (January 1981), 4-23.

Barnfather, Maurice. "More Enterprising Brits." *Forbes* 127 (June 22, 1981), 70+.

Beck, Sanford. "How to Cope with the Corporate Crook." *Journal of Insurance* 42 (March-April 1981), 10-15.

Bennett, James R. "Newspaper Reporting of United States Business Crime in 1980." *Newspaper Research Journal* 3 (October 1981), 45-53.

Bernstein, Paul. "Cheating—The New National Pastime?" *Business* 35 (Oct.-Nov.-Dec. 1985), 24-33.

Braithwaite, John. "Enforced Self-Regulation: A New Strategy for Corporate Crime Control." *Michigan Law Review* 80 (June 1982), 1466-1507.

Braithwaite, John, and G. Geis. "On Theory and Action for Corporate Crime Control." *Crime and Delinquency* 28 (April 1982), 292-314.

Brickman, Bruce K. "The Corporate Computer: A Potential Timebomb." *Financial Executive* 51 (April 1983), 20-24.

Britton, Herchell. "Serious Threats of White Collar Crime." *Vital Speeches of the Day* 47 (June 1, 1981), 485-488.

Brooks, Gary. "Spilled Milk: The Case of the Unintentional Theft." *Journal of Commercial Bank Lending* 66 (May 1984), 61-63.

Bullard, Peter D., and Alan J. Resnik. "Too Many Hands in the Corporate Cookie Jar." *Sloan Management Review* 25 (Fall 1983), 51-66.

Carrington, Tim. "Gilleece Quits Procurement Job at Pentagon." *Wall Street Journal* (August 20, 1985), 60.

Carson-Parker, John. "The Thief Executive—How Serious Is Fraud in the Executive Suite?" *Chief Executive* 26 (Winter 1984), 26-33.

Cogan, John L. "Uncloaking Business Crime." *Management World* 11 (February 1982), 9-13).

"Computer 'Hacking' Is No Longer Just a Lark." *Office* 102 (September 1985), 90+.

Cookingham, Vincent P. "Organized Crime: The Corporation as Victim." *Security Management* 29 (July 1985), 28-31.

Crapnell, Stephen G. "Business Theft: A Private Investigator Opens His Files." *Occupational Hazards* 43 (November 1981), 53-56.

Dee, Joseph M. "White Collar Crime: A Tie That Binds." *Security Management* 29 (January 1985), 18-22.

Duggan, M. A. "Creative Probations are Beneficial in Punishing Corporate Wrongdoers." *Marketing News* 18 (March 30, 1984), 6.

Ewing, David W. "Case of the Rogue Division." *Harvard Business Review* 61 (May-June 1983), 166-168+.

Fromm, Joseph. "New Setback for CIA—And More to Come?" *U.S. News and World Report* 91 (July 27, 1981), 29-30.

Glixon, N. "Un-Collared Crime." *Commonweal* 112 (November 29, 1985), 661-662.

Haskell, Debra L. "Battling the White Collar Crime Wave." *Modern Office Procedures* 26 (May 1981), 66-74.

"In for a Penny: Bank Fraud." *Economist* 280 (July 25-31, 1981), 31+.

Johnson, Michael. "How to Unmask the Data Thieves." *Chief Executive (UK),* (February 1984), 49.

Kelly, Orr. "Corporate Crime, the Untold Story." *U.S. News and World Report* 93 (September 6, 1982), 25-29.

Kennedy, Daniel B. "Theft by Employees." *Security Management* 28 (September 1984), 171-174.

Kramer, Otto P. "Controlling Fraudulent Employee Acts." *CA Magazine (Canada)* 116 (October 1983), 89-92.

Lansing, Paul, and Donald Hatfield. "Corporate Control Through the Criminal System—An Alternative Proposal." *Journal of Business Ethics* 4 (October 1985), 409-414.

Loomis, Carol J. "The Limited War on White-Collar Crime." *Fortune* 112 (July 22, 1985), 90-92+.

McGowan, William. "The Great White-Collar Crime Coverup." *Business and Society Review* 45 (Spring 1983), 25-31.

Mendelson, George J., and Michael A. Lubin. "You've Got Fraud on Your Hands, Now What?" *ABA Banking Journal* 74 (January 1982), 54-57.

Miceli, Marcia P., et al. "Characteristics of Organizational Climate and Perceived Wrongdoing Associated with Whistle-Blowing Decisions." *Personnel Psychology* 38 (Autumn 1985), 525-544.

Nich, David L., and Robert D. Miller. "White-Collar Crime." *Internal Auditor* 41 (December 1984), 24-27.

Parker, Susan T. "Are Thieves Riding High in Oil Country?" *Iron Age* 224 (May 4, 1981), 45-47.

Phillips, David M. "The Commercial Culpability Scale." *Yale Law Journal* 92 (December 1982), 228-290.

Pollack, Harriet, and Alexander B. Smith. "White-Collar v. Street Crime Sentencing Disparity: How Judges See the Problem." *Judicature* 67 (October 1983), 174-182.

Radler, Irving. "Silent Partners: Employees Who Embezzle." *D & B Reports* 29 (July-August 1981), 24+.

Riggs, Carol R. "The Match Game: Arson-for-Profit." *D & B Reports* 29 (July-August 1981), 14+.

Roberts, Johnnie L., and Andy Pasztor. "GE Will Pay Civil Penalty in Fraud Case." *Wall Street Journal* (May 22, 1985), 8.

Rogers, Helene. "How White Collar Pirates Plunder World Shipping." *South* 9 (October 1982), 57-58.

Sandler, Linda. "Chase Action Against Six Ex-Offenders Could Prompt More Negligence Suits." *Wall Street Journal* (October 22, 1984), 5.

Scebra, J. B. "Twenty-Five Ways to Unbutton White Collar Crime." *American School Board Journal* 168 (May 1981), 40-41.

Shaw, Stephen J. "Anatomy of a Computer Sting." *Mini-Micro Systems* 17 (September 1984), 43.

Sloan, Allan. "Only in America." *Forbes* 127 (March 2, 1981), 47.

Stokes, Richard. "Are Your Staff and Secrets Kidnap Proof?" *Personnel Management* 14 (January 1982), 28-32.

Taylor, Robert E. "Laundry Service: More Professionals Like Lawyers, Bankers Said to Hide Drug Loot." *Wall Street Journal* (July 25, 1983), 1+.

Tersine, Richard J., and Roberta S. Russell. "Internal Theft: The Multi-Billion Dollar Disappearing Act." *Business Horizons* 24 (November-December 1981), 11-20.

Trillin, Calvin. "Uncivil Liberties." *Nation* 241 (October 19, 1985), 368.

Vaughan, Diane. "Toward Understanding Unlawful Organizational Behavior." *Michigan Law Review* 80 (June 1982), 1377-1402.

Webster, William H. "Technology Transfer, Industrial Espionage, & Computer Crime: The FBI's Activities." *Computer Security Journal* 3 (Winter 1985), 7-12.

Wells, Joseph T. "White Collar Crime: Myths and Strategies." *Practical Accountant* 1 (August 1985), 43-45.

Wheeler, Stanton, et al. "Sentencing the White-Collar Offender: Rhetoric and Realities." *American Sociological Review* 47 (October 1982), 641-659.

Wheeler, Stanton, and Mitchell L. Rothman. "The Organization as Weapon in White Collar Crime." *Michigan Law Review* 80 (June 1982), 1403-1426.

"White-Collar Criminals on the Run." *Security Management* 29 (November 1985), 29-30.

Will, Ian. "Constructing the Web of Illegality." *Management Today* (July 1983), 76-80.

Zalud, Bill. "Computer Criminals Will Be Prosecuted: Adopting a 'Prevention First' Attitude." *Data Management* 21 (April 1983), 30+.

Women in Organizations

Books

Backhouse, Constance, and Leah Cohen. *Sexual Harassment on the Job: How to Avoid the Working Woman's Nightmare*. Englewood Cliffs, N.J.: Prentice-Hall, 1981.

Baxter, Ralph H., Jr. *Sexual Harassment in the Workplace: A Guide to the Law*. New York: Executive Enterprises, 1981.

Chavkin, Wendy, ed. *Double Exposure: Women's Health Hazards on the Job and at Home*. New York: Monthly Review Press, 1983.

Comparable Worth: A Symposium on the Issues and Alternatives. Washington, D.C.: Equal Employment Advisory Council, 1981.

Davidson, Marilyn, and Cary Cooper. *Stress and the Woman Manager*. Oxford, U.K.: Robertson, 1983.

Freudenberg, Herbert J., and Gail North. *Woman's Burnout*. New York: Doubleday, 1985.

Gutek, Barbara A. *Sex and the Workplace*. San Francisco: Jossey-Bass Pub., 1985.

Kamerman, Sheila B., Alfred J. Kahn, and Paul Kingston. *Maternity Policies and Working Women*. New York: Columbia Univ. Press, 1983.

Kandel, Thelma. *What Women Earn*. New York: Linden Press, 1981.

Leacock, Eleanor, and Helen I. Safa. *Women's Work: Development and the Division of Labor by Sex*. Hadley, Mass.: Bergin & Garvey, 1985.

Pepper, William F., and Florynce R. Kennedy. *Sex Discrimination in Employment*. Charlottesville, Va.: Michie Co., 1982.

Rennick, Helen, ed. *Comparable Worth and Wage Discrimination.* Philadelphia: Temple Univ. Press, 1984.

Roby, Pamela. *Women in the Workplace: Conditions of Women in Blue-Collar Jobs*. Cambridge, Mass.: Schenkman, 1981.

Sacks, Karen, and Dorothy Remy. *My Troubles Are Going to Have Trouble With Me: Everyday Trials and Triumphs of Women Workers*. New Brunswick, N.J.: Rutgers Univ. Press, 1984.

Schlafly, Phyllis, ed. *Equal Pay for Unequal Work: A Conference on Comparable Worth*. Washington, D.C.: Eagle Forum Education, 1983.

Shaw, Lois B., ed. *Unplanned Careers: The Working Lives of Middle-Aged Women*. Lexington, Mass.: Lexington Books, 1983.

Treiman, Donald J. and Heidi I. Hartmann, eds. *Women, Work, and Wages: Equal Pay for Jobs of Equal Value*. Washington, D.C.: National Academy Press, 1981.

Women Workers in Multinational Enterprises in Developing Countries. Geneva: International Labour Office, 1985.

Zabalza, A., and Z. Tzannatos. *Women and Equal Pay*. Cambridge, U.K.: Cambridge Univ. Press, 1985.

Articles

Abarbanel, K. "Sex and the Executive Female." *Executive Female* 7 (July-August 1984), 20-22.

Abowd, John, and Mark R. Killingsworth. "Sex, Discrimination, Atrophy and the Male-Female Wage Differential." *Industrial Relations* 22 (Fall 1983), 387-402.

Adler, Nancy J. "Women Do Not Want International Careers and Other Myths About International Management." *Organizational Dynamics* 13 (Fall 1984), 66-79.

Allegretti, Joseph G. "Sexual Harassment by Nonemployees." *Employee Relations Law Journal* 9 (Summer 1983), 98-111.

Baldwin, James J. "EEOC's New Guidelines on Sexual Harassment: A Further Expansion of Employer Liability." *Business and Economic Review* 27 (December-January 1981), 30-31.

Baron, Alma S. "The Achieving Woman Manager: So Where Are the Rewards?" *Business Quarterly* 49 (Summer 1984), 70-73.

Baron, Alma S. "Do Managers Clone Themselves?" *Personnel Administrator* 26 (March 1981), 53-57.

Baron, Alma S. "What Men Are Saying About Women in Business." *Business Horizons* 25 (January-February 1982), 10-14.

Barry, Janis. "Women Production Workers: Low Pay and Hazardous Work." *American Economic Review* 75 (May 1985), 262-265.

Baxter, Ralph H., Jr. "Judicial and Administrative Protections Against Sexual Harassment in the Work Place." *Employee Relations Law Journal* 7 (Spring 1982), 587-593.

Behrens, Curtiss K. "Co-Worker Sexual Harassment: The Employer's Liability." *Personnel Journal* 63 (December 1985), 12-14.

Bell, Carolyn S. "Comparable Worth: How Do We Know It Will Work?" *Monthly Labor Review* 108 (December 1985), 5-12.

Bellace, Janice R. "Comparable Worth: Proving Sex-Based Wage Discrimination." *Iowa Law Review* 69 (March 1984), 655-704.

Benston, George J. "The Economics of Gender Discrimination in Employee Fringe Benefits." *University of Chicago Law Review* 49 (Spring 1982), 489-542.

Bergmann, Barbara R. "Women's Plight: Bad and Getting Worse." *Challenge* 26 (March-April 1983), 22-26.

Block, Walter, and Walter Williams. "Male-Female Earnings Differentials: A Critical Reappraisal." *Journal of Labor Research* 2 (Fall 1981), 385-388.

Boeker, Warren, et al. "Are the Expectations of Women Managers Being Met?" *California Management Review* 27 (Spring 1985), 148-157.

"Boosting the Careers of B-School Grads." *Business Week* (October 11, 1982), 72.

Boyce, Michael T. "Sexual Harassment: Understanding the Guidelines." *Management World* 12 (June 1983), 14+.

Brinks, James T. "The Comparable Worth Issues: A Salary Administration Bombshell." *Personnel Administrator* 26 (November 1981), 37-40.

Buchele, Robert, and Mark Aldrich. "How Much Difference Would Comparable Worth Make?" *Industrial Relations* 24 (Spring 1985), 222-233.

Bunke, Harvey C. "Anti-Business Sentiments and the Intellectual Community." *Business Horizons* 24 (September-October 1981), 2-8.

Bunzel, John H. "To Each According to Her Worth?" *Public Interest* 67 (Spring 1982), 77-93.

Buono, Anthony F., and Judith B. Kamm. "Marginality and the Organizational Socialization of Female Managers." *Human Relations* 36 (December 1983), 1125-1140.

Bussetti, Laurence, and Laurie McNair. "Comparable Worth: The Issue of the Eighties." *William & Mary Business Review* 6 (1984), 19-24.

Carlson, Barbara M., and Mary Pat McEnrue. "Eliminating the Gender-Based Earning Gap: Two Alternatives." *Business Horizons* 28 (July-August 1985), 76-81.

Carter, Michael F. "Comparable Worth: An Idea Whose Time Has Come?" *Personnel Journal* 60 (October 1981), 792-794.

Chacko, T. I. "Women and Equal Employment Opportunity: Some Unintended Effects." *Journal of Applied Psychology* 67 (February 1982), 119-123.

Cirillo, J. J. "Suit Suite." *Quill* 72 (December 1984), 14-18.

Clynch, Edward J., and Carol A. Gaudin. "Sex in the Shipyards: An Assessment of Affirmative Action Policy." *Public Administration Review* 42 (March-April 1982), 114-121.

Collett, Merrill J. "Comparable Worth: An Overview." *Public Personnel Management* 12 (Winter 1983), 325-331.

Colwill, Nina L. "Sex Roles, Past, Present and Future." *Business Quarterly (Canada)* 47 (August 1982), 18-20.

"Comparable Worth: Disaster or Pay Equality?" *Personnel Journal* 64 (April 1985), 21.

"The Comparable Worth Doctrine: Still in a State of Flux." *CPA Journal* 55 (September 1985), 8-9.

"Comparable Worth: New Concern for Business?" *CPA Journal* 55 (September 1985), 9-11.

Cooper, K. C. "The Six Levels of Sexual Harassment." *Management Review* 74 (August 1985), 54-55.

Cowley, Geoffrey. "Comparable Worth: Another Terrible Idea." *Across the Board* 21 (May 1984), 44-48.

Crew, Bob. "Helping Women Become the Best Man for the Job." *Industrial Management and Data Systems* 14 (January-February 1985), 10-14.

Cuddy, Robert W. "Worthy Adversaries." *Management Focus* 32 (January-February 1985), 31-34.

Dahl, Shirley J., and Karen L. Hooks. "Women Accountants in a Changing Profession." *Journal of Accounting* 158 (December 1984), 108-110.

Dalton, Dan R., and William D. Todor. "Composition of Dyads as a Factor in the Outcomes of Workplace Justice: Two Field Assessments." *Academy of Management Journal* 28 (September 1985), 704-712.

Dalton, Dan R., and Wiliam D. Todor. "Gender and Workplace Justice: A Field Assessment." *Personnel Psychology* 38 (Spring 1985), 133-152.

David, Fred R. "Women Supervisors and Effective Delegation." *Mid-South Business Journal* 3 (April 1983), 24-26.

Dellaverson, JoAnne. "Comparable Worth Keeps Brewing." *ABA Banking Journal* 76 (October 1984), 140-142.

Dobbins, Gregory H. "Effects of Gender on Leaders' Responses to Poor Performers: An Attributional Interpretation." *Academy of Management Journal* 28 (September 1985), 587-598.

Dolecheck, Carolyn C., and Maynard M. Dolecheck. "Sexual Harassment: A Problem for Small Businesses." *American Journal of Small Business* 7 (January-March 1983), 45-50.

Ellis, Evelyn, and Philip Morrell. "Sex Discrimination in Pension Schemes." *Industrial Law Journal* 11 (March 1982), 16-28.

Farnquist, Robert L., David R. Armstrong, and Russell P. Strausbaugh. "Pandora's Worth: The San Jose Experience." *Public Personnel Management* 12 (Winter 1983), 358-368.

Flick, Rachel. "The New Feminism and the World of Rock." *Public Interest* 71 (Spring 1983), 33-44.

Foegen, J. H. "Remaining Sexual Bias: Unconscious or Unconscionable?" *Business Horizons* 26 (November-December 1985), 79-80.

Foster, MarySue. "Moving Women into 'Male' Jobs." *Supervisory Management* 26 (June 1981), 2-9.

Fuentes, Annette, and Barbara Ehrenreich. "The New Factory Girls: Around the Globe Multinationals Use Women to Keep Labor Costs Down and Profits Up." *Multinational Monitor* 4 (August 1983), 5-9.

Fulghum, Judy B. "The Employer's Liabilities Under Comparable Worth." *Personnel Journal* 62 (May 1983), 400-412.

Fulghum, Judy B. "The Newest Balancing Act: A Comparable Worth Study." *Personnel Journal* 63 (January 1984), 32-38.

Geisel, J. "Firms Must Hurry to Change Pension Plans to Aid Women." *Business Insurance* 18 (August 20, 1984), 2+.

Gleason, Sandra E. "Comparable Worth: Some Questions Still Unanswered." *Monthly Labor Review* 108 (December 1985), 17-25.

Green, C. "High-Heeled Power: The Push for Success in the Corporate Arena." *Black Enterprise* 16 (August 1985), 104-107.

Greenbaum, Marcia L., and Bruce Fraser. "Sexual Harassment in the Workplace." *Arbitration Journal* 36 (December 1981), 30-41.

Harel, Gedaliahu H., and Karen Cottledge. "Combatting Sexual Harassment: The Michigan Experience." *Human Resource Management* 21 (Spring 1982), 2-10.

Hauck, Vern E. "Burdine: Sex Discrimination, Promotion, and Arbitration." *Labor Law Journal* 33 (July 1982), 434-441.

Hay, Robert D. "Susan Lewis—A Case of Sexual Harassment." *ABCA Bulletin* 45 (December 1982), 23-26.

Hemming, Heather. "Women in a Man's World: Sexual Harassment." *Human Relations* 38 (1985), 67-79.

Hoffman, Carl, and John S. Reed. "Sex Discrimination?—The XYZ Affair." *Public Interest* 62 (Winter 1981), 21-39.

Hopkins, Carter H., and David A. Johnson. "Sexual Harassment in the Work Place." *Journal of College Placement* 42 (Spring 1982), 30-35.

Howard, Carole. "Moving into Senior Management: Progress? Yes; Success, Sometime." *Vital Speeches of the Day* 51 (December 15, 1984), 148-150.

Huerta, F. L., and T. A. Lane. "Participation of Women in Centers of Power." *Social Science Journal* 18 (April 1981), 71-86.

Hull, Jennifer B. "Female Bosses Say Biggest Barriers Are Insecurity and 'Being a Woman.' " *Wall Street Journal* (November 2, 1982), 31+.

Hurd, Sandra, Paula Murray, and Bill Shaw. "Comparable Worth: A Legal and Ethical Analysis." *American Business Law Journal* 22 (Fall 1984), 407-427.

Jacobson, Beverly. "Comparable Worth: The Working Woman's Issue for the 80's." *National Forum* 61 (Fall 1981), 5-6.

James, Jennifer. "Sexual Harassment." *Public Personnel Management* 10 (Winter 1981), 402-407.

Janjic, Marion. "Diversifying Women's Employment: The Only Way to Genuine Equality of Opportunity." *International Labour Review* 120 (March-April 1981), 149-163.

Jiminez-Butragueno, Maria de los Angeles. "Protective Legislation and Equal Opportunity for Women in Spain." *International Labour Review* 121 (March-April 1982), 185-198.

Johnson, Linnea M. "Sexual Harassment: A Costly Mistake." *Management World* 12 (June 1983), 14-16.

Kaufman, Debra, and Michael L. Fetters. "The Executive Suite: Are

Women Perceived as Ready for the Managerial Climb?" *Journal of Business Ethics* 2 (August 1983), 203-212.

Kelley, Maryellen R. "Discrimination in Seniority Systems: A Case Study." *Industrial and Labor Relations Review* 36 (October 1982), 40-55.

Kener, B. D., et al. "Sex and the Dead-End Job." *Northeast Louisiana Business Review* (Spring-Summer 1983), 11-16.

Kohl, John P., and Paul S. Greenlaw. "The Pregnancy Discrimination Act." *Personnel Journal* 62 (September 1983, 752-756.

Kohl, John P., and Paul S. Greenlaw. "The Pregnancy Discrimination Act and the Hospitality Manager." *Cornell Hotel and Restaurant Administration Quarterly* 23 (November 1982), 72-76.

Kohl, John P., and Paul S. Greenlaw. "The Pregnancy Discrimination Act: Compliance Problems." *Personnel* 60 (November-December 1983), 65-71.

Kohl, John P. "Small Business Compliance With the Pregnancy Discrimination Act." *Journal of Small Business Management* 21 (October 1983), 49-53.

Kotch, Jonathan B., et al. "A Policy Analysis of the Problem of the Reproductive Health of Women in the Workplace." *Journal of Public Health Policy* 5 (June 1984), 213-227.

Kuraitis, Vytenis. "Analyzing the Equal Pay Equation." *Management World* 10 (September 1981), 8+.

Ledgerwood, Donna E., and Sue Johnson-Dietz. "Sexual Harassment: Implications for Employer Liability." *Monthly Labor Review* 104 (April 1981), 45-47.

Levin, Michael. "Comparable Worth: The Feminist Road to Socialism." *Commentary* 78 (September 1984), 13-19.

Linenberger, Patricia, and Timothy J. Keaveny. "Sexual Harassment in Employment." *Human Resource Management* 20 (Spring 1981), 11-17.

Linenberger, Patricia, and Timothy J. Keaveny. "Sexual Harassment: The Employer's Legal Obligations." *Personnel* 58 (November-December 1981), 60-68.

Linenberger, Patricia. "What Behavior Constitutes Sexual Harassment?" *Labor Law Journal* 34 (April 1983), 238+.

Lublin, Joann S. "Fearing Radiation, Pregnant Women Won Transfers from Work on Video Terminals." *Wall Street Journal* (April 6, 1984), 31.

Major, Brenda, and Ellen Konar. "An Investigation of Sex Differences in Pay Expectations and Their Possible Causes." *Academy of Management Journal* 27 (December 1984), 777-792.

Martin, Patricia Y., Dianne Harrison, and Diana Dinitto. "Advancement for Women in Hierarchical Organizations: A Multilevel Analysis of Patterns and Prospects." *Journal of Applied Behavioral Science* 19 (February 1983), 19-33.

Mass, Michael A. "The Pregnancy Discrimination Act: Protecting Men From Pregnancy-Based Discrimination." *Employee Relations Law Journal* 9 (Autumn 1983), 240-250.

May, Larry. "Vicarious Agency and Corporate Responsibility." *Philosophical Studies* 43 (January 1983), 69-82.

McEnery, Jean. "Sexual Harassment in Blue-Collar Jobs: A Problem Unresolved." *Employment Relations Today* 11 (Summer 1984), 205-215.

McGouldrick, Paul. "Why Women Earn Less." *Policy Review* 18 (Fall 1981), 63-76.

Meyer, Peter J., and Patricia L. Maes. "The Reproduction of Occupational Segregation Among Young Women." *Industrial Relations* 22 (Winter 1983), 115-124.

Mikalachki, D. M., and A. Mikalachki. "Women in Business—Going for Broke." *Business Quarterly (Canada)* 50 (Summer 1985), 25-32.

"The More Things Change, the Better Off Women Will Be." *NABW Journal* 59 (January-February 1983), 17-19.

Murray, T. H. "Who Do Fetal-Protection Policies Really Protect?" *Technology Review* 88 (October 1985), 12-13+.

Muson, Howard, "Hard-Hat Women." *Across the Board* 18 (February 1981), 12-18.

Nelson, Debra L., and James C. Quick. "Professional Women: Are Distress and Disease Inevitable?" *Academy of Management Review* 10 (April 1985), 206-218.

Norwood, Janet L. "Perspectives on Comparable Worth: An Introduction to the Data." *Monthly Labor Review* 108 (December 1985), 3-4.

Olson, Craig A., and Brian E. Becker. "Sex Discrimination in the Promotion Process." *Industrial and Labor Relations Review* 36 (July 1983), 624-641.

Ost, Edward. "Comparable Worth: A Response for the 80's." *Personnel Journal* 64 (February 1985), 64-70.

Paoli, Chantal. "Women Workers and Maternity." *International Labour Review* 121 (January-February 1982), 1-16.

Pennar, Karen, and Edward Mervash. "Women at Work." *Business Week* (January 28, 1985), 80-85.

Powell, Gary N. "Sexual Harassment: Confronting the Issue of Definition." *Business Horizons* 26 (July-August 1983), 24-28.

Price, Margaret. "Sex Bias Suits Expand in Scope." *Industry Week* 216 (February 7, 1983), 75-76.

Purdy, Laura M. "In Defense of Hiring Apparently Less Qualified Women." *Journal of Social Philosophy* 15 (Summer 1984), 26-33.

Randall, Donna M. "A Management Dilemma: Regulating the Health of the Unborn." *Journal of Management Case Studies* 1 (Fall 1985), 246-257.

"Recognizing Double Discrimination." *National Business Woman* (February-March 1983), 22+.

Rosen, Benson, Sara Rynes, and Thomas A. Mahoney. "Probing Opinions: Compensation, Jobs, and Gender." *Harvard Business Review* 61 (July-August 1983), 170+.

Rowe, Mary P. "Dealing With Sexual Harassment." *Harvard Business Review* 59 (May-June 1981), 42-44+.

Rozen, Miriam. "Comparable Worth: New Management Bugaboo." *Dun's Business Month* 125 (February 1985), 52-56.

Rubenstein, Michael. "When the Office Romeo Violates the Law." *Personnel Management* 13 (October 1981), 48-51.

Rynes, Sara, Benson Rosen, and Thomas A. Mahoney. "Evaluating Comparable Worth: Three Perspectives." *Business Horizons* 28 (July-August 1985), 82-86.

Rytina, Nancy F. "Occupational Segregation and Earnings Differences by Sex." *Monthly Labor Review* 104 (January 1981), 49-53.

Sample, James O. "Comparable Worth: The Battle Over Sex and Salaries." *Association Management* 37 (May 1985), 54-62.

Scanlon, James P. "Employment Quotas for Women?" *Public Interest* 73 (Fall 1983), 106-112.

Schnebly, John R. "Comparable Worth: A Legal Overview." *Personnel Administrator* 27 (April 1982), 43-48.

Schultz-Brooks, T. "Getting There: Women in the Newsroom." *Columbia Journalism Review* 22 (March-April 1984), 25-31.

Schwartz, Peter. "Women's Work: Is 'Comparable Worth' Good for Women?" *Reason* 14 (July 1982), 40-42+.

"Sexual Harassment." *Ideas and Trends* 84 (February 1985), 17-20.

Shrader, Betty L. "European Banking Women: Still Stuck at the Bottom." *NABW Journal* 59 (January-February 1983), 14-16.

Sorensen, Elaine. "Equal Pay for Comparable Worth: A Policy for

Eliminating the Undervaluation of Women's Work." *Journal of Economic Issues* 18 (June 1984), 465-472.

Spruell, G. "Making It Big—Is It Really Tougher for Women?" *Training and Development Journal* 39 (August 1985), 30-33.

Stevens, George E. "The 'Cruel Trilemma': Sexual Harassment Under Title VII and the Tangible Job Benefit." *American Business Law Journal* 20 (Spring 1982), 109-117.

Studabaker, Anne W. "Controversy: Judge to Decide Sex Discrimination Case." *Madison Avenue* 26 (February 1984), 82-85.

Sutton, Charlotte D., and Kris K. Moore. "Executive Women—20 Years Later." *Harvard Business Review* 63 (September-October 1985), 42-66.

Taylor, Anita. "Women as Leaders: The Skills at Which We Are so Uniquely Qualified." *Vital Speeches of the Day* 50 (April 15, 1984), 445-448.

Thomas, Clarence. "Pay Equity and Comparable Worth." *Labor Law Journal* 34 (January 1983), 3-12.

Tomishige, K. "Pour Tea or Kick the Boss." *Journal of Popular Culture* 17 (Summer 1983), 159-160.

Tosi, Henry L., and Steven W. Einbender. "The Effects of the Type and Amount of Information in Sex Discrimination Research: A Meta-Analysis." *Academy of Management Journal* 28 (September 1985), 712-723.

Trotter, Richard, Susan R. Zacur, and Wallace Greenwood. "The Pregnancy Disability Amendment: What the Law Provides, Part II." *Personnel Administrator* 27 (March 1982), 55-58.

Waks, Jay W., and Michael G. Starr. "Sexual Harassment in the Workplace: The Scope of Employer Liability." *Employee Relations Law Journal* 7 (Winter 1981-82), 369-388.

Waks, Jay W., and Michael G. Starr. "The 'Sexual Shakedown' in Perspective: Sexual Harassment in Its Social and Legal Contexts." *Employee Relations Law Journal* 7 (Spring 1982), 567-586.

Wald, Sara E. "Judicial Construction of the 1978 Pregnancy Discrimination Amendment to Title VII: Ignoring Congressional Intent." *American University Law Review* 31 (Spring 1982), 591-612.

Washbourn, Penelope. "Women in the Workplace." *Word World* 21 (Spring 1984), 159-164.

Webb, Susan L. "Sexual Harassment: Court Costs Rise for a Persistent Problem." *Management Review* 73 (December 1984), 25-28.

Wermiel, Stephen. "Bias Law Applies to Partnerships, High Court Says." *Wall Street Journal* (May 23, 1984), 2.

Whaley, George L. "Controversy Swirls Over Comparable Worth Issue." *Personnel Administrator* 27 (April 1982), 50-61.

"When the Mother-to-Be Is an Executive." *Business Week* (April 11, 1983), 128-132.

"Why More Japanese Career Women Are Moving Abroad." *International Management* 39 (November 1984), 77-79.

Williams, W. "Firing the Woman to Protect the Fetus." *Georgetown Law Journal* 69 (1981), 641-704.

Wolkinson, Benjamin W., Harel, Gedaliahu H., and Dafna N. Izraeli. "Employment Discrimination Against Women: The Israeli Experience." *Employee Relations Law Journal* 7 (Winter 1981-82), 466-489.

Wolkinson, Benjamin W., and Dennis H. Liberson. "The Arbitration of Sex Discrimination Grievances." *Arbitration Journal* 37 (June 1982), 35-44.

"Women: Half Say Job Market Bias Still Exists." *Gallup Report* (August 1982), 22-30.

"Women Managers: A Success Story." *Executive Female* 7 (September-October 1984), 20-22.

"Women Sing the Blues." *Purchasing* 99 (November 21, 1985), 108-109.

Wong, P.T.P., et al. "On the Importance of Being Masculine: Sex Role, Attribution, and Women's Career Achievement." *Sex Roles* 12 (April 1985), 757-767.

"You've Come a Long Way, Baby—But Not as Far as You Thought." *Business Week* (October 1, 1984), 126-131.

The Marketplace

The Marketplace

Accounting

Books

Abdel-Khalik, A. R., ed. *Internal Control and the Impact of the Foreign Corrupt Practices Act*. Gainesville, Fla.: University Presses Fla., 1982.

Briloff, Abraham J. *The Truth About Corporate Accounting*. New York: Harper & Row, 1981.

Merz, C. M., and David F. Graebner. *Toward a Code of Ethics for Management Accountants*. New York: Nat'l. Assoc. Account., 1981.

Rotch, William, and Brandt Allen. *Cases in Management Accounting and Control Systems*. Reston, Va.: Reston Pub., 1983.

Stevens, Mark. *The Big Eight*. New York: Macmillan, 1981.

Articles

"AICPA Ethics Draft Focuses on 'Client,' 'Products' Exposed." *Journal of Accountancy* 156 (November 1983), 9.

Agee, Tom A. "Fraud Challenges in the Utility Industry." *Internal Auditor* 41 (December 1984), 34-38.

Anderson, George D. "A Fresh Look at Standards of Professional Conduct." *Journal of Accountancy* 106 (September 1985), 91-106.

Andresky, Jill. "Indecent Disclosure." *Forbes* 134 (August 13, 1984), 92.

Antle, Rick. "Auditor Independence." *Journal of Accounting Research* 22 (Spring 1984), 1-20.

Aranya, Nissim, and Kenneth R. Ferris. "A Reexamination of Accountants' Organizational-Professional Conflict." *Accounting Review* 59 (January 1984), 1-15.

Arrington, Cecil E., et al. "A Social-Psychological Investigation into Perceptions of Tax Evasion." *Accounting & Business Research* 15 (Summer 1985), 163-176.

Austin, Kenneth R. "How We Audit Ourselves: An Outline of the Self-Regulation Process." *Ohio CPA Journal* 43 (Winter 1984), 15-20.

"Be Warned!" *Accountant* 104 (April 9, 1981), 381.

Beach, John E. "Codes of Ethics: The Professional Catch 22." *Journal of Accounting and Public Policy* 3 (Winter 1984), 311-323.

Benson, Henry. "Standards: The Hallmark of a Profession." *Journal of Accountancy* 15 (February 1981), 45-46.

Benston, George J. "An Analysis of the Role of Accounting Standards for Enhancing Corporate Governance and Social

Responsibility." *Journal of Accounting and Public Policy* 1 (Fall 1982), 5-17.

Berton, Lee. "Goal: Ethical Standards for Accounting Practices." *Wall Street Journal* (May 24, 1984), 32.

Berton, Lee. "Loose Ledgers." *Wall Street Journal* (December 13, 1983), 1+.

Berton, Lee. "Price-Waterhouse Is Urging Formation of Group to Regulate Accounting Firms." *Wall Street Journal* (November 20, 1985), 10.

Boland, Richard J., Jr. "Myth and Technology in the American Accounting Profession." *Journal of Management Studies* 19 (January 1982), 109-127.

Boland, Richard J., Jr. "A Positive View of Management Advisory Services and the Public Well-Being." *Ohio CPA Journal* 42 (Summer 1983), 139-143.

Borst, Duane R. "Accounting vs. Reality: How Wide Is the GAAP?" *Financial Executive* 49 (July 1981), 12-15.

Briloff, Abraham J. "Are Auditors Becoming Too Cozy with Their Clients?" *Business and Society Review* 54 (Summer 1985), 72-76.

Carey, John L. "The Independence Concept Revisited." *Ohio CPA Journal* 44 (Spring 1985), 5-8.

Carter, Roy. "A Contingency Plan for Corporate Fraud Enquiries." *Management Accounting* 63 (July-August 1985), 28-29.

Cassell, Michael N., et al. "An Effective Audit Program for FCPA." *Internal Auditor* 38 (June 1981), 57-62.

Davis, Robert R. "Ethical Behavior Reexamined." *CPA Journal* 54 (December 1984), 32-36.

Deane, Keith. "Tax Fraud and the Client: The Risks and the Penalties." *Accountancy* 92 (May 1981), 122-123.

Delany, John, et al. "The Detection of Fraud and the Management Accountant." *Management Accounting (UK)* 63 (May 1985), 20-21.

De Marco, Victor F. "The Triple Threat Against Fraud." *Internal Auditor* 38 (August 1981), 39-43.

Dougherty, James. "Internal Auditing: Senior Management Pespective." *Retail Control* 52 (November 1983), 32-38.

Dykxhoorn, Hans J., and Kathleen E. Sinning. "The Auditors Independence Problem." *Woman CPA* 45 (October 1983), 10-13.

Ellner, Steve. "Subversion, IMF-Style." *Commonweal* 111 (February 24, 1984), 105-106.

Fern, Richard. "Evaluating Independence." *Journal of Accountancy* 157 (June 1984), 66-70.

Fusco, Cono R. "Ethics and Public Accounting." *Review of Business* 3 (Spring 1982), 12-15.

Goldwasser, Dan L. "Another Look at Accountants' Liability-Part 1." *CPA Journal* 55 (August 1985), 22-29.

Heims, Peter A. "Accounting for Industrial Espionage." *Accountant* 184 (March 19, 1981), 320-321.

Hershman, Arlene, and Henriette Sender. "Cooking the Books." *Dun's Business Month* 121 (January 1983), 40-47.

Hilder, David B. "Accountants' Code Calls Whistleblowing Inappropriate Unless Law Requires It." *Wall Street Journal* (July 21, 1983), 6.

Hill, Richard. "What Should You Tell Clients About Tax Avoidance?" *Accountancy* 92 (April 1981), 91-92.

Hopewell, Rita J., Eileen S. Klink, and Reuben W. Coleman. "Facing the Ethics Involved in Technical Obsolescence." *Management Accounting* 66 (December 1984), 26-29.

Johnson, Kenneth P. "The Auditor's Responsibility to Detect Fraud-IV." *CPA Journal* 51 (March 1981), 22-28.

Kessler, Ellen T. "Advertising Accounting Services: How Effective Has It Been?" *Practical Accountant* 14 (July 1981), 37-44.

Keys, David E., and James A. Hendricks. "The Ethics of Accounting Research." *Journal of Accounting Education* 2 (Fall 1984), 77-88.

Kimmitt, Desmond. "The Meaning of Professionalism." *CA Magazine (Canada)* 115 (October 1982), 72-74.

Kistler, Linda H., and Samuel Klingsbert. "Professional Ethics in a Changing Practice Environment." *Massachusetts CPA Review* 55 (September-October 1981), 15-21.

Knapp, Michael C. "Audit Conflict: An Empirical Study of the Perceived Ability of Auditors to Resist Management Pressure." *Accounting Review* 60 (April 1985), 202-211.

Kovach, Jeffrey L. "A 'Watchdog' Barks Back." *Industry Week* 227 (November 11, 1985), 60.

Kullberg, Duane R. "Reporting to the Public: Who's Responsible?" *Vital Speeches of the Day* 51 (May 1, 1985), 429-431.

"Legislators Consider 'Clarifying' Antibribery Law's Provisions on Accounting and Internal Control." *Journal of Accountancy* 151 (May 1981), 8+.

Loeb, Stephen E. "Codes of Ethics and Self-Regulation for Non-Public

Accountants: A Public Policy Perspective." *Journal of Accounting and Public Policy* 3 (Spring 1984), 1-8.

Long, Douglas P. "Full Service Accounting: A Temptation to Commit a Breach of Ethics." *Tax Executive* 34 (October 1981), 23-30.

Longstreth, Bevis. "SEC Disclosure Policy Regarding Management Integrity." *Business Lawyer* 38 (August 1983), 1413-1428.

Lutz, Edward O. "The Corporate Auditor: An Umpire Chosen by the Home Team." *Business and Society Review* 44 (Winter 1983), 58-61.

McArdle, James H., et al. "CPA-Client Confidentiality Privilege." *Akron Business & Economic Review* 12 (Winter 1981), 42-44.

Merz, C. M. "Toward a Code of Ethics for Management Accountants." *Management Accounting* 63 (December 1981), 60-61.

Misiewicz, Kevin M. "Ethical Guidelines for Tax Practitioners." *CPA Journal* 51 (October 1981), 42-50.

Morgan, Robert G., Jalaleddin Soroosh, and Charles J. Woelfel. "Are Ethics Dangerous to Your Job?" *Management Accounting* 66 (February 1985), 24-32.

"NAA Issues Ethical Conduct Standard for Management Accountants." *W G & L Accounting News* (Fall 1983), 5-7.

"NAA Publishes First Code of Ethics for Management Accountants." *Management Accounting* 65 (September 1983), 68.

O'Riordan, Maureen, and Arthur S. Hirshfield. "Aspects of the Profession's Code of Ethics." *CPA Journal* 52 (August 1982), 30-33.

Pearson, Michael A. "Enhancing Perceptions of Auditor Independence." *Journal of Business Ethics* 4 (February 1985), 53-56.

Previts, Gary J. "Small Talk—Independence: The Cornerstone." *Ohio CPA Journal* 44 (1985), 18.

Puxty, Anthony. "When Moral Issues Can't Be Ignored." *Accountancy* 92 (November 1981), 158-159.

Reckers, Philip M., et al. "Ethics and Auditors: The Issue of 'Fairness.' " *Ohio CPA Journal* 41 (Autumn 1982), 203-207.

Reckers, Philip M., and A. J. Stagliano. "Auditor Independence as Perceived by Financial Analysts." *MSU Business Topics* 29 (Winter 1981), 30-34.

Reilly, Robert F. "Division-Requested Audits: Can They Be Independent and Objective?" *Internal Auditor* 38 (February 1981), 65-69.

Richter, Marshal J. "Fraud: The Accountant as Detective." *National Public Accountant* 29 (April 1984), 18-23.

Root, Steven J. "Foreign Corrupt Practices Act: Where Do We Go From Here?" *Internal Auditor* 40 (April 1983), 28-30.

Rose, Edward M., et al. "The CPA and the Media." *CPA Journal* 55 (March 1985), 11-16.

Rotbart, Dean, and William M. Carley. "Some of Continental Air's Creditors May Try to Close Low-Cost Operations." *Wall Street Journal* (September 29, 1983), 2.

Sandford, Cedric, and Peter Kempton. "What Role for the Practitioner in Curbing Evasion." *Accountancy* 95 (March 194), 84-87.

Sandford, Cedric, and Peter Kempton. "Where Do You Stand on the Tax Evasion Industry?" *Accountancy* 95 (February 1984), 105-107.

Sasseen, Jane. "Take the Cash and Let the Standards Go." *Forbes* 134 (July 2, 1984), 180-182.

Savage, Linda J. "Professionalization of Internal Auditing." *Review of Business* 2 (Spring 1981), 5-6, 22.

Scriven, T. W. "Investigating Employee Crime." *Accountant* 184 (March 19, 1981), 324-325.

Shultis, Robert L. "Ethics for the Management Accountant." *Georgia Journal of Accounting* 3 (Spring 1982), 10-16.

Smith, George T., Jr. "Accounting and Accountability." *Management Focus* 30 (November-December 1983), 29.

Smith, Kimberley C. "Thou Shalt Not Solicit!" *Australian Accountant* 54 (April 1984), 177-178.

St. Pierre, Kent. "Independence and Auditor Sanctions." *Journal of Accounting, Auditing & Finance* 7 (Spring 1984), 257-263.

Stamp, Edward, and Maurice Moonitz. "International Auditing Standards—Part I." *CPA Journal* 52 (June 1982), 24.

"Standards of Ethical Conduct for Management Accountants." *Management Accounting* 65 (September 1983), 69-70.

Steele, Hilliard T., et al. "The Impact of Polygraph Testing on Internal Control." *Internal Auditor* 41 (December 1984), 28-33.

Stern, Richard L. "In Whom Do We Trust?" *Forbes* 131 (April 25, 1983), 38-40.

Wallace, Wanda A. "Internal Control Reporting—950 Negative Responses." *CPA Journal* 51 (January 1981), 33-38.

Williams, Kathy, et al. "Accountants Must Clean Up Their Act: Rep. John Dingell Speaks Out." *Management Accounting* 66 (May 1985), 21-23.

Yang, Catherine. "Watching Pinocchio's Nose." *Forbes* 136 (November 4, 1985), 73.

Zick, John W. "Self-regulation of the Accounting Profession." *Vital Speeches of the Day* 51 (July 15, 1985), 591-584.

Banking and Finance

Books

Boesky, Ivan. *Merger Mania: Arbitrage, Wall Street's Best Kept Money-Making Secret.* New York: Holt, Rinehart and Winston, 1985.

Brickey, Homer, Jr. *Master Manipulator.* New York: Amacom, 1985.

Ferris, Paul. *The Master Bankers: Controlling the World's Finances.* New York: William Morrow & Co., 1984.

Gurwin, Larry. *The Calvi Affair: Death of a Banker.* London, U.K.: Macmillan, 1983.

McClintock, David. *Indecent Exposure: A True Story of Hollywood and Wall Street.* New York: Dell, 1983.

McClintock, David. *Stealing From the Rich: The Story of the Swindle of the Century.* New York: Quill, 1983.

Report on the Study of E D P-related Fraud in the Banking and Insurance Industries. New York: AICPA, 1984.

Stewart, Walter. *Towers of Gold, Feet of Clay: The Canadian Banks.* Toronto: Totem Books, 1983.

U.S. Dept. Justice Bureau of Statistics. *Computer Crime: Electronic Fund Transfer Systems and Crime.* Washington, D.C.: Government Printing Office, 1982.

Walter, Ingo. *Secret Money: The World of International Financial Secrecy.* Lexington, Mass.: Lexington Books, 1985.

Articles

Allen, D. "Real Culprit in Farm Crisis Is Unproductive Debt." *Successful Farming* 83 (October 1985), 11-13.

Anderson, Nicholas. "The Dangers of Insider Trading." *Euromoney (UK),* February 1982), 71.

Bauder, Donald C. "The Trials of J. David." *Barron's* 64 (May 7, 1984), 14+.

Benston, George J. "Discrimination in Home Improvement Loans: A Comment on a Rejoinder." *Journal of Bank Research* 13 (Autumn 1982), 207-208.

Bernzweig, Eli P. "Thy Employee's Keeper." *Financial Planning* 14 (April 1985), 224-227.

Block, Alex B. "Hollywood, Home of the Pigeons." *Forbes* 13 (September 9, 1985), 42-46.

Buchanan, James M. "The Moral Dimension of Debt Financing." *Economic Inquiry* 23 (January 1985), 1-6.

"Busy Banker." *Time* 117 (June 1, 1981), 51.

Carmell, William A., and Robert J. Nobile. "Banks Must Control Sexual Harassment." *ABA Banking Journal* 77 (May 1985), 32-36.

Chimberg, Richard. "Can Performance Have a Conscience?" *Institutional Investor* 19 (October 1985), 191-192.

Clark, Constance J. "Credit Ethics: The Fairness Factor—An Interview with Walter Hunt and Joseph Mathieu." *Credit & Financial Management* 87 (July-August 1985), 28-30.

Coleman, Gilbert E. "Ethics for the Loan Officer: A Community Banker's Pespective." *Journal of Commercial Bank Lending* 64 (October 1981), 37-46.

Davison, J. L. "N.H. Pension Agency Stirs Local Debate by Quitting Amoskeag." *New England Business* 6 (March 19, 1984), 43-44.

Diesel, Paul M. "Beating Legislators to the Punch on 'Basic Banking.' " *Bank Marketing* 17 (June 1985), 16-19.

Edwards, Raoul D. "When E. F. Hutton Talks . . ." *United States Banker* 96 (July 1985), 4-6, 50.

Edwards, Raoul D., et al. "Penn Square—Banking at Its Worst; Penn Square—Evaluating a Troubling Failure." *United States Banker* 93 (September 1982), 4.

Ellis, H. R. "Polygraph: In Search of Truth." *Magazine of Bank Administration* 58 (September 1982), 28-34.

"Ethical Financial Analysis: A First Pass." *Financial Analysts Journal* 39 (May-June 1983), 6.

"Federal Judge Finds Winans, 2 Others Guilty." *Wall Street Journal* (June 25, 1985), 2.

"The Funding of Apartheid." *Business and Society Review* 52 (Winter 1985), 65.

Gillis, John G. "Securities Law and Regulations." *Financial Analysts Journal* 37 (March-April 1981), 14-15+.

Glynn, Lenny. "The Dismantling of Dean Witter." *Institutional Investor* 19 (August 1985), 80-92.

Goldstein, Walter S. "Regulations, Ethics, and Marketing Affecting Personal Financial Planning." *Massachusetts CPA Review* 59 (Summer 1985), 14-18.

Govoni, Stephen J. "The Problem with Churning." *Financial World* 154 (September 17, 1985), 76-78.

Gray, Bonnie, J., and Robert K. Landrum. "What Price Allegiance? A Case of Managerial Ethics." *Business* 31 (January-February 1981), 23-28.

Greenberg, Jonathan. "April Fool's Day Massacre." *Forbes* 128 (July 20, 1981), 35-37.

Heaney, Christopher K. "Stopping Money Launderers in Their Tracks." *ABA Banking Journal* 77 (August 1985), 75-76.

Hendrickson, Robert A. "Ethical Concerns in Multi-Jurisdictional Estate Planning." *Trusts & Estates* 123 (November 1984), 31-42.

Henry, David. "America's Hottest Export—Funny Money Stocks." *Forbes* 136 (September 23, 1985), 38-56.

Hershman, Arlene. "Insider Trading: Why It Can't Be Stopped." *Dun's Business Month* 123 (June 1984), 48-56.

"Hutton Aftermath: A Violation of Business Ethics or Outright Fraud?" *ABA Banking Journal* 77 (July 1985), 30-31.

"Italian Banker Roberto Calvi Found Hanged." *Wall Street Journal* (June 21, 1982), 20.

Kear, Stephen. "Profit Over Principle—The Dark Side of Banking." *Accountancy* 93 (September 1982), 64-66.

Kenna, Gerard J. "Drug Money Laundering Is Now a National Operation." *Bottomline* 2 (April 1985), 41-43.

Klein, Beate. "Banks That Bet on Apartheid." *Business and Society Review* 40 (Winter 1981-82), 49-52.

Lancaster, Eliott. "Fighting Back." *Financial Planner* 14 (May 1985), 59-62.

Levi, Michael. "Giving Creditors the Business: The Criminal Law in Inaction." *International Journal of the Sociology of Law* 12 (August 1984), 321-333.

Levitt, Arthur, Jr. "Self-Regulation at the Amex: Protecting the Endangered Entrepreneur." *Directors & Boards* 6 (Summer 1981), 31-32.

Mahapatra, Sitikantha. "Investor Reaction to a Corporate Social Accounting." *Journal of Business Finance & Accounting* 11 (Spring 1984), 29-40.

"Maintaining CU Ethics." *Credit Union Magazine* 48 (March 1982), 30.

Maneri, K. P. "New Breed of Bank Robber." *D & B Reports* 29 (July 1, 1981), 20-22.

Mangels, John D. "Philosophical Context of Banking in the 80s." *Bankers Monthly* 98 (November 15, 1981), 21-22.

Marinelli, Janet. "Making the Stockmarket Safe for Democracy." *Environmental Action* 1 (September-October 1983), 23-26.

Mellert, Robert B. "Ethics and the Sharing of Credit Information." *Business and Professional Ethics Journal* 1 (Winter 1982), 61-68. Commentary: by Robert E. Morris and Edward G. Roberts, 69.

Miller, G. "Games Raiders Play." *Institutional Investor* 19 (July 1985), 105-106.

Morris, Walter S. "Corporate Takeovers and Professional Investors." *Financial Analysts Journal* 39 (January-February 1983), 75-80.

O'Malley, Kevin F. "The Federal Criminal Liability of Bank Personnel Under the Misapplication Statute." *Banking Law Journal* 99 (February 1982), 100-135.

Patterson, Roger. "The Responsibilities of Banks in Financing Tender Offer Takeovers of Customers." *University of Chicago Law Review* 48 (Spring 1981), 439-461.

Peebles, Lynn. "Moves by Life Insurance Companies into Loan Business Are Attacked." *Chronicle of Higher Education* 31 (November 13, 1985), 13+.

Pennebaker, Kenneth J. "Values Code Invigorates Corporate Mission." *Bank Marketing* 16 (May 1984), 16.

Philips, Michael. "Do Banks Loan Money?" *Journal of Business Ethics* 1 (August 1982), 249-250.

Pol, Louis, and Rebecca F. Guy. "Discrimination in Home Improvement Loans: A Rejoinder." *Journal of Bank Research* 12 (Autumn 1981), 192.

"Price Pessimism Drives Lenders to Fall Closings." *Successful Farming* 83 (October 1985), 10F.

Quirk, William J. "The Citi Never Sleeps: But the Bank Might Be Comatose." *Business and Society Review* 43 (Fall 1982), 16-20.

Rasmus, John C. "Could a Free Lunch Cost You?" *ABA Banking Journal* 77 (August 1985), 60-62.

Rea, Samuel A., Jr. "Arm-Breaking, Consumer Credit and Personal Bankruptcy." *Economic Inquiry* 22 (April 1984), 188-208.

"A Scandal Makes Waves Offshore." *Business Week* (August 16, 1982), 78, 80.

Scholl, Jaye. "Messing with the Syndicate: Street Sharpshooters Target Underwriters." *Barron's* 62 (June 21, 1982), 15, 59.

Smalley, John J. "Ethics and Standards in Foreign Exchange Dealings." *World of Banking* 4 (March-April 1985), 10-11.

"Sneaky Speakers." [Stockbrokers Sales Promotion Methods] *Money* 14 (September 1985), 13.

Streeter, W. W. "Honesty Has No Degrees—You Are Either Honest or Dishonest." *ABA Banking Journal* 77 (June 1985), 6.

Swope, Genilee. "Corporate Ethics—Finance America Has a Plan for Implementation." *Credit* 8 (May-June 1982), 28-30.

Tipgos, Manuel A. "Compliance With the Foreign Corrupt Practices Act." *Financial Executive* 49 (August 1981), 38-40.

"United States: Anti-Apartheid." *Banker* 135 (June 1985), 9+.

"Vermont Bank Values New Code of Ethics." *ABA Banking Journal* 77 (June 1985), 14.

Vohs, Dennis. "The Financial Executive's Role in Computer Security." *Financial Executive* 49 (April 1981), 30-32.

Walker, Robert E. L. "Where Banks Stand in Defending Privacy of Customers." *ABA Banking Journal* 73 (October 1981), 127-128.

Warner, Arthur E., and F. J. Ingram. "A Test for Discrimination in a Mortgage Market." *Journal of Bank Research* 13 (Summer 1982), 116-124.

Weiss, Gary. "Mayor Indicted with Dominelli." *Barron's* 64 (September 24, 1984), 49.

Weiss, Gary. "Rematch: The SEC and First Jersey Clash Again." *Barron's* 65 (November 4, 1985), 79.

"When E. F. Hutton Talks." *U.S. Banker* 96 (July 1985), 4+.

Wimberly, Gerard E., Jr. "Corporate Recovery of Insider Trading Profits at Common Law." *Corporation Law Review* 8 (Summer 1985), 197-250.

"Zeroing in on the Crisis in Agriculture." *ABA Banking Journal* 77 (November 1985), 35-37.

Competition

Books

Bagdikian, Ben H. *The Media Monopoly*. Boston: Beacon Press, 1983.

Borcherding, Thomas E., and Gary W. Dorosh. *The Egg Marketing Board: A Case Study of Monopoly and Its Social Costs*. Vancouver, B.C.: Fraser Institute, 1981.

Bottom, Norman R., Jr., and Robert R. J. Gallati. *Industrial Espionage:*

Intelligence Techniques and Countermeasures. Boston: Butterworths, 1984.

Cetron, Marvin. *The Future of American Business: The U.S. in World Competition*. New York: McGraw-Hill, 1985.

Eells, Richard, and Peter Nehemkis. *Corporate Intelligence and Espionage: A Blueprint for Executive Decision Making*. New York; Macmillan, 1984.

Fuld, Leonard M. *Competitive Intelligence: How to Get It How to Use It*. New York: Wiley, 1985.

Gray, Bradford H., ed. *The New Health Care for Profit: Doctors and Hospitals in a Competitive Environment*. Washington, D.C.: National Academy Press, 1983.

Halamka, John D. *Espionage in the Silicon Valley*. Berkeley, Calif.: SYBEX, 1984.

Heims, Peter A. *Countering Industrial Espionage*. Leatherhead, U.K.: 20th Century Security Educ., 1982.

Johnson, Douglas. *Computer Ethics: A Guide for a New Age*. Elgin, Ill.: Brethren Press, 1984.

Melvern, Linda, Nick Anning, and David Hebditch. *Techno-Bandits*. Boston: Houghton Mifflin, 1984.

Mills, D. Q. *The New Competitors*. New York: John Wiley, 1985.

Mirow, Kurt R., and Harry Maurer. *Webs of Power: International Cartels and the World Economy*. Boston: Houghton Mifflin, 1982.

Noam, Eli M., ed. *Video Media Competition*. New York: Columbia Univ. Press, 1985.

Sammon, William L., Mark A. Kurland, and Robert Spitalnic. *Business Competitor Intelligence: Methods for Collecting, Organizing and Using Information*. New York: Wiley, 1984.

Saunders, Michael. *Protecting Your Business Secrets*. New York: Nichols Pub. Co., 1985.

Stevens, Mark. *The Accounting Wars*. New York: Macmillan, 1985.

Vlahos, Olivia. *Doing Business: The Anthropology of Striving, Thriving and Beating Out the Competition*. New York: Watts, 1985.

Wiseman, Charles. *Strategy and Computers Information Systems as Competitive Weapons*. Homewood, Ill.: Dow Jones-Irwin, 1985.

Articles

Alexander, Charles P. "Going for the Gene Green." *Time* 126 (November 4, 1985), 56.

Alsop, Ronald. "Marketing: Advertising Conflicts Become More Common and Complex." *Wall Street Journal* (May 24, 1984), 35.

"America, the World Trade Predator?" *Business Marketing* 70 (February 1985), 4.

Anderson, Judy. "Off-Air Videotaping: Are You Guilty of Copyright Violations?" *Public Relations Journal* 40 (September 1984), 26-27.

"Apple Counterattacks the Counterfeiters." *Business Week* (August 16, 1982), 82.

"ASCAP, Radio Industry Prepare for Rate Court." *Television/Radio Age* 32 (July 8, 1985), 44-45.

"Assaulting the Competition." *Dun's Business Month* 126 (November 1985), 34.

Battistella, Roger M. "Hospital Receptivity to Market Competition: Image and Reality." *Health Care Management Review* 10 (Summer 1985), 19-26.

Baumol, W. J., and J. A. Ordover. "Use of Antitrust to Subvert Competition." *Journal of Law and Economics* 28 (May 1985), 267-270.

Bennett, Roger C., and Robert G. Cooper." The Misuse of Marketing: An American Tragedy." *Business Horizons* 24 (November-December 1981), 51-61.

Bequai, August. "The Industrial Spy: Red Flags and Recourse." *Security Management* 29 (August 1985), 93-94.

Bequai, August. "Management Can Prevent Industrial Espionage." *Advanced Management Journal* 50 (Winter 1985), 17-19.

Blake, Frederick H. "Black Public Relations Firms: Are They Surviving?" *Public Relations Journal* 39 (October 1983), 31-32.

Brusick, Philipe. "UN Control of Restrictive Business Practices: A Decisive First Step." *Journal of World Trade Law (UK)* 17 (July-August 1983), 337-351.

"Business Intelligence Beehive." *Business Week* (December 14, 1981), 51.

Cannon, James. "An Oligopoly in Western Coal." *Business and Society Review* 41 (Spring 1982), 12-15.

Carrington, Tim. "Scramble in Space: Star Wars Plan Spurs Defense Firms to Vie for Billions of Dollars." *Wall Street Journal* (May 21, 1985), 1.

Chermside, Herbert B. "Some Ethical Conflicts Affecting University Patent Administration. Part 1." *Journal of the Society of Research Administrators* 16 (Winter 1985), 23-24.

Chermside, Herbert B. "Some Ethical Conflicts Affecting University Patent Administration. Part 2." *Journal of the Society of Research Administrators* 16 (Spring 1985), 11-18.

"Competition from Without and Within." *Credit Union Magazine* 49 (November 1983), 22-25.

"Competitive Intelligence Gathering: Keeping Ahead of the Competition." *Small Business Report* 10 (August 1985), 52-56.

"The Consumer Cost of U.S. Trade Restraints." *Federal Reserve New York* 10 (Summer 1985), 1-12.

Cooper, Carol. "The Real Cost of Software Piracy." *Information Age* 6 (April 1984), 98-102.

Couretas, John. "Product Pirates Plunder the Business/Industrial Marketplace." *Business Marketing* 85 (January 1985), 36-47.

DiLorenzo, Thomas J. "Competition: Except Where Prohibited by Law." *Reason* 16 (February 1985), 34-37.

Evangelauf, J. "State Laws Restricting Commercial Ventures by Universities Urged by Trade Associations." *Chronicle of Higher Education* 30 (July 31, 1985), 13.

Flax, Steven. "How to Snoop on Your Competitors." *Fortune* 109 (May 14, 1984), 28-33.

Fuld, L. M. "Sizing Up the Competition." *Canadian Business Review* 12 (Summer 1985), 35-37.

Gilbert, R. J., and D.M.G. Newbery. "Preemptive Patenting and the Persistence of Monopoly." *American Economic Review* 72 (June 1982), 514-526.

Gordon, Ian. "Your Survival Kit: Competitive Intelligence." *Business Quarterly B.C. (Canada)*, (Summer 1982), 65-67.

Gorovitz, Samuel. "Advertising Professional Success Rates." *Business and Professional Ethics Journal* 3 (Spring-Summer 1984), 31-45. Commentaries: by Richard T. De George, 47; Katherine L. Clancy, 53; Alan H. Goldman, 57.

"The Gray Market: Mercedes Tries to Slam on the Brakes." *Business Week* (September 2, 1985), 34.

Greene, Richard. "Never Mind R & D, How About T & G?" *Forbes* 134 (September 24, 1984), 142.

Hertzberg, Daniel. "Policy Fight: Asbestos Lawsuits Spur War among Insurers, with Billions at Stake." *Wall Street Journal* (June 14, 1982), 1.

Hope, A. "Sum of Its Parts." *Car and Driver* 26 (May 1981), 30.

"If It Moves, Sue It." *Economist* 296 (July 20, 1985), 66.

"It Isn't a Glorious Thing to Be a Technology Pirate King." *Across the Board* 21 (May 1984), 36-42.

Johnson, Bob. "Explosion in Industry Lawsuits Seen by '85." *Computerworld* 15 (June 1, 1981), 16.

Kallen, B. "Blaming the Broker." *Forbes* 136 (September 23, 1985), 148.

Kelly, Orr. "How Russia Steals U.S. Secrets Under Our Noses." *U.S. News and World Report* 91 (October 12, 1981), 45-46.

Kempe, Frederick. "Losing Battle: Keeping Technology Out of Soviet Hands Seems to Be Impossible." *Wall Street Journal* (July 24, 1984), 1.

Knoell, William H. " 'Free-Trade' Liquidation of U.S. Industries." *Directors & Boards* 9 (Spring 1985), 14-18.

Kovach, Jeffrey L. "Competitive Intelligence." *Industry Week* 223 (November 12, 1984), 50-53.

Larson, Erik. "Modem Operandi: In High Tech Industry, New Firms Often Get Fast Trip to the Courtroom." *Wall Street Journal* (August 14, 1984), 1.

Levinson, Marc. "Twelve Protectionist Traps." *Across the Board* 22 (September 1985), 24-31.

Maher, Philip. "Corporate Espionage: When Market Research Goes Too Far." *Business Marketing* 69 (October 1984), 50-66.

McDonald, Kim. "Patents Called a Must for Companies Sponsoring University Research." *Chronicles of Higher Education* 25 (November 17, 1982), 12.

McMahon, Gene. "Putting a Lid on Software Piracy." *Management Technology* 2 (June 1984), 57-59.

Meyerowitz, S. A. "Brand X Strikes Back! The Developing Law of Comparative Advertising." *Business Marketing* 70 (August 1985), 81-84.

Michael, Mark. "Patent Rights and Better Mousetraps." *Business and Professional Ethics Journal* 3 (Fall 1983), 13-23.

Michelman, James H. "Some Ethical Consequences of Economic Competition." *Journal of Business Ethics* 2 (May 1983), 79-87.

"The Moral Side of Business Intelligence." *Business Owner* (April 1983), 3+.

Morone, James A. "The Unruly Rise of Medical Capitalism." *Hastings Center Report* 15 (August 1985), 28-31.

Murray, Kevin D. "Corporate Counterspy." *Security Management* 25 (April 1981), 48-53.

"A New Market for Hospital Chains." *Business Week* (April 11, 1983), 124A-124C.

"1984 Was a Good Year for Health Care Competition." *Employee Benefit Plan Review* 40 (July 1985), 86.

O'Hare, Michael. "Copyright: When Is Monopoly Efficient?" *Journal of Policy Analysis and Management* 4 (Spring 1985) 407-418.

O'Reilly, James T. "Confidentiality and TSCA: Can This Marriage Be Saved?" *Chemical Times & Trends* 7 (October 1984), 20-23.

Pollock, Ted. "Sales Ideas That Work—How Should You Talk About Your Competition?" *American Salesman* 27 (December 1982), 26-31.

Pool, Gail, and Michael Comendul. "The Computer Magazines' Puffery Problem." *Columbia Journalism Review* 24 (September/October 1985), 49-51.

"Prescription Drugmakers Try to Cope with a Dose of Adversity." *Business Week* (September 17, 1984), 132-140.

Pugel, T. A., and I. Walter. "U.S. Corporate Interests and the Political Economy of Trade Policy." *Review of Economic Statistics* 67 (August 1985), 465-473.

Ramo, Simon. "Why the U.S. Needs 'Supersized' Companies." *Directors and Boards* 7 (Summer 1983), 18-22.

Romeo, P. "Your Competitor's Latest Ploy: Bribing Customers." *Hotel Motel Management* 198 (May 1983), 6.

Ross, Ian M. "The Global Contest in Industrial Competitiveness Has Just Begun." *Research Management* 28 (May-June 1985), 10-14.

Schiller, Bradley R. " 'Corporate Kidnap' of the Small-Business Employee." *Public Interest* 72 (Summer 1983), 72-87.

Statman, Meir, and Tyzoon T. Tyebjee. "Trademarks, Patents, and Innovation in the Ethical Drug Industry." *Journal of Marketing* 45 (Summer 1981), 71-81.

Stein, R. H., and R. F. Baron. "One Area of Conflict Between Public Higher Education and Private Business: Student Commercial Enterprises." *NASPA Journal* 21 (Summer 1983), 17-22.

Stern, Paula. "Foreign Product Counterfeiting—Private Business Sometimes Needs the Government." *Vital Speeches of the Day* 51 (September 1, 1985), 674-677.

Steward, Robert W., and Michael A. Hiltzik. "Industrial Espionage Is Big Business." *Best of Business* 4 (Fall 1982), 96-104.

Stokes, Robert, and Richard Conniff. "Is Somebody Listening?" *GEO* 5 (November 1983), 42-50+.

Strachan, James L., et al. "The Price Reaction to (Alleged) Corporate Crime." *Financial Review* 18 (May 1983), 121-132.

Straker, T. "Detection and Prevention of Financial Fraud." *Management Accounting* 63 (July-August 1985), 29-30.

Sweezy, Paul M., et al. "Can Socially Responsible Societies Compete Economically?" *Business and Society Review* 52 (Winter 1985), 11-14.

Sweezy, Paul M. "Competition and Monopoly." *Monthly Review* 33 (May 1981), 1-16.

Tracy, Eleanor J. "Selling Software on the Honor System." *Fortune* 110 (October 15, 1984), 146.

Waldholtz, Michael. "Pillbox War: Drug Battle Heats Up Between Brand-Name and Generic Makers." *Wall Street Journal* (August 13, 1984), 1.

Watson, Gary S. "The Patentability of Living Organisms: Diamond v. Chakrabarty, 447 U.S. 303 (1980)." *American Business Law Journal* 20 (Spring 1982), 93-102.

Weidenbaum, Murray L. "The UN as a Regulator of Private Enterprise." *Notre Dame Journal of Law, Ethics and Public Policy* 1 (Winter 1985), 349-363.

Weil, T. P. "Procompetition or More Regulation?" *Health Care Management Review* 10 (Summer 1985), 27-35.

"When Free Markets Throttle Competition." *Economist* 296 (August 24, 1985), 19-20.

Wittrock, Quentin R. "Use of Personal Names in Noncompeting Businesses: Doctrines of Unfair Competition, Trademark Infringement and Dilution." *Iowa Law Review* 70 (May 1985), 995-1019.

Marketing

Books

Asbury, Carolyn H. *Orphan Drugs: Medical Versus Market Value*. Lexington, Mass.: Lexington Books, 1985.

Fenichell, Stephen. *Other People's Money*. Garden City, N.Y.: Anchor Press, 1985.

Laczniak, Gene R., and Patrick E. Murphy. *Marketing Ethics: Guidelines for Managers*. Lexington, Mass.: Lexington Books, 1985.

Articles

Beaver, Bill, and Fred Silvester. "The Gall in Mother's Milk: The Infant Formula Controversy and the WHO Marketing Code . . ." *Journal of Advertising (UK)* 1 (January-March 1982), 1-10.

Chonko, Lawrence B., et al. "Measuring the Importance of Ethical Situations as a Source of Role Conflict." *Journal of Personal Selling & Sales Management* 3 (May 1983), 41-47.

Cooper, Robert. "Marketing Attuned to Ethical Concerns Aids Dentist." *Marketing News* 17 (December 9, 1983), 9.

Couretas, John. "Trade Show Biz Airs 'Kickback.' " *Business Marketing* 69 (August 1984), 8+.

Crosby, Richard. "Uniform Ethical Code Is Impractical Due to Shifting Marketing Research Circumstances." *Marketing News* 15 (September 18, 1981), 16.

Dilenschneider, Robert L. "Ethics in Health Care Marketing." *Vital Speeches of the Day* 51 (June 1, 1985), 494-497.

Dixon, D. F. "The Ethical Component of Marketing: An Eighteenth-Century View." *Journal of Macromarketing* 2 (Spring 1982), 38-56.

"Ethics for Emerging Field a Key Topic Before 1,000 Attending Health Services Marketing Symposium." *Marketing News* 19 (June 7, 1985), 20-21.

Ferrell, O. C., et al. "A Contingency Framework for Understanding Ethical Decision Making in Marketing." *Journal of Marketing* 49 (Summer 1985), 87-96.

Fisher, Walter D., Jr. "North Carolina's Theft of Cable Television Service Statute: Prospects of a Brighter Future for the Cable Television." *North Carolina Law Review* 63 (August 1985), 1296-1316.

Friedman, Hershey H. "Ancient Marketing Practices: The View from Talmudic Times." *Journal of Public Policy & Marketing* 3 (1984), 194-204.

Fritszche, David J., and Helmut Becker. "Ethical Behavior of Marketing Managers." *Journal of Business Ethics* 2 (November 1983), 291-299.

Gillin, Paul, et al. "Early Product Announcements: A Question of Ethics." *Computerworld* 18 (July 9, 1984), 14-15.

Gowans, Christopher W. "Integrity in the Corporation: The Plight of Corporate Product Advocates." *Journal of Business Ethics* 3 (February 1984), 21-28.

Hoffman, Alexander. "Ethical Guidelines That Grow and Adapt." *Direct Marketing* 48 (August 1985), 102-103.

Hoffman, Alexander. "Psychographics Can Be Useful but Sometimes Dangerous." *Direct Marketing* 48 (July 1985), 110.

Hunt, Shelby D., and Lawrence B. Chonko. "Marketing and Machiavellianism." *Journal of Marketing* 48 (Summer 1984), 30-42.

Inhorn, Marcia C. "Riding the Ethical-to-Proprietary Wave." *Drug Topics* 125 (May 1, 1981), 32-36.

Jung, L. S. "Commercialization and the Professions." *Business and Professional Ethics Journal* 2 (Winter 1983), 57-81. Commentaries: by Tibor R. Machan, 83; Sanford A. Marcus, 89.

Laczniak, Gene R. "Framework for Analyzing Marketing Ethics." *Journal of Macromarketing* 3 (Spring 1983), 7-18.

Laczniak, Gene R., Robert F. Lusch, and William A. Strang. "Ethical Marketing: Perceptions of Economic Goods and Social Problems." *Journal of Macromarketing* 1 (Spring 1981), 49-57.

Lee, Kam-Hon. "Ethical Beliefs in Marketing Management: A Cross-Cultural Study." *European Journal of Marketing* 15 (1981), 58-67.

Lee, Susan. "Enough Is Enough." *Forbes* 134 (September 10, 1984), 109-112.

Lefko, Jeffrey J. "New Concepts in Marketing Health Care." *Business and Economic Review* 29 (March 1983), 3-7.

Lipman, Joanne. "Angry Tenants Charge Rouse Co. with Unfair Practices in Its Mall." *Wall Street Journal* (June 18, 1984), 25.

Michelman, James. "Deception in Commercial Negotiation." *Journal of Business Ethics* 2 (November 1983), 255-262.

Mutter, John. "Scandal at the PX: Marketers Go AWOL." *Sales and Marketing Management* 126 (March 16, 1981), 30-37.

Neighbor, Chad. "Nukes and Crumpets: With a Collapsed Domestic Market, the American Nuclear Industry Is Banking on Exports to Britain." *Environmental Action* 15 (June 1983), 12-14.

Nevin, John R., Shelby D. Hunt, and Michael G. Levas. "Legal Remedies for Deceptive and Unfair Practices in Franchising." *Journal of Macromarketing* 1 (Spring 1981), 23-24.

Paskowski, Marianne. "Do Media Buying Services Sell Their Clients Short?" *Marketing and Media Decisions* 20 (August 1985), 49+.

Piasecki, Bruce. "Big Oil's Treacherous Plan to Squeeze America Dry." *Business and Society Review* 45 (Spring 1983), 40-45.

Prillaman, Al. "Aladdin Puts a Bounty on Market Intelligence." *Sales and Marketing Management* 126 (April 6, 1981), 66+.

"Professional Standards Committee Comes to Grip with Issues of

Marketing Ethics." *Marketing News* 16 (September 2, 1982), 10-24.

Reagan, Michael D. "Energy: Government Policy or Market Result?" *Policy Studies Journal* 11 (March 1983), 65-385.

Reddy, Allan C., and C. P. Rao. "Beware Those Pitfalls When Marketing U.S. Technologies in Developing Countries." *Marketing News* 19 (March 1, 1985), 3, 6.

Roberts, Cecily. "Can the Flood of Counterfeit Products Be Stopped?" *Security Management* 29 (October 1985), 32-38.

Rogers, David. "U.S. Tobacco Industry Faces Uncertain Future as Rift Grows Between Farmers, Manufacturers." *Wall Street Journal* (September 30, 1985), 42.

Rudolph, Barbara. "Tobacco Takes a New Road." *Time* 126 (November 18, 1985), 70-71.

Schneider, Kenneth C. "The Role of Ethics in Marketing Research." *Mid-Atlantic Journal of Business* 22 (Winter 1983/84), 11-20.

Sirgy, M. J., et al. "The Question of Value in Social Marketing: Use of a Quality-of-Life Theory to Achieve Long-Term Life Satisfaction." *American Journal to Economics & Sociology* 44 (April 1985), 215-228.

Smith, Scott M. "Marketing Research and Corporate Litigation . . . Where Is the Balance of Ethical Justice?" *Journal of Business Ethics* 3 (August 1984), 185-194.

"Sports Sponsorship Requires Marketing Expertise, Realistic Expectations, and Social Responsibility." *Marketing News* 18 (April 13, 1984), 14.

Werner, Tom. "Despite Industry Outcry IRS Still Wants Lists." *ZIP/Target Marketing* 6 (November 1983), 10, 12.

Whalen, Bernie. "Report Rise in Use of 'J.R.' Research Tactics." *Marketing News (Sect.1)* 18 (May 25, 1984), 1, 30-31.

Wilson, Aubrey, et al. "The Marketing of 'Unmentionables.' " *Harvard Business Review* 59 (January-February 1981), 91-102.

Zinkhan, George M., and Betsy D. Gelb. "Competitive Intelligence Practices of Industrial Marketers." *Industrial Marketing Management* 14 (November 1985), 269-275.

Pricing and Antitrust

Books

Antitrust, the Media and the New Technology. New York: PLI, 1981.

Armentano, Dominick T. *Antitrust and Monopoly: Anatomy of a Policy Failure*. New York: Wiley, 1982.

Atwood, James, and R. Kingman Brewster, Jr. *Antitrust and American Business Abroad*. New York: McGraw, 1981.

Audretsch, David B. *The Effectiveness of Antitrust Policy Towards Horizontal Mergers*. Ann Arbor, Mich.: UMI Research Press, 1983.

Calkins, Richad M. *Antitrust Guidelines for the Business Executive*. Homewood, Ill.: Dow Jones-Irwin, 1981.

Fisher, Franklin M. *Antitrust and Regulation: Essays in Memory of John J. McGowan*. Cambridge, Mass.: MIT Press, 1985.

Articles

Block, Michael K., Frederick C. Nold, and Joseph G. Sidak. "The Deterrent Effect of Anti-Trust Enforcement." *Journal of Political Economy* 89 (June 1981), 429-455.

Carley, William M. "IBM Grant Helped Pay Baxter's Salary During Year's Leave from Teaching Post." *Wall Street Journal* (April 2, 1982), 3.

Feldman, Laurie N. "Employees Discharged in Retaliation for Resisting Employers' Antitrust Violations: The Need for a Federal Remedy." *University of Chicago Law Review* 5 (Spring 1984), 559-580.

Flax, Steven. "The Crackdown on Colluding Roadbuilders." *Fortune* 108 (October 3, 1983), 79-85.

Hoffman, Alexander C. "Ethical Guidelines, MPS: Key DMA Commitments." *Direct Marketing* 46 (February 1984), 126.

Katzman, Robert A. "The Attenuating of Antitrust." *Brookings Review* 2 (Summer 1984), 23-27.

Kosterlitz, Julie. "The Hospital Business." *National Journal* 17 (September 28, 1985), 2180-2187.

Olsen, Randall J. "Price Controls, Price Discrimination and the Market for Petroleum." *Policy Studies Journal* 13 (September 1984), 55-66.

Panneton, Roland L. "Ethics, Due Process and Antitrust." *Life Association News* 76 (October 1981), 159-162.

Sebastian, Pamela. "Street Fight: Linked Deals in Stocks and Futures Contracts Roil Prices, Critics Say." *Wall Street Journal* (October 22, 1985), 1+.

Smith, Thomas B. "Buttering Up Congress and Milking Consumers." *Business and Society Review* 42 (Summer 1982), 34-39.

Tarnoff, S. "PPOs Facing Potential Antitrust Worries." *Business Insurance* 19 (July 22, 1985), 16+.

Taylor, Robert E. "Highway Robbery?: Paving Firms Accused of Rigging Road Bids on Southeast Projects." *Wall Street Journal* (May 29, 1981), 1.

Trombetta, William L. "The Professionals Under Scrutiny: An Antitrust Perspective." *Journal of Consumer Affairs* 16 (Summer 1982), 88-111.

White, Robin. "The Great California Utility Rate Crisis." *Business and Society Review* 42 (Summer 1982), 30-33.

Winkler, John. "Price as a Weapon of War." *Industrial Marketing Digest (UK)* 8 (Second Quarter 1983), 88-93.

Purchasing

Books

Barlow, C.W. *The Buyer and the Law.* New York: Van Nostrand Reinhold, 1982.

Articles

"An Agency View of a Major Problem with Some Purchasing Agents . . . and How to Solve It." *Agency Sales Magazine* 14 (July 1984), 19.

Allerheiligen, Robert, John L. Graham, and Chi-Yuan Lin. "Honesty in Interorganizational Negotiations in the United States, Japan, Brazil, and the Republic of China." *Journal of Macromarketing* 5 (Fall 1985), 4-16.

Bayles, Michael D. "Ethical Issues in Purchasing Management." *Business Quarterly (Canada)* 48 (Spring 1983), 42-47.

Beckenstein, Alan R., H. L. Gabel, and Karlene Roberts. "An Executive's Guide to Antitrust Compliance." *Harvard Business Review* 61 (September-October 1983), 94-102.

Bennett, Joel R. "Antitrust Laws Cover Sham Litigation." *Entrepreneur* 12 (October 1984), 60-62.

Browning, John, and Noel B. Zariskie. "How Ethical Are Industrial Buyers?" *Industrial Marketing Management* 12 (October 1983), 219-224.

Carrington, Tim. "Watered-Down Military Procurement Reforms Will Ensure 'Business as Usual.' " *Wall Street Journal* (August 13, 1985), 60.

"Con Artists Keep Baiting, But Buyers Aren't Biting." *Purchasing* 99 (July 25, 1985), 21-22.

Decker, R. "The Statute of Limitations Won't Allow Time Warps." *Purchasing* 98 (June 13, 1985), 143-144.

"Demise of Unethical Software Hustler Predicted/Get Contract Copies Early, Buyers Told." *Computerworld* 15 (January 26, 1981), SR6.

DeRose, Louis J. "Pseudoethics Do Not Belong in Purchasing." *Purchasing World* 29 (May 1985), 42.

Dubinski, Alan J., and John M. Gwin. "Business Ethics: Buyers and Sellers." *Journal of Purchasing and Materials Management* 17 (Winter 1981), 9-16.

"Ethics of Buying Selling Transportation." *Railway Age* 183 (August 30, 1982), 29-35.

Fiske, Mary Ann. "General Foods Roasted Over Coffee Buying Policy." *Business and Society Review* 49 (Spring 1984), 19-21.

Goodman, Gerson. "Some Caveats for Emptors: Combating Corruption in the Purchasing Department." *D & B Reports* 33 (January-February 1985), 34-35, 53.

Hacker, S. "When a Buying Decision Becomes a Question of Ethics." *Association Management* 37 (May 1985), 143.

Kane, Sid. "Keeping Your Buyers Honest." *Venture* 6 (December 1984), 38-39.

Krishna, V. "Purchase Ethics and Policies." *ASCI Journal of Management (India)* 13 (March 1984), 164-190.

Mason, Roger. "Conflict of Interests in Purchase Decision Making." *Journal of General Management* 9 (Spring 1984), 60-70.

Othmer, Craig. "A Model Procurement Code—New Mexico Style." *Contract Management* 24 (May 1984), 30-35.

Thomas, Michael H. "Know Where You Stand on Ethics." *Purchasing World* 28 (October 1984), 90-91.

Takeovers and Mergers

Books

Carrington, Timothy. *The Year They Sold Wall Street.* Boston: Houghton Mifflin, 1985.

Commons, Dorman L. *Tender Offer: The Sneak Attack in Corporate Takeovers.* Berkeley, Calif.: Univ. Cal. Press, 1985.

Goldberg, Walter H. *Mergers: Motives, Modes, Methods.* New York: Nichols Pub., 1983.

Hartz, Peter F. *Merger: The Exclusive Inside Story of the Bendix-Martin-Marietta Takeover.* New York: Morrow, 1985.

Keenan, Michael, and Lawrence White. *Mergers and Acquisitions: Current Problems in Perspective.* Lexington, Mass.: Lexington Books, 1982.

Lampert, Hope. *Till Death Do Us Part: Bendix vs. Martin Marietta.* New York: Harcourt Brace Jovanovich, 1983.

Organisation for Economic Cooperation and Development. Merger Policies and Recent Trends in Mergers. Paris: O.E.C.D., 1984.

Phalon, Richard. *The Takeover Barons of Wall Street: Inside the Billion-Dollar Merger Game.* New York: Putnam, 1981.

Rhoades, Stephen A. *Power, Empire Building, and Mergers.* Lexington, Mass.: Lexington Books, 1983.

Steinberg, Marc I. *Tender Offers: Developments and Commentaries.* Westport, Conn.: Quorum Books, 1985.

Articles

Adams, Walter. "Mega-Mergers Spell Danger." *Challenge* 25 (March-April 1982), 12-17.

Adler, Herbert S. "The Honeymoon Is the Key to Corporate Marriages." *Management Focus* 28 (November-December 1981), 38-41.

Ahlfeld, William J. "Combatting the Hostile Takeover Attempt." *Business Horizons* 24 (May-June 1981), 70-76.

"American Media: Magazine Merger Mania." *Economist* 294 (March 9, 1985), 71-72.

"American Takeover Bids: More Arms, More Raiders." *Economist* 295 (April 20, 1985), 88+.

Arthur, Thomas C., Tom Kirby, and Bert W. Rein. "Defamation Suits as a Weapon in Corporate Control Battles." *Business Lawyer* 37 (November 1981), 1-25.

Ashton, D. J., et al. "A Partial Theory of Takeover Bids." *Journal of Finance* 39 (March 1984), 167-183.

Batt, Robert. "When Oil Firms Merge, MIS Groups Follow Suit—But Not Without Problems." *Computerworld* 16 (July 19, 1982), 13.

Bittlingmayer, G. "Did Antitrust Policy Cause the Great Merger Wave?" *Journal of Law and Economics* 28 (April 1985), 77-118.

Brownstein, Ronald. "Merger Wars." *National Journal* 15 (July 23, 1983), 1538-1541.

Burck, Arthur. "The Hidden Trauma of Merger Mania." *Business Week* (December 6, 1982), 14.

Carley, William M. "Battle Tactics: Carl Icahn's Strategies in His Quest for TWA Are a Model for Raiders." *Wall Street Journal* (June 20, 1985), 1+.

Carley, William M. "TWA Holder Icahn Has 54.4% of Stake Winning Effective Control of Airline." *Wall Street Journal* (August 8, 1985), 3.

Carney, William J. "Takeover Tussles: The Courts' Tug-of-War with Corporate Boards." *Business and Society Review* 54 (Summer 1985), 64-68.

Commons, Dorman L. "The Tender Trap: The Sneak Attack in Corporate Warfare." *New Management* 2 (Spring 1985), 7-15.

Dewar, Elaine. "Takeover." *Canadian Business* 58 (November 1985), 26-29+.

Drucker, Peter F. "Taming the Corporate Takeover." *Wall Street Journal* (October 30, 1984), 30.

Dugger, W. M. "The Shortcomings of Concentration Ratios in the Conglomerate Age: New Sources and Uses of Corporate Power." *Journal of Economic Issues* 19 (June 1985), 343-353.

Duncan, Charles T. "Regulatory Threat: A Distorted Role for Outside Directors." *Directors & Boards* 8 (Summer 1984), 15, 18-19.

Dunkin, Amy, and Cynthia Green. "Bergerac Lost Revlon—But No Tears, Please." *Business Week* (November 4, 1985), 68-69.

Dwyer, Paula. "Merger Mania: The Courts Finally Start Looking Out for Shareholders." *Business Week* (November 11, 1985), 35.

Field, P. "The Attack on the M and A Barons." *Euromoney* (May 1985), 89.

Foer, Albert A. "The New Antitrust Guidelines: Full Speed Ahead for Business Combinations." *Business and Society Review* 44 (Winter 1983), 23-28.

Fogg, Joseph G., III. "Takeovers: Last Chance for Self-Restraint." *Harvard Business Review* 63 (November-December 1985), 30+.

Forbes, Daniel. "Mergers Shakeup the Job Market." *Dun's Business Month* 126 (November 1985), 48-49.

"Foul Play on a Megamerger?" *Newsweek* 106 (December 30, 1985), 46-48.

Francis, Diane. "Swallowed Alive." *Canadian Business* 54 (July 1981), 54-60.

Gillis, John G. "Ethical Considerations in Takeovers." *Financial Analysts Journal* 4 (March-April 1985), 10-12, 18.

Glasgall, W., et al. "Chapter 11 for Texaco? It's Not Impossible." *Business Week* (December 9, 1985), 36-37.

Greenfield, Jay, and Robert S. Weininger. "Regulators Widen Options in Weighing Mergers." *Mergers & Acquisitions* 20 (September 1985), 54-59.

Greenwald, John, et al. "Today Things Are Getting Badly Out of Hand." *Time* 126 (December 23, 1985), 51.

Halbouty, Michel T. "The Hostile Takeover of Free Enterprise: Respect for Human Dignity." *Vital Speeches of the Day* 51 (August 1, 1985), 613-616.

Hammer, Harold H. "Of 'Blind Loans' and Other Abuses." *Directors & Boards* 9 (Spring 1985), 8.

Hawthorne, Fran. "What Price Divestiture?" *Institutional Investor* 19 (October 1985), 178-179+.

Henry, Gordon M., et al. "The Texaco Star Strikes Out in Houston." *Time* 126 (December 23, 1985), 50.

Hill, G. C., and John D. Williams. "Buyout Boom." *Wall Street Journal* (December 29, 1983), 1+.

"Holding on in a Takeover." *Business Week* (September 27, 1982), 118-120.

"How the New Merger Boom Will Benefit the Economy." *Business Week* (February 6, 1984), 42-43+.

Jensen, Michael C. "Takeovers: Folklore and Science." *Harvard Business Review* 62 (November-December 1984), 109-121.

Jereski, Laura. "The Quick-Draw Takeover." *Forbes* 136 (November 4, 1985), 70-72.

Kavanagh, John. "Heartaches Even in the Friendliest Merger." *Rydge's* (October 1983), 60-62.

Kennedy, L. A. "How to Use Research to Prevent a Takeover." *Public Relations Journal* 41 (May 1985), 31.

Kesner, Idalene F., and Dan R. Dalton. "Antitakeover Tactics: Management 42, Stockholders 0." *Business Horizons* 28 (September-October 1985), 17-25.

Kittrell, C. M. "The Pirates of Profitability." *Vital Speeches of the Day* 51 (May 15, 1985), 453-456.

Lajoux, Alexandra R. "Mergers: The Last Frontier for American Business?" *New Management* 1 (1983), 22-29.

"Let's Make a Deal." *Time* 126 (December 23, 1985), 42-47.

Leukart, Barbara J. "Dealing with Labor When a Company Is Sold." *Mergers & Acquisitions* 19 (Spring 1984), 40-44.

Levin, Doron P., Tim Metz, and Richard B. Schmitt. "Gulf Strategy in Pickens Challenge Hinges on the Timing of the Battle." *Wall Street Journal* (October 20, 1983), 33.

Levin, Doron P., and Richard B. Schmitt. "Pickens Group Appears to Hold 11.5% of Gulf Oil." *Wall Street Journal* (October 24, 1983), 2.

Magnet, Myron. "Is ITT Fighting Shadows—or Raiders?" *Fortune* 112 (November 11, 1985), 25-28.

Manne, Henry G. "In Defense of the Corporate Coup: Why Mergers Make Market Work Better." *Reason* 15 (January 1984), 51-53.

Marinaccio, Charles L. "Forcing Corporate Raiders to Walk the Plank." *Business and Society Review* 53 (Spring 1985), 25-28.

Marks, Mitchell, and Philip Mirvis. "Merger Syndrome: Stress and Uncertainty." *Mergers & Acquisitions* 20 (Summer 1985), 50-55.

Newlin, William R., and Jay A. Gilmer. "The Pennsylvania Shareholder Protection Act: A New State Approach to Deflecting Corporate Takeovers." *Business Lawyer* 40 (November 1984), 111-127.

Pauly, D. "Merger Ethics, Anyone?" *Newsweek* 106 (December 9, 1985), 46-47.

Phalon, Richard. "Fuel for the Flames?" *Forbes* 136 (November 18, 1985), 122+.

Pickens, T. B., Jr. "Shareholders: The Forgotten People." *Journal of Business Strategy* 6 (Summer 1985), 4-5.

Price, M. "Leveraged Buyouts: The Trend Toward Going Public." *Financial World* 154 (October 23, 1985), 10-23.

Proxmire, William. "Hostile Corporate Takeovers and Raids." *Vital Speeches of the Day* 51 (April 15, 1985), 388-395.

Regan, Arthur C., and Arie Reichel. " 'Shark Repellents': How to Avoid Hostile Takeovers." *Long Range Planning* 18 (December 1985), 60-67.

Richman, James E. "Merger Decision Making: An Ethical Analysis and Recommendation." *California Management Review* 27 (Fall 1984), 177-184.

Ricks, Thomas E. " 'Terrible Ted': Turner's Bid for CBS, Viewed as Outlandish, Fits in with His Image." *Wall Street Journal* (April 19, 1985), 1.

Rodino, Peter W., Jr. "Regulatory Relief: A Paean to End Hostile Takeovers." *Directors & Boards* 8 (Summer 1984), 14, 16-17.

Rose, Frederick, et al. "Battle of the Titans: How T. Boone Pickens Finally Met His Match: Unocal's Fred Hartley." *Wall Street Journal* (May 24, 1985), 1+.

Rosen, Corey, and Michael Caudell-Feagan. "Using ESOPs to Thwart Hostile Takeovers: Beware!" *Pension World* 20 (February 1984), 18-20.

Rowan, Roy, and Thomas Moore. "Behind the Lines in the Bendix War." *Fortune* 106 (October 18, 1982), 156-158+.

Samuelson, Robert J. "Merger Mania." *National Journal* 13 (November 28, 1981), 2126.

Saul, Ralph S. "Hostile Takeovers: What Should Be Done?" *Harvard Business Review* 63 (August-September 1985), 18-24.

Sellers, Patricia. "When Clients Merge, Ad Agencies Quake." *Fortune* 112 (November 11, 1985), 101.

"Senators Introduce Bill for Review of Hostile Takeovers." *Broadcasting* 108 (June 24, 1985), 46.

Sinetar, Marsha. "Mergers, Morale and Productivity." *Personnel Journal* 60 (November 1981), 863-867.

Stewart, James B. "CBS Gets $5.41 Billion Takeover Bid from Turner Network's Affiliates, Employees React Negatively." *Wall Street Journal* (April 19, 1985), 3.

"Takeover Defenses: Backlash Against Greenmail." *Mergers & Acquisitions* 20 (Spring 1985), 21.

"Takeover Defenses: Social Concerns in Spotlight." *Mergers & Acquisitions* 20 (Summer 1985), 18-19.

"Tender Offer Law Under Fire." *Mergers & Acquisitions* 20 (Spring 1985), 9-10.

Thackray, John, et al., "Heading Toward Leveraged-Buyout Burnout?" *Across the Board* 21 (December 1984), 30-37.

Treece, James B. "Tokyo Gets Its First Taste of Greenmail." *Business Week* (September 23, 1985), 56.

"Unfriendly Takeovers: Preparing a Battle Plan." *Chain Store Age Executive* 60 (July 1984), 17-20.

Walking, Ralph A., and Michael S. Long. "Agency Theory, Managerial, and Takeover Bid Resistance." *Rand Journal of Economics* 15 (Spring 1984), 54-68.

"The Wasteful Game of America's Corporate Raiders." *Economist* 295 (June 1, 1985), 73-76.

Weberman, B. "Redmail." *Forbes* 136 (October 17, 1985), 173.

Weiss, G. "ABCs of LBOs: What Makes Leveraged Buyouts Popular." *Barron's* 65 (August 19, 1985), 42.

Williams, H. M. "It's Time for a Takeover Moratorium." *Fortune* 112 (July 22, 1985), 133+.

Winkleman, M. "Takeover-Fever Fever." *Public Relations Journal* 41 (May 1985), 22-24.

Work, Clemens P., et al. "Merger Mania Strikes Again in a Frenzy of Takeovers." *U.S. News and World Report* 99 (December 23, 1985), 57.

Worthy, Ford S. "What's Next for the Raiders." *Fortune* 112 (November 11, 1985), 20-24.

Business and Society

Business and Society: General Works

Books

Bornschier, Volker, and Christopher Chase-Dunn. *Transnationals and Underdevelopment*. New York: Praeger, 1985.

Committee for Economic Development. *Investing in Our Children: Business and the Public Schools*. New York: C.E.D., 1985.

Davis, Keith, and William C. Frederick. *Business and Society: Management, Public Policy, Ethics*. 5th ed. New York: Mc-Graw Hill, 1985.

Diebold, John. *The Role of Business in Society*. New York: AMACOM, 1982.

Gevirtz, Donald. *Business Plan for America: An Entrepreneur's Manifesto*. New York: Putnam, 1984.

Hessen, Robert. *Does Big Business Rule America? Critical Commentaries on Charles E. Lindblom's 'Politics and Markets.'* Washington, D.C.: Ethics & Public Policy Center, 1981.

Hochstedler, Ellen, ed. *Corporations as Criminals*. Beverly Hills, Calif.: Sage Pubs., 1984.

Hysom, John L., and William J. Bolce. *Business and Its Environment*. St. Paul: West Publishing Company, 1983.

McFarland, Dalton E. *Management and Society: An Institutional Framework*. Englewood Cliffs, N.J.: Prentice-Hall, 1982.

Sethi, S. P., and C. L. Swanson, eds. *Private Enterprise and Public Purpose: An Understanding of the Role of Business in a Changing Social System*. New York: Wiley, 1981.

Stockdale, James B., et al. *The Ethics of Citizenship*. Dallas, Tex.: Univ. of Texas Press, 1981.

Sturdivant, Frederick D. *Business and Society: A Managerial Approach*. Homewood, Ill.: R. D. Irwin, 1981.

Sturdivant, Frederick D. *Business and Society: A Managerial Approach*. Homewood, Ill.: R. D. Irwin, 1985.

Articles

Blank, Sally J. "Business and the Public Schools." *Management Review* 74 (December 1985), 24-26.

Bond, Kenneth M. "Moral Attitudes of Creighton University Students: A Comparison of Business Administration and Arts & Sciences." *Creighton University Faculty Journal* 2 (April 1983), 26-50.

Burke, Joseph C. "The Academic-Business Partnership: Problems and

Possibilities." *Vital Speeches of the Day* 52 (December 15, 1985), 148-150.

Cavanagh, Gerald F. "Employment and Unemployment." *New Catholic World* 227 (July-August 1984), 161-163.

Chapman, Fern S. "Life-and-Death Question of an Organ Market." *Fortune* 109 (June 11, 1984), 108-118.

"Corporate Money and Co-opted Scholars." *Business and Society Review* 37 (Spring 1980-81), 4-11.

Dobson, Christopher, and Ronald Payne. "Private Enterprise Takes on Terrorism." *Across the Board* 20 (January 1983), 34-41.

Donaldson, Thomas J. "What Is Business in America?" *Journal of Business Ethics* 1 (November 1982), 259-266.

Ewing, David W. "A Bill of Rights for Corporations." *Across the Board* 20 (April 1983), 1-5.

Fahey, Liam, and Richard E. Wokutch. "Business and Society Exchanges: A Framework for Analysis." *California Management Review* 25 (Summer 1983), 128-142.

Furnham, Adrian. "Attitudes Toward the Unemployed Receiving Social Security Benefits." *Human Relations* 36 (February 1983), 135-150.

Gorden, William I. "Organizational Imperatives and Cultural Modifiers." *Business Horizons* 27 (May-June 1984), 76-83.

Harty, Sheila. "Big Business in the Classroom." *Business and Society Review* 38 (Summer 1981), 36-39.

Harty, S. "Hucksters in the Classroom." *Social Policy* 12 (September-October 1981), 38-42.

Hoff, Christina. "When Public Policy Replaces Private Ethics." *Hastings Center Report* 12 (August 1984), 13-14.

Jones, Thomas M. "An Integrating Framework for Research in Business and Society." *Academy of Management Review* 8 (October 1983), 559-564.

Justiz, Manuel J., and V. R. Roskam. "The Students Who Came in from the Cold." *Enterprise* 9 (April 1985), 24-27.

Kruttschnitt, C. "Are Businesses Treated Differently? A Comparison of the Individual Victim in the Criminal Courtroom." *Sociological Inquiry* 55 (Summer 1985), 225-238.

Lancaster, Hal. "Firm Offering Human-Embryo Transfers for Profit Stirs Legal and Ethical Debates." *Wall Street Journal* (March 7, 1984), 33.

Leigh, L. H. "The Criminal Liability of Corporations and Other

Groups: A Comprehensive View." *Michigan Law Review* 80 (June 1982), 1508-1528.

Marx, Herbert L. "Arbitration as an Ethical Institution in Our Society." *Arbitration Journal* 37 (September 1982), 52-55.

McDonald, E. "University/Industry Partnerships: Premonitions for Academic Libraries." *Journal of Academic Librarianship* 11 (May 1985), 82-87.

Miller, Roger L. "Drawing Limits on Liability." *Wall Street Journal* (April 4, 1984), 28.

Mounts, Richard. "The 'Urban Enterprise Zone' Hustle." *Commonweal* 108 (March 13, 1981), 139-142.

Novek, Joel. "University Graduates, Jobs, and University-Industry Linkages." *Canadian Public Policy* 11 (June 1985), 180-195.

O'Cleireacain, Carol. "Unemployment and the Economy." *New Catholic World* 226 (July-August 1983), 155-157.

Post, James E. "Business, Society, and the Reagan Revolution." *Sloan Management Review* 24 (Winter 1983), 67-73.

Reisler, Mark. "Business in Richmond Attacks Health Care Costs." *Harvard Business Review* 63 (January-February 1985), 145-155.

Shapiro, Morton O., and Dennis A. Ahlburg. "Suicide: The Ultimate Cost of Unemployment." *Journal of Post-Keynesian Economics* 5 (Winter 1982-83), 276-280.

Schomer, Howard. "South Africa: Beyond Fair Employment." *Harvard Business Review* 61 (May-June 1983), 145-156.

"Special Report: Small Business." *Wall Street Journal* (May 20, 1985), 1+.

Useem, Michael. "Business Segments and Corporate Relations with U.S. Universities." *Social Problems* 29 (December 1981), 129-141.

Vogel, David. "The Power of Business in America: A Re-appraisal." *British Journal of Political Science* 13, pt.1 (January 1983), 19-43.

Watkins, B. T. "Colleges' Ties With Business Seen Threatening to Academic Freedom." *Chronicle of Higher Education* 24 (June 2, 1982), 14.

Wermiel, Stephen. "Supreme Court Reaffirms It Won't Decide Who Is Liable for Asbestos-Injury Claims." *Wall Street Journal* (March 8, 1983), 16.

Wilber, Charles K. "What Kind of Justice in the U.S. Economy." *New Catholic World* 226 (January-February 1983), 28-31.

Advertising

Books

Advertising Directed at Children. Paris: OECD Pubs. and Info. Ctr., 1982.

Courtney, Alice E., and Thomas W. Whipple. *Sex Stereotyping in Adversiting.* Lexington, Mass.: Lexington Books, 1983.

O'Toole, John. *The Trouble with Advertising.* New York: Chelsea House, 1981.

Rank, Hugh. *The Pitch.* Park Forest, Ill.: Counter-Propaganda Press, 1982.

Rome, Edwin P., and William H. Roberts. *Corporate and Commercial Free Speech: First Amendment Protection of Expression in Business.* Westport, Conn.: Quorum Books, 1985.

Rotzoll, Kim B., et al. *Papers on Advertising and Ethics.* Urbana, Ill.: Univ. of Illinois, 1982.

Schudson, Michael. *Advertising: The Uneasy Persuasion: Its Dubious Impact on American Society.* New York: Basic Books, 1984.

Articles

"Advertising and the Corrupting of America." *Business and Society Review* 41 (Spring 1982), 64-69.

Albert, Sandra J. "International Anguish." *Madison Avenue* 27 (November 1985), 123-124.

Alperowicz, Cynthia. "Toymakers Take Over Children's TV." *Business and Society Review* 49 (Spring 1984), 47-51.

Andreski, S. "Society, Bureaucrats and Businessmen." *Survey* 16 (April 1982), 22-28.

Arrington, Robert L. "Advertising and Behavior Control." *Journal of Business Ethics* 1 (February 1982), 3-12.

"Assuring Responsible Advertising by Your Company." *Chemical Times & Trends* 7 (July 1984), 50-51.

"Attitudes Toward Ads: Some Change Their Minds, Others Change Their Habits." *Marketing and Media Decisions* 20 (August 1985), 8.

Barbow, Fredric L., III, and David M. Gardner. "Deceptive Advertising: A Practical Approach to Measurement." *Journal of Advertising* 11, no.1 (1982), 21-30.

Baysinger, Barry D., and Charles W. Lamb, Jr. "A Consumer Welfare

Standard for FTC Case Selection." *MSU Business Topics* 29 (Winter 1981), 58-64.

Beauchamp, Tom L. "Manipulative Advertising." *Business and Professional Ethics Journal* 3 (Spring-Summer 1984), 1-22. Commentaries: by R.M. Hare, 23; Barry Biederman, 29.

Becker, Boris W. "Injunction Powers of the Federal Trade Commission—Immediate Relief from Deceptive Advertising." *Journal of Advertising* 12, no.3 (1983), 43-45.

Bello, Daniel C., Robert E. Pitts, and Michael J. Etzel. "The Communication Effects of Controversial Sexual Content in Television Programs and Commercials." *Journal of Advertising* 12, no.3 (1983), 32-42.

Berry, Elizabeth J. "Ads Enlist Ambiguity to Target Varied Lifestyles, Values." *Ad Forum* 4 (February 1983), 10-11.

Block, Martin P., and Bruce G. VandenBergh. "Can You Sell Subliminal Messages to Consumers?" *Journal of Advertising* 14, no.3 (1985), 59-62.

Boddewyn, J. J. "The Global Spread of Advertising Regulation." *MSU Business Topics* 29 (Spring 1981), 5-13.

Breed, W., and J. R. DeFoe. "Risk and Alcohol Lifestyle Advertising." *Abstracts and Reviews in Alcohol and Driving* 2 (1981), 5-10.

Caballero, Marjorie, and Paul J. Solomon. "A Longitudinal View of Women's Role Portrayal in Television Advertising." *Journal of the Academy of Marketing Science* 12 (Fall 1984), 93-108.

Carson, Thomas L., Richard E. Wokutch, and James E. Cox, Jr. "An Ethical Analysis of Deception in Advertising." *Journal of Business Ethics* 4 (April 1985), 93-104.

Check, William A. "Prescription Drug Advertising's Inherent Hazards." *Advertising Age* 54 (September 26, 1983), M-22-23.

Childs, James M. "Dialogue with Ross Laboratories: A Chapter in the Infant Formula Controversy." *Trinity Seminary Review* 4 (Fall 1982), 2, 3-18.

Cohen, Dorothy. "Unfairness in Advertising Revisited." *Journal of Marketing* 46 (Winter 1982), 73-80.

Cragin, John P., Y. W. Kwan, and Y. N. Ho. "Social Ethics and the Emergence of Advertising in China: Perceptions from Within the Great Wall." *Journal of Business Ethics* 3 (May 1984), 91-94.

Crawford, Mary Alice. "A 50's Technology Enjoys a Rebirth." *Security Management* 29 (August 1985), 54-56.

Cuperfain, Ronnie, and T. K. Clarke. "A New Perspective of Subliminal Perception." *Journal of Advertising* 14, no.1 (1985), 36-41.

Dreyfack, Madeleine. "How Ethical Is Ethical?" *Marketing and Media Decisions* 18 (August 1983), 60-61.

Durand, Richard M., and Zarrel V. Lambert. "Alienation and Criticisms of Advertising." *Journal of Advertising* 14, no. 3 (1985), 9-17.

Durham, Taylor R. "Information, Persuasion, and Control in Moral Appraisal of Advertising Strategy." *Journal of Business Ethics* 3 (August 1984), 173-180.

Emamalizadeh, Hossein. "The Informative and Pesuasive Functions of Advertising: A Moral Appraisal—A Comment." *Journal of Business Ethics* 4 (Spring 1985), 151-153.

Ferrell, O. C., Mary Zey-Ferrell, and Dean Krugman. "A Comparison of Predictors and Ethical and Unethical Behavior Among Corporate and Agency Advertising Managers." *Journal of Macromarketing* 3 (Spring 1983), 19-27.

Fields, Howard. "Legislative Battle Looms over Proposed Beer, Wine Ad Ban, While FCC Focuses on 'Consolidation.' " *Television/Radio Age* 32 (January 21, 1985), 38-40.

Gavaghan, Paul F. "Alcohol Industry Campaigns Against Alcohol Abuse." *Public Relations Quarterly* 28 (Summer 1983), 11-16.

Gofton, Ken, "Ethicals: Drugs All in a Twist." *Marketing (UK)* 17 (April 12, 1984), 22-24.

Goodpaster, Kenneth E. "Should Sponsors Screen for Moral Values?" *Hastings Center Report* 13 (February 1983), 17-18.

Gratz, J. E. "The Ethics of Subliminal Communication." *Journal of Business Ethics* 3 (August 1984), 181-184.

Grossbart, Sanford L., and Lawrence S. Crosby. "Understanding the Bases of Parental Concern and Reaction to Children's Food Advertising." *Journal of Marketing* 48 (Summer 1984), 79-92.

Grosser, Alfred. "Political, Moral, Social Impact of Advertising." *Direct Marketing* 44 (October 1981), 94-97.

Guyon, Janet. "Health Question: Do Publications Avoid Anti-Cigarette Stories to Protect Ad Dollars?" *Wall Street Journal* (November 22, 1982), 1+.

Haberstroh, Jack. "Can't Ignore Subliminal Ad Charges." *Advertising Age* 55 (September 17, 1984), 42-44.

Hardy, Kenneth G. "Time to Be Heard on Advocacy." *Canadian Business Review* 9 (Spring 1982), 35-39.

Held, Virginia. "Advertising and Program Content." *Business and Professional Ethics Journal* 3 (Spring-Summer 1984), 61-76. Commentaries: by Clifford Christians, 77; Ronald Berman, 81; Norman E. Bowie, 87.

Hoff, Lawrence C. "Advertising Prescription Drugs Direct to the Public: What Are the Issues." *Vital Speeches of the Day* 50 (July 1, 1984), 573-576.

Hoffman, Alexander C. "Tighter Advertising Acceptance Standards." *Direct Marketing* 47 (April 1985), 130-131.

Hubert, Dick. "Public TV Doesn't Deserve Its Halo." *Public Relations Journal* 39 (November 1983), 50-51.

Humphrey, Ronald, and Howard Schuman. "The Portrayal of Blacks in Magazine Advertisements: 1950-1982." *Public Opinion Quarterly* 48 (Fall 1984), 551-563.

Kohn, Paul M., Reginald G. Smart, and Alan C. Ogborne. "Effects of Two Kinds of Alcohol Advertising on Subsequent Consumption." *Journal of Advertising* 13, no.1 (1984), 34-40.

Krasnicka, B., et al. "Portrayals of the Elderly in Magazine Advertisements." *Journalism Quarterly* 59 (Winter 1982), 313-317.

La Barbera, Priscilla. "The Shame of Magazine Advertising." *Journal of Advertising* 10, no.1 (1981), 31-37.

Leffler, K. B. "Persuasion or Information? The Economics of Prescription Drug Advertising." *Journal of Law and Economics* 24 (April 1981), 45-74.

Leiser, Burton M. "Professional Advertising: Price Fixing and Professional Dignity Versus the Public's Right to a Free Market." *Business and Professional Ethics Journal* 3 (Spring-Summer 1984), 93-107. Commentary: by James E. Doughton, 109.

"Log Fake Revenues on Ad Agency's CPU." *Management Information Systems Week* (March 3, 1982), 4+.

Macklin, M. C., and Richard H. Kolbe. "Sex Role Stereotyping in Children's Advertising." *Journal of Advertising* 12, no.2 (1984), 34-42.

Matthews, Leonard S. "Promises, Promises." *Madison Avenue* 26 (July 1984), 18-22.

McCabe, Edward A. "Creativity: Effectiveness, Aesthetics and Morality." *Vital Speeches of the Day* 51 (August 1, 1985), 628-632.

McGann, Anthony F. "Editorial: Off Pricing, Price Fixing and Advertising." *Journal of Advertising* 13, no.1 (1984), 3.

McNeal, James U. "Advertising's Disparagement of American Workers." *Business Horizons* 26 (January-February 1983), 7-12.

Miller, Mark. "New Move to Bridle Television." *Marketing & Media Decisions* 16 (January 1981), 57-59.

Murdock, Gene W., and James M. Peterson. "Strict Product Liability for Advertisers: A Pro/Con Discussion." *Journal of Advertising* 10, no.4 (1981), 5-10.

Norris, Vincent P. "Toward a 'Social Control in the Advertising Agency.' " *Journal of Advertising* 12, no.1 (1983), 30-33.

O' Connor, N. W. "Watch Out for Ads That Trick the Trusting." *Changing Times* 36 (December 1983), 68-69.

O'Toole, John. "Craft or Con?" *Madison Avenue* 26 (August 1984), 32-34.

O'Toole, John. "What Advertising Is—and Isn't." *Across the Board* 19 (April 1982), 32-44.

Paine, Lynda S. "Children as Consumers: An Ethical Evaluation of Children's Advertising." *Business and Professional Ethics Journal* 3 (Spring-Summer 1984), 119-145. Commentaries: by George G. Brenkert, 147; Rita Weisskoff, 155; Lawrence D. Kimmel, 159.

Paskowski, Marianne. "Advertisers Enlist the Syndication Cops." *Marketing & Media Decisions* 20 (August 1985), 64+.

Paskowski, Marianne. "The TV Code Is Dead . . . But the Memory Lingers On." *Marketing & Media Decisions* 18 (December 1983), 64-66.

Perrien, Jean, Christian Dussart, and Paul Francorse. "Advertisers and the Factual Content of Advertising." *Journal of Advertising* 14, no.1 (March 1985), 30-35.

"Pitching Ethical Drugs with Fast Balls." *Chemical Week* 130 (May 12, 1982), 60.

Poltrack, T. "Influencing the Influentials." *Marketing and Media Decisions* 20 (August 1985), 56-57+.

"Proctor & Gamble's Posture on TV Ads Isn't Unusual: Sponsors Often Withdraw." *Wall Street Journal* (June 6, 1981), 6.

"Rabbi Marc Tannenbaum Offers '*Madison Avenue*' a Jewish View of Religion and Advertising." *Madison Avenue* 27 (September 1985), 24+.

Riecken, Glen, et al. "Advertising and the Professions—The Attitudes of Doctors." *International Journal of Advertising (UK)* 3 (1984), 311-319.

Santilli, Paul C. "The Informative and Persuasive Functions of Advertising: A Moral Appraisal." *Journal of Business Ethics* 2 (February 1983), 27-33.

Sasseen, Jane. "If It Ain't Broke, Don't Fix It." *Madison Avenue* 26 (May 1984), 64-66.

Schultze, Q. J. "Professionalism in Advertising: The Origin of Ethical Codes." *Journal of Commerce* 31 (Spring 1981), 64-71.

Shapiro, Irwin A. "Consumers, Health Care Professionals Are Deeply Divided on the Issue of Advertising." *Marketing News* 17 (December 9, 1983), 13.

Soley, L. C., and L. N. Reid. "Baiting Viewers: Violence and Sex in Television Program Advertisements." *Journalism Quarterly* 62 (Spring 1985), 105-110.+.

Stern, Bruce L., and Robert R. Harmon. "Disclaimers in Children's Advertising." *Journal of Advertising* 13, no.2 (1984), 12-16.

Van Auken, Stuart, and Subhash C. Lonial. "Children's Perceptions of Human Versus Animate Characters." *Journal of Advertising* 14, no.2 (1985), 13-22.

Wang, Penelope. "A New Way to Push Drugs." *Newsweek* 106 (December 30, 1985), 34-35.

Watkins, Robert L. "An Advertiser's Perspective on Claim Substantiation." *Journal of Advertising Research* 24 (October-November 1984), I12-14.

Whipple, Thomas W., and Alice E. Courtney. "Female Role Portrayals in Advertising and Communication Effectiveness: A Review." *Journal of Advertising* 14, no.3 (1985), 4-8.

Williams, John K. "And Now, a Pitch for Advertising." *Reason* 15 (September 1983), 29-31.

Wyckham, Robert G., Peter M. Banting, and Anthony K. Wensley. "The Language of Advertising: Who Controls Quality?" *Journal of Business Ethics* 3 (February 1984), 47-53.

Yankelovich, Daniel. "New Rules: Some Implications for Advertising." *Journal of Advertising Research* 22 (October-November 1982), 9-14.

Zanot, Eric J., J. D. Pincus, and E. J. Lamp. "Public Perceptions of Subliminal Advertising." *Journal of Adversiting* 12, no.1 (1983), 39-45.

Agribusiness

Books

Crosson, Pierre R. *The Cropland Crisis—Myth or Reality?* Baltimore: Johns Hopkins, 1981.

Dyson, Lowell K. *Red Harvest: The Communist Party and American Farmers*. Lincoln, Neb.: Univ. Nebraska Press, 1982.

Fite, Gilbert C. *American Farmers: The New Minority*. Indiana University Press, 1981.

Majka, Linda C., and Theo J. Majka. *Farm Workers, Agribusiness, and the State*. Philadelphia: Temple University Press, 1982.

McGregor, Alexander C. *Counting Sheep: From Open Range to Agribusiness on the Columbia Plateau*. Seattle: Univ. Washington Press, 1983.

Articles

Bandow, Doug. "Federal Marketing Orders: Good Food Rots While People Starve." *Business and Society Review* 53 (Spring 1985), 40-47.

Bellew, Patricia A. "Advanced Genetics Bacteria Could Curb Damage from Frost." *Wall Street Journal* (November 9, 1984), 18.

Breimyer, H. F. "Agriculture's Problem Is Rooted in Washington." *Challenge* 28 (May-June 1985), 53-54.

Browne, William P. "Mobilizing and Activating Group Demands: The American Agriculture Movement." *Social Science Quarterly* 64 (March 1983), 19-34.

"Bumper Crop Raises Federal Farm Outlays." *Dun's Business Month* 126 (August 1985), 27.

Byrne, H. S. "Growing Debt: Farmers and Their Banks Have Tough Row to Hoe." *Barron's* 65 (August 19, 1985), 40-45.

Chambers, R. G. "Least-Cost Subsidization Alternatives." *American Journal Agricultural Economics* 67 (May 1985), 251-256.

"Crisis in the Farm Credit System." *Dun's Business Month* 126 (October 1985), 43.

"Down on the Farm System." *Fortune* 112 (November 25, 1985), 6.

Ehrbav, Aloysius. "Facts vs. Furor Over the Farm Policy." *Fortune* 112 (November 11, 1985), 114-120.

"Farm Credit: Shuddering." *Economist* 296 (July 27, 1985), 21-22.

Hart, John. "How Agribusiness Is Destroying Agriculture." *Christianity & Crisis* 45 (March 4, 1985), 130-135.

Hoppe, R. "The Farm Bill: Politics Wins Out Again." *Business Week* (August 19, 1985), 32.

Houston, P., et al. "The Good Earth Is Bad News: Bumper Crops Will Drive Depressed Farm Prices Even Lower." *Business Week* (August 19, 1985), 30-31.

Kominus, Nicholas. "A Sweet Deal for America's Sugar Producers." *Business and Society Review* 44 (Winter 1983), 13-18.

Krohe, J., Jr. "Family-Farm Hogwash." *Across the Board* 22 (May 1985), 3-6.

Leonard, Rodney E. "Meat Inspection Is a Lot of Bull." *Business and Society Review* 47 (Fall 1983), 56-60.

Lepkowski, W. "Science Policy Issues Pervade Debate on 1985 Farm Bill." *Chemical & Engineering News* 63 (June 23, 1985), 20.

McCoy Charles F., and Jeff Bailey. "Blighted Ledgers: Farm Credit System Relies on Accounting that Hides Bad Loans." *Wall Street Journal* (October 7, 1985), 1.

McMenamin, Michael, and Diane Connelly. "How Sunkist Put the Squeeze on the FTC." *Reason* 13 (November 1981), 45-50.

Nadler, P. S. "Blaming the Helper." *Banker's Monthly* 102 (November 1985), 3+.

Pilmer, C. L. "Trouble on the Farm: An Income Analysis Is a Must." *Appraisal Journal* 53 (April 1985), 285-288.

Samuelson, Robert J. "The Farm Mess Forever." *Newsweek* 106 (November 18, 1985), 74.

Sansolo, M. "Farm Bill Fight Flares Up." *Progressive Grocer* 64 (April 1985), 159-160.

Sauve, P. "Farm Wives—the Invisible Force." *Canadian Banker* 92 (August 1985), 18-22.

Schaeffer, Robert. "Are Feedlots Poisoning Our Meat?" *Business and Society Review* 53 (Spring 1985), 48-51.

Schulman, M.D. "Ownership and Control in Agribusiness Corporations." *Rural Sociology* 46 (Summer 1982), 652-668.

Smith, Thomas B. "Food Profits Up, Food Safety Down." *Food Monitor* (September-October 1982), 13-19.

Starleaf, R. R., et al. "The Impact of Inflation on the Real Income of U.S Farmers." *American Journal of Agricultural Economics* 67 (May 1985), 384-389.

Wills, R. L. "Evaluating Price Enhancement by Processing Cooperatives." *American Journal of Agricultural Economics* 67 (May 1985), 183-192.

Bribery and Corrupt Payments

Books

Drew, Elizabeth. *Politics and Money: The New Road to Corruption.* New York: Macmillan, 1983.

Greanias, George C., and Duane Windsor. *The Foreign Corrupt Practices Act: Anatomy of a Statute.* Lexington, Mass.: Lexington Books, 1982.

Noonan, John T., Jr. *Bribes.* New York: Macmillan, 1984.

Proposed Revisions of the Foreign Corrupt Practices Act. Washington, D.C.: American Enterprise Institute, 1981.

Articles

"Administration Backs Changed Bribery Law." *Aviation Week & Space Technology* 114 (May 25, 1981), 22-23.

Aggarwal, Raj, and S. H. Kim. "Should the Foreign Corrupt Practices Act Be Modified?" *Collegiate Forum* (Spring 1982), 7.

Beaudeux, Pierre. "Bribery Business." *World Press Review* 28 (February 1981), 54.

Bishop, B. "Kickback Charges: Former Raytheon Executive Pleads Guilty." *Electronic News* 30 (November 12, 1984), 89.

Brummer, James F. "The Foreign Corrupt Practices Act and the Dilemma of Applied Ethics." *Business and Professional Ethics Journal* 4 (Fall 1985), 17-42. Commentaries: by David P. Schmidt, 43; Kenneth D. Alpern, 47.

Brummer, James J. "The Foreign Corrupt Practices Act and the Imposition of Values." *International Journal of Applied Philosophy* 2 (Spring 1985), 1-17.

Burton, John C. "The Foreign Corrupt Practices Act Is Good for Business." *Hermes (New York)* 9 (Fall 1983), 30-32.

Byron, Christopher, et al. "Big Profits in Big Bribery." *Time* 117 (March 1981), 58-59+.

Carson, Thomas L. "Bribery, Extortion, and 'The Foreign Corrupt Practices Act.' " *Philosophy and Public Affairs* 14 (Winter 1985), 66-90.

Czarnecki, Gerald M. "Internal Controls: Executive Management Responsibility." *Magazine of Bank Administration* 58 (June 1982), 20-24.

D'Andrade, Kendall, Jr. "Bribery." *Journal of Business Ethics* 4 (August 1985), 239-248.

Danley, John R. "Toward a Theory of Bribery." *Business and Professional Ethics Journal* 2 (Spring 1983), 19-39. Commentaries: by Kendall D'Andrade, Jr., v.3 (Fall 1983), 79; Scott Turow, v.3 (Fall 1983), 84.

Denes, Richard F. "Commercial Bribery: The White Collar Crime of the '80s." *Security Management* 29 (April 1985), 56-59.

"Few Are Prosecuted for Overseas Bribes." *Chemical Week* 133 (September 21, 1983), 16.

Garlick, Richard. "Doubtful Deals: How Untainted Is Your Company?" *Chief Executive (UK)*, (May 1982), 16-19.

Georges, William C. "Foreign Corrupt Practices Act Review Procedure." *Cornell International Law Journal* 14 (Winter 1981), 57-93.

Graham, John L. "Foreign Corrupt Practices: A Manager's Guide." *Columbia Journal of World Business* 18 (Fall 1983), 89-94.

Hess, Randall K., et al. "Bribery as an Organizational Response to Conflicting Environmental Expectations." *Journal of the Academy of Marketing Science* 9 (Summer 1981), 206-226.

Hill, Roy. "Questionable Payments Crisis Catches Chairman by Surprise." *International Management* 39 (August 1984), 11.

Holt, Robert N., and Rebecca E. Fincher. "Foreign Corrupt Practices Act." *Financial Analysts Journal* 37 (March-April 1981), 73-76.

Jackson, Brooks. "Mexican Showdown: Was It Bribery When Donald Crawford Sent Money 'to the Folks'?" *Wall Street Journal* (February 23, 1983), 1+.

Johnston, William B. "All in Favor of Bribery, Please Stand Up." *Across the Board* 21 (June 1984), 3-5.

Kim, Suk H. "On Repealing the Foreign Corrupt Practices Act." *Columbia Journal of World Business* 16 (Fall 1981), 16-21.

Kim, Suk H., and Sam Barone. "Is the Foreign Corrupt Practices Act of 1977 a Success or Failure?" *Journal of International Business Studies* 12 (Winter 1981), 123-126.

Lane, Henry W., and Donald G. Simpson. "Bribery in International Business: Whose Problem Is It?" *Journal of Business Ethics* 3 (February 1984), 35-42.

Lieber, J. "Bribery Is Back." *New Republic* 185 (September 30, 1981), 7-9.

Lochner, Scott J. "The Criminalization of American Extraterritorial Bribery." *N.Y.U. Journal International Law & Politics* 13 (Winter 1981), 645-674.

Merten, Alan G., Dennis G. Severance, and Bernard J. White. "Internal Control and the Foreign Corrupt Practices Act." *Sloan Management Review* 22 (Spring 1981), 47-54.

Mino, Hokaji. "Mitsukoshi Scandal Becomes Japan's Story of the Year." *Business Japan* 28 (June 1983), 18-21.

Miya, Yujiro. "Bribery Scandal Finds Roots in Conflicting Policies." *Business Japan* 29 (August 1984), 28-31.

Morganthau, T., et al. "Donovan vs. the Informant." *Newsweek* 98 (December 28, 1981), 39-40.

Moskowitz, Milton R., "Corruption Watchdogs Keep Hong Kong Honest." *Business and Society Review* 50 (Summer 1984), 56-57.

Moskowitz, Milton R. "McDonnell Douglas Makes Peace With the Feds." *Business and Society Review* 40 (Winter 1981-82), 24-27.

Nunn, Arya A. "Closeup: ICPI Insurers Take Action Against Fraud." *Journal of Insurance* 44 (March-April 1983), 30-31.

Philips, Michael. "Bribery." *Ethics* 94 (July 1984), 621-636.

Rauch, Jonathan. "The Foreign Corrupt Practices Act—Anti-Bribery or Anti-Business?" *National Journal* 13 (August 8, 1981), 1422-1425.

Ricchiute, David N. "Foreign Corrupt Practices, Internal Control and the Planning Executive." *Managerial Planning* 29 (May-June 1981), 10-12+.

"Senate Amends Overseas Sales Bribery Law." *Aviation Week & Space Technology* 115 (November 30, 1981), 29.

Siedel, George J. "Corporate Governance Under the Foreign Corrupt Practices Act." *Quarterly Review of Economics and Business* 21 (Autumn 1981), 43-48.

Snyder, Jim. "For Florida: A Fraud Force." *Journal of Insurance* 42 (March-April 1981), 6-9.

Tong, Hsin-Min, and Priscilla Welling. "What American Business Managers Should Know and Do About International Bribery." *Baylor Business Studies* 13 (January 1983), 7-19.

"Turning Back." *Time* 117 (June 1, 1981), 28.

Turow, Scott. "What's Wrong with Bribery?" *Journal of Business Ethics* 4 (August 1985), 249-251.

Vicker, Ray. "Frontier Justice." *Wall Street Journal* (December 3, 1982), 26.

Wadwha, Darshan L. "Questionable Payments—Are They Deductible?" *CPA Journal* 54 (February 1984), 36-41.

Walczak, Lee. "A New Assault on the Bribery Act." *Business Week* (April 18, 1983), 141.

Corporate Social Responsibility

Books

Bertsch, Kenneth A. *Corporate Philanthropy.* Washington, D.C.: Investor Responsibility Research Ctr., 1982.

Bradshaw, Thornton, and David Vogel, eds. *Corporations and Their Critics: Issues and Answers to the Problems of Corporate Social Responsibility.* New York: McGraw-Hill, 1981.

Brown, James K. *Guidelines for Managing Corporate Issues Programs.* New York: Conference Board, 1981.

Buono, Anthony F., and Larry Nichols. *Corporate Policy Values and Social Responsibility.* New York: Praeger, 1985.

Carroll, Archie B. *Business and Society: Managing Corporate Social Performance.* Boston: Little, Brown, and Co., 1981.

Den Uyl, Douglas J. *The New Crusaders: The Corporate Social Responsibility Debate.* Bowling Green, Ohio: Social Phil. & Phil. Ctr., 1984.

French, Peter A. *Collective and Corporate Responsibility.* New York: Columbia Univ. Press, 1984.

Galaskiewicz, Joseph. *Social Organization of an Urban Grants Economy.* New York: Academic Press, 1985.

Goodpaster, Kenneth E., and John B. Matthews, Jr. *Corporate Responsibility as the Decentralization of Conscience.* Boston: Harvard Business School, 1982.

Haire, John R., et al. *Strengthening Liberal Learning: An Opportunity for Corporate Philanthropy.* Washington, D.C.: Assoc. of American Colleges, 1981.

Harvey, Brian, Stephen Smith, and Barry Wilkinson. *Managers and Corporate Social Policy: Private Solutions to Public Problems.* Basingstoke, U.K.: Macmillan, 1984.

Lefever, Ernest W., Raymond English, and Robert L. Schuettinger. *Scholars, Dollars, and Public Policy: New Frontiers in Corporate Giving.* Washington, D.C.: Ethics and Public Policy Ctr., 1983.

Mahon, John F. *The Corporate Public Affairs Office: Structure, Behavior, and Impact.* Boston: Boston University, 1982.

Mauksh, Mary. *Corporate Voluntary Contributions in Europe.* New York: Conference Board, 1982.

Organisation for Economic Cooperation and Development. *Community Business Ventures and Job Creation.* Paris: O.E.C.D., 1984.

Post, James. *Corporate Behavior and Social Change*. Reston, Va.: Reston Pub. Co., 1981.

Preston, Lee E., ed. *Research in Corporate and Social Performance and Policy* (Volumes 3 and 4). Greenwich, Conn.: JAI Press, 1981.

Richardson, Elliot L. *Corporate Responsibility—To Whom and For What*. University Park, Pa.: Penn. State Univ., 1982.

Sonnenfeld, Jeffrey A. *Corporate Views of the Public Interest: Perceptions of the Forest Products Industry*. Boston: Auburn House, 1981.

Tinker, Tony, ed. *Social Accounting for Corporations: Private Enterprise versus the Public Interest*. New York: Markus Wiener Pub. Co., 1984.

Troy, Kathryn. *The Corporate Contributions Functions*. New York: Conference Board, 1982.

Tuleja, Tad. *Beyond the Bottom Line: How Business Leaders Are Turning Principles into Profits*. New York: Facts on File Publ., 1985.

Articles

Akers, John F. "Growth Depends on Ethics." *Canadian Datasystems* 16 (October 1984), 41.

Akhter, H., and A. Hughes. "Marketers Have to Learn How to Head Off Social, Ethical Protest." *Marketing News* 19 (January 20, 1984), 14.

Alexander, Larry D., and William F. Matthews. "The Ten Commandments of Corporate Responsibility." *Business and Society Review* 50 (Summer 1984), 62-66.

Aupperle, Kenneth E., Archie B. Carroll, and John D. Hatfield. "An Empirical Examination of the Relationship Between Corporate Social Responsibility and Profitability." *Academy of Management Journal* 28 (June 1985), 446-463.

Bandow, Doug. "Misdirecting Corporate Philanthropy." *Journal of the Institute for Socioeconomic Studies* 8 (Spring 1983), 57-66.

Barach, Jeffrey A. "Applying Marketing Principles to Social Causes." *Business Horizons* 27 (July-August 1984), 65-69.

Baroody, William J., Jr. "New Corporate Programs in the Public Sector." *Directors & Boards* 6 (Winter 1982), 22-25.

Beattie, L. E. "The New Voluntarism." *Business and Economic Review* 31 (April 1985), 22-23+.

Bell, Gordon H. "Industrial Culture and the School: Some Conceptual and Practical Issues in the Schools-Industry Debate." *Journal of Philosophical Education* 15 (December 1981), 175-190.

Bemis, Judson, and John A. Cairns. "In Minnesota, Business Is Part of the Solution." *Harvard Business Review* 59 (July-August 1981), 85-93.

Birnbaum, Jeffrey H. "Bitter Harvest." *Wall Street Journal* (October 25, 1982), 1+.

Boal, Kimberly B., and Newman Peery. "The Cognitive Structure of Corporate Social Responsibility." *Journal of Management* 11 (1985), 71-82.

Brooks, Leonard J., Jr. "Social Goals for Canadian Business." *Cost & Management* 58 (March-April 1984), 2-8.

Brown, Frank D. "Amandla! The Rallying Cry Against Apartheid." *Black Enterprise* 15 (April 1985), 58-61.

Brummer, James J. "In Defense of Social Responsibility." *Journal of Business Ethics* 2 (May 1983), 111-122.

Buchholz, Rogene. "Business and the Cities: New Directions for the Eighties." *Business Horizons* 26 (January-February 1983), 79-84.

Byron, William J., S.J. "In Defense of Social Responsibility." *Journal of Economics and Business* 34 (1982), 89-192.

Chewning, Richard C. "Can Free Enterprise Survive Ethical Schizophrenia?" *Business Horizons* 27 (March-April 1984), 5-11.

"Chief Executive Officers' Conference on Corporate Social Responsibility." *Response* (November 1981), 8-9.

Chrisman, James J., et al. "Small Business Social Responsibility: Some Perceptions and Insights." *American Journal of Small Business* 9 (Fall 1984), 46-58.

Chrisman, James J., and Archie B. Carroll. "SMR Forum: Corporate Responsibility: Economic and Social Goals." *Sloan Management Review* 25 (Winter 1984), 59-65.

Chrisman, James J., and Fred L. Fry. "Public Versus Business Expectations: Two Views on Social Responsibility for Small Business." *Journal of Small Business Management* 20 (January 1982), 19-26.

Cochran, Philip L., and Robert A. Wood. "Corporate Social Responsibility and Financial Peformance." *Academy of Management Journal* 27 (March 1984), 42-56.

Cowen, Scott S., and Mitchell G. Segal. "Corporate Responsibility Part 1: In the Public: Reporting Social Performance." *Financial Executive* 49 (January 1981), 10-16.

Cramer, J. "Corporations Can Be Real Angels." *American School Board Journal* 169 (March 1982), 36-37.

Dalton, Dan R., and Richard A. Cosier. "The Four Faces of Social Responsibility." *Business Horizons* 25 (May-June 1982), 19-27.

Demers, Louis, and Donald Wayland. "Corporate Social Responsibility: Is No News Good News?" *CA Magazine (Canada)* 115 (January 1982), 42-46.

Desruisseaux, P. "Abuse and Fraud Said to Threaten Matching Gifts." *Chronicle of Higher Education* 30 (July 24, 1985), 1+.

Drucker, Peter F. "A New Look at Corporate Social Responsibility." *McKinsey Quarterly* (Autumn 1984), 17-28.

Drucker, Peter F. "The New Meaning of Corporate Social Responsibility." *California Management Review* 26 (Winter 1984), 53-63.

Farquhar, Carolyn R. "Corporate Sponsorship of the Performing Arts." *Canadian Business Review* 9 (Summer 1982), 30-35.

Fernstrom, Meredith M. "Corporate Public Responsibility: A Marketing Opportunity?" *Management Review* 72 (February 1983), 54-60.

Finlay, J. R. "Toward a Neoenterprise Spirit: The Tasks and Responsibilities of the Public Affairs Function." *Business Quarterly (Canada)* 47 (October 1982), 34-42.

Foley, Ridgway K., Jr. "The Social Role of Business." *Freeman* 32 (October 1982), 611-626.

Foote, Susan B. "Corporate Responsibility in a Changing Legal Environment." *California Management Review* 26 (Spring 1984), 217-228.

Ford, Robert, and Frank McLaughlin. "Perceptions of Socially Responsible Activities and Attitudes." *Academy of Management Journal* 27 (September 1984), 666-674.

Frederick, William C. "Corporate Social Responsibility in the Reagan Era and Beyond." *California Management Review* 25 (Spring 1983), 145-157.

Frederick, William C. "Free Market vs. Social Responbility: Decision Time at the CED." *California Management Review* 23 (Spring 1981), 20-28.

Friedman, Robert, and Matt Miller. "Union Carbide Is Sued by India in U.S. Court." *Wall Street Journal* (April 9, 1985), 8.

Gatewood, Elizabeth, and Archie B. Carroll. "The Anatomy of Corporate Social Response: The Rely, Firestone 500, and Pinto Cases." *Business Horizons* 24 (September-October 1981), 9-16.

Gill, Roger W., and Lisa J. Leinbach. "Corporate Social Responsibility in Hong Kong." *California Management Review* 25 (January 1983), 107-123.

Goddard, Robert W. "The Rise of the New Organization." *Management World* 14 (January 1985), 7-11.

Goodpaster, Kenneth E. "The Concept of Corporate Responsibility." *Journal of Business Ethics* 2 (February 1983), 1-22.

Grcic, Joseph M. "Democratic Capitalism: Developing a Conscience for the Corporation." *Journal of Business Ethics* 4 (April 1985), 145-150.

Hasegawa, Sandra, and Steve Elliott. "Public Spaces by Private Enterprise." *Urban Land* 42 (May 1983), 12-15.

Hathaway, James W. "Business Donations That Don't Help Business." *Business and Society Review* 39 (Fall 1981), 49-52.

Hathaway, James W. "Has Social Responsibility Cleaned Up the Corporate Image?" *Business and Society Review* 51 (Fall 1984), 56-59.

Hayden, Spencer. "Responding to the Changing Face of Corporate Social Responsibility." *Management Review* 72 (September 1983), 49-53.

Herbers, John. "Starved Cities Hunger for Corporate Aid." *Business and Society Review* 45 (Spring 1983), 8-11.

Hildreth, James M. "When Business Comes to Cities' Rescue." *U.S. News and World Report* 93 (August 9, 1982), 42-43.

Hoch, Charles. "Doing Good and Being Right—The Pragmatic Connection in Planning Theory." *Journal of the American Planning Association* 50 (Summer 1984), 335-345.

Hock, Ow C. "The Social Responsibility of Corporations in Singapore." *Singapore Management Review* 3, no.2 (1981), 36-41.

Hunt, Shelby D., and John J. Burnett. "Retailing and Social Responsibility." *Business Forum* 8 (Fall 1982), 30-32.

Jacob, John E. "Black America and U.S. Foreign Policy—A Pluralistic Integrated Society." *Vital Speeches of the Day* 51 (December 1, 1984), 113-116.

Johnson, Elmer W. "How Corporations Balance Economic and Social Concerns." *Business and Society Review* 54 (Summer 1985), 10-14.

Joseph, James A. "Directing the Flow of Corporate Largesse." *Business and Society Review* 42 (Summer 1982), 40-43.

Kane, Stanley P. "How a Company the Size of Early American Life Can Become Involved in Corporate Social Responsibility." *Response* (September 1981), 8-9.

Koch, Frank. "A Primer on Corporate Philanthropy." *Business and Society Review* 38 (Summer 1981), 48-52.

Kramer, Barry. "Bhopal Officials, Residents Say Union Carbide

Hasn't Done Enough for Toxic-Disaster Victims." *Wall Street Journal* (April 2, 1985), 3.

"Kudos for Corporate Angels." *Dun's Business Month* 126 (August 1985), 67.

Lane, Harold E. "The Corporate Conscience and the Role of Business in Society." *Cornell Hotel and Restaurant Administration Quarterly* 23 (November 1982), 8-18.

Lawrence, Melanie. "Social Responsibility: How Companies Become Involved in Their Communities." *Personnel Journal* 61 (July 1982), 502-510.

Leonard, Richard. "Business and South Africa: Pressures Against Apartheid Mount in the U.S.A." *Multinational Business* 3 (1984), 14-22.

Lippke, Richard L. "Setting the Terms of the Business Responsibility Debate." *Social Theory and Practice* 11 (Fall 1985), 355-370.

Logan, John E., Sandra P. Logan, and Jean M. Mille. "Corporate Social Responsibility." *Business and Economic Review* 31 (January 1985), 25-27.

Lundahl, Mats. "Economic Effects of a Trade and Investment Boycott Against South Africa." *Scandinavian Journal of Economics* 86 (1984), 68-83.

Lundeen, Robert W. "A Management Style for the New Policy Issues." *Chemical Times & Trends* 8 (October 1985), 37-39.

MacKinnon, A. M. "Business and the Arts: A Productive Alliance Comes Under Stress." *Management Review* 71 (October 1982), 63-71.

MacMillan, Keith. "Contradictions." *Journal of General Management* 9 (Spring 1984), 3-17.

Manning, Rita C. "Corporate Responsibility and Corporate Personhood." *Journal of Business Ethics* 3 (February 1984), 77-84.

McElroy, K. M., and J. J. Siegfried. "The Effect of Firm Size on Corporate Philanthropy." *Quarterly Review of Economics and Business* 25 (Summer 1985), 18-26.

Meier, Barry. "Union Carbide Chief Criticizes Indians for Rejecting Offer on Bhopal Claims." *Wall Street Journal* (April 25, 1985), 6.

"The Mending of American Education: How Business Can Help." *Enterprise* 8 (April 1984), 6-17.

Meyers, Christopher. "The Corporation, Its Members and Moral Accountability." *Business and Professional Ethics Journal* 3 (Fall 1983), 33-44.

Mintzberg, Henry. "The Case for Corporate Social Responsibility." *Journal of Business Strategy* 4 (Fall 1983), 3-15.

Moskal, Brian B. "Business Meets Its Social Responsibility." *Industry Week* 209 (April 20, 1981), 54-59.

Moskowitz, Milton R. "Company Performance Roundup." *Business and Society Review* 45 (Spring 1983), 65-70.

Moskowitz, Milton R. "The Corporate Responsibility Champs . . . and Chumps." *Business and Society Review* 52 (Winter 1985), 4-10.

Moskowitz, Milton R. "Social Investment Funds: Fortune or Folly?" *Business and Society Review* 49 (Spring 1984), 10-14.

Nanda, Meera. "Secrecy Was Bhopal's Real Disaster." *Science for the People* 17 (November-December 1985), 12-17.

Naor, Jacob. "A New Approach to Multinational Social Responsibility." *Journal of Business Ethics* 1 (August 1982), 219-225.

Naor, Jacob. "Planning and Social Responsibility—A Reexamination." *Journal of Business Ethics* 1 (November 1982), 313-319.

Nash, Laura L. "Ethics Without the Sermon." Harvard Business Review 59 (November-December 1981), 78-90.

Norris, W. C. "Sowing New Seeds for Corporate Responsibility." *FE* 1 July 1985), 16-23.

Ozmon, H. "Adopt-a-School: Definitely Not Business as Usual." *Phi Delta Kappan* 63 (January 1982), 350-351.

Pagan, Rafael D., Jr. "Why Cooperation Succeeds Where Confrontation Fails." *Business and Society Review* 54 (Summer 1985), 27-29.

Parry, Charles W. "My Company—Right or Wrong?: The Best Interest of Business Is Economic." *Vital Speeches of the Day* 51 (August 1, 1985), 632-634.

Payton, R. "The Taming of the Corporation: Private Sector Responsibility." *Change* 17 (January-February 1985), 27-30.

Perry, S. "Professors Can Land Corporate Sponsors for Research—If They Follow the Rules." *Chronicle of Higher Education* 26 (April 20, 1983), 21-22.

Porter, Richard C. "Apartheid, the Job Ladder, and the Evolutionary Hypothesis: Empirical Evidence from South African Manufacturing . . ." *Economic Development & Cultural Change* 33 (October 1984), 117-141.

Preston, Lee E., and James E. Post. "Private Management and Public Policy." *California Management Review* 23 (Spring 1981), 56-62.

"Reassessing the Role of Public Responsibility Committees." *Directors & Boards* 9 (Spring 1985), 22-27.

Rivlin, Catherine A. "Point of View: The Corporate Role in the Not-So-Great Society." *California Management Review* 25 (Summer 1983), 151-159.

Roth, Harold P. "A Role for Small Business in the Social Accounting Area." *Journal of Small Business Management* 20 (January 1982), 27-31.

Schreuder, Hein. "Employees and the Corporate Social Report: The Dutch Case." *Accounting Review* 56 (April 1981), 294-308.

Schutt, Steven R. "Corporate Responsibility Part III: White Collar Crime: The Nation's Largest Growth Industry." *Financial Executive* 49 (February 1981), 16-23.

Seligman, D. "Responsibilism." *Fortune* 112 (December 9, 1985), 150.

Sethi, S. P. "American Business and Social Challenges of the Eighties." *Journal of General Management* 6 (Spring 1981), 31-35.

"Should Criminal Fines Be Released for Charity Gifts?" *Business and Society Review* 50 (Summer 1984), 41-45.

Singer, Alan E. "Planning, Consciousness and Conscience." *Journal of Business Ethics* 3 (May 1984), 113-117.

Sirgy, M. J., et al. "The Interface Between Quality of Life and Marketing: A Theoretical Framework." *Journal of Marketing & Public Policy* 1 (1982), 69-84.

Sohn, Howard F. "Prevailing Rationales in the Corporate Social Responsibility Debate." *Journal of Business Ethics* 1 (May 1982), 139-144.

Sonnenfeld, Jeffrey. "Untangling the Muddled Management of Public Affairs." *Business Horizons* 27 (November-December 1984), 67-76.

Spitzer, Carlton E. "Can Business Take Up the Social Slack?" *Business and Society Review* 42 (Summer 1982), 16-17.

Spitzer, Carlton E. "Lobbying, Ethics and Common Sense." *Public Relations Journal* 38 (February 1982), 34-36.

Spitzer, Carlton E. "Should Government Audit Corporate Social Responsibility?" *Public Relations Review* 7 (Summer 1981), 13-28.

Stead, Bette A. "Corporate Giving: A Look at the Arts." *Journal of Business Ethics* 4 (June 1985), 215-222.

Stephenson, D. R. "Internal PR Efforts Further Corporate Responsibility: A Report from Dow Canada." *Public Relations Quarterly* 28 (Summer 1983), 7-10.

Stevens, George F. "Business Ethics and Social Responsibility: The Responses of Present and Future Managers." *Akron Business & Economic Review* 15 (Fall 1984), 6-11.

Surdam, Robert M. "Investing in Social Welfare: How the Detroit Bank Does It." *Directors & Boards* 6 (Summer 1982), 18-27.

Taylor, Allan R. "Business and the Community: Is There a Corporate Santa Claus?" *Vital Speeches of the Day* 51 (December 15, 1984), 154-157.

Thibodeaux, Mary S., and James D. Powell. "Exploitation: Ethical Problems of Organizational Power." *Advanced Management Journal* 50 (Spring 1985), 42-44.

Tilson, Donn J., and Donald Vance. "Corporate Philanthropy Comes of Age." *Public Relations Review* 11 (Summer 1985), 26-33.

Tombari, Henry J. "The Limits of Corporate Responsibility." *Business and Public Affairs* 8 (Spring 1982), 51-63.

Tretiak, J. S., and D. S. Anderson. "Brewers and Colleges: Strange Bedfellows?" *Journal of College Student Personnel* 24 (January 1983), 91-92.

Tuzzolino, Frank, and Barry R. Armandi. "A Need-Hierarchy Framework for Assessing Corporate Social Responsibility." *Academy of Management Review* 6 (January 1981), 21-28.

Ullmann, A. A. "Data in Search of a Theory." *Academy of Management Review* 10 (July 1985), 540-547.

Van Auken, Philip M., and R. D. Ireland. "Plain Talk About Small Business Social Responsibility." *Journal of Small Business Management* 20 (January 1982), 1-3.

Velasquez, Manuel G., S.J. "Why Corporations Are Not Morally Responsible for Anything They Do." *Business and Professional Ethics Journal* 2 (Spring 1983), 1-18. Commentaries: by Kenneth E. Goodpaster, vol.2, no.4, 100; Thomas A Klein, vol.3, no.4, 69.

Walton, Clarence C. "Corporate Social Responsibility: The Debate Revisited." *Journal of Economics and Business* 34 (1982), 173-187.

Weidenbaum, Murray L. "The True Obligation of the Business Firms to Society." *Management Review* 70 (September 1981), 21-22.

Weissman, George. "Social Responsibility and Corporate Success." *Business and Society Review* 51 (Fall 1984), 67-68.

Wilbur, James E. "The Foundations of Corporate Responsibility." *Journal of Business Ethics* 1 (May 1982), 145-155.

"A Word from Our Sponsor: Increasing Ties between Big Business and the Art World Raise Some Delicate Questions." *Newsweek* 106 (November 25, 1985), 96-98.

Zalud, Bill. "IBM Chief Urges DP Education, Social Responsibility." *Data Management* 22 (September 1984), 30, 74.

Environmental Issues and Nuclear Safety

Books

Ackerman, Bruce A., and W. T. Hassler. *Clean Coal/Dirty Air*. New Haven: Yale University Press, 1981.

Brodeur, Paul. *Outrageous Misconduct: The Asbestos Industry on Trial*. New York: Pantheon, 1985.

Brown, Michael. *Laying Waste: The Poisoning of America by Toxic Chemicals*. New York: Washington Square Press, 1981.

Brunner, David L., Will Miller, and Nan Stockholm. *Corporations and the Environment: How Should Decisions Be Made?* Stanford, Calif.: Stanford University, 1981.

Davis, Lee N. *The Corporate Alchemists: Profit Takers and Problem Makers in the Chemical Industry*. New York: Morrow, 1984.

Gilbreath, Kent. *Business and the Environment: Toward Common Ground*. 2d ed. Washington, D.C.: Conservation Foundation, 1984.

Moore, Robert. *The Social Impact of Oil: The Case of Peterhead*. Boston: Routledge & Kegan Paul, 1982.

Nader, Ralph, et al. *Who's Poisoning America: Corporate Polluters and Their Victims in the Chemical Age*. San Francisco: Sierra Club Books, 1981.

Organisation for Economic Cooperation and Development. *Environment and Economics*. Paris: O.E.C.D., 1985.

Regenstein, Lewis. *America the Poisoned*. Washington, D.C.: Acropolis Books, 1982.

Shrivastava, Paul. *Industrial Crisis: A Strategic Analysis of the Bhopal Tragedy*. Cambridge, Mass.: Ballinger, 1985.

Stoler, Peter. *Decline and Fall: The Ailing Nuclear Power Industry*. New York: Dodd, Mead, 1985.

U.N. Centre on Transnational Corps. *Environmental Aspects of the Activities of Transnational Corporations: A Survey*. New York: U.N. Agent, 1985.

Whelan, Elizabeth M. *Toxic Terror: Exploding the Myths of the Environmental Fanatics*. Ottawa, Ill.: Jameson Books, 1985.

Willens, Harold. *The Trim Tab Factor: How Business Executives Can Help Solve the Nuclear Weapons Crisis*. New York: Morrow, 1984.

Articles

Alexander, Tom. "A Simpler Path to a Cleaner Environment." *Fortune* 103 (May 4, 1981), 234-254.

Alterman, Eric R. "No-Nuke Execs Fight for Peace." *Business and Society Review* 49 (Spring 1984), 31-34.

Ameiss, Albert P. "Environmental Concerns for Top Management: Corrupt Practices and Social Responsibility." *Managerial Planning* 32 (September-October 1983), 21+.

Anderson, Eugene. "The Financial Executive and Toxic Substance Litigation." *Financial Executive* 51 (November 1983), 48-53.

Applegate, Howard G., et al. "Hazardous and Toxic Substances in U.S.-Mexico Relations." *Texas Business Review* 57 (September-October 1983), 229-234.

Bernstein, Peter W. "A Nuclear Fiasco Shakes the Bond Market." *Fortune* 105 (February 11, 1982), 100-115.

Bleiberg, Robert M. "End of the Fallout? Three Mile Island's Start-Up Is a Milestone for Nuclear Power." *Barron's* 65 (October 7, 1985), 11.

Bleiberg, Robert M. "EPA's Formaldehyde Scare." *Barron's* 64 (May 21, 1984), 11.

Boland, John C. "Nader Crusade: The Anti-Business Lobby Is Alive and Kicking." *Barron's* 61 (October 12, 1981), 11, 16-26.

Borowski, Patricia A. "Is Another Crisis Looming?" *National Underwriter (Property/Casualty)* 88 (May 11, 1984), 27+.

Bremer, K. D. "Wildlife Wins, Honeywell Loses." *Progressive* 49 (October 1985), 16-17.

Brenner, Lynn. "The Toxic Waste Time Bomb." *Institutional Investor* 18 (February 1984), 163+.

Brewster, James N. "Love Canal: Redefining Disaster." *Christian Century* 99 (August 4-11, 1982), 829-830.

Brooks, K., et al. "Slow Action on a Carbide Leak." *Chemical Week* 137 (August 21, 1985), 7-8.

Brown, Michael. "Arresting the Spread of Chemical Garbage." *Business and Society Review* 42 (Summer 1982), 56-60.

Brummer, James J. "Love Canal and the Ethics of Environmental Health." *Business and Professional Ethics Journal* 2 (Summer 1983), 1-22. Commentary: by June Fessenden-Raden and Stuart M. Brown, 23.

Byrd, Robert C. "Surviving Acid Rain." *Public Utilities Fortnightly* 114 (December 1984), 15-17.

Cahan, Vicky, and Maria Recio. "Forcing Chemical Makers to Come Clean on Hazards." *Business Week* (December 7, 1985), 86H.

Cameron, Catherine M. "Hope for a Less Toxic Future." *Christian Century* 100 (August 17-24, 1983), 747-749.

Cantilli, Edmund J., and Raymond D. Scanlon. "Death on Wheels: Hazardous Materials Transport: An Explosive National Problem." *Journal of Insurance* 42 (July-August 1981), 2-7.

Caufield, Catherine. "How Hamburgers Destroy Tropical Forests." *Business and Society Review* 39 (Fall 1981), 29-32.

Cheek, Leslie, III. "An Insurance Perspective on Proposals for Hazardous Substance Compensation." *Chemical Times & Trends* 7 (July 1984), 33-38.

Cheek, Leslie, III. "Pollution: The Peril Around Us." *Journal of Insurance* 42 (September 1981), 2-7.

Chern, Michael J. "Union Carbide's Plant at Institute, W.Va.: Lessons from Bhopal." *EPA Journal* 11 (July-August 1985), 21-23.

Cohn, J. P. "Creating a Conservation Ethic." *Americas* 37 (November/December 1985), 12-15.

"A Council for Hazardous Waste Treaters." *Chemical Week* 135 (September 19, 1984), 60-65.

Crandall, Robert W. "An Acid Test for Congress?" *Regulation* 8 (September/December 1984), 21-28.

Cuneo, Alice. "The Uproar Over Burning Toxic Wastes Offshore." *Business Week* (September 16, 1985), 124E-124H.

Curry, Michael. "The Inevitability of Bhopal." *Science for the People* 17 (November-December 1985), 7+.

Del Duca, Patrick. "The Clean Air Act: A Realistic Assessment of Cost Effectiveness." *Harvard Environmental Law Review* 5 (1981), 184-203.

Drabble, N. "Pesticide Legislation Reform: Accord Between Industry and Environmentalists." *Environment* 27 (December 1985), 4-5).

Dwyer, Paula. "The EPA's Eye in the Sky Has Companies Seeing Red." *Business Week* (October 28, 1985), 90.

"Economics and the Environment: Not Conflict but Symbiosis." *OECD Observer* 130 (September 1984), 30-34.

Emshwiller, John R. "Power Struggles: Environmental Group, in Change of Strategy, Is Stressing Economics." *Wall Street Journal* (September 28, 1981), 1+.

Engler, Rick. "The New Jersey 'Right to Know Campaign: The Nation's Toughest Toxics Law." *Health and Medicine* 2 (Winter 1983-84), 10-12.

Evans, Bob, and John Seavey. "Workers of Conscience." *Across the Board* 21 (March 1984), 7-8.

Feuer, Dale. "Protecting the Public: How Much Training Is Enough?" *Training* 22 (November 1985), 22-28.

"Final Approval Given for Asbestos Claims Facility." *Best's Review (Property/Casualty)* 86 (August 1985), 5-6.

Fisher, M. J. "U.S. Asked to Pay Part of Asbestos Bill." *National Underwriter (Property/Casualty)* 89 (September 13, 1985), 3+.

Fisher, Sidney T. "The Hazards of Nuclear Power Generation—The Case for Survival." *Long Range Planning* 16 (February 1983), 77-83.

Flavin, Christopher. "The Demise of Nuclear Power." *Challenge* 27 (July-August 1984), 38-45.

"Foreign Firms Feel the Impact of Bhopal Most." *Wall Street Journal* (November 26, 1985), 24.

"Forest Firms Get Awards for Energy Environment." *Forest Industries* 112 (August 1985), 10.

Freeman, Alix M. "Firms Curb Hazardous Waste to Avoid Expensive Disposal." *Wall Street Journal* (May 31, 1985), 25.

Gabel, H. L. "Reform of the Clean Air Act—Another Decade of Waste?" *Sloan Management Review* 23 (Fall 1981), 69-75.

Giltenan, Edward F. "Hazardous Waste Control Keeps the Beat." *Chemical Business* (September 1984), 42-44.

Goldstein, Mark L. "Acid Rain." *Industry Week* 223 (November 26, 1984), 64-65.

Gould, Jay M. "Toxic Waste and Cancer: The Link Is Getting Stronger." *Council on Economic Priorities Newsletter* (September 1984), 1-6.

Gunn, Bruce. "Capitalism or Competruism." *Vital Speeches of the Day* 48 (September 15, 1982), 720-722.

Hamilton, Robert A. "What Will We Do When the Well Runs Dry?" *Harvard Business Review* 62 (November-December 1984), 28-40.

Hanson, David. "Multimedia Approach to Pollution Control Urged." *Chemical and Engineering News* 62 (November 26, 1984), 26-27.

Hartung, Bill. "Would a Nuclear Freeze Bomb the Economy?" *Business and Society Review* 47 (Fall 1983), 34-39.

"Hazardous Materials." *Distribution* 83 (December 1984), 50.

Hebert, James, and Jane Teas. "Urban Third World Children: Toxic Exposure and Malnutrition." *Science for the People* 17 (November-December 1985), 18-22.

Hoffman, John S. "Contingency Planning for a Hotter Earth." *Directors & Boards* 7 (Fall 1982), 34-38.

Holub, Kay M., and James E. Levin. "Strategic Waste Management Considerations in Siting Industrial Facilities." *Industrial Development* 153 (December 1984), 4-13.

Huber, Peter. "The I Ching of Acid Rain." *Regulation* 8 (September-December 1984), 15-20.

Hughey, Ann. "Poison Problem: Fearing Love Canal, Chemical Firms Stress Safer Disposal of Hazardous Waste." *Wall Street Journal* (June 30, 1983), 58.

"The Hunt for Illegal Skins and Furs." *Business Week* (March 7, 1983), 70-71.

"India's Tragedy—A Warning Heard Around the World." *U.S. News and World Report* 97 (December 17, 1984), 25-27.

"It Was Like Breathing Fire." *Newsweek* 104 (December 28, 1984), 26-44.

Joseph, Raymond A. "Recurring Hazard: Cleanup at New England Asbestos Dump Shows Costs Can Offset Health Factors." *Wall Street Journal* (September 13, 1983), 60.

Jubak, Jim. "They Are the First." *Environmental Action* 14 (February 1983), 9-14.

Katz, D. M. "Bhopal and Public Right to Know." *National Underwriter (Property/Casualty)* 89 (August 2, 1985), 3+.

Kirkland, Richard I., Jr. "Union Carbide: Coping with Catastrophe." *Fortune* 111 (January 7, 1985), 50-53.

Knowles, L. "$225,000 TMI Settlement Awaits Approval." *Business Insurance* 18 (August 20, 1984), 78.

Lahey, James W. "Hazardous Wastes and the Small Company." *National Safety News* 130 (November 1984), 36-37.

Landrigan, P.J., and R. L. Gross. "Chemical Wastes—Illegal Hazards and Legal Remedies." *American Journal of Public Health* 71 (September 1981), 985-987.

Lanouette, William J. "Industry Goliath, Environmental David Girding for Battle Over Nuclear Power." *National Journal* 15 (April 9, 1983), 737-739.

Lappe, Alyssa A. "Will Coal Finally Clean Up Its Act?" *Forbes* 136 (July 29, 1985), 78-82.

"Living, Dangerously, with Toxic Wastes." *Time* 126 (October 14, 1985), 86-90.

MacDougall, William L. "Private Money Pours in to Save Green Space." *U.S. News and World Report* 91 (October 26, 1981), 64.

Magnuson, Ed, et al. "A Problem That Cannot Be Buried." *Time* 126 (October 14, 1985), 76-78+.

Main, Jeremy. "The Hazards of Helping Toxic Waste Victims." *Fortune* 108 (October 1983), 158-170.

"Major Acid Rain Study Launched." *Public Utilities Fortnightly* 115 (June 27, 1985), 58-59.

"Managing Hazardous Waste." *Enterprise* 7 (November 1983), 5-18.

"Many Victims of Pollution Are Shortchanged." *Conservation Foundation Newsletter* (January 1981), 1-8.

Maxwell, Jane. "Exporting Lung Cancer." *Science for the People* 17 (July-August 1985), 15-17.

Mays, Richard H. "Dioxin: Deadly or Deceptive?" *Environmental Forum* 2 (February 1984), 13-21.

Meier, Barry. "Union Carbide Stresses U.S. Plant Safety, but Questions about India Site Remain." *Wall Street Journal* (December 12, 1984), 3.

Meier, Barry, and Andy Pasztor. "Risky Business." *Wall Street Journal* (June 26, 1984), 1+.

Miller, William H. "Friendly 'Foe': Industry's Favorite Environmental Group." *Industry Week* 224 (February 4, 1984), 31-33.

Mojtabai, A. G. "Pantex's Nuclear Bombs: America's Doomsday Factory." *Business and Society Review* 43 (Fall 1982), 21-25.

Morrison, Alan B. "Executive Privilege Has Its Place." *Wall Street Journal* (May 27, 1983), 22.

Morrison, Alan B. "Executive Privilege Has Its Place." *Wall Street Journal* (May 27, 1983), 22.

Munson, Richard. "Dealing the Death Blow to Nuclear Power." *Business and Society Review* 53 (Spring 1985), 55-58.

Nute, Leslie F. "Compensation for Exposure to Hazardous Substances." *Chemical Times & Trends* 7 (January 1984), 27-30.

Odell, Rice. "Pollution's Victims Rarely Get Compensated." *Business and Society Review* 39 (Fall 1981), 23-28.

O'Reilly, James T. "What's Wrong With the Right to Know?" *Across the Board* 22 (April 1985), 24-29.

O'Sullivan, Dermot A. "European Concern About Acid Rain Is Growing." *Chemical and Engineering News* 63 (January 28, 1985), 12-18.

Peters, Ted. "The Ethics of Radwaste Disposal." *Christian Century* 99 (March 17, 1982), 271-273.

Peterson, Jeffrey K. "Community Right to Know: Creating the Balance That Works." *Chemical Times & Trends* 8 (April 1985), 28-29.

Pettinger, Thomas, Jr. "Trial Begins on 1978 Amoco Cadiz Wreck for Liability in History's Worst Oil Spill." *Wall Street Journal* (May 5, 1982), 23.

Pilot, Larry R., and Roger D. Middlekauff. "Chemicals, Carcinogens and Common Sense." *Chemical Times & Trends* 7 (January 1984), 55-57.

Pollitti, N. "Licence to Kill Renewed." *New Statesman* 104 (August 27, 1982), 6-7.

Powell, William J., Jr., William B. Glaberson, and Resa W. King. "Union Carbide Points the Finger at Itself." *Business Week* (April 1, 1985), 32-33.

"Preserving Wildlife and Land: 'It's Good Business.' " *Chemical Week* (October 24, 1984), 30-34.

Proom, Burt C. "Nuclear Insurance: What's Ahead?" *Journal of Insurance* (July-August 1981), 9-14.

"RCRA Weeds Out Waste Facilities." *Chemical Week* 137 (November 6, 1985), 46-48.

"Rainy Weather." *Fortune* 112 (October 14, 1985), 8.

Reamer, F. G., and S. J. Schaffer. "Duty to Warn: An Uncertain Danger." *Hastings Center Report* 15 (February 1985), 15+.

Recio, M. "Everybody Will Probably Pay to Clean Up Toxic Waste." *Business Week* (November 4, 1985), 30.

Reilly, William K. "Cleaning Our Chemical Waste Backyard." *Wall Street Journal* (May 31, 1984), 30.

Rich, L. A., and J. Trewhitt. "Fall Calls for Environmental Legislation." *Chemical Week* 137 (September 4, 1985), 37-38.

Ripstein, Diane. "Chemical Waste Beneath a Massachusetts Town." *Business and Society Review* 41 (Spring 1982), 46-47.

Ruckelshaus, William D. "Risk in a Free Society." *Risk Analysis* 4 (September 1984), 157-162.

Russell, Robert J. "Energy and Values." *New Catholic World* 224 (May-June 1981), 100-103.

Salzman, Lorna. "Bad Solutions to Radioactive Pollution." *Business and Society Review* 41 (Spring 1982), 33-35.

Sands, Roberta G., Larry Newby, and Richard A. Greenberg. "Labeling of Health Risk in Industrial Settings." *Journal of Applied Behavioral Science* 17 (July-September 1981), 359-374.

Savage, J. A. "The Timber Titan with a Tiny Heart." *Business and Society Review* 54 (Summer 1985), 69-71.

Sayre, Kenneth. "Morality, Energy, and the Environment." *Environmental Ethics* 3 (Spring 1981), 5-18.

Schaeffer, Robert. "The Fire Storm Over Toxic Smoke." *Business and Society Review* 45 (Spring 1983), 56-62.

Schmitt, Richard B. "Some Dallas Residents Are Angry at EPA over Agency's Handling of Alleged Hazard." *Wall Street Journal* (April 13, 1983), 29.

Shue, H. "Exporting Hazards." *Ethics* 91 (July 1981), 579-606.

Silcox, Marcia F., and Joseph H. Highland. "Chemical Technology, Values and Economic Quality." *New Catholic World* 224 (May-June 1981), 123-126.

Silverman, E. B. "Robots Set to Move into Nuclear Plant Safety." *National Underwriter (Property/Casualty)* 89 (August 2, 1985), 20-21.

Smith, R. J. "Privatizing the Environment." *Policy Review* 20 (Spring 1982), 11-50.

Spalding, B. J. "If Acid Rain's a Problem, Who Pays for Solving It?" *Chemical Week* 136 (April 17, 1985), 20-21.

Speth, James G. "Questions for a Critical Decade." *Columbia Journal of World Business* 19 (Spring 1984), 5-9.

Spurgeon, W. A., and T. P. Fagan. "Criminal Liability for Life-Endangering Corporate Conduct." *Journal of Criminal Law and Criminology* 72 (Summer 1981), 400-433.

Stafford, H. A. "Environmental Protection and Industrial Location." *Annals American Assn. Geographers* 75 (June 1985), 227-240.

Stanfield, Rochelle L. "Environmentalists Try the Backdoor Approach to Tackling Acid Rain." *National Journal* 17 (October 19, 1985), 2365-2368.

Stanfield, Rochelle L. "Politics Pushes Pesticide Manufacturers and Environmentalists Closer Together." *National Journal* 17 (December 14, 1985), 2846-2851.

Stead, Jean, and W. E. Stead. "The Dollar Cost of Cancer." *Business and Society Review* 37 (Spring 1980-81), 68-69.

Stevens, Christine. "Importers Poach Profits on Endangered Species." *Business and Society Review* 50 (Summer 1984), 26-29.

Stickle, Warren E. "Emerging Challenges for the Mid-80's: Groundwater and Federal Community Right to Know." *Chemical Times & Trends* 8 (October 1985), 59-64.

Stoler, Peter. "Turning to New Technologies: Incenerators and Voracious Bacteria Help Dispose of Waste." *Time* 126 (October 14, 1985), 90.

Storck, William J., and David Webber. "Carbide's Anderson Explains Post-Bhopal Strategy." *Chemical and Engineering News* 63 (January 21, 1985), 9-15.

Street, Annie. "El Caso Pennwalt: Mercury Pollution in Nicaragua." *Business and Society Review* 40 (Winter 1981-82), 21-23.

Tanzer, Michael. "Stealing the Third World's Nonrenewable Resources: Lessons from Brazil." *Monthly Review* 35 (April 1984), 26-35.

Tasini, Jonathan. "The Nuclear Issue That Won't Die." *Business Week* (May 6, 1985), 110F-110G.

Tell, Lawrence. "Grassroots Trouble." *Barron's* 64 (September 24, 1984), 14+.

Tenorio, Vyvyan, and Mimi Bluestone. "Initial Data on Bhopal Survivors." *Chemical Week* 137 (December 4, 1985), 12.

Thompson, Paul B. "Need and Safety: The Nuclear Power Debate." *Enrivonmental Ethics* 6 (Spring 1984), 57-69.

"The Threat That's Stirring Carbide's Survival Instincts." *Business Week* (September 16, 1985), 29.

Tiller, M. H. "Environmental Exposures: Out of the Closet." *National Underwriter (Property/Casualty)* 89 (August 2, 1985), 18-19+.

Tirman, John. "Nuclear Industry, Heal Thyself." *Wall Street Journal* (December 30, 1983), 8.

Trauberman, Jeffrey. "Compensating Victims of Toxic Substances Pollution: An Analysis of Existing Federal Statutes." *Harvard Environmental Law Review* 5 (1981), 1-29.

Trost, Cathy. "Hooker Chemical's Michigan Mess." *Business and Society Review* 40 (Winter 1981-82), 32-39.

Turner, Tom. "Scuttling Environmental Progress." *Business and Society Review* 42 (Summer 1982), 48-52.

"Union Carbide Says Managerial Errors Led to Leak at Institute." *Chemical Marketing Reporter* 228 (August 26, 1985), 3+.

Vaidyanathan, A. "Accountability Is Bad for Business." *Science for the People* 17 (November-December 1985), 9-11.+

Vermeulen, James E., and Daniel M. Berman. "Asbestos Companies Under Fire." *Business and Society Review* 42 (Summer 1982), 21-25.

"Victim Compensation: Paying for the Damage Caused by Toxic Wastes." *Chemical Week* 132 (March 9, 1983), 22.

Viscusi, W. K. "Phosphates and the Environmental Free Lunch." *Regulation* 8 (September-December 1984), 53-55.

Wallinger, R. S. "Industry Commitment to Reforesting Public Lands Is Crucial to the Future." *Pulp & Paper* 59 (July 1985), 72-74.

Wehr, Elizabeth. "Action Expected Next Year on System for Compensating Victims of Asbestos Disease." *Congressional Quarterly Weekly Report* 40 (October 23, 1982), 2729-2733.

Weinberg, Alvin M. " 'Immortal' Energy Systems and Intergenerational Justice." *Energy Policy (UK)* (February 1985), 51-59.

Wells, Ken. "Unlikely Alliance: In Distinct Departure, Environmental Group Woos Big Business." *Wall Street Journal* (February 7, 1983), 1+.

Wenner, Lettie M. "Interest Group Litigation and Environmental Policy." *Policy Studies Journal* 11 (June 1983), 671-683.

Wenz, Peter W. "Ethics, Energy Policy, and Future Generations." *Environmental Ethics* 5 (Fall 1983), 95-209.

Zeusse, Eric. "Love Canal: The Truth Seeps Out." *Reason* 12 (February 1981), 16-33.

Zuckerman, Ed. "Corporate Defense Against Nuclear Attack." *Business and Society Review* 41 (Spring 1982), 60-63.

Families and Work

Books

Axel, Helen. *Corporations and Families: Changing Practices and Perspectives.* New York: Conference Board, 1985.

Berry, Peggy. *The Corporate Couple: Living the Corporate Game* New York: Watts, 1985.

Bohen, Halcyone H. *A Corporate Reader: Work and Family Life in the 1980s.* Washington, D.C.: Children's Defense Fund, 1983.

Borman, Kathryn M., et al. *Women in the Workplace: Effects on Families.* Norwood, N.J.: Ablex, 1984.

Cooper, Cary L. *Executive Families Under Stress: How Male and Female Managers Can Keep Their Pressures Out of Their Homes.* Englewood Cliffs, N.J.: Prentice-Hall, 1981.

Danco, Katy. *From the Other Side of the Bed: A Woman Looks at Life in the Family Business.* Cleveland: Ctr. for Family Business, 1981.

Finch, Janet. *Married to the Job: Wives' Incorporation in Men's Work.* London, U.K.: Allen & Unwin, 1983.

Gerson, Kathleen. *Hard Choices: How Women Decide About Work, Career, and Motherhood.* Berkeley, Calif.: Univ. Calif. Press, 1985.

Articles

Bains, Leslie E. "Banks Must Cope With Dual-Career Marriages." *ABA Banking Journal* 77 (October 1985), 117-120.

Banbury-Masland, Brooke, and Daniel J. Brass. "Careers, Marriage and Children: Are Women Changing Their Minds?" *Business Horizons* 28 (May-June 1985), 81-86.

Buss, Dale D. "Auto Firms' Blue-Collar Transfers Result in Troubles at Work, Home." *Wall Street Journal* (May 15, 1984), 31.

"Corporations and Two Career Families." *Human Ecology Forum* 12 (Winter 1982), 6-7.

Derr, C. B., and Claire J. Turner. "Careers in Collision?: The Changing Role of the Executive Wife." *Business* 32 (April-June 1982), 18-22.

Foegen, J. H. "Big Motherism." *Business and Society Review* 41 (Spring 1982), 73-74.

Foegen, J. H. "Is There Life after 5?" *Business Horizons* 27 (May-June 1984), 33-36.

Gomez, F. "Why Women Must Make a Choice Between Business and Home Life." *International Management* 40 (July 1985), 52.

Grayson, J. P. "The Effects of a Plant Closure on the Stress Levels and Health of Workers' Wives." *Journal of Business Ethics* 2 (August 1983), 221-225.

Green, Donna H., and Thomas J. Zenisek. "Dual Career Couples: Individual and Organizational Implications." *Journal of Business Ethics* 2 (August 1983), 171-184.

Greenhaus, Jeffrey H., and Nicholas J. Beutell. "Sources of Conflict Between Work and Family Roles." *Academy of Management Review* 10 (January 1985), 76-87.

Gullotta, Thomas P., et al. "Preventing Family Distress During Relocation: Initiatives for Human Resource Managers." *Personnel Administrator* 27 (December 1982), 37-43.

Harvey, Michael G. "The Executive Family: An Overlooked Variable in International Assignments." *Columbia Journal of World Business* 20 (Spring 1985), 84-92.

Holmstrom, Nancy. "Women's Work, the Family and Capitalism." *Science and Society* 45 (Summer 1981), 186-211.

Immerwahr, John. "Building a Consensus on the Child Care Problem." *Personnel Administrator* 29 (February 1984), 31-37.

Jackson, Susan E., Sheldon Zedeck, and Elizabeth Summers. "Family Life Disruptions: Effects of Job-Induced Structural and Emotional Interference." *Academy of Management Journal* 28 (September 1985), 574-586.

LeRoux, Margaret. "Liability Insurers Are Abandoning Day Care Centers Across the U.S." *Business Insurance* 19 (June 10, 1985), 2, 37.

Levitan, Sar A., and Richard S. Belous. "Working Wives and Mothers: What Happens to Family Life?" *Monthly Labor Review* 104 (September 1981), 26-30.

Lyman, Amy, Matilde Salganicoff, and Barbara Holland. "Women in Family Business: An Untapped Resource." *Advanced Management Journal* 50 (Winter 1985), 46-49.

Madlin, N. "The Venture Survey: Is Your Business Your Spouse's Business?" *Venture* 7 (June 1985), 16.

Magnet, Myron. "What Mass-Produced Child Care Is Producing." *Fortune* 108 (November 28, 1983), 157-174.

Pave, I. "A Lot of Enterprise Is Staying in the Family These Days." *Business Week* (July 1, 1985), 62-63.

"Working Around Motherhood." *Business Week* (May 24, 1982), 188.

Zoppetti, Leighsa. "The Single Parent and Unemployment Economy." *New Catholic World* 226 (July-August 1983), 166-169.

Government and Business Relations

Books

Adams, Gordon. *The Politics of Defense Spending.* New Brunswick, N.J.: Transaction Books, 1982.

Badaracco, Joseph L., Jr. *Loading the Dice: A Five-Country Study of Vinyl Chloride Regulation.* Boston: Harvard Bus. School Press, 1985.

Blackburn, John D., et al. *Legal Environment of Business: Public Law and Regulation.* Homewood, Ill.: R.D. Irwin, 1982.

Block, Walter. *Competition Versus Monopoly: Combines Policy in Perspective.* Vancouver, B.C.: Fraser Institute, 1982.

Boggs, Thomas, and Katherine R. Boyce. *Corporate Political Activity.* New York: Marcel Bender, 1984.

Brooks, Harvey, Lance Liebman, and Corinne Schelling. *Public-Private Partnership: New Opportunities for Meeting Social Needs.* Cambridge, Mass.: Ballinger, 1984.

Butler, Stuart M. *Privatizing Federal Spending: A Strategy to Eliminate the Deficit.* New York: Universe Books, 1985.

Cooling, Benjamin F., ed. *War, Business and World Military-Industrial Complexes.* Port Washington, N.Y.: Kennikat, 1981.

The Corporation in Politics: PACs, Lobbying Laws, and Public Officials. New York: Practising Law Institute, 1983.

Etzioni, Amitai. *Capital Corruption: The New Attack on American Democracy.* San Diego, Calif.: Harcourt Brace Jovanovich, 1984.

Fisse, Brent, and Peter A. French, eds. *Corrigible Corporations and Unruly Law.* San Antonio: Trinity University Press, 1985.

Gardner, Bruce L. *The Governing of Agriculture: Studies in Government and Public Policy.* Univ. Press of Kansas, 1981.

Goodwin, Jacob. *Brotherhood of Arms: General Dynamics and the Business of Defending America.* New York: Random House, 1985.

Grefe, Edward A. *Fighting to Win: Business Political Powers.* New York: Law & Business, Inc., 1981.

Levine, Marsha, ed. *The Private Sector in the Public School.* Washington, D.C.: American Enterprise Institute, 1985.

Lynton, Ernest A. *The Missing Connection Between Business and the Universities.* New York: Macmillan, 1984.

Mann, Kenneth. *Defending White Collar Crime: A Portrait of Attorneys at Work.* New Haven: Yale Univ. Press, 1985.

Monsen, Joseph, and Kenneth Walters. *Nationalized Companies: A Threat to American Business.* New York; McGraw-Hill, 1983.

Neal, Alfred C. *Business Power and Public Policy.* New York: Praeger, 1981.

Poole, Robert W., Jr. *Instead of Regulation: Alternatives to Federal Regulatory Agencies.* Lexington, Mass.: Lexington Books, 1982.

Quirk, Paul J. *Industry Influence in Federal Regulatory Agencies.* Princeton, N.J.: Princeton Univ. Press, 1981.

Sethi, S. P. *Push Button Politics and American Business: How Referendum Process Works.* Cambridge, Mass.: Oelgeschlager, Gunn, & Hain, 1981.

Shapiro, Susan. *Wayward Capitalists: Target of the Securities and Exchange Commission.* New Haven: Yale University Press, 1984.

Shippen, Frank, and Marianne M. Jennings. *Business Strategy for the Political Arena.* Westport, Conn.: Quorum Books, 1984.

Solo, Robert A. *The Positive State.* Cincinnati: South-Western Pub. Co., 1982.

Stokes, McNeil, ed. *Conquering Government Regulations: Business Guide.* New York: McGraw-Hill, 1982.

Tupper, Allan. *Public Money in the Private Sector: Industrial Assistance Policy and Canadian Federalism.* Kingston, Ont.: Queen's University, 1982.

U.S. Congress Jt. Econ. Committee. *Privatization of the Federal Government. Part 1.* Washington, D.C.: Gov't. Printing Office, 1984.

Useem, Michael. *The Inner Circle: Large Corporations and the Rise of Business Political Activity in the U.S. and U.K.* New York: Oxford Univ. Press., 1984.

Walter, Edward. *The Immorality of Limiting Growth.* Albany: S.U.N.Y. Press, 1981.

Weidenbaum, Murray L. *Business, Government, and the Public.* Englewood Cliffs, N.J.: Prentice-Hall, 1981.

Wilson, Graham K. *Business and Politics: A Comparative Introduction.* London, U.K.: Macmillan Education, 1985.

Wilson, Graham K. *Interest Groups in the U.S.* Oxford, U.K.: Clarendon, 1981.

Wolfson, Nicholas. *The Modern Corporation: Free Market versus Regulation.* New York: Free Press, 1984.

Articles

Adams, Gordon, and Geoff Quinn. "The Politics of Defense Spending." *Business and Society Review* 40 (Winter 1981-82), 28-31.

"AIDS, Hepatitis, and the National Blood Policy." *Regulation* 9 (July-August 1985), 5-7.

Alexander, Herbert E., and Mike Eberts. "Political Action Committees: A Practical Approach." *Business Forum* 9 (Winter 1984), 67+.

Alterman, Eric R. "How Pentagon Spending Undermines the Economy." *Business and Society Review* 52 (Winter 1985), 50-55.

Amacher, Ryan, et al. "The Behavior of Regulatory Activity Over the Business Cycle: An Empirical Test." *Economic Inquiry* 23 (January 1985), 7-19.

Audres, G. J. "Business Involvement in Campaign Finance." *P S* 18 (Spring 1985), 213-220.

Bandow, Doug. "Corporate America: Uncle Sam's Favorite Welfare Client." *Business and Society Review* 55 (Fall 1985), 48-54.

Barry, John M. "Biotech: Will the U.S. Lose Its Edge?" *Dun's Business Month* 124 (August 1984), 58-61.

Bensman, David. "The Government Buys a Bank." *Commonweal* 111 (September 7, 1984), 462-464.

Berman, Phillis. "Shark Swallows Whale." *Forbes* 126 (November 4, 1985), 60-65.

Bingham, Richard D., and John P. Blair. "Leveraging Private Investment With Federal Funds: Use and Abuse." *Policy Studies Journal* 11 (March 1983), 458-464.

Birnbaum, Philip H. "Political Strategies of Regulated Organizations as Functions of Context and Fear." *Strategic Management Journal* 6 (April-June 1985), 135-150.

Bluestone, Mimi, et al. "Chemical Companies Face Up to Hazard Communication." *Chemical Week* 137 (November 20, 1985), 65-71.

Boddewyn, J. J. "Advertising Regulation: Fiddling with the FTC While the World Burns." *Business Horizons* 28 (May-June 1985), 32-40.

Bollier, David. "The Deregulation of Carcinogens." *Business and Society Review* 48 (Winter 1984), 13-18.

Boulding, Kenneth E. "The Role of Government in a Free Economy." *Review of Social Economy* 40 (December 1982), 417-426.

Bowser, Georgia W. "Who Seeks Management Assistance: A Study of Minority Entrepreneurs." *Journal of Small Business Management* 19 (October 1981), 24-28.

Boyd, Bruce, and Hans B. C. Spiegel. "Financing Community Organizations: The Business Option." *Journal of Community Action* 1 (1983), 9-13.

Brown, Andrew C. "For Sale: Pieces of the Public Sector." *Fortune* 108 (October 31, 1983), 78-84.

Brown, Peter C. "New 'Public' Markets for the Private Sector." *Enterprise* 6 (July 1982), 2-5.

Brown, William S. "Unfettered Free Enterprise: It Can't Happen Here." *Management World* 10 (October 1981), 40, 44.

"Business May Get a Crack at Federal R & D." *Dun's Business Month* 126 (October 1985), 44.

Cannon, James S. "Federal Aid to Dependant Coal Users." *Business and Society Review* 43 (Fall 1982), 55-59.

Carley, William M. "Ruling in AT&T—MCI Case Indicates Courts' Confusion on Predatory Pricing." *Wall Street Journal* (January 21, 1983), 7.

Carlucci, Frank C. "An Economic Defense of the Defense Budget." *Directors & Boards* 7 (Winter 1983), 24-27.

Carrington, Tim. "Navy Penalizes General Dynamics Corp. but Doesn't Bar Officials from Contracts." *Wall Street Journal* (May 22, 1985), 2.

Carrington, Tim, and Daniel Mortimer. "FDIC, in a Bailout of Continental Illinois, Would Buy $4.5 Billion in Problem Loans." *Wall Street Journal* (July 24, 1984), 3.

Castle, Michael N. "The Public-Private Partnership and the States." *Vital Speeches of the Day* 51 (October 1, 1985), 738-741.

Chiles, Lawton. "PACs: Congress on the Auction Block." *Journal of Legislation* 11 (Summer 1984), 193-217.

Chilton, Kenneth W., and Murray L. Weidenbaum. "Government Regulation: The Small Business Burden." *Journal of Small Business Management* 20 (January 1982), 4-10.

Clark, Timothy B. "Demands for Government Assistance Not Limited to Old 'Smokestack' Industries." *National Journal* 15 (February 26, 1983), 444-452.

Clark, Timothy B. "Tax and Price Support Issues Causing Tobacco Interests' Solidarity to Crack." *National Journal* 17 (October 26, 1985), 2423-2427.

Cohen, David. "How Business Can Influence Government Credibility." *Journal of Business Ethics* 1 (May 1982), 109-114.

Cohen, Stephen. "Justification for a Doctrine of Strict Liability." *Social Theory and Practice* 8 (Summer 1982), 213-229.

Cooper, Ann. "Senate Immigration Bill Singles Out Western Growers for Special Treatment." *National Journal* 17 (October 19, 1985), 2162-2164.

Corrigan, Richard. "A Setback for a Computer Company." *National Journal* 14 (December 18, 1982), 2154-2156.

Crapnell, Stephen G. "Asbestos: Legal Battles Escalate—Will Congress Act?" *Occupational Hazards* 43 (April 1981), 99-102.

Daneke, Gregory A. "Regulation and the Sociopathic Firm." *Academy of Management Review* 10 (January 1985), 15-20.

Davis, Joseph A. "Hazardous Waste Measures Affect Smaller Operations." *Congressional Quarterly Weekly Report* 41 (August 20, 1983), 1701-1704.

Davison, J. L. "U.S. Surgical Seeks to Rebuild Following After SEC Settlement." *New England Business* 6 (September 17, 1984), 72-76.

Demac, Donna A. "The OMB: Making Government Safe for Business." *Business and Society Review* 53 (Spring 1985), 29-32.

Demkovich, Linda E. "The Delaney Clause Comes Under the Gun as Critics Ask, How Safe Is Safe?" *National Journal* 13 (October 13, 1981), 1950-1952.

Deringer, Dorothy K., and Andrew R. Molnar. "University, Industry, Federal Cooperation—A Case Study." *Science, Technology and Human Values* 8 (Fall 1983), 40-45.

Dewey, Martin. "Prisoners Who Work for Private Companies." *Across the Board* 18 (September 1981), 82-84.

"The Dialogue That Sometimes Happens: Government and Business Reflect on Business and Government." [Special Supplement] *Business Quarterly (Canada)* (Summer 1985), 61-118.

Dickson, Douglas. "Corpacs: The Business of Political Action Committees." *Across the Board* 18 (November 1981), 13-22.

"Dole Says Manville Filing to Affect Review of U.S. Bankruptcy Code by Senate Panel." *Wall Street Journal* (August 30, 1982), 3.

Donovan, William J. "The Government's Ban on GE Defense Work Was a Symbolic Move." *New England Business* 7 (May 20, 1985), 60-63.

Drucker, Meyer, and Mark A. Segal. "Penalties for Federal Tax Crimes." *Management Accounting* 66 (July 1984), 32-37.

Duffy, Susan M. "Breaking into Jail." *Barron's* 64 (May 14, 1984), 20+.

Dunn, Matthew J., et al. "The Campaign Finance Reform Act: A Measured Step to Limit the PACs." *Journal of Legislation* 11 (Summer 1984), 497-520.

Easley, Allen K. "Buying Back the First Amendment: Regulation of Disproportionate Corporate Spending in Ballot Issue Campaigns." *Georgia Law Review* 17 (Spring 1983), 675-758.

Eberle, James A. "Deregulation Catches the Eye of Justice Department Watchdogs." *Bottomline* 2 (January 1985), 31-33+.

Edsall, Thomas B. "Campaign Financing: An Answer to the PAC Debate." *Management (University of California at L.A.)* 3 (Spring 1984), 10-14+.

Englehardt, K. "Conversion of Military Research and Development: Realism or Wishful Thinking?" *International Labour Review* 124 (March-April 1985), 181-192.

Etzioni, Amitai. "Do Defense Contractors Map Our Military Strategy?" *Business and Society Review* 51 (Fall 1984), 29-34.

Evans, M. S. "Yes, We Have No Oranges." *Consumer's Research* 67 (December 1984), 20-21.

Falvey, James M. "Problems of Regulation." *Journal of Business Ethics* 1 (August 1982), 179-184.

Feldinger, Frank. "How the Bell System Avoids Taxes." *Business and Society Review* 40 (Winter 1981-82), 56-60.

Fialka, John G. "Concern Grows Over Foreign Stake in Companies Doing Defense Work." *Wall Street Journal* (January 8, 1982), 25.

Fielding, Fred F. "What to Do When the White House Calls." *Directors & Boards* 7 (Spring 1983), 6-15.

Fields, Howard. "Stations Can Expect Less Oversight from Commission." *Television/Radio Age* 32 (April 15, 1985), 47-50.

"Flouting the Law, Serving the Poor." *Reason* 17 (June-July 1985), 29-35.

Foglesong, Richard E. "Business Against the Welfare State." *Challenge* 26 (November-December 1983), 38-45.

Freedman, Craig, and David Makofsky. "Supporting the Rich." *California Management Review* 23 (Summer 1981), 49-54.

Freeman, Brian, and Barrett Seaman. "The Case for Messy Bailouts." *Fortune* 108 (October 3, 1983), 243-254.

Gage, Theodore. "Cops, Inc." *Reason* 14 (November 1982), 23-28.

Garment, Suzanne. "Toxic-Liability Bills Plant a Time-Bomb of Liability Costs." *Wall Street Journal* (June 3, 1983), 20.

Garvin, David A. "Deregulating and Self-Regulating." *Wharton* 5 (April 1981), 57-63.

Gigot, Paul A. "Favored Friends: In Philippines, to Be President's Pal

Can Be Boon for a Businessman." *Wall Street Journal* (November 4, 1983), 1.

Goldberg, Nicholas. "Shakedown in the Boardroom: How PACs Raise Their Money May Be as Corrupting as How They Spend It." *Washington Monthly* 15 (December 1983), 14-19.

Gollub, Erica. "Clearing Carcinogenic Contraceptives Through the FDA." *Business and Society Review* 46 (Summer 1983), 67-70.

Gowa, J. "Subsidizing American Corporate Expansion Abroad: Pitfalls in the Analysis of Public and Private Power." *World Politics* 37 (January 1985), 180-203.

Graves, Florence. "The Runaround." *Common Cause Magazine* 8 (June 1982), 18-23.

Greene, C. S., and Paul Miesing. "Public Policy, Technology, and Ethics: Marketing Decisions for NASA's Space Shuttle." *Journal of Marketing* 48 (Summer 1984), 56-67.

Grove, Gary A. "The Supreme Court Ruling Shattering the Confidentiality Code." *National Public Accountant* 30 (April 1985), 26-31.

Guiley, Rosemary. "Business, Labor Clash Over Regulating Computer Terminals in Workplace." *Management Review* 73 (December 1984), 37-39.

Guzzardi, Walter J. "Reagan's Reluctant Deregulators." *Fortune* 105 (March 8, 1982), 34-40.

Haggerty, Alfred G. "California Commissioner Wants Widespread Changes." *National Underwriter (Property/Casualty)* 88 (June 15, 1984), 40.

Harding, C.S.P. "European Communities and Control of Criminal Business Activities." *International and Comparative Law Quarterly* 31 (1982), 246-262.

Harris, M. "Fatal Fire Followed Firm's Free Enterprise." *New Statesman* 102 (September 18, 1981), 2-3.

Harrison, Bennett, and Barry Bluestone. "The Incidence of Regulation of Plant Shutdowns." *Policy Studies Journal* 10 (December 1981), 297-320.

Hickel, James. "Lemon Aid: Debunking the Case of the Chrysler Bail Out." *Reason* 14 (Mach 1983), 37-39.

Hill, G. C., and Jeff Bailey. "Bankers See Continental Illinois' Future Dependent on an FDIC-Assisted Merger." *Wall Street Journal* (May 25, 1984), 6.

Holland, Joe. "Free Trade or Protectionism?" *New Catholic World* 227 (July-August 1984), 157-160.

Horton, Thomas R. "If Right to Fire Is Abused, Uncle Sam May Step In." *Wall Street Journal* (June 11, 1984), 24.

Horwick, Sandy. "New York Plays Robin Hood to Loft Industries . . ." *Planning (APA)* 48 (November 1982), 18-21.

"How Contractors Can Survive Government Allegation of Fraud." *Security Management* 29 (August 1985), 58-60.

"How Russia Snares High-Technology Secrets." *Business Week* (April 27, 1981), 128-131.

Ingersoll, Bruce. "SEC Probe of Searle Options Raises Questions of Ethics, Inside Trades." *Wall Street Journal* (February 27, 1984), 29.

Jackson, Brooks, and Edward F. Pound. "Legislative Lucre: Fees for Congressmen from Interest Groups Doubled in Past Year." *Wall Street Journal* (July 28, 1983), 1.

Johnson, Robert. "Steel Theft Becoming Widespread: FBI and Firms Investigate Truckers." *Wall Street Journal* (April 5, 1983), 33.

Johnson, Robert. "Steel-Theft Plot Is Said Broken by an FBI Probe." *Wall Street Journal* (March 22, 1983), 10.

Kastiel, D. L. "Washington Mandates Asbestos Cleanup Training." *Business Insurance* 19 (August 5, 1985), 24.

Kerr, Lorin E., James L. Weeks, and Maier B. Fox. "Reckless Deregulation in the Coal Mines." *Business and Society Review* 44 (Winter 1983), 52-57.

Kidwell, Roland. "Handicapping an Innovator." *Reason* 13 (August 1981), 39-46.

Kirkland, Richard I., Jr. "Taxing the Business Lobby's Loyalty." *Fortune* 106 (October 18, 1982), 141+.

Kosterlitz, Julie. "The Money Behind the MX." *Common Cause Magazine* 11 (March-April 1985), 14-17.

Krajick, Kevin. "Punishment for Profit: Can Private Enterprise Do a Better Job of Running Our Prisons Than the Government?" *Across the Board* 21 (March 1984), 20-27.

Laderman, Jeffrey M. "The Epidemic of Insider Trading: The SEC Is Fighting a Losing Battle to Halt Stock-Market Abuses." *Business Week* (April 29, 1985), 78-81+.

Langley, Monica. "Ma Bell's Shepherds: AT&T Sends a Horde of Lobbyists to Fight a Phone-Bill Proposal." *Wall Street Journal* (November 4, 1983), 1.

Lanouette, William J. "Beyond Bailouts." *National Journal* 13 (December 19, 1981), 2251.

Larson, Merle D. "Chain Saw Makers Chop at Government Red Tape." *Business and Society Review* 45 (Spring 1983), 63-64.

Lashbrooke, E. C., Jr. "Suits Against International Organizations in Federal Court: OPEC, a Case Study." *California Western International Law Journal* 12 (Spring 1982), 305-324.

Leefeldt, Ed. "Rise in 'Greenmail' Payoffs Spurs Challenges in Courts and Congress." *Wall Street Journal* (May 2, 1984), 33.

Lehrer, Linda. "Designers Want More Protection from Imitators." *Wall Street Journal* (October 1, 1985), 35.

Lekachman, Robert. "Privatization." *Christianity and Crisis* 45 (April 29, 1985), 150-151.

"Limit Campaign Donations by PACs." *U.S. News & World Report* 96 (May 28, 1984), 51.

Lo, C.Y.H. "Theories of the State and Business Opposition to Increased Military Spending." *Social Problems* 29 (April 1982), 424-438.

Lodge, George C., and William R. Glass. "The Desperate Plight of the Underclass." *Harvard Business Review* 60 (July-August 1982), 60-71.

Loevinger, Lee. "Making Washington Work." *Directors & Boards* 8 (Winter 1984), 34-37.

Lydenberg, Steven. "Business Big-Spenders Hit the Referenda Votes." *Business and Society Review* 47 (Fall 1983), 53-55.

MacArthur, Malcolm D., et al. "What Are Your Limits in Restricting Association Membership?" *Association Management* 35 (April 1983), 91-93.

"Making a Few Corrections in the Prison Business." *Reason* 17 (May 1985), 17.

Manne, Henry G. "Insider Trading and Property Rights in New Information." *Cato Journal* 4 (Winter 1985), 933-943.

Markowitz, Steven. "Ethical Rules for Corporate PAC-Men." *Business and Society Review* 50 (Summer 1984), 21-25.

Masters, Marick F., and Barry D. Baysinger. "The Determinants of Funds Raised by Corporate Political Action Committees: An Empirical Examination." *Academy of Management Journal* 28 (September 28, 1985), 654-664.

Mautz, Robert K., and Alan G. Merten. "Business Diversity and Government Regulation." *Financial Executive* 49 (November 1981), 20-28.

McCraw, Thomas K. "Business and Government: The Origins of the

Adversary Relationship." *California Management Review* 26 (Winter 1984), 33-52.

McCue, Lisa J. "Taking Your Regulator to Court. Is It a Good Idea?" *Bottomline* 2 (January 1985), 23-28.

McEntee, Gerald W. "City Services: Can Free Enterprise Outperform the Public Sector?" *Business and Society Review* 55 (Fall 1985), 43-47.

McIntyre, Douglas I., and James C. Renick. "Purchase of Service: Forging Public-Private Partnerships in the Human Services." *Urban and Social Change Review* 16 (Winter 1983), 21-26.

McKenzie, Floretta D. "A Merger with Dividends: D.C. Public Schools Are Looking for Business Partners." *Enterprise* 9 (March 1985), 22-24.

Metz, Tim. "SEC Investigates Insider Trading on Takeover Bids." *Wall Street Journal* (July 23, 1984), 2.

Miller, Frederic A., et al. "South Africa—The Screws Are Tightening on U.S. Companies." *Business Week* (February 11, 1985), 38-40.

Miller, William H. "An End to Defense Scandals?" *Industry Week* 226 (September 16, 1985), 55-58.

Monnett, A. A., Jr. "Perspective on Protectionism: One View from American Business." *Social Education* 48 (January 1984), 37-39.

Mulkern, John R., Edward Handler, and Lawrence Godtfredsen. "Corporate PACs as Fundraisers." *California Management Review* 23 (Spring 1981), 49-55.

Mullins, James P. "Integrating Military and Industrial Complex: A New War Production Board." *Vital Speeches of the Day* 51 (October 15, 1984), 7-11.

Naar, J. L. "Open Corporate Politics, a New Problem." *American Journal of Economics and Sociology* 40 (April 1981), 221-223.

Nagel, Steve H., and John L. Hagan. "The Sentencing of White Collar Criminals in Federal Courts: A Socio-Legal Exploration of Disparity." *Michigan Law Review* 80 (June 1982), 1427-1465.

Nolan, Joseph T. "Political Surfing When Issues Break." *Harvard Business Review* 63 (January-February 1985), 72-81.

"Now That the TV Code Is Dead." *Marketing and Media Decisions* 18 (May 1983), 72-74.

O'Connor, Charles A., III, and Bonnie A. Sullivan. "Regulating Export of Toxic and Hazardous Chemicals." *Chemical Times & Trends* 4 (April 1981), 57-61.

O'Reilly, James T. "Free Business Secrets: With Love, From Uncle Sam." *Across the Board* 20 (June 1983), 8-12.

"PBGC as a Watchman, Not a Foreman." *Employee Benefits Plan Review* 39 (June 1985), 86.

Paltrow, Scot J. "Order in Case on DeLorean Angers Press." *Wall Street Journal* (April 21, 1983), 35+.

Pasztor, Andy. "House Panel Members Seek Resignation of Operating Chief for Synfuels Program." *Wall Street Journal* (April 4, 1984), 8.

Pasztor, Andy P. "U.S. Synfuels Program Appears to Be Stalled as Congress Moves to Probe Ethics Charges." *Wall Street Journal* (April 30, 1984), 3.

Payne, Seth. "Washington Turns Up the Heat on General Dynamics." *Business Week* (March 18, 1985), 30-31.

Perry, L. G. "The SEC's Enforcement Activities." *CPA Journal* 54 (April 1984), 9-13.

Pertschuk, Michael. "Confessions of an FTC Commissioner: Lessons Learned and Unlearned." *Across the Board* 20 (March 1983), 26-33.

Pertschuk, Michael. "Regulatory Back Pedaling (sic) on Public Health." *Business and Society Review* 43 (Fall 1982), 60-62.

Peterson, William H. "It's a Company Town." *Reason* 13 (October 1981), 38-39.

Poole, Dennis L. "The Future of Public-Private Sector Partnerships for the Provision of Human Services." *Journal of Applied Behavioral Science* 21 (1985), 393-406.

Posner, Michael. "Privatisation: The Frontier Between Public and Private." *Policy Studies* 5 (July 1984), 22-23.

Pound, Edward T. "Investigators Detect Pattern of Kickbacks for Defense Business." *Wall Street Journal* (November 11, 1985), 1.

Ramsey, Bruce. "Forest Socialism: Nationalized Forests Are Socialized Forests and Corporate America Wants It That Way." *Reason* 17 (August 1985), 33-37.

"Retired Corporate Aides Say Regulation Needed to Prevent Misdeeds, Poll Finds." *Wall Street Journal* (May 16, 1983), 12.

Reynolds, Larry. "Foundations of an Institutional Theory of Regulation." *Journal of Economic Issues* 15 (June 1981), 641-656.

Rich, Laurie A. "Turning Hazardous Waste into Energy." *Chemical Week* 137 (December 4, 1985), 38-41.

Richards, Eric L. "In Search of Consensus on the Future of Campaign Finance Laws." *American Business Law Journal* 20 (Summer 1982), 243-267.

Richman, Tom. "Growing, Going, Gone: To Stay in Business, Wallace Forman Had to Stay Small at Any Cost." *Inc.* 6 (March 1984), 103+.

Rickover, Hyman G. "The Scandals of Military Contracting." *Business and Society Review* 41 (Spring 1982), 48-52.

Robertson, J. "GTE Admits Using Secret DOD Data." *Electronic News* 31 (September 16, 1985), 68.

Roeder, Edward. "Business Financing of the Repressive Right." *Free Inquiry* 1 (Fall 1981), 6-10.

Ruffin, David C., and Earl G. Graves. "An Interview with Vice President George Bush." *Black Enterprise* 16 (September 1985), 49-52+.

Ruttenberg, Ruth. "Regulation Is a Boon for Business." *Business and Society Review* 41 (Spring 1982), 53-57.

"SEC Sues First Jersey." *Dun's Business Month* 126 (December 1985), 22.

Salem, Hanan. "Paper Industry PACs Are a Growing Factor in 1984 Political Fund Raising." *Pulp & Paper* 58 (November 1984), 86-88.

Scheibla, Shirley H. "Breakthrough in Drugs: The U.S. Is About to Make It Easier to Export Them." *Barron's* 65 (September 30, 1985), 40+.

Schilling, S. "Incentives and Barriers to Private Sector Involvement in Public Schools: A Corporation's Perspective." *Educational Computer Magazine* 3 (September 1983), 42-45.

"Senate Looks at DEE." *Engineering-News Record* 215 (November 28, 1985), 68.

"Senator's Bill Would Halt Leveraged Hostile Takeovers." *Electronic News* 31 (April 29, 1985), 6.

Sethi, S. P. "Corporate Political Activism." *California Management Review* 24 (Spring 1982), 32-42.

Shackleton, J. R. "Privatization: The Case Examined." *Quarterly Review (National Westminster Bank)* (May 1984), 59-73.

Sheler, Jeffrey L. "Is Congress for Sale?" *U.S. News and World Report* 96 (May 28, 1984), 47-50.

Shiner, Roger A. "Review Essay: Deregulation and Distributive Justice." *Journal of Business Ethics* 3 (August 1984), 235-255.

Slater, Robert E. "Private Jobs for Public Offenders." *Business and Society Review* 43 (Fall 1982), 32-36.

Smith, R. N. "Are Futures PACs Getting Funds to Favorite Candidates?" *Futures* 14 (August 1985), 66+.

Smith, Rodney N. "Spendthrift PACs: Where the Money Doesn't Go." *Barron's* 64 (June 4, 1984), 32-33.

Stamper, Malcolm T. "Crisis Without a Cause: A Champion Is Needed." *Vital Speeches of the Day* 51 (July 15, 1985), 601-603.

Stanley, Guy. "Could Markets Run the Social Services?" *Canadian Business Review* 12 (Spring 1985), 48-50.

"Superfund Law Spurs Cleanup of Abandoned Sites." *Occupational Hazards* 43 (April 1981), 67.

Swaim, C. R. "Public-Private Relations: The Arts and Humanities." *Policy Studies Journal* 11 (March 1983), 465-472.

"Symposium on Small Business and Public Policy." [Entire Issue] *Policy Studies Journal* 13 (June 1985).

Tarnoff, S. "Despite Antitrust Threat, PPOs Can Foster Competition." *Business Insurance* 19 (July 22, 1985), 22.

Taylor, Robert E. "House Votes $10 Billion Superfund Bill: Taxes on Oil, Chemical Firms to Increase." *Wall Street Journal* (December 11, 1985), 17.

Tenneriello, Bonnie. "The SEC Plays Hide-And-Seek with Executive Pay." *Business and Society Review* 49 (Spring 1984), 35-48.

Tinker, Anthony M. "Theories of State and the State of Accounting." *Journal of Accounting and Public Policy* 3 (Spring 1984), 55-74.

Tobin, Gary A. "The Public/Private Sector Partnership in the Redevelopment Process." *Policy Studies Journal* 11 (March 1983), 473-482.

"Top Execs Urge Management Defense Reform." *Management Review* 74 (November 1985), 6.

Towell, Pat. "Lawmakers Scrutinizing Spare Parts Practices: Beyond the Horror Stories, an Attempt to Cut Costs." *Congressional Quarterly Weekly Report* 42 (March 24, 1984), 671-674.

Travis, Laurence F., III, and Edward J. Latessa, Jr. "The Role of Private Enterprise in Institutional Corrections: A Call for Caution." *Urban Resources* 2 (Summer 1985), 25-29.

Trost, Cathy. "Occidental Petroleum Flexes Its Political Muslces." *Business and Society Review* 43 (Fall 1982), 46-49.

Tupper, Allan, and G. B. Doern. "Understanding Public Corporations in Canada." *Canadian Business Review* 9 (Autumn 1982), 33-39.

"UNR Sues U.S. in Bid to Share Liability for Asbestos Damage." *Wall Street Journal* (January 17, 1984), 8.

"U.S. Grants Limited Immunity to Veliotis in Exchange for Date on Navy Fraud Case." *Wall Street Journal* (May 11, 1984), 12.

Useem, Michael. "Beyond the Corporation: Who Represents Business to the Government and Public?" *Business Horizons* 28 (May-June 1985), 21-26.

Wallace, Cynthia. "Control Through Disclosure Legislation: Foreign Multinational Enterprises in Industrialised States." *International and Comparative Law Quarterly* 32 (1983), 141-174.

Walsh, Frank E. "Corporate Election Campaigns: In Conflict with the Law or Not?" *Public Relations Review* 9 (Summer 1983), 7-17.

"Warning on Ethics at Mutual Funds Is Issued by SEC." *Wall Street Journal* (April 4, 1983), 24.

Wermiel, Stephen, and Robert S. Greenberger. "Justices Uphold Exposure Limits on Cotton Dust." *Wall Street Journal* (June 18, 1981), 3.

Westin, Alan F. "Michigan's Law to Protect the Whistleblowers." *Wall Street Journal* (April 18, 1981), 18.

White, James A. "AT&T Sees Possible Financial Problems if Plan to Share Any Damages Is Rejected." *Wall Street Journal* (May 25, 1983), 7.

"Will Entrepreneurs Be America's Economic Saviors?" *Business and Society Review* 53 (Spring 1985), 4-14.

Windsor, Duane. "Regulation and the Corporate Environment." *Texas Business Review* 57 (January-February 1983), 1-5.

Yudken, Joel. "Industrial Conversion: Beating Swords into Plowshares." *Business and Society Review* 49 (Spring 1984), 26-30.

Zardkoohi, A. "On the Political Participation of the Firm in the Electoral Process." *Southern Economic Journal* 51 (January 1985), 804-817.

Zimay, Max. "Reagan Stacks the Deck at the NLRB." *Business and Society Review* 45 (Spring 1983), 26-39.

Zonana, Victor F. "Appeals Court Rules Apple Software Is Subject to Copyright Law Protection." *Wall Street Journal* (September 2, 1983), 2.

Investment Policy and Shareholder Responsibility

Books

Block, Dennis J., and Harvey L. Pitt. *Hostile Battles for Corporate Control* [2 vols.]. New York: Practising Law Institute, 1984.

Domini, Amy L., and Peter D. Kinder. *Ethical Investing*. Boston: Addision-Wesley, 1984.

O'Neal, F. H. *O'Neal's Oppression of Minority Shareholders*. 2d ed. Wilmette, Ill.: Callaghan, 1985.

Articles

Andresky, Jill. "Cold Comfort." *Forbes* 136 (November 18, 1985), 223-224.

Andresky, Jill. "A Matter of Privity." *Forbes* 136 (September 23, 1985), 122.

Antilla, Susan. "Socially Responsible Investments." *Working Woman* 10 (April 1985), 38-41.

Arnott, Robert D., et al. "Divestiture Risks Can Be Reduced with Planning, Eye to the Issues." *Pensions & Investment Age* 13 (August 5, 1985), 21.

"Backlash Against Greenmail." *Mergers & Acquisitions* 20 (Spring 1985), 21.

Baldwin, William. "Morality Plays." *Forbes* 136 (July 29, 1985), 42-43.

Baysinger, Barry D., Gerald D. Keim, and Carl P. Zeithaml. "An Empirical Evaluation of the Potential for Including Shareholders in Corporate Constituency Programs." *Academy of Management Journal* 28 (March 1985), 180-200.

Bloch, H. R., and T. J. Laureau. "Should We Invest in Socially Irresponsible Firms?" *Journal of Portfolio Management* 11 (Summer 1985), 27-31.

Brudney, Victor. "Business Corporations and Stockholders' Rights Under the First Amendment." *Yale Law Journal* 91 (December 1981), 235-295.

Christman, E. "Two Believe Events Justify Policies." *Pensions Investment Age* 13 (August 5, 1985), 34.

Coston, Carol. "A Positive Alternative for Religious Investors." *Commonweal* 111 (December 14, 1984), 683-685.

Day, Sam. "How to Invest in Peace." *Witness* 68 (March 1985), 15.

DeAngelo, Harry, Linda DeAngelo, and Edward M. Rice. "Going Private: Minority Freezeouts and Stockholder Wealth." *Journal of Law and Economics* 27 (October 1984), 367-401.

Dennis, Anita. "Church Agency Sells AT&T, GE Shares, Cites Military Work." *Wall Street Journal* (February 10, 1983), 22.

Dickson, Douglas N. "Sugar Babies and the Sisterhood—A Business Case Study." *Across the Board* 19 (January 1982), 40-46.

Domini, Amy L., and Peter D. Kinder. "Your Money or Your Ethics: A Choice Investors No Longer Have to Make." *Environmental Action* 17 (July-August 1985), 16-20.

Fritzsche, David J., and Wesley Ehler. "How 'Ethical Investors' Attempt to Influence Corporate Social Behavior." *Business Forum* 7 (Winter 1982), 19-25.

Greene, R. "Greenmail—The Backlash." *Forbes* 136 (December 2, 1985), 86+.

Greenwald, John. "The Popular Game of Going Private." *Time* 126 (November 4, 1985), 54-55.

Gregg, Gail. "Warding Off the Big Chill: Ethical Investing for Profit." *Barron's* 64 (May 21, 1984), 1.

Irwin, Robin J. "Clean and Green." *Sierra* 70 (November-December 1985), 50-56.

"Is Greenmail Obsolete?" *Institutional Investor* 19 (May 1985), 208.

Keef, Stephen P. "Rights Issues: A Plea for the Private Shareholder." *Accountancy* 92 (September 1981), 132-133.

Langston, Maxine M. "Selective Investing Based on Conscience and Still a Normal Return." *Engage/Social Action* 11 (September 1983), 2-5.

Lowry, Ritchie P. "Social Investing: Doing Good While Doing Well." *Futurist* 16 (April 1982), 22-28.

Lydenberg, Steven. "High Noon for Social Proxy Activists." *Business and Society Review* 46 (Summer 1983), 62-66.

Lydenberg, Steven. "Moving Money in Step with Conscience: Social Criteria for Investments." *Christianity and Crisis* 44 (May 28, 1984), 206-210.

Mares, J. W. "Social Activism: Should It Play a Part in the Pension Fund Decision?" *FE* 1 (September 1985), 43-48.

Moskowitz, Milton R. "Investors Who Seek Virtue with Their Cash." *Business and Society Review* 39 (Fall 1981), 33-39.

Moskowitz, Milton R. "The Massachusetts Portfolio Purification." *Business and Society Review* 45 (Spring 1983), 71-72.

Muckley, Joseph E. "Dear Fellow Shareholder." *Harvard Business Review* 62 (March-April 1984), 46+.

Pyko, K., and R. Rosenfeld. "Unions Avoid Divestiture; Churches Take Harder Line." *Pensions Investment Age* 13 (August 5, 1985), 32.

Robinson, J.W. "Predicting Shareowner Support of Shark-Repellent Proposals." *Directors & Boards* 9 (Winter 1985), 47-49.

Rudd, Andrew. "Social Responsibility and Portfolio Performance." *California Management Review* 23 (1981), 55-61.

Rudnitsky, Howard. "Whoops!" *Forbes* 131 (June 6, 1983), 60-68.

Scheibla, Shirley H. "A Mickey for Greenmail: The Disney Affair Spurs Congress to Action." *Barron's* 64 (June 18, 1984), 8-9+.

Shanklin, William L., and John K. Ryan, Jr. "Should the Board Consider This Agenda Item?" *MSU Business Topics* 29 (Spring 1981), 35-42.

Simison, Robert L. "Capuchins Oppose Consumers Power on Nuclear Project." *Wall Street Journal* (March 23, 1984), 20.

Simon, William E., et al. "The South Africa Investment Debate: Divestiture or Stockholder Pressure?" *Business and Society Review* 50 (Summer 1984), 4-16.

Smock, Audrey C. "A Blow to Corporate Democracy: The SEC Acts to Shut Out Shareholders." *Christianity and Crisis* 43 (November 14, 1983), 432-435.

"South African Investment Debate: Divestiture or Stockholder Pressure?" *Business and Society Review* 50 (Summer 1984), 4-6.

Stein, Benjamin J. "Going Private Is Unethical." *Fortune* 112 (November 11, 1985), 169-170.

"Study Finds Ethical Investing by California Funds Is Safe." *Pension World* 17 (January 1981), 36-37.

Swann, Jerre B. "Current Issues Between Corporations and Shareholders: Shareholder Litigation." *Business Lawyer* 36 (March 1981), 783-790.

"Thayer, Associate Get Four Years in Insider Trading Case." *Aviation Week & Space Technology* 122 (May 13, 1985), 25.

Tracy, E. J. "A New Greenmailer Swings into Action." *Fortune* 112 (August 5, 1985), 71.

Train, John. "Responsible or Irresponsible." *Forbes* 128 (July 6, 1981), 176.

Williams, Edward E., and M. C. Findlay, III. "Corporate Governance: A Problem of Hierarchies and Self-Interest." *American Journal of Economics and Sociology* 43 (January 1984), 19-36.

Yarrow, G. K. "Shareholder Protection, Compulsory Acquisition and the Efficiency of the Takeover Process." *Journal of Industrial Economics* 34 (September 1985), 3-16.

Young, S. D. "Insider Trading: Why the Concern?" *Journal of Accounting, Auditing & Finance* 8 (Spring 1985), 178-183.

Minorities and Justice

Books

Fevre, Ralph. *Cheap Labour and Racial Discrimination.* Aldershot, U.K.: Gower Publishing Co., 1984.

King, A. T. *Discrimination in Mortgage Lending: A Study of Three Cities.* New York: New York Univ., 1981.

Minority Business Development Agency, ed. *New Perspectives on Minority Business Development.* San Antonio: The Science, 1984.

Roos, Patricia A. *Gender and Work.* Albany: State Univ. New York, 1985.

Schafer, Robert, and Helen F. Ladd. *Discrimination in Mortgage Lending.* Cambridge, Mass.: MIT Press, 1981.

Scott, William C., Antonio Furino, and Eugene Rodriguez, Jr. *Key Business Ratios of Minority-Owned Businesses: Analysis and Policy Implications.* San Antonio: University of Texas, 1981.

Sowell, Thomas. *The Economics and Politics of Race.* New York: Morrow, 1983.

Sowell, Thomas. *Markets and Minorities.* New York: Basic Books, 1981.

Ward, Robin, and Richard Jenkins, eds. *Ethnic Communities in Business: Strategies for Economic Survival.* Cambridge, U.K.: Cambridge Univ. Press, 1984.

Weintraub, Sidney, and Stanley R. Ross. *'Temporary' Alien Workers in the United States: Designing Policy from Fact and Opinion.* Boulder, Colo.: Westview, 1982.

Work, John W. *Race, Economics and Corporate America.* Wilmington, Del.: Scholarly Resources, 1984.

Articles

Alexandre, Laurien. "Whose Development?: Women Strategize." *Christianity and Crisis* 45 (September 16, 1985), 344-349.

Alsop, Ronald. "Firms Still Struggle to Devise Best Approach to Black Buyers." *Wall Street Journal* (October 25, 1984), 64.

Anderson, Harry. "A Steel Town's Fight for Life." *Newsweek* 101 (March 28, 1983), 49-50.

Appleman, Jeff T. "Vis-à-Vis Visas: How to Employ Foreign-Born Workers Legally." *Personnel Journal* 64 (July 1985), 44-50.

"Are the Policies of Life Insurance Companies Sexist?" *Business and Society Review* 47 (Fall 1983), 40-42.

Beranek, William. "The Illegal Allien Work Force, Demand for Unskilled Labor, and the Minimum Wage." *Journal of Labor Research* 3 (Winter 1982), 89-99.

Bergmann, Barbara R., and William Darity, Jr. "Social Relations, Productivity, and Employer Discrimination." *Monthly Labor Review* 104 (April 1981), 47-49.

Burnett, Nancy, and Jill Neimark. "DP and the Disabled." *Datamation* 31 (January 1985), 22-30.

Campbell, Everett J. "Discrimination: Market or Societal?" *International Journal of Social Economics* 11 (1984), 14-23.

Cardenas, Gilbert. "Mexican Illegal Immigration in the Southwest: Issues for the 1980s." *Adherent* 8 (November 1981), 53-62.

Chipman, Lauchlan. "Australia's Future—The Coming Clash of Ideals." *Practising Manager (Australia)* 3 (April 1983), 22-29.

Christopher, M. "Minorities Eye Role in Cap Cities Selloff." *Advertising Age* 56 (May 27, 1985), 50.

Conrad, Thomas. "Computers Programmed for Racism." *Business and Society Review* 42 (Summer 1982), 61-64.

Corcoran, Mary E., and Paul N. Courant. "Sex Role Socialization and Labor Market Outcomes." *American Economic Review* 75 (May 1985), 275-278.

"Effect of Gratuitous Transfer to Corp. by Shareholder." *Journal of Taxation* 63 (July 1985), 17.

"Feds Condemn States That Use DBE Quotas." *Engineering News-Record* 215 (July 25, 1985), 58.

"Female and Minority Practitioners See Teaching as a Good Career, Not a Bed of Roses." *Public Relations Quarterly* 30 (Spring 1985), 12-16.

Firth, Michael. "Racial Discrimination in the British Labor Market." *Indusrial and Labor Relations Review* 34 (January 1981), 265-272.

"The Forgotten Americans: Minority Joblessness Is Stubbornly High—But There Are Ways to Help." *Business Week* (September 2, 1985), 50-55.

Fulwood, Sam. "Paving the Way for Big Money Contracts." *Black Enterprise* 15 (February 1985), 119-122.

Gillis, William R., and Ron E. Shaffer. "Targeting Employment Opportunities Toward Selected Workers." *Land Economics* 61 (November 1985), 433-444.

Haner, Lisa G. "The New Wave: Strangers in Our Land." *Business Horizons* 26 (May-June 1983), 2-6.

Harrop, Mark D. "The Fast-Ticking Time Bomb in South African Mines." *Business and Society Review* 49 (Spring 1984), 52-55.

Hoffheimer, Daniel J. "Employment Discrimination Against Resident Aliens by Private Employers." *Labor Law Journal* 35 (March 1984), 142-147.

Hudson, James L. "The Ethics of Immigration Restriction." *Social Theory and Practice* 10 (Summer 1984), 201-239.

Humphreys, Marie A., and Jacquetta McClung. "American Indian Entrepreneurs in the Southwest." *Texas Business Review* 56 (July-August 1982), 187-192.

"Illegal Workers Follow Building-Boom Trail." *Engineering News-Record* 215 (August 29, 1985), 10.

Johnson, P. L. "The Black Entrepreneur." *Crisis* 92 (April 1985), 16-21+.

Kovach, Jeffrey L. "Minority Sell: Ads Target Blacks, Hispanics, but . . ." *Industry Week* 227 (November 11, 1985), 29-31.

La Porte, Vincent. "Discrimination in Business Dealings: Do You Do It?" *Credit and Financial Management* 83 (September 1981), 34-35.

Latos, Charles J. "Racial Discrimination in Labor Markets: A Job Filtering Hypothesis." *Review of Black Political Economy* 11 (Summer 1982), 413-427.

Lautzenheiser, B. J. "Will Sex Survive in the States?" *Journal of the American Society C.L.U.* 39 (July 1985), 11-12.

LaVan, Helen. "Employment Discrimination Against Hispanics: A Survey of Litigated Cases." *Employment Relations Today* 10 (Winter 1983-84), 414-424.

Lydenberg, Steven. "Minority Banks Gasp for Corporate Accounts." *Business and Society Review* 50 (Summer 1984), 30-33.

Marion, Peggy. "High Tech Takes Root in the Ghetto." *Venture* 7 (June 1985), 134-137.

Marsden, Lorna, and Lorne J. Tepperman. "The Migrant Wife—Worst of All Worlds." *Journal of Business Ethics* 4 (June 1985), 205-214.

"Minority Ownership Issues Explored at Syracuse Conference." *Broadcasting* 109 (August 5, 1985), 70-72.

Morrison, Julian. "The Quiet Success of Hispanic Business." *Nation's Business* 72 (July 1984), 62-64.

Pellegrino, Eric T., and Barry L. Reece. "Perceived Formative and

Operational Problems Encountered by Female Entrepreneurs in Retail and Service Firms." *Journal of Small Business Management* 20 (April 1982), 15-24.

Peterson, Richard L. "An Investigation of Sex Discrimination in Commercial Banks' Direct Consumer Lending." *Bell Journal of Economics* 12 (Autumn 1981), 547-561.

Picard, Earl. "The Corporate Intervention Strategy and Black Economic Development." *Black Scholar* 16 (September-October 1985), 14-22.

Piontek, S. "Unisex Fight Moves to the States: Apex Hit." *National Underwriter (Life/Health)* 89 (July 6, 1985), 17.

Poe, Randall. "America's Immigration Hangup." *Across the Board* 21 (July-August 1984), 12-21.

Pomer, Marshall I. "Mobility of Women into the Economic Mainstream." *Journal of Business Ethics* 2 (August 1983), 185-189.

Reimers, Cordelia W. "Labor Market Discrimination Against Hispanic and Black Men." *Review of Economics and Statistics* 65 (November 1983), 570-579.

Seligman, Daniel. "Insurance and the Price of Sex." *Fortune* 107 (February 21, 1983), 84-85.

"Sex and the Insurance Policy." *Business Week* (February 7, 1983), 83+.

Shear, W. B., and A. M. Yezer. "Discrimination in Urban Housing Finance: An Empirical Study Across Cities." *Land Economics* 61 (August 1985), 292-302.

Shulman, Steven. "Competition and Racial Discrimination: The Employment Effects of Reagan's Labor Market Policies." *Review of Radical Political Economics* 16 (Winter 1984), 111-128.

Smith, Bennett W. "The Black Economic Giant Flexes Its Mighty Muscles." *Business and Economic Review* 53 (Spring 1985), 35-37.

Sowell, Thomas. "Affirmative Action Harms the Disadvantaged." *Wall Street Journal* (July 28, 1981), 28.

Steck, Robert N. "America's Newest Entrepreneurs." *D & B Reports* 33 (July-August 1985), 18-20, 39.

Swinton, David H. "Orthodox and Systemic Explanations for Unemployment and Racial Inequality: Implications for Policy." *Review of Black Political Economy* 12 (Spring 1983), 9-25.

Taylor, Charlotte. "Woman Entrepreneurs: The New Immigrants." *NABW Journal* 57 (March-April 1981), 17-21.

"We've All Been Victims: It's Time We Helped Each Other." *Personnel Journal* 64 (January 1985), 14-15.

Wilhelm, Sidney M. "Black-White Equality: An Economic Doctrine for White Supremacy." *Journal of Black Studies* 12 (December 1981), 142-165.

Yim, Marian. "Sex Discrimination: The Changing Status of Private Clubs." *Cornell Hotel and Restaurant Administration Quarterly* 23 (February 1983), 23-27.

Multinational Corporations

Books

Akeroyd, Anne, et al. *European Business and South Africa: An Appraisal of the EC Code of Conduct.* Munchen: Kaiser, 1981.

Cavanagh, John, and Frederick F. Clairmonte. *Alcoholic Beverages: Dimensions of Corporate Power.* New York: St. Martin's Press, 1985.

Dlugos, Gunter, and Klaus Weiermair, eds. *Management Under Differing Value Systems.* Berlin: Walter de Gruyter, 1981.

Frith, Stan W. *The Expatriate Dilemma: How to Relocate and Compensate U.S. Employees Assigned Overseas.* Chicago: Nelson-Hall, 1981.

Horn, Norbert, ed. *Legal Problems of Codes of Conduct for Multinational Enterprises.* Boston: Kluwer, 1980.

Ives, Jane H., ed. *The Export of Hazard: Transnational Corporations and Environmental Control Issues.* London, U.K.: Routledge and Kegan Paul, 1985.

Kline, John M. *International Codes and Multinational Business: Setting Guidelines for International Business Operations.* Westport, Conn.: Quorum, 1985.

Leape, Jonathan, Bo Baskin, and Stefan Underhill. *Business in the Shadow of Apartheid: U.S. Firms in South Africa.* Lexington, Mass.: Lexington Books, 1985.

Medawar, Charles, and Barbara Freese. *Drug Diplomacy.* London, U.K.: Social Audit, 1982.

Michaud, Lucien, ed. *Multinational Corporations and Regional Development: Conflicts and Convergences.* Rome: Herder, 1983.

Norris, Ruth, and A. K. Nahed. *Pills, Pesticides, and Profits.* Croton-on-Hudson, N.Y.: North River Press, 1982.

O'Mahony, Patrick J. *Multinationals and Human Rights.* Great Wakering, U.K.: Mayhew-McCrimmon, 1980.

Poynter, Thomas A. *Multinational Enterprises and Government Intervention.* London, U.K.: Croom Helm, 1985.

Silverman, Milton, Philip R. Lee, and Mia Lydecker. *Prescriptions for Death: The Drugging of the Third World.* Berkeley, Calif.: Univ. of California Press, 1982.

Sincere, Richard E., Jr. *The Politics of Sentiment: Churches and Foreign Investment in South Africa.* Washington, D.C.: Ethics and Public Policy Ctr., 1984.

Tavis, Lee A., ed. *Multinational Managers and Poverty in the Third World.* Notre Dame, Ind.: Notre Dame Press, 1982.

Taylor, Peter. *The Smoke Ring: Tobacco, Money, and Multinational Politics.* New York: Pantheon Books, 1984.

Tuomi, Helena, and Raimo Vayrynen. *Transnational Corporations, Armaments and Development.* Aldershot, U.K.: Gower, 1982.

U.N. Centre on Transnational Corporations. *Transnational Corporations in the Pharmaceutical Industry of Developing Countries.* New York: United Nations, 1984.

Articles

Adelman, Kenneth L. "Biting the Hand That Cures Them." *Regulation* 6 (July-August 1982), 16-18.

Adler, Nancy J. "Expecting International Success." *Columbia Journal of World Business* 19 (Fall 1984), 79-85.

Ahmed, Karim, and Jacob Scherr. "Poisons for Export." *Business and Society Review* 40 (Winter 1981-82), 4-8.

Anthony, R. B. "Multinational Corporations and Global Awareness." *Social Studies* 75 (March-April 1985), 59-81.

Ashour, Ahmed S. "Self-Serving Practices of Multinational Corporations in Less Developed Countries." *Management International Review,* no.3 (1981), 67-79.

Bamber, Derek. "South Africa: Caught in the Golden Vice." *Euromoney* (December 1983), 122-125.

Barkey, David W., and D. S. Eitzen. "Toward an Assessment of Multinational Corporate Social Expenditures." *Inter-American Economic Affairs* 34 (Spring 1981), 77-90.

Beeman, Don R., and Sherman A. Timmins. "Who Are the Villains in International Business?" *Business Horizons* 25 (September-October 1982), 7-10.

Bendick, Marc, Jr., and Mary Lou Egan. "Providing Industrial Jobs in the Inner City." *Business* 32 (January-March 1982), 2-9.

Benson, Stuart E. "The U.N. Code on Restrictive Business Practices: An International Antitrust Code Is Born." *American University Law Review* 30 (Summer 1981), 1031-1048.

Berleant, Arnold. "Multinationals, Local Practice and the Problem of Ethical Consistency." *Journal of Business Ethics* 1 (August 1982), 185-193.

Beswick, Albert L. "Corporate Compliance with the FCPA." *Syracuse Journal of International Law & Commerce* 9 (Fall 1982), 301-313.

Bray, Howard. "Puerto Rico's One Note Samba." *Across the Board* 2 (January 1985), 3-4.

"Bribery in International Business: Whose Problem Is It?" *Journal of Business Ethics* 3 (February 1984), 35-42.

Burridge, A. L. "Impact of U.S. Multinational Companies in the Philippines: They Diffuse Industrial Technology and Managerial Expertise." *Business Journal (Manila)* 61 (June 1985), 6+.

Busch, Edgar T. "How Europe's Philosophies Affect American Human Resource Management." *Personnel Administrator* 28 (September 1983), 72-76.

Buss, Martin D. J. "Legislative Threat to Transborder Data Flow." *Harvard Business Review* 62 (May-June 1984), 111-118.

Carlson, Barbara, and Roger R. House, III. "More U.S. Companies Shedding Their Ties with South Africa." *New England Business* 5 (November 7, 1983), 34-38.

Caron, Sandra L. "Politics and International Business; The Impact of the Foreign Corrupt Practices Act." *Journal of Contemporary Business* 10 (1981), 17-28.

Chadwin, Mark L. "Europe Debates the Vredeling Concept." *Personnel Administrator* 28 (September 1983), 62-70.

Chafee, John H. "Doing Business Overseas: Clarifying the Bribery Question." *Enterprise* 5 (December 1981), 2-5.

Coombe, George W., Jr., and Susan L. Kirk. "Privacy, Data Protection and Transborder Data Flow: A Corporate Response to International Expectations." *Business Lawyer* 39 (November 1983), 33-66.

Dickson, Douglas N. "Case of the Reluctant Multinational." *Harvard Business Review* 83 (January-February 1983), 6-18.

Dobrow, Davis B., et al. "MNE Disclosure Alternatives and Their Consequences." *Journal of World Trade Law* 18 (September-October 1984), 437-454.

"Dole and Del Monte Are Staying Put No Matter What." *Business Week* (November 18, 1985), 58-59.

Donaldson, Thomas. "Multinational Decision-Making: Reconciling International Norms." *Journal of Business Ethics* (August 1985), 357-366.

Ebert-Miner, Allan. "Haitians Slave to Hatch Our Baseballs." *Business and Society Review* 45 (Spring 1983), 12-13.

Goodstein, Leonard D. "Commentary: Do American Theories Apply Abroad? American Business Values and Cultural Imperialism." *Organizational Dynamics* 10 (Summer 1981), 49-54.

Gray, Andrew. "Repatriation at the Burr Hamilton Bank." *Business Horizons* 25 (March-April 1982), 13-14.

Hagg, Claes. "The OECD Guidelines for Multinational Enterprises: A Critical Analysis." *Journal of Business Ethics* 3 (February 1984), 71-76.

Hagg, Claes. "Sources of International Business Ethics." *Management International Review* 23 (1983), 73-78.

Harvey, Michael G. "The Multinational Corporation's Expatriate Problem: An Application of Murphy's Law." *Business Horizons* 26 (January-February 1983), 71-78.

Helfgott, Roy B. "American Unions and Multinational Companies: A Case of Misplaced Emphasis." *Columbia Journal of World Business* 18 (Summer 1983), 81-86.

Hill, Roy. "Are Multinationals Aliens in the Third World?" *International Management* 36 (January 1981), 12-16.

Hoerr, John, et al. "South Africa: Botha Gives U.S. Business One More Reason to Leave." *Business Week* (September 2, 1985), 42-43.

Holstein, William J., Jim Jones, and Boyd France. "U.S. Companies Are Pulling Out—But Apartheid Is Likely to Stay." *Business Week* (June 24, 1985), 56-57.

Kapstein, Jonathan, John Hoerr, and Elizabeth Weiner. "Leaving South Africa." *Business Week* (September 23, 1985), 104-112.

Katz, David M. "Political Risk: Are We the Problem?" *National Underwriter (Property/Casualty)* 89 (September 6, 1985), 6, 69.

Kendall, D. W. "Repatriation: An Ending and a Beginning." *Business Horizons* 24 (November-December 1981), 21-25.

Kessler, Felix. "Goodyear Toughs It Out." *Fortune* 112 (September 30, 1985), 24-26.

Kirkpatrick, Jeane J. "Global Paternalism: The UN and the New International Regulatory Order." *Regulation* 7 (January-February 1983), 17-22.

Kobrin, Stephen J. "Assessing Political Risk Overseas." *Wharton Magazine* 6 (Winter 81-82), 24-31.

Krauthammer, Charles, et al. "Does Business Love Foreign Dictators?" *Business and Society Review* 41 (Spring 1982), 4-11.

Kwame, Safro. "Doin' Business in an African Country." *Journal of Business Ethics* 2 (November 1983), 263-268.

Laczniak, Gene R., and Jacob Naor. "Global Ethics: Wrestling with the Corporate Conscience." *Business* 33 (July-September 1985), 3-10.

Lansing, Paul. "Divestment of United States Companies in South Africa and Apartheid." *Nebraska Law Review* 60 (1981), 304-326.

Latta, Geoffrey W., et al. "Making the Corporation Transparent: Prelude to Multinational Bargaining." *Columbia Journal of World Business* 18 (Summer 1983), 73-80.

Lee, R. H. "The Role of the Private Sector as a Catalyst for Change in South Africa." *African Affairs* 82 (October 1983), 455-463.

"The MNC Record in South African Employment." *Multinational Business* 2 (1985), 33-35.

"Managers Wrestle with Ethical Conflicts Worldwide." *International Management (UK)* 38 (February 1983), 52-53.

Marks, Leonard, Jr. "Multinational Corporations and Third World Poverty." *Review of Social Economy* 40 (December 1982), 438-453.

McCann, D. P. "Liberation and the Multinationals." *Theology Today* 41 (April 1984), 51-60.

McMillion, C. "Automate, Emigrate or Evaporate: America's Choices in the Global Economy." *Futurist* 19 (April 1985), 45-57.

Medawar, Charles, and Barbara Freese. "Drug Multinationals in the Third World." *Business and Society Review* 38 (Summer 1981), 22-24.

Meier, Barry. "Carbide Suits May Affect Industry Norms: Chemical Makers Look at Safety Overseas." *Wall Street Journal* (April 5, 1985), 6.

Mufson, Steve. "Businessmen Pressure South Africa's Botha to Modify Apartheid." *Wall Street Journal* (September 13, 1985), 1+.

Newman, Barry. "Border Dispute." *Wall Street Journal* (November 30, 1983), 1+.

Nielsen, John. "Time to Quit South Africa?" *Fortune* 112 (September 30, 1985), 18-23.

Ogle, George. "Multinational Corporations: An Ethical Perspective." *Engage/Social Action* 10 (May 1982), 12-17.

Pagan, Rafael D., Jr. "Carrying the Fight to the Critics of Multinational Capitalism—Think and Act Politically." *Vital Speeches of the Day* 48 (July 15, 1982), 589-591.

Pontojas Garcia, Emilio. "Puerto Rico: The Making of a Corporate Paradise." *Multinational Monitor* 5 (October-November 1984), 12-15.

"Racism or Reason: The Corporations That Refuse to Sign the Sullivan Principles." *Business and Society Review* 46 (Summer 1983), 42-45.

"Reckoning with Reality in South Africa." *Business Week* (September 23, 1985), 144.

Reid, Brad, and E. Timmerman. "Marketing, Morality and Multinational Firms." *Collegiate Forum* (Spring 1982), 5.

Robinson, William. "Fluor: Apartheid's Energy Partner." *Business and Society Review* 37 (Spring 1980-81), 59-61.

Rowan, Richard L., et al. "The Attempt to Regulate Industrial Relations Through International Codes of Conduct." *Columbia Journal of World Business* 18 (Summer 1983), 64-72.

Rubin, Seymour J. "Transnational Corporations and International Codes of Conduct." *American University Law Review* 30 (Summer 1981), 903-921.

Russell, James W. "U.S. Sweatshops Across the Rio Grande." *Business and Society Review* 50 (Summer 1984), 17-20.

Sahelnikov, L. "No Holds Barred." *New Times (Moscow)* 22 (May 1983), 18-20.

Schmidt, Elizabeth. "Greasing the Wheels of Apartheid: How Administration and US Corporations Bolster S. African Regime." *Sojourners* 12 (October 1983), 10-12.

Sherman, Stratford P. "Scoring Corporate Conduct in South Africa." *Fortune* 110 (July 9, 1984), 168-172.

Simon, William E. "Our Most Powerful Weapon Against Apartheid." *Across the Board* 22 (February 1985), 13-14.

Simpson, James R. "Ethics and Multinational Corporations Vis-à-Vis Developing Nations." *Journal of Business Ethics* 1 (August 1982), 227-237.

Slater, Robert B. "Companies That Hide Behind the Sullivan Principles." *Business and Society Review* 49 (Spring 1984), 15-18.

Stone, Marvin. "Doing Business Abroad." *U.S. News & World Report* 90 (June 22, 1981), 88.

Street, Anne M. "Multinationals Square Off Against Central American Workers." *Business and Society Review* 52 (Winter 1985), 45-49.

Sullivan, Leon. "Agents for Change: The Mobilization of Multinational Companies in South Africa." *Law and Policy Intern. Business* 15 (1983), 427-444.

"The Sullivan Principles after Six Years: Compliance and Non-Compliance." *Business and Society Review* 44 (Winter 1983), 29-31.

Sullivan, Stewart. "Beware of Vredeling: A Big-Brother Directive Tells Multinational Corporations How to Run Their Employee Relations." *Enterprise* 8 (February 1984), 21-22.

Takamiya, Makoto. "Japanese Multinationals in Europe: Internal Operations and Their Public Policy Implications." *Columbia Journal of World Business* 16 (Summer 1981), 5-17.

Tavis, Lee A. "Multinational Corporate Responsibility for Third World Development." *Review of Social Economy* 40 (December 1982), 427-437.

Tell, Lawrence J. "The Apartheid Factor." *Barron's* 65 (August 15, 1985), 18, 20+.

Walter, Gordon A. "The Morning After." *Cornell Executive* 8 (Summer 1982), 15-19.

Webber, D. "U.S. Chemical Producers Weigh Anti-Apartheid Tack in South Africa." *Chemical and Engineering News* 63 (June 17, 1985), 20-23.

Weir, David, and Mark Schapiro. "Pesticide Pollution Goes Multinational." *Business and Society Review* 37 (Spring 1981), 47-53.

Welles, Nancy. "The Growing Dilemma of Locating Internationally." *Institutional Investor* 16 (May 1982), 231-232.

Whitt, John D. "Budgeting Social Responsibility of Affiliates in Latin America." *Managerial Planning* 31 (May-June 1983), 32-34.

Whitt, John D. "Latin American Subsidiaries and Social Responsibility." *Arizona Business* 28 (April 1981), 19-23.

Wisniewski, Kathleen. "Corporations Prepare Future Generation of Cross-Cultural Employees." *Marketing News* 18 (September 14, 1984), 43.

Young, Gay. "Women, Development, and Human Rights: Issues in Integrated Transnational Production." *Journal of Applied Behavior Science* 20 (1984), 383-402.

Zevin, Robert B. "The Corporations Must Kowtow." *Across the Board* 22 (February 1985), 14-15.

New Directions in Business and Society

Books

Bowden, Elbert V. *Revolution in Banking*. Richmond: Robert F. Dame, Inc., 1980.

Bradley, Keith. *Worker Capitalism: Managing Industrial Decline through the Market*. Boston: Harvard Business School, 1984.

Bradley, Keith, and Alan Gelb. *Worker Capitalism: The New Industrial Relations*. Cambridge, Mass.: MIT Press, 1985.

Kuwahara, Satoshi. *The Changing World Information Industry*. Boston: Rowman & Allenheld, 1985.

Mattera, Philip. *Off the Books: The Rise of the Underground Economy*. New York: St. Martin's Press, 1985.

Menzel, Paul T. *Medical Costs, Moral Choices: A Philosophy of Health Care Economics in America*. New Haven: Yale University Press, 1983.

Naisbitt, John. *Megatrends: Ten New Directions Transforming Our Lives*. New York: Warner Books, 1982.

Phillips, Kevin P. *Staying on Top: The Business Case for a National Industrial Strategy*. New York: Random House, 1984.

Rothwell, Roy, and Walter Zegveld. *Industrial Innovation and Public Policy: Preparing for the 1980s and 1990s*. Westport, Conn.: Greenwood Press, 1981.

Saks, Daniel H. *Distressed Workers in the Eighties*. Washington, D.C.: Nat'l. Planning Assn., 1983.

Shapiro, Irving S., and Carl B. Kaufman. *America's Third Revolution: Public Interest and the Private Role*. New York: Harper and Row, 1984.

Thurow, Lester. *The Zero-Sum Solution: Building a World Class American Economy*. New York: Simon & Schuster, 1985.

Wohl, Stanley. *The Medical Industrial Complex*. New York: Harmony Books, 1984.

Zolotas, Xenophon. *Economic Growth and Declining Social Welfare*. New York: New York Univ. Press, 1982.

Zukin, Sharon, ed. *Industrial Policy: Business and Politics in the United States and France*. New York: Praeger, 1985.

Articles

Albrecht, Sandra L. "Industrial Home Work in the U.S.: Historical

Dimensions and Contemporary Perspective." *Economic and Industrial Democracy* 3 (November 1982), 413-420.

Bach, Marilyn L., Martin E. Finch, and Cynthia L. Crist. "A Medical Mecca in the Making." *Business Health* 3 (November 1985), 43-46.

Baden, John, and Tom Blood. "Abracadabra Prosperity." *Reason* 16 (September 1984), 38-42.

Barrett, Nancy S. "Part-Time Work Will Increase, Bringing Change to Social Mores and Standards of Compensation." *Personnel Administrator* 28 (December 1983), 94+.

Bartlett, Bruce R. "Industrial Policy: Crisis for Liberal Economics." *Fortune* 108 (November 14, 1983), 83-86.

Bedrosian, John C. "The Investor-Owned Hospital as the Community Hospital: Can It Care for the Rich and Poor Alike?" *Vital Speeches of the Day* 52 (October 15, 1985), 7-11.

Bernstein, Aaron. "Is Big Labor Playing Global Vigilante?" *Business Week* (November 4, 1985), 92-96.

"Big Business Buys Everything But the Farm." *Dollars and Sense* (May-June 1982), 13-15.

"Biotech Comes of Age: What Gene-Splicing's Second Wave May Deliver." *Business Week (Ind./Tech. Ed.)* (January 23, 1984), 84-94.

"Biotechnology: Scientific Miracle or Pandora's Box." *Business and Society Review* 55 (Fall 1985), 29-33.

Blair, John P., Rudy Fichtenbaum, and James Swaney. "The Market for Jobs: A New Approach to Solving Unemployment." *Futurist* 18 (April 1984), 54-59.

Brown, William S. "Industrial Policy and Corporate Power." *Journal of Economic Issues* 19 (June 1985), 487-496.

Bryant, Alan W. "Replacing Punitive Discipline with a Positive Approach." *Personnel Administrator* 29 (February 1984), 79-87.

Calton, Jerry M. "Industrial Policy, International Competitiveness, and the World Auto Industry." *Journal of Contemporary Business* 11 (Spring 1982), 63-82.

Calvez, Jean-Yves, Shlomo Avineri, and Norman Birnbaum. "Are We Entering a Post-Marxist Age?" *Commonweal* 111 (October 5, 1984), 524-529.

Chapman, Fern S. "Going for Gold in the Baby Business." *Fortune* 110 (September 17, 1984), 41-47.

Colwill, Nina L. "Designing a Corporate Response to Terrorism." *Police Chief* 52 (February 1985), 22-24.

Cooper, Robert. "Some Remarks on Theoretical Individualism, Alienation, and Work." *Human Relations* 36 (August 1983), 717-723.

Cox, Patrick. "Space Entrepreneurs." *Reason* 16 (January 1985), 23-26.

Crouter, Ann C. "Spillover from Family to Work: The Neglected Side of the Work-Family Interface." *Human Relations* 37 (June 1984), 425-441.

DeNoble, Alex, and Donald M. Moliver. "The Small Business Dilemma: Can Cooperation Help?" *American Journal of Small Business* 7 (January-March 1983), 51-58.

Deveny, Kathleen, et al. "Should Profit Drive Artificial Hearts?" *Business Week* (December 10, 1984), 38-39.

Diebold, John. "Technology Outrunning Policy: The Biorevolution." *Journal of Institute for Socioeconomic Studies* 9 (Autumn 1984), 71-85.

Duff, Andrew, and Stephen Cotgrove. "Social Values and the Choice of Careers in Industry." *Journal of Occupational Psychology* 55 (June 1982), 97-107.

Eckstein, Albert J., and Dale M. Heien. "Causes and Consequences of Service Sector Growth: The U.S. Experience." *Growth and Change* 16 (April 1985), 12-17.

Edmondson, B. "The Market for Medical Self-Care." *American Demographics* 7 (June 1985), 34-37+.

Freedenberg, Sam. "Vanguard: Monitoring Indicators of Change." *Association Management* 33 (November 1981), 110-111.

Garlitz, Gladys. "Temporary Workers: A Changing Industry." *Personnel Administrator* 28 (March 1983), 47-48.

"Genentech's Drug Problem: The Perils of Marketing a Synthetic Hormone." *Newsweek* 106 (November 25, 1985), 70.

Greene, Richard. "Tracking Job Growth in Private Industry." *Monthly Labor Review* 105 (September 1982), 3-9.

Griffith, Mark, Jr. " 'New Morality' Forces Agency to Take a Hard Look at Claims." *Rough Notes* 126 (January 1983), 40-45.

Grout, Jack M. "A New Look at School Support." *Enterprise* 7 (June 1983), 24-25.

Guest, Donald B. "Is America's Medical Industry Incurably Ill?" *Business and Society Review* 55 (Fall 1985), 21-28.

Guest, Robert H. "Management Imperatives for the Year 2000." *Vital Speeches of the Day* 51 (March 15, 1985), 338-341.

Hall, Trish. "Industry Headache: Americans Drink Less and Makers of Alcohol Feel a Little Woozy." *Wall Street Journal* (March 14, 1984), 1+.

Harvey, Michael. "A New Corporate Weapon Against Terrorism." *Business Horizons* 28 (January-February 1985), 42-47.

Hatfield, Mark O. "America's Need for an 'Ethical Renaissance.' " *Journal of Business Ethics* 1 (May 1982), 99-108.

Hechinger, Fred. "Turnaround for the Public Schools?" *Harvard Business Review* 63 (January-February 1985), 136-144.

Heilbroner, Robert L. "The Future of Capitalism." *Challenge* 25 (November-December 1982), 32-39.

Hodson, R., and T. A. Sullivan. "Totem or Tyrant? Monopoly, Regional and Local Sector Effects on Worker Commitment." *Social Forces* 63 (March 1985), 716-731.

Holland, Jeffrey R. "The Value of Values: Shared Tasks for Business and Education in the 1980's." *Vital Speeches of the Day* 48 (January 15, 1982), 205-208.

Jarboe, K. P. "A Reader's Guide to the Industrial Policy Debate." *California Management Review* 27 (Summer 1985), 198-219.

Lacey, Dan. "Exploring the Potentials of Decentralized Work Settings." *Personnel Administrator* 29 (February 1984), 48-52.

Lancaster, Hal. "Groups Battle to Be Voice of Gene Firms." *Wall Street Journal* (March 2, 1984), 29.

Leach, John J., and B. J. Chakiris. "The Dwindling Future of Work in America." *Training and Development Journal* 39 (April 1985), 44-46.

Lehman-Wilzig, Sam N. "Frakenstein Unbound: Towards a Legal Definition of Artificial Intelligence." *Futures (UK)* 13 (December 1981), 442-457.

Lyman, Francesca. "New Life Forms for Fun and Profit." *Business and Society Review* 40 (Winter 1981-82), 40-44.

Matulich, S. "Professors on the Corporate Board of Directors." *Journal of General Education* 35 (1983), 110-118.

McKenna, Patrick J. "Management's Key Strategic Issues in the Turbulent Eighties: Part II." *Canadian Manager* 6 (May-July 1981), 4-7.

Miller, Russell. "Is There a 'New Federalist' Industrial Policy?" *Management Review* 74 (March 1985), 61-62.

Murray, Thomas H. "Thinking the Unthinkable About Genetic Screening." *Across the Board* 20 (June 1983), 34-39.

Neef, Marian G. "An Industrial Policy: What Does It Mean?" *Business Horizons* 27 (November-December 1984), 43-49.

Otten, Alan L. "Doctors Dilemma: As Medicine Advances, Hastings

Center Tries to Solve Ethical Issues." *Wall Street Journal* (November 23, 1983), 1.

Packer, James S. "How Will You Cope with Workers of the 80's?" *Association Management* 35 (July 1983), 126-129.

Paul, Karen. "Business Environment/Public Policy Problems for the 1980's." *Business and Society* 20 (Winter 81–Spring 82), 11-16.

Peirce, Neal R., and Deborah Sagen. "Business Increasingly Sees Quality Education as Vital to Its Interests." *National Journal* 15 (October 15, 1983), 2109-2113.

Pine, Art. "The Outlook: Protected Industries May Have to Modernize." *Wall Street Journal* (February 3, 1984), 1.

Porter, Jack. "Corporations That Grant Degrees." *Business and Society Review* 41 (Spring 1982), 41-45.

Relman, Arnold S. "The New Medical-Industrial Complex." *Across the Board* 18 (February 1981), 27-35.

Rosow, Jerome M., and Robert Zagar. "Work in America Institute's Recommendations Grapple with the Future of the Older Worker." *Personnel Administrator* 26 (October 1981), 47+.

Samuelson, Robert J. "Industrial Suicide." *National Journal* 13 (October 24, 1981), 194.

Schank, J. T. "Let's Resume Debate on U.S. Industrial Policy." *Management Review* 74 (August 1985), 57-58.

Schiff, Frank W. "Flexiplace: Pros and Cons." *Futurist* 17 (June 1983), 32-33.

Scobie, W. "No Business Like 'Snow' Business." *Maclean's* 94 (May 4, 1981), 33-34.

Shanker, Albert. "Business Is Welcome in School." *Across the Board* 21 (April 1984), 59-61.

Shapiro, Steven L. "Pfizer's Corporate Campus Builds Skills and Morale." *Personnel Administrator* 28 (June 1983), 49-53.

Sheler, Jeffrey L. "Where Jobs Go Begging Amid Recession." *U.S. News and World Report* 92 (December 6, 1982), 81+.

Skloot, Edward. "Special Report: Should Not-for-Profits Go Into Business?" *Harvard Business Review* 61 (January-February 1983), 20-26.

Smith, Harold T. "The Future: 1990's Office Will Need Human Focus." *Association Management* 36 (March 1984), 193-202.

Spruell, Geraldine. "Two Degrees of Distinction." *Training and Development Journal* 39 (October 1985), 59-64.

Steck, Robert N. "Critics of Designer Genes Are Holding Up Production." *D & B Reports* 22 (July-August 1984), 44-45, 57.

Stein, Herbert. "Don't Fall for Industrial Policy." *Fortune* 108 (November 14, 1983), 64-78.

Strobel, Frederick R. "The U.S. Banking Corporate Structure: Some Implications for Industrial Policy." *Journal of Economic Issues* 19 (June 1985), 541-549.

Susman, Gerald I. "Planned Change: Prospects for the 1980s." *Management Science* 27 (February 1981), 139-154.

"Unemployment: The Failure of Private Enterprise?" *Monthly Review* 35 (June 1983), 1-9.

Weigand, R. E. "National Industrial Recovery Act: America's Flirtation with Socialism." *Marketing News* 19 (May 10, 1985), 8-9.

Willis, Rod. "Fear and Hope in Youngstown." *Management Review* 74 (March 1985), 24-32.

Wohl, Stanley. "Is Corporate Medicine Healthy for Medicine?" *Business and Society Review* 51 (Fall 1984), 16-20.

Wolfgram, Tammara H. "Working at Home: The Growth of the Cottage Industry." *Futurist* 18 (June 1984), 31-34.

Wolozin, H. "Corporate Power in an Aging Economy: Labor Force Policy." *Journal of Economic Issues* 19 (June 1985), 475-486.

Plant Closings and Business Failure

Books

Bluestone, Barry, and Bennett Harrison. *The Deindustrialization of America: Plant Closings, Community Abandonment, and the Dismantling of Basic Industry.* New York: Basic Books, 1982.

Buss, Terry F., and F. S. Redburn. *Mass Unemployment: Plant Closings and Community Mental Health.* Beverly Hills, Calif.: Sage, 1983.

Buss, Terry F., and F. S. Redburn. *Shutdown at Youngstown: Public Policy for Mass Unemployment.* Albany: S.U.N.Y. Press, 1983.

Erickson, Jon. *Plant Closings: Impact, Causes, and Policies.* Chicago: Council of Planning Librarians, 1983.

Gordus, Jeanne P., Paul Jarley, and Louis A. Ferman. *Plant Closings and Economic Dislocation.* Kalamazoo, Mich.: W.E. Upjohn Institute, 1981.

McKenzie, Richard B. *Fugitive Industry: The Economics and Politics of Deindustrialization*. Cambridge, Mass.: Ballinger Pub. Co., 1984.

McKenzie, Richard B., ed. *Plant Closings: Public or Private Choices?* Washington, D.C.: Cato Institute, 1982.

McKenzie, Richard B. *The Right to Close Down: The Political Battle Shifts to the States*. Los Angeles: International Institute for Economic Research, 1982.

Raines, John C., Lenora E. Berson, and David Gracie. *Community and Capital in Conflict: Plant Closings and Job Loss*. Philadelphia: Temple Univ. Press, 1982.

Shutdown: A Guide for Communities Facing Plant Closings. Washington, D.C.: Northeast-Midwest Inst., 1982.

Articles

Auerbach, Joseph. "The Poletown Dilemma." *Harvard Business Review* 63 (May-June 1985), 93-99.

Barker, Lawrence. "There Is a Better Way." *Labor Law Journal* 32 (August 1981), 453-458.

Carroll, Archie B. "When Business Closes Down: Social Responsibilities and Management Actions." *California Management Review* 26 (Winter 1984), 125-140.

Cater, Morrow. "Manville Bankruptcy Case May Prompt Congress to Close 'Loophole' in Law." *National Journal* 14 (November 27, 1982), 2029-2030.

Chrisman, James J., and Archie B. Carroll. "What's Wrong with Plant Closing Legislation and Industrial Policy?" *Business Horizons* 28 (September-October 1985), 28-27.

Dickinson, Roger. "Business Failure Rate." *American Journal of Small Business* 6 (October-December 1981), 17-25.

Doan, Michael. "How Battered Firms Are Surviving Slumps." *U.S. News and World Report* 93 (August 9, 1982), 29-30.

Duncan, Joseph W. "Private Sector Data on Business Failures." *Review of Public Data Use* 11 (March 1983), 29-35.

Felsten, Gary J. "Current Considerations in Plant Shutdowns and Relocations." *Personnel Journal* 60 (May 1981), 369-372.

Fenton, Thomas P. "Plant Closed, Moved to Asia." *Maryknoll* (April 1982), 50+.

Fottler, Myron D., and Dennis W. Shuler. "Reducing the Economic and Human Costs of Layoffs." *Business Horizons* 27 (July-August 1984), 9-16.

Fulmer, William E. "A Resurrection Plan for Dying Factories." *Business and Society Review* 54 (Summer 1985), 50-55.

Gillett, Richard W. "Plant Closures: Major New Issue." *Witness* 64 (January 1981), 4-7.

Harrison, Bennett, and Barry Bluestone. "The Incidence and Regulation of Plant Shutdowns." *Policy Studies Journal* 10 (December 1981), 297-320.

Hoyt, Michael. "How to Make Steel: Agitate and Organize." *Christianity and Crisis* 45 (March 4, 1985), 62-65.

Jacobs, Sally. "Everybody Loses." *New England Business* 7 (May 6, 1985), 88-95.

Jones, Mary E. "Twelve States Mull Laws on Closing of Plants." *Automotive News* (February 22, 1982), 162.

Lustig, R. J. "The Politics of Shutdown: Community, Property, Corporatism." *Journal of Economic Issues* 19 (March 1985), 125-132.

"Many Plant Closings Reflect Switch in Strategy as Well as Poor Economy." *Wall Street Journal* (October 15, 1982), 37.

McKenzie, Richard B. "Hostage Factories." *Reason* 14 (April 1983), 35-39.

Metzgar, J. "Johnstown, Pa.: Ordeal of a Union Town." *Dissent* 32 (Spring 1985), 160-163.

O'Connor, Matt. "Harvester Ready to Close Plant, Take a Charge." *Wall Street Journal* (September 25, 1984), 20.

"Plant Shutdowns: States Take a New Tack." *Business Week* (October 24, 1983), 72+.

Roe, Mark J. "Bankruptcy and Mass Tort." *Columbia Law Review* 84 (May 1984), 846-922.

Rotbart, Dean. "Manville Filing Expected to Have a Wide Effect." *Wall Street Journal* (August 30, 1982), 3.

Schweickart, David. "Is There an Answer to Plant Closings?: A Philosophical Reflection." *New Catholic World* 226 (July-August 1983), 180-183.

Senia, Al M. "A Dark Cloud of Plant Closings Hangs Over Sunny California." *Iron Age* 226 (March 16, 1983), 28-31.

Sheehan, Michael F. "Plant Closings and the Community: The Instrumental Value of Public Enterprise in Countering Corporate Flight." *American Journal of Economics & Sociology* 44 (October 1985), 423-433.

Southwick, Holly S. "Business Bankruptcy and Business Failure: Utah, Mountain States Region and the United States, 1978-1985." *Utah Economic and Business Review* 45 (July-August 1985), 1-14.

Stavro, Barry. "Fort Wayne: 'It Was Hell, but I Survived.' " *Forbes* 134 (October 22, 1984), 66-74.

Strohmeyer, John. "The Agonizing Ordeal of a One-Company Town." *Business and Society Review* 54 (Summer 1985), 45-49.

Woods, M. "A Look at Smyrna: The Nissan Impact One Year Later." *Public Management* 67 (June 1985), 19.

Yoder, Dale, and Paul D. Staudohar. "Management and Public Policy in Plant Closures." *Sloan Management Review* 26 (Summer 1985), 45-57.

Product Safety and Quality

Books

Coffin, Sharon. *Product Hazards: A Case History Guidebook.* Washington, D.C.: Washington Business Info., 1981.

Eads, George, and C. P. Reuter. *Designing Safer Products: Corporate Responses to Product Liability Law and Regulation.* Santa Monica, Calif.: Rand Inst. for Civil Justice, 1983.

Freedman, Warren. *Products Liability for Corporate Counsels, Controller, and Product Safety Executives.* New York: Van Nostrand Reinhold, 1984.

Organisation for Economic Cooperation and Development. *Product Safety: Measures to Protect Children.* Paris: O.E.C.D., 1984.

Smith, Charles O. *Products Liability: Are You Vulnerable?* Englewood Cliffs, N.J.: Prentice-Hall, 1981.

Strobel, Lee P. *Reckless Homicide? Ford's Pinto Trial.* South Bend, Ind.: And Books, 1980.

Swit, David, and Richard Hadley. *Product Survival: Lessons of the Tylenol Terrorism.* Washington, D.C.: Washington Business Info., 1982.

Viscusi, W. K. *Regulating Consumer Product Safety.* Washington, D.C.: American Enterprise Inst., 1984.

Articles

"A.H. Robins Hauls a Judge into Court." *Business Week* (July 16, 1984), 27-28.

"Are Those Labels Ready?" *Industry Week* 227 (November 25, 1985, 37+.

Avlonitis, George, J. "Ethics and Product Elimination." *Management Decision* 21 (1983), 37-45.

"Babies at Risk: Companies Still Violate Infant Formula Code." *Multinational Monitor* 6 (December 1984 – January 1985), 10-12.

Baker, James C. "The International Infant Formula Controversy: A Dilemma in Corporate Social Responsibility." *Journal of Business Ethics* 4 (June 1985), 181-190.

Beltramini, Richard F., Robert A. Peterson, and George Kosmetsky. "Concerns of College Students Regarding Business Ethics." *Journal of Business Ethics* 3 (August 1984), 195-200.

Berger, Peter L. "New Attack on the Legitimacy of Business." *Harvard Business Review* 59 (September-October 1981), 82-89.

Clark, Alistair. "Strict Liability for Product Defects." *Journal of Business Law* (March 1983), 130-141.

Cooper, Russell, et al. "Product Warranties and Double Moral Hazard." *Rand Journal of Economics* 16 (Spring 1985), 103-113.

Crozier, J. A. "Pesticide Labeling: In Search of Space." *Chemical Times & Trends* 8 (April 1985), 20-21+.

De George, Richard T. "Ethical Responsibilities of Engineers in Large Organizations: The Pinto Case." *Business and Professional Ethics Journal* 1 (Fall 1981), 1-14. Commentary: by Hart T. Mankin, 15.

"Doing Business Amid Scientific Controversy: The Impact of the AOAC Use-Dilution Test." *Chemical Times & Trends* 8 (July 1985), 17-36.

Duffy, Susan M. "Toxic Shock: Makers of Tampons Are the Target of Heavy Legal Attack." *Barron's* 64 (March 16, 1984), 8-9.

Dworkin, Terry M. "The Constitutionality and Application of the Indiana Product Liability Act." *Indiana Business Review* 56 (August 1981), 11-14.

Dworkin, Terry M. "Enterprise Liability—Increasing the Manufacturer's Burden." *Business Horizons* 24 (May-June 1981), 77-82.

Eisman, Deborah E. "Product Liability: Who Should Bear the Burden?" *American Economist* 27 (Spring 1983), 54-57.

Epstein, Richard A. "Manville: The Bankruptcy of Product Liability Law." *Regulation* 6 (September-October 1982), 14-19.

Fields, Samuel S. "Does Blame for Handgun Crime Lie at the Factory Gate?" *Business and Society Review* 45 (Spring 1983), 51-55.

Filios, Vassilios P. "Assessment of Attitudes Toward Corporate Social Responsibility in Britain." *Journal of Business Ethics* 4 (June 1985), 155-173.

Filios, Vassilios P. "Corporate Social Responsibility and Public Accountability." *Journal of Business Ethics* 3 (November 1984), 305-314.

Fisher, Roger. "He Who Pays the Piper: Settling Cases Out of Court." *Harvard Business Review* 63 (March-April 1985), 150-159.

"GM Accused by U.S. Aide of Withholding Data Linked to Safety of '80 X-Car Brakes." *Wall Street Journal* (August 24, 1984), 7.

Garvin, David A. "What Does 'Product Quality' Really Mean?" *Sloan Management Review* 26 (Fall 1984), 25-44.

Glaberson, William B. "Did Searle Close Its Eyes to a Health Hazard: Lawsuits Claim It Is Selling an IUD That Causes Infection and Sterility." *Business Week* (October 14, 1985), 120-122.

Greany, Thomas F., Jr. "Getting Off the Roller Coaster of Product Liability Insurance." *Chemical Times & Trends* 8 (January 1985), 41-43.

Hamilton, Lynn. "Infant Formula: Beyond the Nestle Announcement." *Food Monitor* (May-June 1982), 9-10.

Harsha, Mary R. "Assuring Proper Consumer Product Use." *Chemical Times & Trends* 7 (April 1984), 20-21+.

Hartwick, Nanci. "Infant Formula: A Threat to Third World Babies." *Graduate Woman* 75 (November-December 1981), 26-32.

Head, George. "An Asbestos CEO." *National Underwriter (Life/Health)* 86 (November 1982), 19, 42-43.

Heywood, Donald L. "Assure Proper Industrial Product Use." *Chemical Times & Trends* 7 (April 1984), 22-23+.

Hickel, James. "Infant Formula: WHO Mixes It Up." *Reason* 13 (December 1981), 41-45+.

Jacobson, Charles M. "So Your Product Is Being Misused." *Chemical Times & Trends* 7 (April 1984), 16+.

Johnston, William B. "The Product Liability Follies." *Across the Board* 21 (July-August 1984), 5-7.

Jovanovic, B. "Truthful Disclosure of Information." *Bell Journal of Economics* 13 (Spring 1982), 36-44.

Keller, Bruce P. "Tricks Aren't for Kids." *Madison Avenue* 26 (November 1984), 12-16.

Keller, H. A. "Behind WHO's Ban on Baby Formula Ads." *Wall Street Journal* (June 29, 1981), 20.

Kelley, Ben. "How to Make Driving Safer." *Business and Society Review* 41 (Spring 1982), 22-28.

Kipnis, Kenneth. "Engineers Who Kill: Professional Ethics and the

Paramountcy of Public Safety." *Business and Professional Ethics Journal* 1 (Fall 1981), 77-91. Commentary: by James F. Fairman, 93.

Krulwich, Andrew S. "Recalls: Legal and Corporate Responses to FDA, CPSC, NHTSA, and Product Liability Considerations." *Business Lawyer* 39 (February 1984), 757-780.

Lancianese, Frank W. "Congress Passes Product Liability Reform Bill." *Occupational Hazards* 43 (November 1981), 47-50.

Leibman, Jordan H. "Legal Horizons: Liability for the Unknowable." *Business Horizons* 26 (July-August 1983), 35-40.

Leibman, Jordan H. "The Manufacturer's Responsibility to Warn Product Users of Unknowable Dangers." *American Business Law Journal* 21 (Winter 1984), 403-438.

Malott, Robert H. "Let's Restore Balance to Product Liability Law." *Harvard Business Review* 61 (May-June 1983), 66-74.

Malott, Robert H. "Product Liability: The Law of Hazards." *Enterprise* 7 (December 83 – January 84), 22-24.

Meese, George P. E. "The Sealed Beam Case: Engineering in the Public and Private Interest." *Business and Professional Ethics Journal* 1 (Spring 1982), 1-20. Commentary: by Robert D. Knoll, 21.

Merrill, Richard A. "CPSC Regulation of Cancer Risks in Consumer Products: 1972-1981." *Virginia Law Review* 67 (October 1981), 1261-1375.

Miller, Judith, and Mark Miller. "Testing Fraud: Federal Indictments Send Tremors Through Chemical Industry." *Focus/Midwest* 15 (August 1982), 10-12.

Mintz, Morton. "At Any Cost: Corporate Greed, Women, and the Dalkon Shield." *Progressive* 49 (November 1985), 20-25.

Mokhiber, Russell, ed. "Special Issue: Export of Hazards." *Multinational Monitor* 5 (September 1984), 3-22.

"The Moral Minefield of Cigarette Advertising." *Business and Society Review* 51 (Fall 1984), 13-15.

Nelson-Horchler, Joani. "Fighting a Boycott." *Industry Week* 220 (January 23, 1984), 54-55.

Policano, Christopher. "Case Study: A.H. Robins and the Dalkon Shield." *Public Relations Journal* 41 (March 1985), 16-23.

Post, James E. "Assessing the Nestle Boycott: Corporate Accountability and Human Rights." *California Management Review* 27 (Winter 1985), 113-131.

Razook, Nim. "Merging Comparative Fault and Strict Products

Liability: The Case for Judicial Innovation." *American Business Law Journal* 20 (Winter 1983), 511-523.

Roberts, Verne L. "The Origins of Product Safety." *Journal of Product Liability* 7 (1984), 19-30.

Rodricks, Joseph V. "Risk Assessment and Product Misuse." *Chemical Times & Trends* 7 (April 1984), 18-19+.

Schmeltzer, David. "CPSC's Assessment of Consumer Product Labelling." *Chemical Times & Trends* 8 (April 1985), 22-23+.

Schmidt, Frederick. "Food Industry Shakes Off Sodium Labeling." *Business and Society Review* 49 (Spring 1984), 57-59.

Sibbison, J. "Pushing New Drugs—Can the Press Kick the Habit?" *Columbia Journalism Review* 24 (July-August 1985), 52-54.

Simon, M. J. "Imperfect Information, Costly Litigation, and Product Liability." *Bell Journal of Economics* 12 (Spring 1981), 171-184.

Simon, M. J., et al. "Product Safety, Liability Rules and Retailer Bankruptcy." *Southern Economic Journal* 51 (April 1985), 1130-1141.

Specter, H. A. "Product Liability Act: A Uniform Return to Caveat Emptor." *Trial* 18 (November 1982), 6.

Stewart, Robert M. "Morality and the Market in Blood." *Journal of Applied Philosophy* 1 (October 1984), 227-238.

Timmerman, Ed, and Brad Reid. "The Doctrine of Invited Misuse: A Societal Response to Marketing Promotion." *Journal of Macromarketing* 4 (Fall 1984), 40-48.

"Unsafe Products: The Great Debate over Blame and Punishment." *Business Week* (April 30, 1984), 96+.

Verespej, Michael A. "Which Theory Applies?" *Business Insurance* 16 (April 5, 1982), 12-13.

Vicker, Ray. "Rise in Chain-Saw Injuries Spurs Demand for Safety Standards, but Industry Resists." *Wall Street Journal* (August 23, 1982), 17.

Viscusi, W. K. "Market Incentives for Safety." *Harvard Business Review* 63 (July-August 1985), 133-138.

Vos, Kenneth D., and Douglas E. Kenney. "Combating Inhalation Abuse: An Industry Responds." *Chemical Times & Trends* 8 (October 1985), 9-13.

Waters, Craig R. "The Private War of James Sullivan." *Inc.* 4 (July 1982), 41+.

Weinberg, Nancy. "Product Liability Litigation and Legislation: Recent Trends." *Chemical Times & Trends* 7 (July 1984), 21-24.

Weinstein, Kenneth W., and Donna Diamond. "Liability Resulting from Product Misuse." *Chemical Times & Trends* 7 (April 1984), 49-51.

Public Relations and the Business Image

Books

Bock, Betty, et al. *The Impact of the Modern Corporation.* New York: Columbia Univ. Press, 1984.

Burden, Tom, et al. *Business in Society: Consensus and Conflict.* Boston: Butterworths, 1981.

Dickson, Douglas N., ed. *Business and Its Public.* New York: Wiley, 1984.

Hartley, Robert F. *Marketing Mistakes.* Columbus, Ohio: Grid Pub., 1981.

Lesley, Philip. *Overcoming Opposition: A Survival Manual for Executives.* Englewood Cliffs, N.J.: Prentice-Hall, 1984.

Lusterman, Seymour. *Managerial Competence: The Public Affairs Aspect.* New York: Conference Board, 1981.

MacDougall, Kent. *Ninety Seconds to Tell It All: Big Business and the News Media.* Homewood, Ill.: Dow Jones-Irwin, 1981.

McClosky, Herbert, and John Zaller. *The American Ethos: Public Attitudes Toward Capitalism and Democracy.* Cambridge, Mass.: Harvard University Press, 1984.

McDowell, Duncan, ed. *Advocacy Advertising: Propaganda or Democratic Right?* Ottawa: Conference Board in Canada, 1982.

Moskowitz, Milton, and Michael Katz, ed. *Everybody's Business Scoreboard: Corporate America's Winners, Losers, and Also-Rans.* San Francisco: Harper Row, 1983.

Saxon, Charles. *Honesty Is One of the 'Better' Policies: Saxon's World of Business.* New York: Viking, 1984.

Sellers, James H., and Edward E. Milam. *Accounting Student Perceptions of Business and Professional Ethics.* University, Mo.: Univ. Missouri, 1981.

Sethi, S. P. *Corporate Free Speech: Advocacy/Issue Advertising by Business.* Cambridge, Mass.: Oelgeschlager, Gunn & Hain, 1982.

Steckmest, Francis W. *Corporate Performance: The Key to Public Trust.* New York: McGraw-Hill, 1982.

Theberge, Leonard J., ed. *Crooks, Conmen and Clowns: Businessmen in TV Entertainment: A Study.* Washington, D.C.: Media Institute, 1981.

Watts, Emily S. *The Businessman in American Literature.* Athens, Ga.: Univ. of Georgia Press, 1982.

Articles

Alexander, Larry D. "The Seven Deadly Sins of Corporate Doubletalk." *Business and Society Review* 48 (Winter 1984), 41-44.

"Are MBAs More Than Quantitative Robots?" *Business and Society Review* 44 (Winter 1983), 4-12.

Baida, P. "Saving the Businessman's Soul." *American Heritage* 36 (October-November 1985), 18+.

Banks, L. "Why the Media Look Less Fearsome." *Fortune* 112 (October 14, 1985), 205+.

Bartha, Peter F. "Tuning in on Issues Management." *Canadian Business Review* 11 (Summer 1984), 25-27.

Bell, Howard. "Advocating Advocacy Advertising." *Madison Avenue* 26 (May 1984), 26+.

Bennett, Charles P. "The Ethical Quandary in Business." *Review of Business* 3 (Fall-Winter 1981), 19-20+.

Bennett, James R. "Corporate Sponsored Image Films." *Journal of Business Ethics* 2 (February 1983), 35-41.

Bennett, James R. "Saturday Review's Annual Advertising Awards." *Journal of Business Ethics* 2 (May 1983), 73-78.

Berry, Waldron. "Overcoming Public Distrust of Business." *Business Forum* 9 (Winter 1984), 15-19.

Brouillard, Joseph. "Corporate Reputation Counts." *Advertising Age* 54 (November 1983), M-46.

Brown, Daniel J., and Jonathan B. King. "Small Business Ethics: Influences and Perceptions." *Journal of Small Business Management* 20 (January 1982), 11-18.

Bryant, B. E. "Data Manipulation Technologies Erode Public Trust in Survey Confidentiality." *Marketing News* 19 (March 1, 1985), 24.

Bulkeley, William M., et al. "Toxic Waste Disposal Companies Facing a Profitable Future Despite Bad Publicity." *Wall Street Journal* (June 10, 1983), 33+.

"CG Poll: Sharp Divisions Over Moral Issues." *National Underwriter (Life/Health)* 85 (April 25, 1981), 2+.

"CSPI Awards Its Non-Awards." *Marketing and Media Decisions* 20 (August 1985), 26.

"Campaign Seeks to Change Negative Public Perceptions About Advertising." *Marketing News* 18 (April 27, 1984), 6.

Chilton, Kenneth W. "What Should Government Do for Small Business?" *Journal of Small Business Management* 22 (January 1983), 1-3.

Cialdini, Robert. "Persuasion Principles." *Public Relations Journal* 41 (October 1985), 12-16.

Clavier, David E., and Frank B. Kalupa. "Corporate Rebuttals to 'Trial by Television.' " *Public Relations Review* 9 (Spring 1983), 24-36.

Coe, Barbara J. "The Effectiveness Challenge in Issue Advertising Campaigns." *Journal of Advertising* 12 (1983), 27-35.

Corbett, Harold J. "The Best of the Thieves." *Vital Speeches of the Day* 51 (March 1985), 349-350.

"Crooks, Conmen, and Clowns." *Across the Board* 18 (October 1981), 62-73.

Cullather, James L. "Has the Laughter Died? Musings on the *New Yorker*'s Business Ethics Cartoons." *Business Horizons* 26 (March-April 1983), 30-33.

Cullather, James L. "Learning to Love the Modern Corporation." *Business and Society Review* 42 (Summer 1982), 18-20.

Cullen, Francis T., Bruce G. Link, and Craig W. Polanzi. "The Seriousness of Crime Revisited: Have Attitudes Toward White-Collar Crime Changed?" *Criminology* 20 (May 1982), 83-103.

Divelbiss, R. I., and Maurice R. Cullen, Jr. "Business, the Media, and the American Public." *MSU Business Topics* 29 (Spring 1981), 21-28.

Donaldson, Thomas. "Ethically, 'Society Expects More from a Corporation.' " *U.S. News and World Report* 93 (September 1982), 30.

Donovan, William J. "When a Story Offends Should Its Subject Attack the Reporter?" *New England Business* 6 (October 1, 1984), 60.

"Don't Harm Us to Help Us, Say South African Blacks." *Reason* 17 (May 1985), 16.

Dreschsel, Robert E., and Deborah Moon. "Corporate Libel Plaintiffs and the News Media: An Analysis of the Public-Private Figure Distinction after Gertz." *American Business Law Journal* 21 (Summer 1983), 127-156.

Dreier, P. "The Corporate Complaint Against the Media." *Quill* 71 (November 1983), 17-20+.

Eisendrath, Craig, and Pauline Young-Eisendrath. "Pseudo-Patriarch: An Image of the American Corporate Leader." *Anima* 8 (Spring 1982), 123-130.

Evans, Fred J. "The Politics of the Press." *Business Horizons* 27 (March-April 1984), 22-29.

Fine, Gary A. "The Goliath Effect: Corporate Dominance and Mercantile Legends." *Journal of American Folklore* 98 (January-March 1985), 63-84.

Fisher, Peter. "Investment Tax Credits, Capital Gains Taxation, and Reindustrialization of the U.S. Economy." *Journal of Economic Issues* 15 (June 1981), 769-773.

Fox, James F. "Communicating on Public Issues: The CEO's Changing Role." *Public Relations Review* 9 (Spring 1983), 11-23.

Fox, Karen, F., and Bobby J. Calder. "The Right Kind of Business Advocacy." *Business Horizons* 28 (January-February 1985), 7-11.

Gallese, Liz R. "MBA Blues: Business Schools Run Into Problems Delving Into Firms' Problems." *Wall Street Journal* (December 24, 1981), 1+.

Gibson, W. D. "How the Indians View Carbide." *Chemical Week* 137 (December 18), 1985), 12-13.

Gibson, W. D. "The Plant Manager Reaches Out to His Publics." *Chemical Week* 137 (November 13, 1985), 19-21.

Gitlin, Todd. "The Image of Business on Prime Time Television." *California Management Review* 26 (Winter 1984), 64-73.

Gonzales, Paula W. "Advertising and the Public Image of Business." *Business and Public Affairs* 7 (Spring 1981), 49-53.

Guerrasio, Michael E. "How the Accounting Profession Is Viewed by Users." *CPA Journal* 54 (October 1984), 96-98.

Heath, R. L., and R. A. Nelson. "Image and Issue Advertising: A Corporate and Public Policy Perspective." *Journal of Marketing* 49 (Spring 1985), 58-68.

Hockaday, Irvine O., Jr. "Journalists and Businessmen Have a Lot in Common: They Are Distrusted by the Public." *Vital Speeches of the Day* 51 (February 1, 1985), 244-246.

Howell, L. "For Nestle's Auditors, the Test Is Yet to Come." *Christianity and Crisis* 42 (September 20, 1982), 261-265.

Hutchinson, Charles T. "A Serenade to the U.S. Corporation." *Business Horizons* 25 (January-February 1982), 15-18.

Johnson, Douglas. "A Glimpse at Nestle's Anti-Boycott Strategy." *Business and Society Review* 37 (Spring 1980-1981), 65-67.

Johnson, Robert, and Betsy Morris. "Northwest Industries Plan Faces Difficulties: Leveraged Buyout Proposal Must Overcome Concerns Related to India Disaster." *Wall Street Journal* (December 12, 1984), 3.

Judd, Larry R. "A New Militancy." *Public Relations Journal* 40 (November 1984), 15-16.

Katz, David M. "J and H Exec Urges Ethics Code to Brighten Industry's Image." *National Underwriter (Property/Casualty)* 86 (October 1982), 3+.

Keim, Gerald, and Valerie Zeithaml. "Improving the Return on Advocacy Advertising." *Financial Executive* 49 (November 1981), 40-44.

Kelley, David. "Critical Issues for Issue Ads." *Harvard Business Review* 60 (July-August 1982), 80-87.

Kleinfield, N. R. "A New Breed of C.E.O. Enters the Public Eye." *New York Times Magazine* (December 1, 1985), 76-77.

Komisarjevsky, Christopher P. "Trial by Media." *Business Horizons* 26 (January-February 1983), 36-43.

Kuechle, David. "Crisis Management an Executive Quagmire." *Business Quarterly* 50 (Spring 1985), 53-70.

Lagerfeld, S. "Anti-Business Business Magazine." *Policy Review* 17 (Summer 1981), 59-75.

Lanouette, William J. "Civiletti et al Face Eizenstat et al." *National Journal* 13 (November 7, 1981), 1982-1984.

Levitt, Lee. "Public Relations as a Source of Power." *Public Relations Review* 11 (Fall 1985), 3-9.

Lutz, William D. "Corporate Doublespeak: Making Bad News Look Good." *Business and Society Review* 44 (Winter 1983), 19-22.

Machan, Tibor P. "Profits with Honor." *Reason* 15 (May 1983), 30-33+.

Makin, Claire. "Ranking Corporate Reputations." *Fortune* 107 (January 10, 1983), 34-44.

" 'Managing' Company Lawsuits to Stay Out of Court." *Business Week* (August 23, 1982), 54+.

Marti, Eric. "Protect Us from the Protectionists." *Reason* 17 (December 1985), 10-12.

Marty, Martin E. " 'Satanism: No Soap': The Story of the Rumor Behind the Seal of Proctor and Gamble." *Across the Board* 19 (December 1982), 8-14.

McCammond, Donald B. "A Matter of Ethics." *Public Relations Journal* 39 (November 1983), 46-47.

McConnell, Jon P. "Apparent Agency: Caught by Illusion." *Cornell Hotel and Restaurant Administration Quarterly* 26 (August 1985), 28-33.

McDowell, Duncan. "And Now a Word from Our Sponsor . . . Ottawa Turns to Advocacy Advertising." *Canadian Business Review* 9 (Autumn 1982), 29-32.

McGrew, T. J. "When the Advertiser Strikes Back: The Case for Counter-Advertising." *Ad Forum* 6 (May 1985), 15.

McKay, John. "The Challenge of Public Affairs." *Journal of General Management* 8 (Fall 1982), 58-68.

McNitt, George C. "Profits, Pocketbooks and 'Ralph Naders': How to Advocate Business to the Public." *Business Marketing* 70 (February 1985), 57-64.

Miller, Gregory. "The Fine Art of the Proxy Nastygram." *Institutional Investor* 19 (October 1985), 172-174.

Milmo, Sean. " 'Issue' Ads React, Score Gains." *Business Marketing* 70 (February 1985), 12+.

"Mobil Takes on the Media: Chairman Rawleigh Warner Leads a Combative Campaign against the Press and TV." *International Management* 36 (August 1981), 10-12+.

Moore, Ellen M., William O. Bearden, and Jesse E. Teel. "Use of Labeling and Assertions of Dependency in Appeals for Consumer Support." *Journal of Consumer Research* 12 (June 1985), 90-96.

Muson, Howard. "Not 'Crooks, Conmen, and Clowns' This Time: 'Enterprise' Surprises." *Across the Board* 19 (January 1982), 2-7.

Nichols, Donald K. "Speechwriters: The Myth of Corporate Excellence." *Vital Speeches of the Day* 52 (November 1, 1985), 54-57.

Olasky, Marvin N. "Chemical Giant Goodwinks the Press." *Business and Society Review* 54 (Summer 1985), 60-63.

Olasky, Marvin N. "Inside the Amoral World of Public Relations: Truth Molded for Corporate Gain." *Business and Society Review* 52 (Winter 1985), 41-44.

Olasky, Marvin N. "The 1984 Public Relations Scam Awards." *Business and Society Review* 51 (Fall 1984), 42-46.

O'Neil, R. F. "The Artist's Perception of the Typical Businessman: Selfish, Greedy, Conniving and Thoroughly Amoral." *International Journal of Social Economics (UK)* 8 (1981), 31-39.

Patti, Charles H., and John P. McDonald. "Corporate Advertising: Process, Practices and Perspectives (1970-1989)." *Journal of Advertising* 14 (March 1985), 42-49.

Paulk, Mahlon S. "Positive Images." *Life Association News* 80 (May 1985), 151-152.

Perry, Nancy J. "America's Most Admired Companies." *Fortune* 109 (January 9, 1984), 50-62.

Podhoretz, Norman. "The New Defenders of Capitalism." *Harvard Business Review* 59 (March-April 1981), 96-106.

Pressley, Milton M., and David E. Blevins. "Student Perceptions of Job Politics as Practised by Those Climbing the Corporate Ladder." *Journal of Business Ethics* 3 (May 1984), 127-138.

"A Qualified Audit." *Economist* 296 (August 17, 1985), 15-16.

Ricklefs, Roger. "Executives and the General Public Say Ethical Behavior Is Declining in the U.S." *Wall Street Journal* (Oct. 31 – Nov. 3, 1983), 1.

Roff, L. L., and E. L. Klemmack. "Employers' Responsibility for Social Services: Public Perceptions." *Social Work* 30 (September-October 1985), 445-447.

Roper, Burns W., and Thomas A. Miller. "Americans Take Stock of Business." *Public Opinion* 8 (August-September 1985), 12-15.

Rothschild, M. "No Place for Scruples: What Counts Is Turning a Buck—Any Which Way You Can." *Progressive* 49 (November 1985), 26-28.

Samuelson, Robert J. "A False Religion." *National Journal* 14 (November 20, 1982), 1992.

Schwartz, Harry. "The UN System's War on the Drug Industry." *Regulation* 6 (July-August 1982), 19-24.

Sebba, Leslie. "Attitudes of New Immigrants Toward White-Collar Crime: A Cross-Cultural Exploration." *Human Relations* 36 (December 1983), 1091-1110.

Sellerberg, A. M. "On Modern Confidence." *Acta Sociologica* 25 (1982), 20-26.

Sethi, S. P. "Becoming a Better Advocate." *Directors & Boards* 9 (Fall 1984), 12-13.

Sethi, S. P. "Serving the Public Interest: Corporate Political Action Strategies for the 1980's." *Management Review* 70 (March 1981), 8-11.

Sethi, S. P., and Nobuaki Namiki. "Managing Public Affairs: The Public Backlash against PACs." *California Management Review* 25 (Spring 1983), 133-144.

Siddon, Patrick. "Business and Journalism: Bedfellows or Mortal Enemies?" *Business Horizons* 28 (September-October 1985), 3-7.

Smith, Ward. "Business and the Media: Sometimes Partners, Sometimes Adversaries." *Vital Speeches of the Day* 52 (November 1, 1985), 49-51.

Socolovsky, A. "In the Public Eye: As the Public Becomes More Aware of the Electronics Industry, Managers Face an Ethical Responsibility." *Electronic Business* 9 (June 1983), 200.

Spilker, Bert. "Myths and Misconceptions about Drug Industry Ethics." *International Journal of Applied Philosophy* 2 (Fall 1984), 1-11.

Stephenson, D. R. "Internal PR Efforts Further Corporate Responsibility: A Report from Dow Canada." *Public Relations Quarterly* 28 (Summer 1983), 7-10.

Straughan, Dulcie, Bill Chamberlin, and Carol Reuss. "For Corporate Libel Plaintiffs: Life After Gertz?" *Public Relations Review* 10 (Fall 1984), 47-70.

Strier, Franklin. "Business vs. Academia: How They Perceive Each Other." *Business and Public Affairs* 8 (Spring 1982), 9-17.

Towers, Alan. "Striking a Balance in the Public Mind: How People View a Company Can Be Vital to Its Success." *Advertising Age* 53 (June 21, 1982), M-48.

Traylor, Mark B., and Alicia M. Mathias. "The Impact of TV Advertising Versus Word of Mouth on the Image of Lawyers: A Projective Experiment." *Journal of Advertising* 12 (1983), 42-49.

Ward, Howard H. " 'We Have Lost the Trust of Many . . ." *National Underwriter* 85 (August 21, 1981), 25, 29.

"Was Mobil Wise to Blacklist the Wall Street Journal?" *Business and Society Review* 53 (Spring 1985), 38-39.

"Will a Few Bad Apples Spoil the Core of Big Business?" *Business and Society Review* 55 (Fall 1985), 4-15.

Wright, Donald K., and Chester Burger. "Ethics in Public Relations." *Public Relations Journal* 38 (December 1982), 12-17.

Young, Lewis H. "Business and the Media/Part II: A Distorted Image?" *FE* 1 (April 1985), 28-32.

Social Activism and Consumer Concerns

Books

Aram, John D. *Managing Business and Public Policy: Concepts, Issues, and Cases*. Marshfield, Mass.: Pitman, 1982.

Buchholz, Rogene. *Business Environment and Public Policy: Implications for Management.* Englewood Cliffs, N.J.: Prentice-Hall, 1982.

Burt, Dan M. *Abuse of Trust: A Report on Ralph Nader's Network.* Chicago: Regnery/Gateway, 1982.

Dunlop, John T. *Business and Public Policy.* Cambridge, Mass.: Harvard University Press, 1981.

Janger, Allen R., and Ronald E. Berenbeim. *External Challenges to Management Decisions: A Growing International Business Problem.* New York: Conference Board, 1981.

Luthans, Fred, and Richard M. Hodgetts. *Social Issues in Business: Strategic and Public Policy Perspectives.* 4th ed. New York: Macmillan, 1984.

Martin, David, and Peter Mullen, eds. *Unholy Warfare: The Church and the Bomb.* Oxford, U.K.: Blackwell, 1983.

Meyer, Jack A., ed. *Meeting Human Needs: Toward a New Public Philosophy.* Washington, D.C.: American Enterprise Inst., 1982.

Miles, Robert. *Coffin Nails and Corporate Strategies.* Englewood Cliffs, N.J.: Prentice-Hall, 1982.

Pertschuk, Michael. *Revolt Against Regulation: The Rise and Pause of the Consumer Movement.* Berkeley, Calif.: Univ. Calif. Press, 1982.

A Promise Unfulfilled: Consumer Protection. Princeton, N.J.: Center for Analysis of Public Issues, 1982.

Suthers, John W., and Gary L. Shupp. *Fraud and Deceit: How to Stop Being Ripped Off.* New York: Arco Pubs., 1982.

Articles

Achampong, Francis. "Will the D.C. No-Fault Law Serve the Consumer?" *CPCU Journal* 38 (March 1985), 40-47.

Agege, Charles O. "Dumping of Dangerous American Products Overseas: Should Congress Sit and Watch?" *Journal of World Trade Law* 19 (July-August 1985), 403-410.

Altschul, James S. "Counting the Cost of the Atom: Construction of US Nuclear Plants Has Been Hit by Vast Cost Overruns." *Euromoney (UK),* (November 1984), 96+.

Anderson, Wayne C. "Academia and Business: Public Policy and Social Issues." *Vital Speeches of the Day* 52 (November 1, 1985), 57-60.

Andres, William A. "The Case for Open Trade: Speaking Out for the Consumer." *Vital Speeches of the Day* 51 (August 1, 1985), 623-626.

Antil, John H. "Socially Responsible Consumers: Profile and Implications for Public Policy." *Journal of Macromarketing* 4 (Fall 1984), 18-39.

Asinof, Richard. "Rate Shock: Can Business and Consumers Fight Back Together?" *Environmental Action* 16 (January-February 1985), 12-15.

Beach, John E. "Codes of Ethics: Court Enforcement Through Public Policy." *Business and Professional Ethics Journal* 4 (Fall 1985), 53-64. Commentaries: by William G. Snead, 65; Scott F. Turow, 69.

Bearden, William O., et al. "Self-Monitoring, Norms, and Attitudes as Influences on Consumer Complaining." *Journal of Business Research* 9 (September 1981), 255-266.

Belk, Russell W. "Materialism: Trait Aspects of Living in the Material World." *Journal of Consumer Research* 12 (December 1985), 265-280.

Bofarull, Ignacio U. "The Spanish Act on the Protection of the Rights of Consumers and Users." *Journal of Consumer Policy* 8 (June 1985), 169-172.

Borrie, Gordon, et al. "Where Directors Are at Risk/If Consumers Get Outraged." *Director (UK)* 38 (May 1985), 47-50.

Braithwaite, J. "Corporate Crime Research: Why Two Interviewers Are Needed." *Sociology* 19 (February 1985), 136-138.

Brimelow, Peter. "Shock Waves from Whoops Roll East." *Fortune* 108 (July 25, 1983), 46-48.

Burgenmaier, Beat. "Consumer Protection in Switzerland: Strengthening Countervailing Power or Competition?" *Journal of Consumer Policy* 8 (March 1985), 45-52.

Calais-Auloy, Jean. "Towards New Laws for Consumer Protection: Proposal of the French Reform Commission." *Journal of Consumer Policy* 8 (March 1985), 53-67.

"The Case against Depo-Provera." [Special Issue] *Multinational Monitor* 6 (February-March 1985), 3-22.

Chadwick-Brown, David. "Litigation as Private Formulation of Public Policy." *Journal of Contemporary Business* 10 (1981), 119-127.

Chapman, Fern S. "Deciding Who Pays to Save Lives." *Fortune* 111 (May 27, 1985), 58-70.

Copulos, Milton. "It's Effective—But Is It Safe?" *Reason* 16 (March 1985), 24-32.

Crable, Richard E., and Steven L. Vibbert. "Managing Issues and Influencing Public Policy." *Public Relations Review* 11 (Summer 1985), 3-16.

Enck, Judith. "Anti-Litter Activists Bottle Up the Container Industry." *Business and Society Review* 43 (Fall 1982), 37-41.

Evers, Myrlie. "Consumerism in the Eighties." *Public Relations Journal* 39 (August 1983), 24-26.

Federspiel, Benedicte. "Consumer Organizations and Their Influence." *Journal of Consumer Policy* 8 (June 1985), 187-189.

Fiski, John F. "Dangerous Territory: The Societal Marketing Concept Revisited." *Business Horizons* 28 (July-August 1985), 42-47.

Fleming, John E. "Corporate Response to Social Actions." *Business* 32 (January-March 1982), 10-14.

Forbes, James D. "Organizational and Political Dimensions of Consumer Pressure Groups." *Journal of Consumer Policy* 8 (June 1985), 105-131.

Glezen, G. W., and Paul H. Schwinghammer. "Why No Public Oversight Boards?" *Directors & Boards* 8 (Winter 1984), 8-9.

Golonka, Nancy. "The Many Faces of Consumerism." *Journal of Insurance* 42 (January-February 1981), 26-30.

Harris, Marlys. "What Have Consumer Groups Done for You Lately?" *Money* 11 (October 1982), 218-220.

Harrop, Mark D. "Banning Krugerrands: Debasing the Currency of Apartheid." *Business and Society Review* 47 (Fall 1983), 48-52.

Haru, Terry T. "Moral Obligations and Conceptions of World Hunger: On the Need to Justify Correct Action." *Applied Behavior Science* 20 (1984), 363-382.

Henell, Olof. "Alcoholization—The Biggest Consumer Problem." *Journal of Consumer Policy* 8 (March 1985), 69-78.

"How to Avoid Business-Opportunity Frauds." *Consumer's Research* 67 (December 1984), 35-37.

Hughes, G. D. "Can Business and Consumer Interests Merge?" *Chemical Times & Trends* 5 (January 1982), 7-11.

Hunt, Shelby D., and John R. Nevin. "Why Consumers Believe They Are Being Ripped Off." *Business Horizons* 24 (May-June 1981), 48-52.

Jackson, Brooks. "Anti-PAC Group Launches Attack." *Wall Street Journal* (March 5, 1984), 56.

Jacobson, Michael F., Robert Atkins, and George Hacker. "Booze Merchants Cheer on Teenage Drinking." *Business and Society Review* 46 (Summer 1983), 46-50.

Kemper, Vicki. "A Campaign of Persuasive Pressure: The Movement to End U.S. Support of S.A. Injustice." *Sojourners* 14 (February 1985), 18-20.

Kerton, Robert R. "The Business of Organized Consumers: National and International." *Canadian Business Review* 8 (Autumn 1981), 31-33.

Lamm, Richard D. "Anti-Social Ethics: Health Care Costs." *Vital Speeches of the Day* 51 (March 15, 1985), 325-327.

Lee, Mike. "Unemployed: The Road from Toxteth Riots." *Management Today (UK)* (November 1981), 43-44, 48.

Lee, S. M. "Business Pressure on Consumer Educators." *Journal of Home Economics* 75 (Winter 1983), 11-13.

Leonard, H. A. "Consumers Talk—The ACLI Listens." *Best's Review (Life/Health)* 86 (August 1985), 24+.

Liebman, Bonnie. "Nouveau Junk Food: Consumers Swallow the Back to Nature Bunk." *Business and Society Review* 51 (Fall 1984), 47-51.

Linck, Sandra. "What Happened to Values in Consumer Education and Research?" *Journal of Consumer Affairs* 16 (Winter 1982), 389-393.

Loescher, Samuel M. "Public Interest Movements and Private Interest Systems: A Healthy Schizophrenia." *Journal of Economic Issues* 15 (June 1981), 557-568.

Maremont, Mark. "Fire on Campus, Tremors in the Boardroom." *Business Week* (April 29, 1985), 98-99.

McKenzie, Richard B. "Caution: Consumer Protection May Be Hazardous to Your Health." *Reason* 12 (January 1981), 38-41+.

Miller, John A. "The Health Care Cost Epidemic." *Best's Review (Life/Health)* 84 (April 1984), 26-32.

Nelson, J. R. "Corporations and Social Action." *Christian Century* 99 (November 24, 1982), 1191-1192.

Paltrow, Scot J. "Alluring Bait: Swindlers Often Use Ads on Financial Pages to Appear Respectable." *Wall Street Journal* (April 29, 1982), 1+.

"The Pressure Builds: Reagan's Shift on Sanctions Adds to a Mounting Issue of Urgency for Change." *U.S. News and World Report* 99 (September 23, 1985), 20-21.

Preston, Lee E., and Paul N. Bloom. "The Concerns of the Rich/Poor Consumer." *California Management Review* 26 (Fall 1983), 100-119.

Richins, Marsha L., and Bronislaw J. Verhage. "Seeking Redress for Consumer Dissatisfaction: The Role of Attitudes and Situational Factors." *Journal of Consumer Policy* 8 (March 1985), 29-41.

"Right-to-Know: Wave of the Future?" *National Safety and Health News* 132 (November 1985), 26-31.

Rogers, Ray. "How to Confront Corporations." *Business and Society Review* 38 (Summer 1981), 60-64.

Rongine, Nicholas M. "Toward a Coherent Legal Response to the Public Policy Dilemma Posed by Whistleblowing." *American Business Law Journal* 23 (Summer 1985), 281-297.

Samli, A. C., et al. "Marketers Can Become Social Activists with These Guidelines." *Marketing News* 17 (April 1, 1983), 5-6.

Samuels, Warren J. "A Consumer View on Financing Nuclear Plant Abandonments." *Public Utilities Fortnightly* 115 (January 10, 1985), 26-32.

Scanlon, Terrence M. "Revving Up a Regulatory Merry-Go-Round." *Wall Street Journal* (July 11, 1984), 30.

Scherhorn, Gerhard. "The Goal of Consumer Advice: Transparancy or Autonomy?" *Journal of Consumer Policy* 8 (June 1985), 133-151.

Schmalz, Richard A. "Problems of Insurance Availability—'Redlining.' " *CPCU Journal* 34 (March 1981), 25-36.

Schneider, Kenneth C., and Cynthia K. Holm. "Deceptive Practices in Marketing Research: The Consumer's Viewpoint." *California Management Review* 24 (Spring 1982), 89-96.

Shuman, Eric. "Potentially Hazardous Merchandise: Domestic and International Mechanisms for Consumer Protection." *Vanderbilt Journal of Transnational Law* 16 (Winter 1983), 179-229.

Smith, J. A., III. "Committee for Energy Awareness: Fronts for Nuclear Power." *Business and Society Review* 50 (Summer 1984), 51-55.

Stewart, James B. "Wake of Disaster: Controversy Surrounds Payments to Plaintiffs in Hyatt Regency Case." *Wall Street Journal* (July 3, 1984), 1.

Taylor, Bernard, and Luigi Ferro. "Key Social Issues for European Business." *Long Range Planning* 16 (February 1983), 42-69.

Thomas, Michael J. "Social Marketing, Social-Cause Marketing, and the Pitfalls Beyond." *Quarterly Review of Marketing (UK)* 9 (October 1983), 1-5.

Ursic, Michael L. "A Model of the Consumer Decision to Seek Legal Redress." *Journal of Consumer Affairs* 19 (Summer 1985), 20-36.

Valaskakis, Kimon. "The Conserver Society: Emerging Paradigm of the 1980s?" *Futurist* 15 (April 1981), 5-13.

Warner, Gregory D. "Morals in the Marketplace: The TV Coalition in Context." *Christian Century* 100 (April 13, 1983), 342-345.

Weidenbaum, Murray L. "Politicizing Business Is Bad Business." *Directors & Boards* 8 (Winter 1984), 28-29.

Weis, William L. "A Smoke Cloud Over Tobacco's Future." *Business and Society Review* 52 (Winter 1985), 37-40.

"When Sanctions Work." *Economist* 296 (September 14, 1985), 15-16.

Wines, Michael. "Administrational Critics Play Legal Cat and Mouse Game on Agency Rules." *National Journal* 14 (December 18, 1982), 2157-2160.

Wogaman, J. P. "The Ethical Premise for Social Activism." *Business and Society Review* 54 (Summer 1985), 30-36.

Wood, James R. "Poverty in America." *Business Horizons* 25 (July-August 1982), 85-90.

Wood, John A. "Consumer Advocacy: Ethics in Political Action." *Review and Expositor* 81 (Spring 1984), 225-233.

Wright, T., et al. "Corporate Interests, Philanthropies, and the Peace Movement." *Monthly Review* 36 (February 1985), 19-31.

Technology: Its Impact on Society

Books

Braun, Ernest. *Wayward Technology*. Westport, Conn.: Greenwood Press, 1984.

Faunce, William A. *Problems of an Industrial Society*. 2d ed. New York: McGraw-Hill, 1981.

Florman, Samuel C. *Blaming Technology: The Irrational Search for Scapegoats*. New York: St. Martin's Press, 1981.

Hall, Peter, and Ann Markusen. *Silicon Landscapes*. Boston: Allen & Unwin, 1985.

Lapham, Lewis H., ed. *High Technology and Human Freedom*. Washington, D.C.: Smithsonian Inst. Press, 1985.

Mahon, Thomas. *Charged Bodies*. New York: New American Library, 1985.

Minsky, Marvin, ed. *Robotics*. Garden City, N.Y.: Anchor Press, 1985.

Robertson, James. *Future Work: Jobs, Self-Employment and Leisure After the Industrial Age*. London, U.K.: Gower Pub. Co., 1985.

Rybczynski, Witold. *Taming the Tiger: The Struggle to Control Technology*. New York: Viking Press, 1983.

Unger, Stephen H. *Controlling Technology: Ethics and the Responsible Engineer*. New York: Holt, Rinehart, & Winston, 1982.

Zand, Dale E. *Information, Organization and Power: Effective Management in the Knowledge of Society.* New York: McGraw-Hill, 1981.

Articles

Aggarwal, Vimla, and Sumer C. Aggarwal. "High Technology: Economic Hope or Hoax?" *Business Horizons* 27 (January-February 1984), 47-51.

Akers, John F. "SMR Forum: A Responsible Future—An Address to the Computer Industry." *Sloan Management Review* 26 (Fall 1984), 53-57.

Albus, J. S. "Robots and the Economy." *Futurist* 17 (December 1984), 38-44.

Blunden, Margaret. "Futures Essay—Technology and Values: Problems and Options." *Futures (UK)* 16 (August 1984), 418-424.

Brandt, Richard, et al. "Those Vanishing High-Tech Jobs." *Business Week* (July 15, 1985), 30-31.

Bumstead, Richard. "Opening Up High Technology Careers to Women." *Occupational Outlook Quarterly* 25 (Summer 1981), 26-31.

Byrne, Edmund F. "Displaced Workers: America's Unpaid Debt." *Journal of Business Ethics* 4 (February 1985), 31-41.

Chase, Marty, and Mary Jo Foley. "High Tech and Apartheid: The South African Connection." *Electronic Business* 11 (May 1, 1985), 30-36.

Coates, Vary T. "The Potential Impacts of Robotics." *Futurist* 17 (February 1983), 28-32.

Dray, James, and Joseph A. Menosky. "Computers and the New World Order . . ." *Technology Review* 86 (May-June 1983), 12-16.

Everard, Bertie. "The Social and Ethical Problems of Work and Unemployment in Technological Society." *Industrial & Commercial Training (UK)* 13 (September 1981), 298-304.

Forest, Robert B. "Howard Bromberg's Electronic Cottage." *Infosystems* 28 (June 1981), 98.

Geiser, Kenneth. "The Low Side of High-Tech: Chemical Hazards in the Electronics Industry." *Business and Society Review* 52 (Winter 1985), 60-63.

Gilchrist, Bruce, and Arlaana Shenkin. "Disappearing Jobs: The Impact of Computers on Unemployment." *Futurist* 15 (February 1981), 44-49.

Hollon, Charles J., and George N. Rogol. "Now Robotization Affects People." *Business Horizons* 28 (May-June 1985), 74-80.

Hornig, Lilli S. "Women in Science and Engineering: Why so Few?" *Technology Review* 87 (November-December 1984), 29-41.

Jackson, Auzville, Jr. "High Tech's Influence on Our Lives: Adapting to Change." *Vital Speeches of the Day* 51 (January 1, 1985), 164-166.

Jennings, Lane. "Work and Leisure in Computopia." *National Forum* 62 (Summer 1982), 34-36.

Jordan, Michael H. "Humanism in a Technological Age: A Change from Driver to Coach." *Vital Speeches of the Day* 51 (January 15, 1985), 210-213.

Krass, Peter. "Computers That Would Program People." *Business and Society Review* 37 (Spring 1980-81), 62-64.

Lukaszewski, Charles T. "The Quest for Convenience: Value Growth." *Vital Speeches of the Day* 51 (August 15, 1985), 649-650.

Marx, Gary T. "The New Surveillance." *Technology Review* 88 (May-June 1985), 42-48.

McDonald, Dennis D. "Copyright Can Survive the New Technologies." *Bulletin of ASIS* 10 (October 1983), 19-22.

McGowan, William. "Can High-Tech Retraining Cure the Terminally Unemployed?" *Business and Society Review* 46 (Summer 1983), 52-56.

McLuhan, Marshall, and B. Powers. "Electronic Banking and the Death of Privacy." *Journal of Communication* 31 (Winter 1981), 164-169.

Noble, David F. "Is Progress What It Seems to Be?" *Datamation* 30 (November 15, 1984), 141-154.

Patterson, William P. "Technology: The Great Genetics Debate." *Industry Week* 223 (December 10, 1984), 42-48.

Roessner, J. D. "Forecasting the Impact of Office Automation on Clerical Employment, 1985-2000." *Technological Forecasting and Social Change* 28 (November 1985), 203-216.

Rubins, David. "Telecommuting: Will the Plug Be Pulled?" *Reason* 16 (October 1984), 24-32.

Salomon, Jean Jacques. "Technology and Economic Policy in a Changing World." *Research Management* 24 (January 1981), 36-41.

Spence, Lewis H. "Technology and the Poor." *Technology Review* 85 (August-September 1982), 10-12.

Wiener, Hesh. "The OPM Scandal Unmasked." *Datamation* 29 (September 1983), 34-36+.

Theoretical and Applied Ethics

Theoretical and Applied Ethics

Cases and Texts

Books

Allen, William R., and Louis K. Bragaw. *Social Forces and the Manager: Readings and Cases.* New York: John Wiley, 1982.

Barry, Vincent. *Moral Issues in Business.* 2d ed. Belmont, Calif.: Wadsworth Pub. Co., 1983.

Beauchamp, Tom L. *Case Studies in Business, Society, and Ethics.* Englewood Cliffs, N.J.: Prentice-Hall, 1983.

Beauchamp, Tom L., and Norman E. Bowie. *Ethical Theory and Business.* Englewood Cliffs, N.J.: Prentice-Hall, 1983.

Brickey, Kathleen F. *Corporate Criminal Liability: A Treatise on the Criminality of Corporations, Their Officers and Agents.* Wilmette, Ill.: Callaghan, 1984.

Buchholz, Rogene, William D. Evans, and Robert A. Wagley. *Management Response to Public Issues: Concepts and Cases in Strategy Formulation.* Englewood Cliffs, N.J.: Prentice-Hall, 1985.

De George, Richard T. *Business Ethics.* New York: Macmillan, 1982.

Donaldson, Thomas, ed. *Case Studies in Business Ethics.* Englewood Cliffs, N.J.: Prentice-Hall, 1984.

Donaldson, Thomas, and Patricia H. Werhane. *Ethical Issues in Business: A Philosophical Approach.* Englewood Cliffs, N.J.: Prentice-Hall, 1983.

Farmer, Richard N., and W. D. Hogue. *Corporate Social Responsibility.* 2d ed. Lexington, Mass.: Lexington Books, 1985.

Hay, Robert D., and Edmund R. Gray. *Business and Society: Cases and Text.* 2d ed. Cincinnati: South-Western Pub. Co., 1981.

Hoffman, W. M., and Jennifer M. Moore. *Business Ethics: Readings and Cases in Corporate Morality.* New York: McGraw-Hill, 1984.

Jones, Donald G., ed. *Doing Ethics in Business; New Ventures in Management Development.* Cambridge, Mass.: Oelgeschlager, Gunn & Hain, 1982.

Matthews, John B., Kenneth E. Goodpaster, and Laura L. Nash. *Policies and Persons: A Casebook in Business Ethics.* New York: McGraw-Hill, 1985.

Owens, James. *Ethical Theory and Business Decisions.* Tantallon, Md.: Management Educ. Ltd., 1982.

Parker, Donn B. *Ethical Conflicts in Computer Science and Technology.* Arlington, Va.: AFIPS Press, 1981.

Partridge, Scott H. *Cases in Business and Society*. Englewood Cliffs, N.J.: Prentice-Hall, 1982.

Regan, Tom, ed. *Just Business: New Introductory Essays in Business Ethics*. Philadelphia: Temple University Press, 1984.

Regan, Tom, and Donald Van DeVeer, eds. *And Justice for All: New Introductory Essays in Ethics and Public Policy*. Totowa, N.J.: Biblio Distr. Centre, 1982.

Sethi, S. P. *Up Against the Corporate World: Modern Corporations and Social Issues of the Eighties*. Englewood Cliffs, N.J.: Prentice-Hall, 1982.

Steiner, George A., and John F. Steiner. *Business, Government and Society: Text and Cases*. New York: Random House, 1985.

Sturdivant, Frederick D. *The Corporate Social Challenge: Cases and Commentaries*. 3d ed. Homewood, Ill.: R. D. Irwin, 1985.

Sturdivant, Frederick D., and Larry M. Robinson, eds. *The Corporate Social Challenge: Cases and Commentaries*. Rev. ed. Homewood, Ill.: R. D. Irwin, 1981.

Torrington, Derek, and Trevor Hitner. *Management and the Multi-Racial Work Force: Cases in Employment Practice*. London, U.K.: Gower Pub. Co., 1982.

Troy, Kathryn, *Studying and Addressing Community Needs: A Corporate Case Book*. New York: Conference Board, 1985.

Velasquez, Manuel G., S.J. *Business Ethics: Concepts and Cases*. Englewood Cliffs, N.J.: Prentice-Hall, 1982.

Articles

English, Gary. "Case Studies on Business Ethics." *Student Activities Programming* (May 1981), 32-38.

Ethics, Economics, and Justice

Books

Benne, Robert. *The Ethic of Democratic Capitalism: A Moral Reassessment*. Philadelphia: Fortress Press, 1981.

Block, Walter, and Donald Shaw, eds. *Theology, Third World Development and Economic Justice*. Regina, Sask.: Fraser Institute, 1985.

Buchanan, Allen E. *Ethics, Efficiency and the Market*. Totowa, N.J.: Rowman & Allanheld, 1985.

Carens, Joseph H. *Equality, Moral Incentives, and the Market: An Essay in Utopian Politico-Economic Theory*. Chicago: University of Chicago Press, 1981.

Drucker, Peter F. *Toward the Next Economics*. New York: Harper & Row, 1981.

Dyke, C. *Philosophy of Economics*. Englewood Cliffs, N.J.: Prentice-Hall, 1981.

Hochschild, Jennifer L. *What's Fair? American Beliefs About Distributive Justice*. Cambridge, Mass.: Harvard University Press, 1981.

Maital, Shlomo, and Sharone L. Maital. *Economic Games People Play*. New York: Basic Books, 1984.

Murchland, Bernard. *Humanism and Capitalism: A Survey of Thought on Morality and the Economic Order*. Washington, D.C.: American Enterprise Inst., 1984.

Novak, Michael. *The Spirit of Democratic Capitalism*. New York: Simon & Schuster, 1982.

Posner, Richard A. *The Economics of Justice*. Cambridge, Mass.: Harvard University Press, 1981.

Schweickart, David. *Capitalism or Worker Control?: An Ethical and Economic Appraisal*. New York: Praeger, 1980.

Scott, John. *Corporations, Classes, and Capitalism*. 2d ed. London, U.K.: Hutchinson Educ., 1985.

Steedman, Ian, et al. *The Value Controversy*. London, U.K.: Verso Eds. & New Left Bks, 1981.

Strinati, Dominic. *Capitalism, the State and Industrial Relations*. London, U.K.: Croom, Helm, 1982.

Weeks, John. *Capital and Exploitation*. Princeton, N.J.: Princeton University, 1981.

Yamani, Ahmed Z. *Some Thoughts on the Morals of Trade*. Berkeley, Calif.: Univ. of California, 1980.

Zelizer, Viviana A. R. *Morals and Markets: The Development of Life Insurance in the United States*. New Brunswick, N.J.: Transaction Books, 1983.

Articles

Aharoni, Yair. "Towards an Age of Humility." *California Management Review* 24 (Winter 1981), 49-59.

Bachelder, Robert S. "The Gospel of Equality and the Gospel of Efficiency." *Christian Century* 101 (April 11, 1984), 368-370.

Baumol, William J. "Marx and the Iron Law of Wages." *American Economic Review* 73 (May 1983), 303-308.

Beauchamp, Tom L. "The Ethical Foundations of Economic Justice." *Review of Social Economy* 40 (December 1982), 291-300.

Bennett, John G. "Ethics and Markets." *Philosophy and Public Affairs* 14 (Spring 1985), 195-204.

Billings, Donald B. "The Moral Case for Competitive Capitalism." *Freeman* 33 (July 1983), 413-419.

Birch, Thomas D. "Marshall and Keynes Revisited." *Journal of Economic Issues* 19 (March 1985), 194-200.

Bliss, Michael. "The Battle that Business Lost." *Canadian Business* 55 (November 1982), 48-50+.

Boarman, Patrick M. "Business and Ethics: Contemporary Capitalism." *Vital Speeches of the Day* 48 (June 15, 1982), 532-535.

Burt, John (Bishop). "Bottom Line: People and Jobs." *Witness* 64 (March 1981), 5-6.

Campbell, William J., D. Richardson, and George Monsma. "Impoverished Wealth, Affluent Poverty, or Economic Wisdom: Three Economists Look at Gilder's Views." *Christianity Today* 27 (February 4, 1983), 28-29.

Cavanagh, Gerald F. "Free Enterprise Values." *Review of Social Economy* 40 (December 1982), 330-339.

Cotter, John J. "Ethics and Justice in the World of Work." *Review of Social Economy* 40 (December 1982), 393-406.

Daly, Herman E. "Economics, Ethics, and Cost-Benefit Analysis." *Human Systems Management* 2 (April 1981), 7-12.

Danner, Peter L. "Exchange Value in the Value Hierarchy." *International Journal of Social Economics (UK)* 8, no.4 (1981), 70-84.

Darrity, William A., Jr., and Rhonda Williams. "Peddlers Forever?: Culture, Competition and Discrimination." *American Economic Review* 75 (May 1985), 256-261.

Donaldson, Thomas. "What Justice Demands." *Review of Social Economy* 40 (December 1982), 301-310.

Ellin, Joseph S. "The Justice of Collective Responsibility." *University of Dayton Review* 15 (Winter 1981-82), 17-27.

Evans, J. W. "Ethics and the Capitalist-Liberal Organization: Implications for a Social Economy in the United States." *International Journal of Social Economics* 8, no.4 (1981), 85-96.

Freeman, R. E., and Dan Maitland. "Ethics and Economics: A Management Reply to the Catholic Bishops." *Minnesota Management Review* 4 (March 1985), 1+.

Gordon, Scott. "Equality." *Business Horizons* 25 (July-August 1982), 73-77.

Gramm, Warren S. "Property Rights in Work: Capitalism, Industrialism, and Democracy." *Journal of Economic Issues* 15 (June 1981), 363-375.

Hagg, Claes. "Just Price and Equal Opportunity." *Journal of Business Ethics* 2 (November 1983), 269-272.

Harrington, Michael. "Is Capitalism Still Viable?" *Journal of Business Ethics* 1 (November 1982), 281-284.

Harrison, Beverly. "Social Justice and Economic Orthodoxy." *Christianity and Crisis* 44 (January 21, 1984), 513-515.

Higler, George J. "The Pleasures and Pains of Modern Capitalism." *Across the Board* 20 (June 1983), 53-59.

Hirschman, Albert O. "Rival Interpretations of Market Society: Civilizing, Destructive, or Feeble?" *Journal of Economic Literature* 20 (December 1982), 1463-1484.

Hoaglund, John. "Ethical Theory and Practice: Is There a Gap?" *Journal of Business Ethics* 3 (August 1984), 201-205.

Hodgson, Bernard. "Economic Science and Ethical Neutrality: The Problem of Teleology." *Journal of Business Ethics* 2 (November 1983), 237-253.

Hosmer, LaRue T. "Managerial Ethics and Microeconomic Theory." *Journal of Business Ethics* 3 (November 1984), 315-325.

Kahn, Alfred E. "Economethics." *Across the Board* 18 (April 1981), 93-97.

Keeney, Ralph L. "Ethics, Decision Analysis, and Public Risk." *Risk Analysis* 4 (June 1984), 117-129.

Kelman, Steven. "Cost-Benefit Analysis: An Ethical Critique." *Across the Board* 18 (July-August 1981), 74-82.

Khoury, Sarkis J. "Profits: A Blessing or a Curse." *Managerial Planning* 33 (January-February 1985), 37-46.

Kirk, Russell. "Is Capitalism Still Viable?" *Journal of Business Ethics* 1 (November 1982), 277-280.

Laney, James T. "The Other Adam Smith." *Economic Review* 66 (October 1981), 26-29.

Lindblom, C. E. "Market as Prison." *Journal of Politics* 44 (May 1982), 324-336.

Lindgren, J. R. "The Irrelevance of Philosophical Treatments of Affirmative Action." *Social Theory and Practice* 7 (Spring 1981), 1-19.

Lodge, George C. "The Connection Between Ethics and Ideology." *Journal of Business Ethics* 1 (May 1982), 85-98.

MacLeod, Alistair M. "Distributive Justice, Contract, and Equality." *Journal of Philosophy* 81 (November 1984), 709-718.

McCann, Dennis P. "Empowering the Poor: A Catholic Agenda for Welfare Justice." *New Catholic World* 227 (July-August 1984), 168-172.

McGuire, Joseph W. "Business, Economics and Ethics: A Research and Action Agenda for the Future." *Review of Social Economy* 40 (December 1982), 454-462.

McKee, Arnold F. "Social Economics and Values." *International Journal of Social Economics* 9 (1982), 5-19.

McMahon, Christopher. "Morality and the Invisible Hand." *Philosophy and Public Affairs* 10 (Summer 1981), 247-277.

McMurtry, John. "Free Enterprise, Rationality and Competition." *Journal of Business Ethics* 3 (February 1984), 43-46.

McNichols, Charles W., and Thomas W. Zimmerer. "Situational Ethics: An Empirical Study of Differentiation of Student Attitudes." *Journal of Business Ethics* 4 (June 1985), 175-180.

Moyer, John. "Call for Justice in Economic Life." *Witness* 66 (October 1983), 15-17.

Nielsen, Richard P. "Arendt's Action Philosophy and the Managers as Eichmann, Richard III, Faust, or Institution Citizen." *California Management Review* 26 (Spring 1984), 191-201.

Nielsen, Richard P. "Toward an Action Philosophy for Managers Based on Arendt and Tillich." *Journal of Business Ethics* 3 (May 1984), 153-161.

O'Brien, John C. "Ayres, the Pragmatist, and the New Mode of Thinking." *International Journal of Social Economics* 9, no.4 (1982), 60-78.

O'Brien, John C. "The Economist's Quandary: Ethical Values." *International Journal of Social Economics* 8, no.3 (1981), 26-46.

O'Brien, John C. "Gunnar Myrdal and the Moral Philosopher." *International Journal of Social Economics* 9, no.4 (1982), 3-19.

O'Brien, John C. "Karl Marx and Bourgeois Morality." *International Journal of Social Economics* 9, no.4 (1982), 42-59.

O'Brien, John C. "The Noble Tawney's Appeal to Principles." *International Journal of Social Economics* 9, no.4 (1982), 20-41.

O'Brien, John C. "The Role of Economics and Ethics in Civilisation and Progress." *International Journal of Social Economics* 8, no.4 (1981), 1-20.

Oswald, Andrew J. "Threat and Morale Effects in the Theory of Wages." *European Economic Review* 16 (June-July 1981), 269-283.

Penn, William Y., Jr., and Boyd D. Collier. "Current Research in Moral Development as a Decision Support System." *Journal of Business Ethics* 4 (April 1985), 131-136.

Pilon, Roger. "Capitalism and Rights: An Essay Toward Fine-Tuning the Moral Foundations of a Free Society." *Journal of Business Ethics* 1 (February 1982), 29-42.

Rasmussen, Douglas B. "Ethics and the Free Market." *Listening* 16 (Winter 1982), 77-88.

Rees, Ray. "The Theory of Principal and Agent: Part 2." *Bulletin of Economic Research* 37 (May 1985), 75-95.

Rosenfield, Harry N. "The Free Enterprise System." *Antioch Review* 43 (Summer 1985), 352-363.

Schelling, Thomas C. "Economic Reasoning and the Ethics of Policy." *Public Interest* 63 (Spring 1983), 37-61.

Schlossberger, Eugene. "How to Fix the Economy Without Really Trying." *Commonweal* 110 (February 11, 1983), 72-73.

Sefler, George F. "Elements in a Theory of Collective Responsibility." *University of Dayton Review* 15 (Winter 1981-82), 29-32.

Shaviro, Sol. "A Critique of Consumer Cooperation." *American Journal of Economics & Sociology* 41 (January 1982), 29-42.

Shenfield, Arthur. "Capitalism Under the Test of Ethics." *Imprimis* (December 1981), 4.

Shin, Bong G., and Elliot Zashin. "Management and the New Egalitarianism: McGuire Revisited." *California Management Review* 24 (Summer 1982), 5-13.

Smith, Gary S. "The Spirit of Capitalism Revisited: Calvinists in the Industrial Revolution." *Journal of Preservation History* 59 (Winter 1981), 481-497.

Starr, William C. "Codes of Ethics—Towards a Rule-Utilitarian Justification." *Journal of Business Ethics* 2 (May 1983), 99-106.

Stein, Herbert. "Conservatives, Economists and Neckties." *Business Economics* 18 (January 1983), 5-9.

Steinfels, Peter. "Does Capitalism Equal Pluralism Equal Democracy?" *Commonweal* 110 (February 11, 1983), 79-85.

Stevenson, Rodney. "Corporate Power and the Scope of Economic Analysis." *Journal of Economic Issues* 19 (June 1985), 333-341.

Stewart, Ross E. "Sismondi's Forgotten Critique of Early Capitalism." *Journal of Business Ethics* 3 (August 1984), 227-234.

Sufrin, Sidney C. "How Moral Can a Business Be?" *Christian Century* 100 (March 2, 1983), 186-188.

Surber, Jere. "Individual and Corporate Responsibility: Two Alternative Approaches." *Business and Professional Ethics Journal* 2 (Summer 1983), 67-68. Commentary: by Peter A. French, 89.

Tomlinson, J. D. "Economic and Sociological Theories of Free Enterprise and Industrial Democracy." *British Journal of Sociology* 35 (December 1984), 591-605.

Tool, Marc R. "Equational Justice and Social Value." *Journal of Economic Issues* 17 (June 1983), 335-344.

Tornblom, Kjell Y. "Reversal in Preference Responses to Two Types of Injustice Situations: A Methodological Contribution to Equity Theory." *Human Relations* 35 (November 1982), 991-1014.

Walton, Clarence C. "The Connected Vessels: Economics, Ethics, and Society." *Review of Social Economy* 40 (December 1982), 251-290.

Waters, William R., and Thomas A. Busch. "Ethics and Economics: Retrospect and Prospect." *Review of Social Economy* 40 (December 1982), 247-262.

White, Terrence H. "Productivity and the Nature of Work." *Journal of Business Ethics* 3 (February 1984), 55-61.

Wilson, Fred. "Mill's Proof that Happiness Is the Criterion of Morality." *Journal of Business Ethics* 1 (February 1982), 59-72.

Wilson, Fred. "Mills' 'Proof' of Utility and the Composition of Cause." *Journal of Business Ethics* 2 (May 1983), 135-155.

Worland, S. T. "Exploitative Capitalism: The Natural-Law Perspective." *Social Research* 48 (Summer 1981), 277-305.

Wuthnow, Robert. "The Moral Crisis in American Capitalism." *Harvard Business Review* 60 (March-April 1982), 76-84.

Religion and Business Ethics

Books

Abdul-Rauf, Muhammed. *A Muslim's Reflections on Democratic Capitalism.* Washington, D.C.: American Enterprise Inst., 1984.

Blackburn, Tom. *Christian Business Ethics: Doing Good While Doing Well.* Chicago: Fides/Claretian, 1981.

Block, Walter, Geoffrey Brennan, and Kenneth Elzinga. *Morality of the Market: Religious and Economic Perspectives.* Vancouver, B.C.: Fraser Institute, 1985.

Church, State and Corporation: A Report of the Impact of Religious Organizations on Corporate Policy. New York: Burson Marsteller, 1982.

Commission on Churches' Participation in Development. *CCPD Documents 21.* Geneva: World Council of Churches, 1982.

Cumbler, John T. *A Moral Response to Industrialism: The Lectures of Reverend Cook in Lynn, Massachusetts.* Albany: S.U.N.Y. Press, 1982.

Griffiths, Brian. *Morality and the Marketplace.* London, U.K.: Hodder and Stoughton, 1982.

Hallam, Arthur F. *Christian Capitalism.* Akron, Ohio: Capitalist Press, 1981.

Hallam, Arthur F. *Christian Capitalist Sermons One Through Twenty-Six.* Akron, Ohio: Capitalist Press, 1983.

Hare, J. E., and Carey B. Joynt. *Ethics and International Affairs.* New York: St. Martin's Press, 1982.

Houck, John W., and Oliver F. Williams. *Co-Creation and Capitalism: John Paul II's 'Laborem Exercens.'* Washington, D.C.: Univ. Press of America, 1983.

Jones, Donald G., ed. *Business, Religion, and Ethics: Inquiry and Encounter.* Cambridge, Mass.: Oelgeschlager, Gunn & Hain, 1982.

Kuhn, Robert L., and George T. Feis. *The Firm Bond: Linking Meaning and Mission in Business and Religion.* New York: Praeger, 1984.

Kuttner, Robert. *The Economic Illusion: False Choices Between Prosperity and Social Justice.* Boston: Houghton Mifflin, 1984.

Lee, Robert. *Faith and the Prospects of Economic Collapse.* Atlanta: John Knox Press, 1981.

Morano, Roy W. *The Protestant Challenge to Corporate America: Issues of Social Responsibility.* Ann Arbor, Mich.: UMI Research Press, 1984.

Mueller, Franz H. *The Church and the Social Question.* Washington, D.C.: American Enterprise Inst. 1984.

Novak, Michael. *Toward a Theology of the Corporation.* Washington, D.C.: American Enterprise Inst., 1981.

Novak, Michael, and John W. Cooper, eds. *The Corporation: A Theological Inquiry.* Washington, D.C.: American Enterprise Inst., 1981.

Oden, Thomas C. *Conscience and Dividends: Churches and the Multinationals*. Washington, D.C.: Ethics and Public Policy Center, 1985.

Poggi, Gianfranco. *Calvinism and the Capitalist Spirit: Max Weber's 'Protestant Ethic.'* London, U.K.: Macmillan, 1983.

Reeck, Darrell. *Ethics for the Professions: A Christian Perspective*. Minneapolis: Augsburg, 1982.

Royal, Robert, ed. *Challenge and Response*. Washington, D.C.: Ethics and Public Policy Center, 1985.

United Church of Christ. *Corporate Social Responsibility Actions, 1979-1981*. New York: United Church of Christ, no date given.

Williams, Oliver F., and John W. Houck. *The Judeo-Christian Vision and the Modern Corporation*. Notre Dame, Ind.: Univ. Notre Dame Press, 1982.

World Council of Churches. *Transnational Corporations, the Churches, and the Ecumenical Movement*. Geneva: World Council of Churches, 1982.

Articles

Albin, Peter S. "Exclusionary Economics: Two Systems Side by Side." *Christianity and Crisis* 41 (March 30, 1981), 81-85.

Alperovitz, Gar, and Jeff Faux. "The Budget and the Economy." *Christianity and Crisis* 41 (April 13, 1981), 100-103.

Armstrong, A. J. "The Maturing of Church Corporate Responsibility Programs." *Business and Society Review* 54 (Summer 1985), 6-9.

Barrett, Nancy. "The Case for Collaboration." *Commonweal* 112 (June 21, 1985), 363-365.

Baum, Gregory. "A Canadian Perspective on the U.S. Pastoral." *Christianity and Crisis* 44 (January 21, 1985), 516-518.

Baum, Gregory. "Capital Bishops and Unemployment." *New Catholic World* 226 (July-August 1983), 158-162.

Block, Walter. "The Jews and Capitalism: The Free Market Place." *Vital Speeches of the Day* 51 (February 15, 1985), 283-288.

Brown, Lester R. "Toward a Sustainable Society: The Need for New Values." *Christianity and Crisis* 41 (November 30, 1981), 327-332.

Buchholz, Rogene A. "The Protestant Ethic as an Ideological Justification of Capitalism." *Journal of Business Ethics* 2 (February 1983), 51-60.

Buss, Terry F., and F. S. Redburn. "Religious Leaders as Policy Advocates: The Youngstown Steel Mill Closing." *Policy Studies Journal* 11 (June 1983), 640-647.

Byron, William J., S.J. "Christianity and Capitalism." *Review of Social Economy* 40 (December 1982), 311-322.

Calian, Carnegie S. "Between Recession and Recovery." *Theology Today* 91 (April 1984), 47-50.

Carroll, James. "On Not Skipping the Sermon." *Commonweal* 111 (November 2-16, 1984), 603-605.

Cavanagh, John. "Debt and Development: An Action Agenda." *Christianity and Crisis* 45 (October 14, 1985), 394-397.

"The Church and Capitalism." *Business Week* (November 12, 1984), 104-112.

Cieply, Michael. "How Many Divisions Do They Have?" *Forbes* 131 (April 1983), 50-56.

Clapp, Rodney. "Where Capitalism and Christianity Meet." *Christianity Today* 27 (February 4, 1983), 22-28.

Coffman, Richard B., Hershey H. Friedman, and Morris Yarmish. "Some Economic Implications of Talmudic Busines Ethics/ Talmudic Business Ethics Versus Economic Efficiency—A Reply." *Akron Business and Economic Review* 13 (Spring 1982), 24-29.

Cox, Harvey G. "Imagining an Economy Based on Shalom: The Bishops Draft Pastoral." *Christianity and Crisis* 44 (January 21, 1985), 509-512.

Crotty, James R., and James R. Stormers, S.J. "The Bishops on the U.S. Economy." *Challenge* 28 (March-April 1985), 36-41.

Davis, Winston. "Japan as 'Paradigm': Imitation vs. Insight." *Christianity and Crisis* 42 (September 20, 1982), 254-260.

De Rosen, Leon. "The World of Business and the Church." *Ecumenical Review* 37 (January 1985), 47-52.

Dombrowski, Daniel A. "Benne and Novak on Capitalism." *Theology Today* 91 (April 1984), 61-65.

Douglas, R. B. "At the Heart of the Letter." *Commonweal* 112 (June 21, 1985), 359-363.

Erteszeh, Jan J. "Corporate Entrepreneurship and Christian Ethics." *Review of Social Economy* 40 (December 1982), 323-329.

"Faith and Economics: Comments from Sixty Years." *Commonweal* 111 (November 2-16, 1984), 613-625.

Faulhaber, Robert W. "The Church and Culture—John Paul II's 'On Human Work.' " *Listening* 18 (Spring 1983), 103-118.

Finn, Daniel R. "Christian Ethics and the Debate Over Economic Planning." *New Catholic World* 227 (July-August 1984), 148-151.

"Freeing the Fortune 500?" *Commonweal* 108 (August 28, 1981), 451-452.

Freudberg, David. "Ministering to the Corporation." *Across the Board* 21 (November 1984), 14-19.

Friedman, Hershey H. "Ethical Behavior in Business: A Hierarchical Approach from the Talmud." *Journal of Business Ethics* 4 (Spring 1985), 117-129.

Friedman, M. "Capitalism and the Jews: Confronting a Paradox." *Encounter* 63 (June 1984), 74-79.

Gillett, Richard W. "The Reshaping of Work: A Challenge to the Churches." *Christian Century* 100 (January 5-12, 1983), 10-13.

Graham, W. F. "America's Other Religion." *Christian Century* 99 (March 17, 1982), 306-308.

"Guarding Wall Street's Morals." *Economist* 296 (July 27, 1985), 24.

Gunnemann, Jon P. "Christian Ethics in a Capitalist Society." *Word World* 5 (Winter 1985), 49-59.

Harrington, Michael. "The Future of Poverty." *Commonweal* 111 (November 2-16, 1984), 625-632.

Hodiak, Bohdan. "Prophets in Steeltown." *Christian Century* 102 (May 8, 1985), 460-462.

Hug, James E. "Call to Cultural Conversion: Moral Reflections on U.S. Economy." *New Catholic World* 226 (July-August 1983), 170-175.

Hug, James E. "Joining the Prophetic Process." *New Catholic World* 227 (July-August 1984), 152-156.

Hug, James E. "A Preferential Option for the Entrepreneur." *Christianity and Crisis* 44 (January 21, 1985), 518-520.

Hug, James E., Gregory Baum, and Larry Rasmussen. "The Bishops and the Economy: Three Appraisals." *Christianity and Crisis* 45 (November 25, 1985), 470-476.

Hussain, Jane. "Islam: Faith and Ideology." *Commonweal* 111 (April 6, 1984), 214-218.

Kavanaugh, John. "Challenging a Commodity Culture." *Commonweal* 111 (November 2-16, 1984), 606-612.

Kerr, Hugh T. "Symposium: Business and Religion." *Theology Today* 41 (April 1984), 42-77.

Krietemeyer, Ronald T. "U.S. Bishops on Employment and Economic Justice." *New Catholic World* 226 (July-August 1983), 176-179.

Lacinak, Michael. "Religion and Labor Make Common Cause." *Christian Century* 99 (August 18-25, 1982), 845-846.

Langan, John. "The Bishops & the Bottom Line." *Commonweal* 111 (November 2-16, 1984), 586-592.

Lekachman, Robert. "Paul and the Bishops on Dignity and Community." *Christianity and Crisis* 44 (January 21, 1985), 507-509.

Lekachman, Robert, et al. "Continuing Discussion: 'A Strategy for Economic Revival.' " *Christianity and Crisis* 42 (October 4, 1982), 283-287.

Lens, Sidney. "Averting Economic Catastrophes." *Christian Century* 101 (July 18-25, 1984), 707-710.

Logue, John J. "The Law of the Sea at Low Tide." *Commonweal* 108 (August 28, 1981), 460-463.

Long, Grace C. "The Marketing of Health Care." *Christian Century* 101 (February 29, 1984), 222-224.

Magaziner, Ira C. "A Strategy for Economic Revival." *Christianity and Crisis* 42 (August 9, 1982), 229-235.

Martin, Keith D. "Setting Economic Policy in the Real World." *Christianity and Crisis* 44 (April 16, 1984), 130-133.

Mayer, Ann E. "Economics and the Koran." *Wharton Magazine* 6 (Winter 1981-82), 41-45.

McBrien, Richard P. "American Economy: Some Ecclesiological Considerations." *New Catholic World* 227 (July-August 1984), 164-167.

McClenahan, J. S. "When Religion and Business Collide." *Industry Week* 226 (August 19, 1985), 38-41.

McCoy, Bowen. "A Test Case in Communication." *Theology Today* 91 (April 1984), 42-46.

McMahon, Thomas F. "The Contributions of Religious Traditions to Business Ethics." *Journal of Business Ethics* 4 (August 1985), 341-349.

McSwain, Larry L. "Christian Ethics and the Business Ethos." *Review and Expositor* 81 (Spring 1984), 197-207.

"Morality and Capitalism." *Society* 18 (September-October 1981), 24-72.

Nagle, Robin. "How Pope John Paul II and Other Religious Leaders View Advertising/ . . . and When the Churches Themselves Advertise." *Madison Avenue* 27 (September 1985), 18-28.

Neff, David. "Jacques Ellul's Money and Power." *Christianity Today* 29 (February 15, 1985), 26-30.

Noyce, Gaylord. "The Dilemmas of Christians in Business." *Christian Century* 98 (August 12-19, 1981), 802-804.

Olivarez, Graciela. "The Poor You Shall Always." *New Catholic World* 227 (July-August 1984), 183-187.

Pellauer, Mary. "Porn Is Big Business." *Christianity and Crisis* 45 (May 13, 1985), 174-175.

Pellauer, Mary. "Self-Esteem, Salaries, and Subjectivity." *Christianity and Crisis* 45 (September 30, 1985), 336-367.

Pemberton, Prentiss L., and Daniel R. Finn. "Economics & Christian Values." *Commonweal* 111 (November 2-16, 1984), 597-602.

Pichler, Joseph A. "The Pastoral Letter and Employment." *New Catholic World* 227 (July-August 1984), 179-182.

Pinyan, Charles. "Pressure From the Pulpit." *Chemical Week* 137 (December 11, 1985), 14-15.

Pohl, Keith J. "The Ethics of Disinvestment." *Christian Century* 102 (August 28 – September 4, 1985), 759-760.

Powelson, John P. "Holistic Economics." *Theology Today* 91 (April 1984), 66-77.

Preston, Ronald H. "Pope John Paul II on Work." *Theology* 86 (January 1983), 19-24.

Raines, John C. "Conscience and the Economic Crisis." *Christian Century* 99 (September 1-8, 1982), 883-887.

Ribuffo, Leo P. "Jesus Christ as Business Statesman." *American Quarterly* 33 (Summer 1981), 206-231.

Rowland, Chris, and Rich Preuss. "Christianity in the Marketplace." *Scholastic* 123 (May 1982), 16+.

Rule, James B. "The Undiscussable Assumption." *Commonweal* 111 (November 2-16, 1984), 596-597.

Sadowsky, James A. "Capitalism, Ethics, and Classical Catholic Social Doctrine." *This World* 6 (Fall 1983), 115-125.

Scheibner, Anne. "The Wine Skins Are Bursting: Plant Closings, Economic Dislocation and the Response of the Religious Community." *New Catholic World* 226 (July-August 1983), 163-165.

Schotte, Jan P. "The Social Teaching of the Church." *Review of Social Economy* 40 (December 1982), 340-370.

Sethi, S. P. "Church Activism and Corporate America." *Business and Society Review* 54 (Summer 1985), 4-5.

Sethi, S. P. "The Conflict Between Business and the Church." *Business and Society Review* 36 (Winter 1980-81), 23-29.

Sethi, S. P. "The Righteous and the Powerful: Differing Paths to Social Goals?" *Business and Society Review* 54 (Summer 1985), 37-44.

Sklar, Holly. "Co-missionaries for Top-down Capitalism." *Christianity and Crisis* 43 (January 21, 1985), 521-523.

Slack, Kenneth. "Coal Miners' Strike Ends." *Christian Century* 102 (April 3, 1985), 317-319.

Smith, Sue. "Economics of Shelter." *Commonweal* 111 (November 2-16, 1984), 610-611.

Smith, Timothy N. "Church Activists in the 1980s: The Conscience of Corporate America." *Business and Society Review* 54 (Summer 1985), 15-20.

"South Africa: Crisis and Hope." [Special Issue] *Christianity and Crisis* 45 (February 4 & 8, 1985).

"South Africa: Crisis and Hope." [Special Issue] *Christianity and Crisis* 45 (November 11, 1985).

Sowe, Kathy. "To Talk or Not to Talk—And Who to . . ." *One World* 67 (June 1981), 7, 19.

Steidle-Meier, Paul, et al. "The Church and the Economy: Four Responses to the Draft of the Pastoral." *Commonweal* 111 (November 30, 1984), 650-654.

Steinfels, Peter. "Michael Novak and His Ultrasuper Democraticapitalism." *Commonweal* 110 (January 14, 1983), 11-16.

Sturm, Douglas. "Education for Profit." *Christianity and Crisis* 44 (April 16, 1984), 125-126.

Thompson, Robert W. "Ministering to the Unemployed." *Christian Century* 99 (September 1-8, 1982), 888-890.

Umholtz, Thomas F. "Vocation at Work." *Christian Century* 102 (August 28 – September 4, 1985), 767-768.

U.S. Catholic Bishops Council. "Catholic Social Teaching and the U.S. Economy." *Origins* 14 (November 15, 1984).

Vanek, Jaroslav. "Testimony to the Catholic Bishops' Economy Committee." *New Catholic World* 227 (July-August 1984), 173-178.

Wall, James M. "Campbell Boycott Decision Nears." *Christian Century* 101 (November 7, 1984), 1027-1028.

Wilde, Alexander. "Ideology at the IAF." *Commonweal* 111 (February 10, 1984), 72-74.

Williams, Oliver F. "Being a Christian in the Business World: The Challenge and the Promise." *Horizons* 11 (Fall 1984), 383-392.

Williams, Oliver F. "Catholic Bishops Take on Economics." *Business and Society Review* 54 (Summer 1985), 21-26.

Williams, Oliver F. "Religion: The Spirit or the Enemy of Capitalism." *Business Horizons* 26 (November-December 1983), 6-13.

Williams, Oliver F. "Who Cast the First Stone?" *Harvard Business Review* 62 (September-October 1984), 151-160.

"The World Council of Churches Takes on the Corporations: An Interview with Marcos Arruda." *Multinational Monitor* 3 (August 1982), 13-15.

Wright, Peter. "Doing Business in Islamic Markets." *Harvard Business Review* 59 (January-February 1981), 34-40.

Teaching and Training in Ethics

Books

Dickie, Robert B., et al. *Teaching Management Ethics in an M.B.A. Core Course*. Boston: Harvard University, 1981.

Articles

Arledge, Elizabeth. "Harvard Business School Angst." *Rolling Stone* (October 1, 1981), 43+.

Arledge, Elizabeth. "How Do You Pass a Course in Corporate Ethics?" *Rolling Stone* (October 1, 1981), 43.

Arlow, Peter, and Thomas A. Ulrich. "Business Ethics and Business School Graduates." *Akron Business and Economic Review* 16 (Spring 1985), 13-17.

Arlow, Peter, and Thomas A. Ulrich. "Can Ethics Be Taught to Business Students?" *Collegiate Forum* (Spring 1983), 17.

Bahm, Archie J. "Teaching Ethics Without Ethics to Teach." *Journal of Business Ethics* 1 (February 1982), 43-47.

Boyd, David P. "Improving Ethical Awareness Through the Business and Society Course." *Business and Society* 20-2, 21-1 (Winter-Spring 1981-1982), 27-31.

Britell, Jenne K. "Ethics Courses Are Making Slow Inroads." *New York Times Magazine* (April 26, 1981), 44.

Buchholz, Rogene. "Ethics and Management Education." *Business Forum* 7 (Winter 1982), 6-10.

Carlson, P. "Updating Individualism and the Work Ethic: Corporate Logic in the Classroom." *Curriculum Inquiry* 12 (Summer 1982), 125-160.

Cooper, David E. "Cognitive Development and Teaching Business Ethics." *Journal of Business Ethics* 4 (August 1985), 313-329.

Cuilla, Joanne B. "Do MBA Students Have Ethics Phobia?" *Business and Society Review* 53 (Spring 1985), 52-54.

Culbertson, Hugh M. "How Public Relations Textbooks Handle Honesty and Lying." *Public Relations Review* 9 (Summer 1983), 65-73.

Cumming, W. K. "Educational Ethics for Survival." *Vital Speeches of the Day* 51 (October 15, 1985), 13-16.

"Do Business Schools Teach Absolute Rot?" *Business and Society Review* 40 (Winter 1981-1982), 61-65.

Evanson, Randall M. "Ethics in the Business Curriculum: How Transmissable Is the Indefinable?" *Collegiate News and Views* 38 (Fall-Winter 1984), 27-29.

George, Richard J. "An Interdisciplinary Business Ethics Course Should Be Required of All Business Majors." *Marketing Educator* 3 (Winter 1984), 102.

Gini, A. R. "The Case Method: A Perspective." *Journal of Business Ethics* 4 (August 1985), 351-352.

Golen, Steven, Celeste Powers, and M. A. Titkemeyer. "How to Teach Ethics in a Basic Business Communications Class." *Journal of Business Communication* 22 (Winter 1985), 75-83.

Goodwin, H. E. "News Media Ethics—Where Should It Be Taught and by Whom?" *Mass Communication Review* 8 (Spring 1981), 11-16.

Greenberg, Karen. "The Business of Ethics." *Advanced Management Journal* 47 (Summer 1982), 21-22.

Hamilton, Patricia. "Teaching Business Ethics." *D & B Reports* 29 (July 1, 1981), 38-41.

Hiley, D., and W. Layton. "What Is a Corporate Executive Like You Doing in a Philosophy Class Like This?" *Liberal Education* 71 (Spring 1985), 77-80.

Hoffman, W. M. "Ethics in Business Education: Working Toward a Meaningful Reciprocity." *Journal of Business Ethics* 3 (November 1984), 259-268.

Hoffman, W. M., and Jennifer M. Moore. "Results of a Business Ethics Curriculum Survey Conducted by the Center for Business Ethics." *Journal of Business Ethics* 1 (May 1982), 81-83.

Hollander, Stanley C., and Roger Dickinson. "Some Ethical Questions in Teaching Marketing and Retailing." *Journal of Marketing Education* 7 (Summer 1985), 2-12.

Horwitt, Liz. "Corporate Ethics 101." *American Way* (September 1981), 29-32.

Hosmer, LaRue T. "The Other 338: Why a Majority of Our Schools of Business Administration Do Not Offer a Course in Business Ethics." *Journal of Business Ethics* 4 (February 1985), 17-22.

Jones, Donald G. "Teaching Business Ethics to Executives." *Teaching Philosophy* 6 (July 1983), 205-220.

Kreitner, Robert. "Needed: Formal Instruction in Business Ethics for Managers." *Journal of Management Development (UK)* 2 (1983), 16-25.

Krohn, Franklin B. "A General Semantics Approach to Teaching Business Ethics." *Journal of Business Communication* 22 (Summer 1985), 59-66.

Krohn, Franklin B. "Teaching of Legal and Ethical Standards for Marketing Research." *Journal of Marketing Education* 4 (Spring 1982), 31-34.

Lombardi, Louis G. "A Quick Justification for Business Ethics." *Journal of Business Ethics* 4 (August 1985), 353-356.

Long, John D. "The Responsibility of Schools of Business to Teach Ethics." *Business Horizons* 27 (March-April 1984), 2-4.

Martin, T. R. "Do Courses in Ethics Improve the Ethical Judgment of Students?" *Business and Society* 20-2, 21-1 (Winter-Spring 1981-1982), 17-26.

McCammond, Donald B. "The Growth of Ethical Awareness." *Public Relations Journal* 41 (February 1985), 8-9.

McDaniel, C.-G. "How to Teach Ethics in the Intro Course." *Journalism Education* 38 (Autumn 1983), 16-19.

Miller, William E. "The Untaught Skill." *Collegiate News and Views* 37 (Winter 1983-1984), 19-20+.

Moore, Thomas. "Industrial Espionage at the Harvard B-School." *Fortune* 106 (September 6, 1982), 70-76+.

Moskowitz, Daniel B., and John A. Byrne. "Where Business Goes to Stock Up on Ethics." *Business Week* (October 14, 1985), 63+.

Murphy, Patrick E., and Gene R. Laczniak. "How Marketing Educators, Text Authors Can Give Higher Priority to Ethical Issues." *Marketing News* 16 (July 23, 1982), 14.

Nash, Laura L. "Ethics in the Business Curriculum." *Selections* 2 (1985), 3-7.

Oelgeschlager, Max. "Philosophical Therapy for Business Managers." *Southwestern Philosophical Studies* 6 (April 1981), 98-104.

Owens, James. "Business Ethics in the College Classroom." *Journal of Business Education* 58 (April 1983), 258-262.

Pastin, Mark. "Business Ethics, by the Book." *Business Horizons* 28 (January-February 1985), 2-6.

Paul, Karen. "Business Ethics Steamroll the Professors." *Business and Society Review* 39 (Fall 1981), 40-41.

Payne, S. "Exploring Values and Ethics in Management Education: A Term Project Assignment." *Journal of Business Education* 59 (March 1984), 249-251.

Petrof, John V., Elie E. Sayegh, and Pandelis I. Vlahopoulos. "The Influence of the School of Business on the Values of Its Students." *Journal of the Academy of Marketing Science* 10 (Fall 1982), 500-513.

Posner, Barry Z., and J. M. Munson. "Comparing Value Systems of College Students, Faculty, and Corporate Recruiters." *Psychological Reports* 48 (February 1981), 107-113.

Pruitt, Dennis. "Can Ethics Be Taught?" *Student Activities Programming* (May 1981), 28-31.

Razzouk, Nabil Y. "Cover Ethics in Management Courses." *Marketing News* 16 (July 23, 1982), 1, 14.

Saul, George K. "Business Ethics: Where Are We Going?" *Academy of Management Review* 6 (April 1981), 269-276.

Schneider, Kenneth C. "Teaching Ethics in Marketing Research: An Experiential Approach." *Journal of Marketing Education* 5 (Fall 1983), 27-34.

Stevens, George E. "Ethical Inclinations of Tomorrow's Citizens: Actions Speak Louder?" *Journal of Business Education* 59 (January 1984), 147-152.

Stratton, William E., W. R. Flynn, and George A. Johnson. "Moral Development and Decision Making: A Study of Student Ethics." *Journal of Enterprise Management* 3 (1981), 35-41.

Sullivan, Roger. "Learning to Think Ethically." *Student Activities Programming* (May 1981), 24-27.

Williams, Oliver F. "Business Ethics: A Trojan Horse." *California Management Review* 24 (Summer 1982), 14-24.

Subject Index

Subject Index

Author Index

Author Index